Racing & Football Outlook

FLAT RACING GUIDE 2020

Interviews • Statistics • Results
Previews • Training centre reports

Contributors: Richard Birch, James Burn, Tom Collins, Steffan Edwards, Jack Haynes, Dylan Hill, Bruce Jackson, Andrew King, David Milnes, Justin O'Hanlon, James Thomas, Nick Watts

Designed and edited by Nick Watts and Dylan Hill

Published in 2020 by Raceform Ltd
27 Kingfisher Court, Hambridge Road, Newbury RG14 5SJ

A catalogue record for this book is available from the British Library.

ISBN 978-1-83950-042-8

Printed by CPI Group (UK) Ltd, Croydon, CRO 4YY

RACING & FOOTBALL **Outlook**

Contents

Editor's introduction

FOR all the highs – Enable's battle with Crystal Ocean in the King George, Magical's heroics all through a long year, Pinatubo being the best two-year-old in 25 years – an objective assessment of the 2019 Flat season has it down as one of the worst on record.

Enable, Waldgeist and Crystal Ocean shared world champion honours at the World's Greatest Racehorse Rankings and their mark of 128 was the lowest for any world champion in more than 40 years of the awards taking place.

Furthermore, the mark awarded to champion three-year-old Sottsass was the lowest in the history of the awards by 2lb, the French colt having been put in his place by Enable and Waldgeist in the Prix de l'Arc de Triomphe.

But the good news is that such a dearth of talent among the youngsters has seemingly tempted connections of our old favourites to come back for more in 2020.

AGONY: Enable's bid for history in the Prix de l'Arc de Triomphe was denied

PINATUBO (left): the best two-year-old since Celtic Swing 25 years earlier

Amazingly, having come up agonisingly short in her bid for an unprecedented third Arc last year, Enable will try again as she stays in training as a six-year-old. En route to Longchamp, that might also mean we can look forward to more memorable clashes with her old rival Magical, who was retired at the end of last season but could return, with Coolmore reconsidering their decision at the time of writing.

If we were short of a superstar three-year-old last year, that certainly couldn't be said for the two-year-olds. Pinatubo was simply breathtaking and by any measurement he was the best juvenile since Celtic Swing in 1994. It will be fascinating to see how he fares this year.

Celtic Swing is perhaps the warning as he was caught up by his peers at three. While Pinatubo has at least proved he has the versatility in terms of ground conditions that Celtic Swing lacked, our ante-post king Steffan Edwards is keen to take him on this year – be sure not to miss his views on the Classics in this book.

We also have our regional experts bringing you all the news on which other big names will leave their mark this year and no doubt there will be more pearls like Jerry M's tips for Magna Grecia to win the 2,000 Guineas and Anthony Van Dyck to win the Derby from 12 months ago.

We've spoken to two trainers we expect to have big seasons. Michael Dods gets stronger and stronger at the top end of the game and has myriad prospects for the season's big sprints, while Grant Tuer is aiming to build on a breakthrough campaign in 2019.

Pedigree expert James Thomas gives his take on the year, while Nick Watts has searched far and wide for his list of 30 horses to follow.

As well as that, we have invaluable stable insight from Tom Collins and Richard Birch; Time Test brings you all the key speed figures; and Dylan Hill guides you through last season's leading form.

Then there are the stats, reams and reams of winner-finding numbers detailing the top trainers and jockeys also broken down course by course so you know who to follow at your local track.

Once again we have every base covered for a year packed with bumper profits – and don't forget to buy your copy of the RFO every week for the very latest news and tips.

Profiles for punters
Michael Dods

MICHAEL DODS: has a remarkable conveyor belt of top sprinting talent

Profile by Dylan Hill

MICHAEL DODS could be forgiven for approaching this season with a bit of trepidation.

For the last couple of years his standout performer has been Mabs Cross, the brilliant sprinter whose CV included victory in a Prix de l'Abbaye, successive wins in the Palace House Stakes and an agonising defeat in a Nunthorpe Stakes, but she has now been retired to the paddocks, leaving a significant hole for Dods to fill.

However, the trainer has become known for churning out a remarkable conveyor belt of sprinting talent to the extent that Pricewise supremo Tom Segal last year described him as the best trainer of sprinters in Britain. Even more impressively, he has done it for relatively little money.

The homebred Mabs Cross, bought back for breeders David and Emma Armstrong after reaching just £3,000 in the ring, herself filled the void left by another Group 1 winner in 16,00gns purchase Mecca's Angel, who won back-to-back runnings of the Nunthorpe in 2015 and 2016, and there are several candidates to become the latest sprinting sensation at Dods's County Durham base.

Dakota Gold progressed through the ranks last year and very nearly signed off with a Group 3 win at Newbury even when conditions were against him; flying females Que Amoro and Queens Gift have already finished second in Listed races and have never stopped improving; the apple of Dods's eye, Pendleton, finally made the strides expected last autumn with big performances in a couple of major three-year-old handicaps; and Cornwallis Stakes winner Good Vibes is a new arrival, sent here by Qatar Racing after they paid 390,00gns for her.

This sort of strength in depth has become par for the course for Dods, who will be aiming for a 15th successive season with at least 38 winners having never once got to such a tally until 2006 – a full 16 years after he took out his licence.

"We'll miss Mabs Cross, who's gone to stud," says Dods, "but we've still got a lot of nice horses this year. It's very exciting."

However, asked which of the flying five mentioned above is most likely to be the next Mabs Cross, Dods is understandably coy.

"You can't say which of them will be able to win a Group 1 at this stage because it's such a jump. You have to go through the grades, Listed races and Group races, and we want them to be competitive in those first. But Good Vibes has already won her Group 3 and we'll be looking at that level at some point, the same for Dakota Gold. Hopefully something will be able to come through."

If any of these horses have it in them to get to the top then Dods can clearly get it out – so just what is the key to his success with sprinters?

According to the trainer, it's all about getting them right mentally as much as physically, as he explains: "Sprinters are like coiled springs. You really see them change in the parade ring when the jockey gets on and if you buzz them up it's hard to bring them back down, so you need to get inside their heads and keep them chilled.

MABS CROSS: off to the paddocks

"That means you have to train them differently to other horses and we'd give sprinters a lot less work than other horses – even if that means they don't always look as fit. Some of them do very little galloping and just canter, but they'll often be fitter than you might think from looking at them."

The horses

Amplification 5yo gelding
Lonhro – Our Drama Queen

He won a couple of times for Ed Dunlop and we picked him up for 27,000gns at the horses-in-training sale in 2018. Unfortunately he missed most of last season with a slight injury, but he came back with a good run on the all-weather earlier this year. He'll be helped by going up to a mile.

Arch Moon 3yo gelding
Sea The Moon – Archduchess

He's a lovely horse who showed promise last year, looking a bit unlucky not to win, but was always going to be a better three-year-old. The handicapper has taken no chances with his opening mark of 83 but he's definitely open to improvement.

Brunch 3yo gelding
Harbour Watch – Granola

He's an exciting prospect. He's so laid-back that he got detached first time out and the race passed him by a bit, but then he won well at Newcastle, doing exactly what we expected. I have high hopes for him this year.

Camacho Chief 5yo gelding
Camacho – Passage To India

I thought he did really well to win at Doncaster last summer as he's not the biggest of horses and was carrying 9st 12lb. He ran well without winning after that and would have finished closer a couple of times with a bit more luck. I think he's still improving and will do well over a stiff 5f on soft ground.

Challet 3yo gelding
Clodovil – Eileenlilian

He was a big, weak horse last year and it took him a while to mature, but he still did well and was placed a couple of times. He's wintered well and I expect him to make into a lovely three-year-old. He should do quite well.

DAKOTA GOLD: wins at Ascot after the ground just found him out at Newbury

Commanche Falls 3yo gelding
Lethal Force – Joyeaux

He won at Thirsk first time out last year and I was a bit disappointed he didn't really kick on from that, but he was still not beaten far at Ayr and I couldn't fault him when sixth in a valuable sales race at Newmarket. He'll get an extra furlong and that should help him to find a bit more.

Dakota Gold 6yo gelding
Equiano – Joyeaux

He kept surprising us all through last year and ended up winning five times. The first three were in handicaps, including two in the space of five days in August, and he was quite a short price for the Ayr Gold Cup at that point, but I didn't want to run him under a big weight in that as he's not a great big horse. We went down the Listed route instead and he won twice at that level at York and Ascot as well as finishing second in a Group 3 at Newbury. The ground was a bit quick that day and I'd like to think he can do even better as he needs some cut, especially at 5f.

Danielsflyer 6yo gelding
Dandy Man – Warm Welcome

He came here from David Barron's yard at the start of last year but unfortunately he was quite badly handicapped. He did well to get close to winning a few times and his mark is becoming better now. I think we'll step him up in trip, maybe to a mile and a quarter, and that should help him.

Gale Force Maya 4yo filly
Gale Force Ten – Parabola

She did really well last year and the way she races probably helped with her mark. She only just does enough and that meant the handicapper couldn't do too much to her, so she was able to win three in a row at Carlisle and then she was second in good races at Pontefract and Newmarket. She has to improve again to stay ahead of the handicapper but I think she can do it.

Good Vibes 3yo filly
Due Diligence – Satsuma

She's a nice filly who won the Cornwallis for David Evans last year before being bought by Qatar Racing and sent here. She's been very straightforward since we got her and looks well. It's never easy with three-year-old sprinters, especially fillies, but I'd hope she trains on and does well.

Heath Charnock 4yo colt
Showcasing – Bayleaf

He won two of his first three races but has had soundness issues and hasn't quite done it since then. We dropped him back to 5f towards the end of last season and I think that will be his trip eventually, but the penny hadn't quite dropped enough at that stage. He'll do well when everything drops into place.

Jawwaal 5yo gelding
Bahamian Bounty – Avenbury

We got him from John Gosden last year and I think he was a bit unlucky not to win. He came close a few times and on some other occasions he didn't get the cover he needs. Physically, he looks like he could develop into a 5f horse and we'll campaign him as a sprinter with a bit of cut in the ground.

John Kirkup 5yo gelding
Assertive – Bikini

He's an interesting horse. He's won his last two races when he gets soft or heavy ground but he needs it proper soft and struggles to get competitive otherwise. He'll do well again when he gets his conditions.

Pendleton 4yo gelding
Garswood – Anglezarke

He frustrated me for most of last season as he was blowing everything out of the way at home but wasn't doing it on the track.

QUEENS GIFT (near side): has been sharpened up by cheekpieces

I just think he was a bit slow in the head and not as switched on in races as he needed to be, but he learned as the year went on and came good in the autumn when he won at Ascot and was second to the unbeaten Bielsa in another valuable handicap at Doncaster. The ground also helped as it was soft and heavy in those races. He's growing up mentally all the time and I think there's more to come.

Que Amoro **4yo filly**
Es Que Love – Onomatomania

She's an exciting horse. We thought she'd be very good right from the start but it took her until last summer to really deliver. The key to her was to let her get on with it as I'd felt she needed restraint and was getting frustrated, but then we decided not to hang about at York in July and she loved it. She won by seven lengths that day, followed up at the Ebor meeting and then finished a half-length second in a Listed race at Ayr on her last run. She's a big filly and should have more improvement in her.

Queens Gift **5yo mare**
Canford Cliffs – Jawaaneb

She really improved as last season went on and I think cheekpieces made a big difference to her. She took a lot longer than she should have done to win her race at Doncaster, so we put cheekpieces on when she went to Ripon and she was much sharper and won again, then she was second in a couple of Listed races at Beverley and Doncaster. She's a decent mare and looks really well this year.

Rapid Russo **3yo gelding**
Coach House – Rapid Recruit

He won at Catterick last year but has paid a bit of a price. It fell into his lap as they went too hard in front and he was able to pick them off, but the handicapper took the form literally and he's still rated too high on 74. He's a nice sprinter in the making but will have to find his mark.

Road Rage 3yo gelding
Requinto – Grid Lock

He seems fine now after getting jarred up at Newmarket on his final run last year. He'd won on soft ground at Haydock before that, rightly getting the race in the stewards' room, and he'll need some cut this year. He should win off his mark.

Tombolo 3yo colt
Le Havre – Sandbar

He's a very nice horse. He ran a blinder to finish second on his debut at Haydock last year and then we put him away. He was a bit weak last year but he's strengthened up now and will stay further. I like him a lot.

Troubador 3yo gelding
Poet's Voice – Eastern Destiny

He was a superstar for us last year, winning four races and finishing second in three. That's caused its own issues, though, as he'll have to improve to be competitive off 101 – I thought it was very harsh of the handicapper to hike him up 8lb for finishing second at the Ebor meeting. However, he's looking very well this year so I'm hopeful he can overcome that.

Unifier 3yo gelding
Showcasing – Miss Chicane

He was second at 66-1 on his last run at York in September but I wouldn't say it was that much of a surprise. He'd been working very well before his debut at Carlisle but just got bogged down on bad ground. He's a nice horse and will improve again.

Wahoo 5yo gelding
Stimulation – Shohrah

We have to be careful with this horse as he can't go on quick ground – he has won on good to firm at Haydock in 2018, but even then I was worried until I walked the course and there was no jar in it. He won at Redcar on good ground last year but was a bit disappointing in the autumn. He's down to a good mark again now, though, and I hope he'll do well.

TROUBADOR (right): looking well ahead of his three-year-old campaign

Profiles for punters
Grant Tuer

GRANT TUER: rewarded for a breakthrough 2019 with a much bigger team

Profile by Dylan Hill

IT'S been a long, hard road, but Grant Tuer finally seemed to make a big breakthrough as a trainer last year – and, perhaps more tellingly, it wasn't through a single horse but rather sheer weight of winners.

Tuer had done well in 2018, with eight winners doubling his previous best tally. Then last year he stormed past that total, finishing with 21 winners at a hugely impressive strike-rate of 17 per cent, and now he is confident of kicking on again.

That's because Tuer puts his progress down to simple economics, with his initial success attracting more and bigger owners, and that process has continued apace, with a much bigger team of horses now in place for 2020.

"We were delighted with how last year went," he reflects. "We'd found it hard to attract owners, but we begged, stole and borrowed a few last year and ended up with more horses, including plenty of well-handicapped ones.

"We did all right with them, especially as we had a virus in May that set us back a bit, and now we've got a much bigger team again. We had about 25 horses last year and ran 20 of them – there were a few two-year-olds who didn't make it to the track. This year we've got 37 or 38, with 17 two-year-olds, which is very exciting. Three of them have been sent here by Geoff Turnbull of Elwick Stud, we've bought seven or eight, and we're leasing four from some breeders who kept hold of some of their fillies."

And it's not just youngsters among the new recruits as Tuer has also bought a trio of more experienced handicappers to fill a void in his yard.

"I wanted some Saturday horses in the yard so we've bought a few who will hopefully take us to some of the bigger races this year. We got Bolder Bob out of David Barron's yard, Illusionist out of Archie Watson's yard, and then in February we paid 30,000gns for Mutafani from Simon Crisford's yard. That now gives us three horses rated in the 90s, which isn't something we've had before."

In general, though, it's no doubt there is a significant youth policy at Tuer's yard, which is somewhat out of kilter with his background. Indeed, if you're still relatively unfamiliar to him as a trainer, you might well remember him better as an amateur jump jockey, finishing placed in the Foxhunter at Cheltenham (Trade Dispute in 2000) and its equivalent over the Grand National fences at Aintree (Son Of Anshan in 2002).

He first took out a training licence in 2002 and again focused primarily on the jumps, but since returning from an eight-year hiatus in 2016 the jumpers haven't had a look in. That switch began with his father Edwin, upon whose retirement Tuer returning to training, and since then he has had no interesting in rekindling his jumps passion.

The North Yorkshire trainer said: "I had unfinished business training. When we trained before we had tried to be predominantly a jumps yard and I can make all of the excuses in the world, but I felt when we tried to do it the northern jump

TRADE DISPUTE: third in the 2000 Cheltenham Foxhunter

racing scene was on a decline and it was very, very difficult to try to persuade people to own a horse and run on a Tuesday at Sedgefield in February, which is why I haven't got a jumps licence now.

"I'm Flat only and I find it a much more saleable product when we are so close to the likes of Thirsk, Catterick, Ripon, Pontefract and York – they're all within an hour or so of here. I've had in the last year one or two horses on the Flat who would go jumping and I've sold them – I find that much easier. I'd much rather train two-year-olds."

And no wonder when things are going this well.

The horses

Angels Faces 3yo filly
Gutaifan – Worthington

She ended up being quite disappointing last year because we really liked her early on. She was knocked sideways when making her debut and then really pleased us when third at Haydock, which told us we were on the right track. However, she ran three times after that and wasn't finishing her races at all. We've tried a few things with her during her time off and I'm hoping that will do the trick as she shows a lot more than her mark at home. It would be no surprise if she proved well handicapped.

Arabic Culture 6yo gelding
Lonhro – Kydd Gloves

He's done most of his racing on the all-weather and did well again this winter, but we've given him a little break since his last run at the end of January with a view to starting a turf campaign in May. He was a very good second at Newmarket last autumn on soft ground and he'd want a bit of cut.

Athabasca 3yo filly
Nathaniel – Sibaya

She's a nice filly. She had a couple of runs late last year and was a decent fifth at Newcastle. I'd be hopeful for her once she goes handicapping and the further she goes the better she'll be.

Bolder Bob 6yo gelding
Big Bad Bob – Semiquaver

He's a really good horse who won four times for David Barron before missing last year. He's over his injury and I'm hoping he'll be able to start back at the Dante meeting at York. He's not fully exposed by

BOLDER BOB: four-time could be Grant Tuer's much-desired Saturday horse

any means over a mile and a half and I'm also hoping he might get a bit further than that. I think we can get him back and have plenty of fun with him.

Etikaal 6yo gelding
Sepoy – Hezmah

Although he won at Yarmouth last summer, he tends to find things a bit harder on turf. The key to him is to be dropped out and covered up, so you need a really strong pace for him to go at. That often happens at Newcastle, where he's done well again this winter, but less so on turf. I'd be keen for him to go over a mile again.

Forus 3yo gelding
Mukhadram – Anbella

We picked him up for 12,000gns at the horses-in-training sale last October. He'd just won a nursery at Chelmsford for Jamie Osborne and he looks a decent horse. His win came over a mile and he could run over a mile and a quarter or even further. He's strong and I expect him to progress as a three-year-old.

Illusionist 3yo gelding
Hot Streak – Irishstone

He was fifth in the Windsor Castle for Archie Watson last year but disappointed a couple of times after that and we were able to pick him up quite cheaply at 13,000gns. I suspect that's more because he's not the biggest, so we've taken a bit of a punt on him, but he's really fast, an out-and-out sprinter, and there are lots of good three-year-old sprint handicaps to aim at.

Kaafy 4yo gelding
Alhebayeb – Serene Dream

He ran lots of good races last year but was quite frustrating as he'd then go and put in a poor run – basically, he was a typical three-year-old colt as his mind wasn't always on the job. He's been gelded since then, which should help, and we've also ironed out a few other little problems. He's a good-looking horse, so much so he looks like he should be rated 20lb higher than he is, so he has the potential to do well this year.

Kermouster 4yo filly
Garswood – Rise

She's a big filly and never stopped growing last year, so she did well to win four times, including a golden patch in the middle of the summer when she completed a hat-trick in a month. Her latest mark of 72 wouldn't be beyond her by any stretch of the imagination. We could possible step her up in trip a little bit and there muat be more improvement in her.

Lezardrieux 3yo gelding
Due Diligence – M'selle

He won a couple of nurseries on the all-weather towards the end of last year, but I fear they were pretty weak races and he probably wouldn't be thrown in now. That said, I could still see him winning a couple of sprints in the north. He'll be fine on fast ground.

Mutafani 5yo gelding
Exceed And Excel – Hokkaido

We went out looking for a Saturday horse at the Tattersalls sale in February and found him for 30,000gns. He'd been a good two-year-old for Simon Crisford in 2018, winning twice, and although he didn't show as much last year he'd been gelded and had a wind op before going on the all-weather this winter, when he was second at Chelmsford on his last run. We'll probably start him off at the Dante meeting at York and I'd like to think he'll be competitive in something like the Thirsk Hunt Cup. I'm sure we can find a nice handicap for him.

Out Of Breath 3yo gelding
Bated Breath – Parisi

He's a half-brother to Champarisi, who was an absolute superstar for us last year,

CHAMPARISI: a star for Grant Tuer, who bought her half-brother Out Of Breath

winning five times, before being retired to the paddocks. Because of that I'd followed him closely for Jamie Osborne last year and, when he put him in a seller at Leicester, I thought I'd take a chance on him. He soon won for us at Musselburgh and ran another good race when second at Redcar. He ran badly on his only run after that, but I should never have run him as he'd had a hard season. He should be competitive in handicaps this year, although he wouldn't have a mountain in hand. I can see him stepping up to a mile and a quarter.

So Macho 5yo gelding
Camacho – Turban Heights

He won at Brighton last summer but it was a terrible race and he's not been the most reliable. He's a big, strong horse, though, and I'm hoping he'll progress when we step him up in trip.

Swinging Eddie 4yo gelding
Swiss Spirit – Bling Bling

We got him for just £6,000 out of Kevin Ryan's yard at the horses-in-training sale last summer and got him started on the all-weather this year. Although he's had a fair bit of experience, he's still quite green and needs to learn to settle. The engine is there, though, and he's at the right end of the handicap to do well this summer.

Termonator 4yo gelding
Monsieur Bond – Easy Terms

He was bred by my dad and we were quite disappointed with him last year. However, he might have been running over insufficient trips as he never went beyond a mile and his dam won over a mile and a half at the Dante meeting in 2012. We'll step him up in trip sooner rather than later and he should progress the further he goes. He'll want some cut in the ground.

Unnamed 2yo colt
War Command – Malayan Mist

He'd be the pick of my two-year-olds – certainly the nicest long-term prospect, although he'll also be ready early . He's a half-brother to Moonlight In Paris, who won very nicely for John Gosden at the backend of last year, and we did well to get him for 27,000gns. We might wait for the 6f maidens with him.

Pedigrees for punters by James Thomas

THE ultimate arbiter of a stallion's success will always be what his runners achieve on the track, but some big hints about who will shine have been dropped long before each sire fields his first racecourse representatives.

Every stallion relies on support from breeders, so the number of mares covered – and subsequently foals produced – will ultimately dictate how many winners he is capable of producing in any given crop, while the quality of those mares – most commonly expressed through the number of stakes performers in his book – can also help guide our expectations.

Further down the line, experts such as bloodstock agents, owners and trainers will already have had the chance to assess the stock of new stallions at the yearling sales, so the sums their progeny achieved at auction – particularly when compared against the fees they were conceived at – can often tell us plenty.

But when assessing each year's new cohort of stallions, the covering fees at which they bred their debut crops is often a revealing starting point – and by that measurement, the first-season sires for 2020 really do lack a standout performer.

In 2019, the debut crop of Golden Horn hit the track having been bred at £60,000. Twelve months earlier Kingman's first two-year-olds, conceived at £55,000, did the same, while in 2016 Frankel's offspring made their first racecourse appearances, having been bred for £125,000.

This year's first-season sire with the highest introductory covering fee stood for just €27,500 when his first two-year-olds were conceived. That honour belongs to **Shalaa**, though it could be argued that such a fee undersells his credentials.

He was a top-class two-year-old for John Gosden and Al Shaqab Racing, winning two Group 1s, namely the Middle Park Stakes and the Prix Morny, and he also bagged a brace of Group 2s in the July Stakes and Richmond Stakes.

He retired to his owner's Haras de Bouquetot in France and covered a star-studded debut book of 158 mares. His yearlings proved in high demand at the sales, with his European average price of £103,860 comfortably the highest of any first-crop sire (with a double-figure representation at public auction) last year.

Shalaa is responsible for one of the most highly anticipated two-year-olds of the 2020 season as his daughter Paris is the second foal of none other than two-time Prix de l'Arc de Triomphe heroine Treve. The blue-blooded filly has gone into training with Andre Fabre.

Invincible Spirit's emergence as a sire of sires – with sons such as Kingman and Australia's I Am Invincible having made sizeable impressions – has been a running theme in recent seasons and there is every reason to think Shalaa can continue the trend.

However, while Shalaa undoubtedly has enough ammunition in Britain and Ireland to make an impression – with Richard

Hannon, Roger Varian and Ralph Beckett among the trainers with his progeny – it may just be that his biggest guns ply their trade in France.

Another former Al Shaqab colour-bearer set to field his first runners is Tally-Ho Stud's **Mehmas**, winner of the July and Richmond Stakes. With 146 two-year-olds on the ground, including a £260,000 half-brother to Golden Horde (bred at £12,500), he looks to hold solid claims of taking the leading first-season sire title (by number of winners) in Britain and Ireland.

Galileo, who claimed his 11th champion sire crown in 2019, boasts a growing number of sire sons, with the likes of Frankel, Nathaniel, New Approach and Teofilo all having supplied multiple Group 1 winners at stud. This year, **The Gurkha** will bid to join that list as his first runners appear.

It is hard to know exactly how precocious The Gurkha was himself as he didn't run until his three-year-old season, though he quickly made up for lost time by winning the Poule d'Essai des Poulains on just his third start and added a second Group 1 when landing the Sussex Stakes on his sixth and final outing.

What we can be more certain about is that his debut crop includes 117 two-year-olds conceived at a fee of €25,000, while his yearlings averaged £54,075. His first book of mares contained 49 (28 per cent) stakes performers, pointing to quality as well as quantity among his offspring. He also looks set to benefit from strong home support from Coolmore, with MV Magnier signing for The Gurkha's most expensive yearling, the €525,000 colt out of Larceny, who is now in training at Ballydoyle.

Another Classic winner among this year's first-season sires is Derrinstown Stud's **Awtaad**, whose finest hour came when landing the Irish 2,000 Guineas for Shadwell and Kevin Prendergast. His yearlings caused something of a stir at the sales, as confirmed by an average of £74,110 having been bred at just €15,000.

The pricest of those was the half-brother to Izzy Bizu who was bought by Sackville-Donald for 350,000gns, while Shadwell secured the half-brother to fellow Irish

SHALAA: the most expensive first-crop sire, albeit at just €27,500

2,000 Guineas scorer Phoenix Of Spain for €400,000. His debut crop numbers 93 foals, which came from a book of mares that included 29 (24 per cent) stakes performers.

Darley's **Territories** is another son of Invincible Spirit with plenty to recommend him now he begins his second career. The Prix Jean Prat winner hails from the same family as star sires Shamardal (sire of Blue Point, Earthlight and Pinatubo) and Street Cry (sired Winx and Zenyatta), and he has a squad of 110 two-year-olds to represent him. Noted judges such as Alex Elliott and the Blandford Bloodstock team gave six-figure sums for his yearlings, results which helped contribute to an average of £46,525 for youngsters bred at £12,000.

The team at Ballylinch Stud are behind one of the most upwardly mobile young stallions in Europe in Lope De Vega, who has risen from a fee of €12,500 to a high of €100,000 in 2020 having supplied ten Group/Grade 1 winners.

This year the operation sees **New Bay**'s first runners hit the track. The Group 1-winning son of Dubawi, who shares his sire with 2019's breakthrough freshman Night Of Thunder, has 77 two-year-olds to represent him, a bunch that brought an average price of £41,150 having been bred at €20,000.

Speaking of Lope De Vega, his son **Belardo** is also among this year's first-crop sires. The Kildangan Stud resident has a team of 92 juveniles who brought an average at £35,040 at the yearling sales having been conceived at €15,000. Early whispers suggest he is passing on plenty of the talent that helped him win the Dewhurst at two and Lockinge Stakes at four.

Breeders lost access to an old ally when Chelevey Park Stud retired Kyllachy in late 2017, but the Thompsons' operation may have found an heir in his son **Twilight Son**, winner of the Sprint Cup and Diamond Jubilee. With 122 juveniles in his armoury, who sold at an average of £29,325, he has the kind of ammunition required to make his mark with his first runners.

The Aga Khan's **Harzand** may not boast the kind of profile usually associated with champion first-season sires, but given he

THE GURKHA: has been given strong home support from Coolmore

was a top-class racehorse, winning the Derby and the Irish equivalent, it will be fascinating to see how the son of Sea The Stars fares nonetheless.

Despite his exemplary race record, he began life at stud at just €15,000 and produced 72 two-year-olds – a figure that pales in comparison to many of his peers. Given they come from a book of mares that contained 27 per cent stakes performers – and averaged £41,030 – there is every reason to believe his progeny can still have an impact, even if they don't prove to be especially early types.

The first-season sires mentioned above seem the most likely to make the biggest impression, but in a wide-open year the likes of **Adaay**, **Bobby's Kitten**, **Buratino**, **Charming Thought**, **Coulsty**, **Estidhkaar**, **Fascinating Rock**, **Kodi Bear**, **Markaz**, **The Last Lion** and **Vadamos** should not go totally overlooked, having also come in for their fair share of support.

With so many stallions having something to recommend them, it will be intriguing to see who rises to the top.

Ante-post preview by Steffan Edwards

2,000 Guineas

IT'S been a while since Godolphin were the team to beat in the Guineas, but that's how it looks this year – and not just because of the brilliant unbeaten favourite **Pinatubo**.

Pinatubo won all six starts last term, highlighted by a mightily impressive 9l win in the National Stakes at the Curragh. That performance earned him an official rating of 128, 10lb clear of the second best two-year-old, and on breeding he should also be suited by the step up to a mile. Granted normal improvement over the winter, he undoubtedly sets a high standard for the rest to aim at.

That's reflected in his short odds, though, and judged by his wins either side of the National Stakes (RPRs of 121 and 122) he perhaps he isn't as far clear of the opposition as that outlier performance suggests.

Godolphin's second string **EARTH LIGHT** looks a decent bet to turn over the favourite.

Like Pinatubo, he was unbeaten at two and won twice in Group 1 company. He raced exclusively over sprint distances, but that wasn't through design. He looked ready for a step up to 7f when taking the Prix Morny, and Andre Fabre said afterwards it would be the Dewhurst next, but then that became Pinatubo's target and he was rerouted to the Middle Park.

He won comfortably at Newmarket, if not by far, but he's by Shamardal out of a New Approach mare and there has to be great potential for improvement over further this year.

Fabre said he's likely to have a prep run before the Guineas and trainer history suggests it will be in the Prix Djebel, the trial taken in by Zafonic and Pennekamp prior to their Guineas wins, and also by Al Wukair, who finished third to Churchill three years ago.

Fabre's other potential candidate is **Victor Ludorum**, who was impressive in winning each of his three starts last year including the Prix Jean-Luc Lagardere. He travels well and can quicken, and would be an interesting contender, but all signs point to him going the Poulains-Prix du Jockey Club route. He raced exclusively over a mile on turning tracks at two, so it makes sense to keep him at home for similar races.

With Godolphin having such a strong hand already, it was a surprise to read that Saeed bin Suroor intends to run **Military March** in the race, especially as he is bred more for middle distances. He said he sees him as a Derby horse as well, so it wouldn't be a shock if plans changed and he was rerouted to the Dante.

Al Suhail is another who will be suited by further than a mile this year, while

Boccaccio looked good winning both his starts last year and should make up into a smart miler but will surely be targeted elsewhere with Appleby already having Pinatubo.

Aidan O'Brien has dominated this Classic, winning it in ten of the last 22 years, including four of the last five. However, his shortest-priced contender this time around is 16-1.

Arizona was well beaten by Pinatubo in the National Stakes but had another crack at him in the Dewhurst and finished a lot closer, despite his trainer being concerned about the soft ground. He has the size to progress from two to three so there is a chance he will overtake the Godolphin colt, and he looks the pick of the Ballydoyle horses.

Armory was progressing nicely before he bumped into Pinatubo in the National Stakes. He was then beaten in the Lagardere and in a match for the Criterium International, but the ground was against him in France and he can do better back on a decent surface. It wouldn't be a surprise to see him take his chance at Newmarket.

Wichita ran out a 7l winner of the Group 3 Tatersalls Stakes but then found the ground against him in the Dewhurst, in which he finished third. A winter's break and getting back on decent ground could see him step up.

Vatican City couldn't be better bred for the race, being a brother to Gleneagles, Marvellous and Happily, and he got some experience of the track when fifth on his debut behind Kinross before getting off the mark in comfortable fashion at Dundalk. However, he lacks the experience of his trainer's previous Guineas winners and would have to show something in the trial at Leopardstown to be of interest.

Royal Dornoch edged out Kameko to win the Royal Lodge but on balance looks a second-tier contender from the yard. The same goes for **Lope Y Fernandez** and **Royal Lytham**.

Monarch Of Egypt may not stay as well as his pedigree promises as he is a keen-going type who's shown plenty of speed, whereas **Mogul** and **Innisfree** look more like Derby horses in the making.

John Gosden has yet to win the 2,000 Guineas and looks a bit light on potential runners.

Palace Pier is probably the best of

EARTHLIGHT: Godolphin star can turn over the operation's first string Pinatubo

AL MADHAR (left): fascinating contender for the Richard Hannon team

them, but he wasn't seen again after picking up an injury to his tibia during his second win at Sandown. Gosden had intended to run him in the Lagardere next, and when that had to be shelved he mentioned the Greenham as a likely starting off point this year, the race he reintroduced Kingman in before the Guineas. It was also meant to be Too Darn Hot's prep race for last year's Guineas, so it looks significant that he nominated the race so far out.

He could be a springer in the market if all goes well at Newbury, but he does carry his head a bit high and might just lack the experience required for the Guineas.

It's not out of the question that **Waldkonig** or **Cape Palace** could run in the Guineas, but if they do it will probably be as a prep for the Derby, for which they are more suitably bred.

Siskin was unbeaten in his four starts last year, including a win on unsuitably soft ground in the Group 1 Phoenix Stakes. He had to be withdrawn from the Middle Park after playing up badly in the stalls, which is slightly concerning, and I'm not convinced he will be a miler this year. He has plenty of speed and it could be that the Commonwealth Cup becomes his main early-season target.

The Royal Ascot sprint could also be the target for the Mill Reef winner **Pierre Lapin** and Middle Park runner-up **Golden Horde**.

Kameko took his form to a new level when winning the Vertem Futurity. He has to prove that wasn't just because the race was switched to the Tapeta as he is bred to go well on synthetics, but there was plenty to like about the way he travelled into contention and pulled clear of the Ballydoyle contingent. Andrew Balding has said he plans to give him a prep either back at Newcastle or in the Craven.

The beaten favourite in the Vertem Futurity was **Kinross**, who had demolished a good field at Newmarket on his debut. He fell a bit short on the step up in class but retains plenty of potential, although a hold-up means this is likely to be too soon.

Positive didn't go a yard on the soft ground in the Dewhurst but had previously beaten Kameko in the Solario Stakes. Although he is by Dutch Art, he's out of a 1m4f winner so should get a mile all right.

Highest Ground impressed in winning on his debut given the ground he lost at the start. He wouldn't be able to get away with that sort of thing in the Guineas and, with the race coming so soon in the season, he might just lack the experience needed. An outing in the Craven would be a big plus.

Kenzai Warrior beat a subsequent

Group 3 winner on his debut at Salisbury, and built on that when taking the Horris Hill in November, looking very much at home in the testing ground. The Guineas will demand a lot more, but his trainer Roger Teal knows what it takes having sent out 50-1 shot Tip Two Win to finish runner-up in 2018.

The Richard Hannon stable is always worth respecting in the Guineas. Over the past ten years, in addition to Night Of Thunder, who won it in 2014, the yard has had seven horses finish placed in the race and all apart from Barney Roy were sent off at double-figure odds. Even he had been 20-1 before he won the Greenham on his reappearance. This year the stable has three contenders of note.

Threat improved steadily all year and defied a penalty to win the Champagne Stakes only to run below par in the Middle Park. It's possible that was just one run too many at the end of a long season and his trainer has long maintained that he's a Guineas horse in the making, so he could bounce back. The Greenham looks a likely starting point, and then the question will be whether he stays a mile. His pedigree suggests he should.

Mums Tipple won a strong novice at Ascot on his debut but no-one could have predicted what he would do at York next time, where he made every yard to win a 21-runner sales race by 11l. Sent off 3-1 for the Middle Park on the back of that impressive performance, he disappointed, but it later transpired he was lame having been kicked while he was in the stalls, presumably by Siskin who was withdrawn after getting upset in the stall next door. He looks the type to progress from two to three, but whether he'll be wanting to go as far as a mile is another question.

Perhaps it's just a coincidence, but since 2014, when Richard Hannon took over the licence from his father, three of the four horses to have made the frame for the yard were lightly raced at two, contrasting with the previous placed runners. Night Of Thunder had a couple of starts including a Listed win, Barney Roy only had a maiden win to his name and King Of Change had been beaten in both his starts.

AL MADHAR fits the profile this year. He wasn't seen again after winning his maiden at Newmarket in July but it was a strong race, with Al Suhail in second and plenty of subsequent winners down the field. He was strong at the finish over 7f and stepping up to a mile will only see him in a better light. He is definitely worth backing at 33-1.

2,000 Guineas

Newmarket, 2 May

	Bet365	*Betfred*	*Betway*	*Coral*	*Hills*	*Lads*	*PPower*	*SkyBet*
Pinatubo	10-11	10-11	Evs	Evs	Evs	11-10	11-10	**5-4**
Earthlight	**8**	**8**	**8**	**8**	**8**	7	**8**	**8**
Siskin	10	12	12	10	12	10	**14**	**14**
Arizona	10	**16**	14	14	12	14	**16**	10
Kameko	**16**	14	14	12	12	10	**16**	12
Palace Pier	14	16	16	14	16	16	**20**	14
Kinross	16	16	16	16	16	16	**20**	14
Victor Ludorum	14	16	14	16	14	14	**20**	-
Mogul	20	20	20	**25**	16	20	-	14
Wichita	**25**	**25**	20	20	20	16	20	20
Threat	**33**	25	18	16	25	16	20	20
Al Madhar	25	**33**	25	-	-	-	**33**	-
Armory	16	25	25	25	25	25	**33**	**33**
Mums Tipple	25	**33**	28	**33**	20	**33**	25	20

each-way 1/5 odds, 1-2-3

Others on application, prices correct at time of going to press

1,000 Guineas

THE market prefers the milers' form, that of the Fillies' Mile and Prix Marcel Boussac, to that of those who contested the Cheveley Park over 6f, but I'm not so sure and am going to take one from each division.

Raffle Prize didn't run a bad race all season and, despite being beaten into second, emerged with plenty of credit from the Cheveley Park, in which she helped to force a strong pace. If she can carry her speed to a mile she will be a huge player in the Guineas, but that is the doubt because, while her pedigree offers some hope, her style of racing leaves me with doubts.

The one who took advantage of the good gallop in the Cheveley Park was the Jessica Harrington-trained **Millisle**, who was outpaced at halfway but finished strongly to win convincingly. She was aided by getting a lovely run against the favoured stands' rail, but even so it was a performance that suggests she will have no issues stepping up to 7f. A mile is another question, though, as she is by a speedier sire than her siblings who stayed a mile-plus.

ALBIGNA: potential contender but could return to France instead

In third was **TROPBEAU**, who was dropping back in distance having won her previous three starts over 7f.

After her win in the Group 2 Prix du Calvados Andre Fabre had been considering the Marcel Boussac over a mile for her next start, but in the event she travelled over to Newmarket, perhaps for the better ground, which was expected to suit, and also to give her experience of the track, which is something Fabre always likes to do with his Guineas contenders. Outpaced at the back of the field early on, she didn't enjoy the clearest of runs as she closed from off the pace and her momentum was also checked by the weakening runner-up in the closing stages. She was unlucky not to finish second and looks sure to benefit from a return to further.

On breeding she wouldn't be sure to get a mile, but her form suggests otherwise as she was strong at the end of her races over 7f and again in a well-run race at Newmarket over 6f, while the fact Fabre was considering the Marcel Boussac suggests he has no doubts either. Dismissive quotes of 33-1 look far too big.

Harrington had a very strong bunch of two-year-old fillies last year and, in addition to winning the Cheveley Park with Millisle, she took the Prix Marcel Boussac with **Albigna**.

I'm not convinced she enjoyed the soft ground that day, but she was strong at the finish and won comfortably nevertheless. Sent to the Breeders' Cup afterwards, she ran well to take fourth given how much ground she had to make up from the turn in, once again putting in her trademark strong finish. I think a mile at Newmarket will suit her well, but the question is whether her trainer will run both fillies or split

CHEVELEY PARK: underrated as a trial, with third-placed Tropbeau a huge price

them up. The concern in backing Albigna is that she is the one with Longchamp form so would be the natural choice to take to France.

Harrington also trains **Alpine Star**, who was a gutsy winner of the Debutante Stakes and was all set to go for the Boussac, but a pulled muscle put an end to that plan and Albigna took her place. Yet another high-class prospect from the yard, she is a half-sister to Alpha Centauri, but given she is by Sea The Moon it's likely she will be at her best beyond a mile this year, while her jockey Shane Foley has said she needs cut in the ground.

Albigna and Alpine Star are both owned by the Niarchos family so it's reasonable to expect connections will be keen to keep them apart as well.

Harrington has said she has the Irish Guineas in mind for **Cayenne Pepper**, who didn't handle the Dip at Newmarket in the Fillies' Mile. She rallied well on the run to the line to regain fourth, but it is easy to see why her trainer might favour the Curragh for the filly, especially given the way she won the Flame of Tara there on her previous start.

Roger Charlton's **Quadrilateral** came a long way in three starts last year, bolting up in a conditions race at Newbury second time out and then getting up late to win the Fillies' Mile. The daughter of Frankel has a good attitude and clearly stays a mile well, but she was done for a bit of speed on easy ground at Newmarket before rallying late and it is likely she will need further to be seen at her best this year.

The Fillies' Mile runner-up **POWERFUL BREEZE** arguably shaped better with the Guineas in mind as she travelled comfortably and quickened to the front looking the likely winner only to falter close home. She more than confirmed her May Hill form with **Boomer** and has the scope to progress from two to three.

James Doyle will no doubt be keen to deliver her challenge a bit later in the Guineas. Her trainer Hugo Palmer has said she will go to the race without a prep run, which is what he did when he won the 2,000 Guineas with Galileo Gold four years ago.

Back in third was **Love**, who has a few similarities with last year's Guineas winner Hermosa. Both were a little short of the best around at two but showed steady improvement throughout the season. They are also bred along the same lines, by Galileo out of a Pivotal mare, and it isn't hard to imagine Love similarly improving the few pounds required to be in with a shout at Newmarket, although I suspect she will be at her best over middle distances.

Of Aidan O'Brien's other contenders, **Peaceful** won her maiden very easily on her second start at Thurles and then ran a close second in Listed company at Newmarket at the backend of the year. The ground was heavy that day and I doubt that suited her, but she got some experience of the track and there is potential for improvement this year on a quicker surface. She could emerge as a contender via the Leopardstown trial.

Etoile won a Group 3 on her debut in May but didn't really build on that in two subsequent starts, albeit in top company. She could still make the grade.

So Wonderful has so far appeared to have more ability than she is willing to show, carrying her head a bit high and yet to get off the mark in eight starts despite improving enough to be placed in Group 1 company. If she shows up she might be worth a place-only bet at a wild price.

The Freddy Head-trained **Khayzaraan** was an impressive winner of a maiden and a conditions race last year and was being considered for the Marcel Boussac afterwards. Although she missed out through injury there, she remains an exciting prospect. She's fairly high up in the betting for the Guineas, but at this stage I'd be surprised if she travelled over, the Pouliches looking a far more likely option.

Roger Varian's **Daahyeh** was a good two-year-old, winning the Albany and the Rockfel as well as finishing second in a couple of races at the top level. She got the mile pretty well at the Breeders' Cup, although Santa Anita is a sharp track and there would have to be a doubt about her getting the trip in a well-run race at Newmarket judged on her pedigree. In addi-

CLOAK OF SPIRITS: could be a springer in the market for the Guineas

tion, she isn't the biggest and it remains to be seen whether she trains on.

Close behind Daahyeh in the Rockfel were the smart maiden **Stylistique**, a stablemate of the winner, and Richard Hannon's **Cloak Of Spirits**. I don't think we've seen the best of the latter, a daughter of Invincible Spirit who impressed when winning on her debut at Ascot but then disappointed as favourite in the May Hill when too keen. Her better run at Newmarket afterwards suggests she could yet make the grade and she could be a springer in the market if she shows up well in one of the trials.

White Moonlight shapes like a middle-distance filly in the making, both on breeding and in the way she races, and the same goes for **Born With Pride**, **Fancy Blue** and **New York Girl**, while I suspect the Guineas will come too soon for the likes of **Heiress** and **Spring Of Love**, who won well at Newmarket in the autumn but are lacking in experience.

After a promising start to her campaign during which she was an early favourite for the Guineas, the wheels rather fell off for **Summer Romance**, who was comfortably held in her last two starts in Group 3 company. It is too early to write off this half-sister to Rizeena, who won the Coronation Stakes, but she has a lot to prove now.

Another with something to prove is the Sir Michael Stoute-trained **Melnikova**. She won a strong Kempton maiden on her debut despite taking a wider trip than ideal and was sent off favourite against Quadrilateral in a conditions race at Newbury only to be beaten 9l. She is by Frankel out of a daughter of Russian Rhythm, so is bred to win a Guineas, but she will need to bounce back in a big way to be a player at Newmarket.

Her stablemate **Soffika** overcame greenness to make a winning debut over 6f and then stayed on well to finish second in the Sweet Solera over 7f. There is more to come from her over a mile-plus but she needs to improve a good bit to be considered for the Guineas.

In **Pocket Square**, connections of Quadrilateral have a back-up option. Winner of a Group 3 in heavy ground at Deauville last autumn, she had previously quickened up well to win her novice at Ascot on good to firm, so she is clearly versatile, and she would merit her place in the line-up at Newmarket.

However, if all is well with the ante-post favourite it isn't hard to imagine them being kept apart and Pocket Square travelling back to France for the Pouliches.

1,000 Guineas

Newmarket, 3 May

	Bet365	*Betfred*	*Betway*	*Coral*	*Hills*	*Lads*	*PPower*	*SkyBet*
Quadrilateral	**6**	5	5	5	11-2	5	5	**6**
Powerful Breeze	**10**	8	9	8	**10**	8	7	**10**
Albigna	**14**	12	9	12	12	10	10	10
Khayzaraan	**16**	-	**16**	**16**	-	**16**	-	-
Daahyeh	16	16	**20**	**20**	16	**20**	**20**	16
Love	16	**20**	18	**20**	10	**20**	**20**	14
Raffle Prize	20	20	20	16	20	20	**25**	20
Millisle	14	-	16	14	16	12	**25**	20
Alpine Star	**33**	-	22	20	25	20	-	25
Tropbeau	25	-	25	20	20	20	**33**	25
Summer Romance	**33**	20	20	**33**	**33**	25	20	20
Cloak Of Spirits	**33**	25	25	20	**33**	25	**33**	**33**
Cayenne Pepper	20	-	28	**33**	25	**33**	**33**	20
Etoile	25	20	25	**40**	20	33	25	25

each-way 1/5 odds, 1-2-3

Others on application, prices correct at time of going to press

Derby

THE Derby looks wide-open, especially as the favourite **Pinatubo** can be taken on. He looks far too pacey to stay the trip and, if he goes beyond a mile this year, it will probably be later in the season. It's 14-1 bar so there is a winner lurking at a big price somewhere.

The Vertem Futurity winner **Kameko** looks a questionable stayer on pedigree and, being by Kitten's Joy, was hugely favoured by having the race switched to the Tapeta at Newcastle. I expect one or more of the Ballydoyle colts who chased him home that day to reverse the form if they meet at Epsom.

Speaking of which, Aidan O'Brien has the usual glut of possible runners, but he lacks a standout candidate at the moment, several having run to a smart level without separating themselves from the pack.

Mogul and **Innisfree** finished close to each other at Newcastle on the back of winning in Group 2 company and are both bred to stay well. The market currently prefers Mogul, who cost 3.4 million guineas and is a brother to Japan and Secret Gesture, but Innisfree finished the stronger behind Kameko. Their overall form is similar and there doesn't seem to be much between them.

Armory, **Royal Dornoch** and **Lope Y Fernandez** are unlikely to stay, whereas **Arthur's Kingdom** might need further.

Dawn Rising, who made his debut in the Group 3 Eyrefield Stakes at Leopardstown in October, is quite interesting. Although finishing last of five, he wasn't beaten far despite being quite green. It's notable that Donnacha O'Brien took the ride that day and he wasn't unfancied, being sent off 5-1 against more experienced rivals who had already shown decent form. A brother to last year's surprise Irish Derby winner Sovereign, he could take a big step up this spring.

Like last year when Sir Dragonet came from nowhere to go off favourite on the day, I wouldn't be surprised if the number one contender from Ballydoyle was

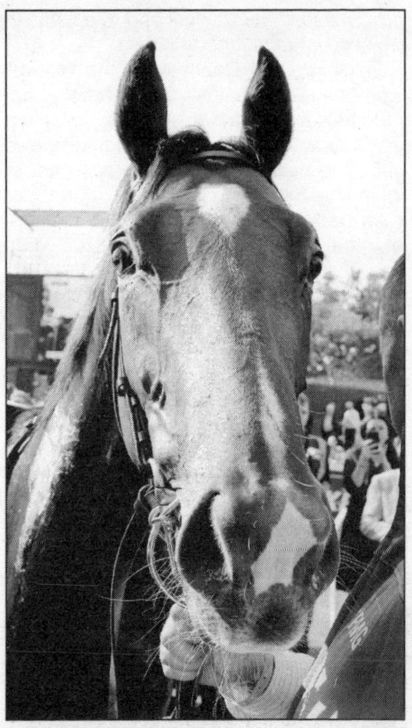

MOGUL: cost 3.4 million guineas but yet to separate himself from the pack

unraced at two. One name to look out for is **Gauntlet**, who is by Galileo and a half-brother to Arc winner Danedream.

Incidentally, in his first season training at David Wachman's old yard, Donnacha O'Brien also has an interesting unraced colt in **Star Of Juniper**, who is by Deep Impact and the first foal of a Group 3-winning sister to Minding.

Joseph O'Brien's **Degraves** has a nice combination of speed and stamina in his pedigree. A smooth traveller who can quicken, he has improved with every start and won the Eyrefield Stakes over 1m1f far easier than the winning margin suggests, idling in front. Being by Camelot, he should stay this far and his trainer suggested he'd reappear in a Derby trial this year. He isn't currently entered at Epsom so would have to be added in the spring.

There are a few questions to answer when it comes to who will represent John Gosden this year. **Palace Pier** isn't short of speed and looks more of a Guineas horse; **Enemy**, though a half-brother to Magic Wand and Chicquita, is by the sprinter Muhaarar, so it's unlikely he'll get the trip; and **Hypothetical** quickened right away to win over a mile on his debut at Chelmsford but his pedigree also raises doubts about his stamina.

Cape Palace won in great style on his debut at Newcastle, pulling 8l clear of a rival who won his next two starts including in Listed company. The trouble is he then blew out in the Haynes, Hanson & Clark next time out, racing a bit keenly and managing only third having been sent off a short-priced favourite. He didn't run again and it's likely that wasn't him at his best. While he has a bit to prove now, he could easily bounce back, and his pedigree gives hope he'll get the Derby trip.

The one from the yard who appeals most is **WALDKONIG**, who made a winning debut at Wolverhampton in December. It was a slowly run race and he didn't beat a great deal, but there was plenty to like about the way he overcame greenness to quicken up on the turn in and pull 9l clear in no time.

He is a half-brother to Arc winner Waldgeist but by a speedier sire in Kingman, which was evident in his ability to quicken at Wolverhampton. It might be that he has a bit too much speed, but ideally a Derby horse has a mixture of speed and stamina and, with the other side of his pedigree so stamina-laden (dam is a half-sister to St Leger winner Masked Marvel) there is every chance he will stay.

Five years ago Jack Hobbs won first

CAPE PALACE: not the only John Gosden hope to impress on the all-weather last season – Waldkonig was another and makes even more Derby appeal

Derby

Epsom, 6 June

	Bet365	*Betfred*	*Betway*	*Coral*	*Hills*	*Lads*	*PPower*	*SkyBet*
Pinatubo	6	**7**	11-2	6	5	6	**7**	**7**
Kameko	**14**	12	10	10	12	10	10	10
Mogul	12	10	12	**14**	12	**14**	12	12
Military March	16	**20**	16	16	16	16	**20**	16
Waldkonig	16	16	16	16	14	16	**20**	**20**
Palace Pier	20	**25**	20	16	20	16	**25**	20
Innisfree	**25**	20	20	**25**	**25**	20	20	20
Armory	14	16	20	20	**33**	20	20	25
Brentford Hope	28	**33**	**33**	25	**33**	25	**33**	**33**
Al Suhail	**33**	-	**33**	**33**	**33**	**33**	**33**	28
Enemy	**33**	**33**	**33**	**33**	**33**	**33**	**33**	**33**
Cape Palace	**40**	25	33	**40**	25	**40**	**40**	25
Highest Ground	**50**	33	33	33	33	33	**50**	33
Satono Japan	**50**	-	**50**	**50**	**50**	**50**	-	**50**

each-way 1/5 odds, 1-2-3

Others on application, prices correct at time of going to press

time out for the yard in a December Wolverhampton maiden and he came back the following year to finish second in the Derby, so it's a path the stable has taken before.

A slight concern is that Waldkonig has a bit of a knee action, but generally you don't win like he did on Tapeta and then need soft ground on turf and in any case Epsom is always well watered these days.

If anything, Gosden might have a more interesting bunch of unraced Derby contenders than Aidan O'Brien. It will be worth keeping an eye out in particular for **Darain**, who cost a whopping 3.5 million guineas and is a brother to Too Darn Hot, So Mi Dar and Lah Ti Dar. **Atheel**, the first foal of Oaks winner Taghrooda, and a couple of Anthony Oppenheimer-owned colts named **Golden Rules** and **Mr Curiosity** are also bred for the job.

The Saeed bin Suroor-trained **Military March** was two from two last year and strong at the finish in both races. His Autumn Stakes win looks solid form and his pedigree – brother stayed 2m – confirms the impression that he can only improve for a step up in distance this year. He wintered in Newmarket rather than Dubai, which is probably a plus, and has plenty to recommend him on paper.

Al Suhail improved with racing last year and is bred to come into his own over middle distances. He is a keen-going sort who wears a hood, though, and his half-brother Telecaster, who won the Dante and went off 5-1 for last year's Derby, got rather worked up beforehand, failed to settle in the race itself and dropped away to finish last. His dam Shirocco Star also tended to race keenly and failed to add to a maiden win despite being good enough to place on more than one occasion in Group 1 company, including the Oaks. I didn't like the way Al Suhail failed to win the Solario despite having a pacemaker set things up perfectly for him and he was outbattled by Military March in the Autumn Stakes.

Sir Michael Stoute's **Highest Ground** made an eyecatching debut at Leicester in September, blowing the start and giving his rivals a head start before coming through to win by 2¾l. It was an impressive performance and he has a bright future, but the vast majority of his siblings have been at their best over shorter and the trip is a question mark for me.

Stamina shouldn't be an issue for stablemate **Law Of One**, who went close to winning on his debut at Chelmsford despite not having much go his way. He is a half-brother to Cloth Of Stars, who twice finished placed in the Arc, but might prove more of a longer-term project.

The same is probably true of **Satono Japan**, a son of Deep Impact who did well to quicken up and win on his debut at Kempton despite being unfancied in the market. The form is nothing special but he is bred for middle distances and is open to plenty of improvement.

BRENTFORD HOPE is an interesting candidate. Richard Hughes started training in 2015 and this colt looks the best he has had so far. Making his debut in a backend Newmarket maiden, he cruised through from the back of the field before quickening clear to win easily.

By Camelot out of a half-sister to Beautiful Romance, who was beaten a neck by Vazirabad in the Dubai Gold Cup over 2m, he will clearly be primarily about stamina, so the fact that the race was over 1m2f on soft ground played to his strengths, but he showed pace as well in travelling smoothly and settling things quickly. With that combination of speed and stamina, he has all the attributes you would want in a Derby horse and is worth chancing at a price.

Hukum won from an impossible position at Kempton on his second start. He looks good but is a half-brother to Kasbaan, whose all-weather form is on a different level to his turf efforts, so there is a danger the same could be true for him.

Via De Vega came home strongly to win on his debut at Sandown and was then pitched into Group 1 company at Saint-Cloud, where he finished well held in bad ground. He can be forgiven that, but whether he is a Derby horse is open to question as none of his seven winning siblings ever raced beyond 1m3f and most proved at their best at up to a mile.

Stamina isn't going to be a problem for Ralph Beckett's **Max Vega**, who powered home to win the 1m2f Zetland Stakes on his third start. He relished the soft ground that day, though, and lacks size, so might find a few improving past him this season.

Beckett could have a more interesting contender in **Jacksonian**, who is by Frankel out of a Kahyasi mare and showed a good level of ability when chasing home Military March on his debut at Newmarket in July but didn't run again.

HUKUM (right): looks good but might not be quite as effective on turf

FANCY BLUE (near): Oaks contender is the pick of Donnacha O'Brien's yard

Oaks

THE obvious place to start is with the Fillies' Mile principals and Newmarket winner **Quadrilateral** heads the market. Both her pedigree and the way she rallied to win suggest she will relish stepping up to middle distances this year.

I can't argue with her place at the head of the market, but neither can I get excited about prices no bigger than 10-1.

Of the placed horses at Newmarket, **Powerful Breeze** is likely to be more at home sticking to a mile but **Love** is a sister to Flattering, who won at up to 1m4f, and Peach Tree, who won over 1m6f, so it's reasonable to expect improvement from her up once she steps up in distance.

Of the Jessica Harrington-trained fillies, it's not out of the question that **Albigna** will get the trip, but I see her more as a 1m-1m2f type for the time being. She is a strong finisher in her races but did win twice over 6f last year, including in Group 2 company, so is not short of speed.

Cayenne Pepper didn't handle the Dip at Newmarket in the Fillies' Mile but was rallying on the run to the line. She is by Australia and promises to stay, but perhaps the Irish Oaks at the Curragh will suit her better than Tattenham Corner and the camber at Epsom.

Alpine Star has the form in the book to be a player and, being by Sea The Moon, she should be well suited by middle distances this term, but it is thought that she is happiest with some ease in the ground.

William Haggas has a couple of interesting prospects on his hands.

Born With Pride was set a stiff task on her debut in the Listed Montrose Stakes, but she made most of the running and galloped on strongly to win narrowly from the more experienced Ballydoyle filly Peaceful and the Group 3-placed Run Wild.

It was a fine effort and she is bred to stay well, being a half-sister to Raheen House, who has won at up to 1m6f, but I do think she was suited by the testing conditions that day and might not be as effective on a quicker surface. Haggas also suggested Epsom might not be her track.

The more interesting contender from the yard is **DOMINO DARLING**, who won her novice in stylish fashion at Doncaster in October. She moved smoothly into contention and only had to be pushed out to take the measure of the 6-4 favourite **Gold Wand**, the pair drawing clear of the rest.

The time was good and already the form has started to work out well, with the third, fifth and sixth all getting off the mark since.

Domino Darling and Gold Wand are both by Golden Horn, but Domino Darling is the more stoutly bred of the pair on the dam's side, being a half-sister to Namibian, who won the Queen's Vase over 2m. While the ground was heavy at Doncaster, she looks the type who will be happier on a sounder surface.

As well as Love, Aidan O'Brien has a couple of others worthy of a mention.

Peaceful wouldn't be a certain stayer on the dam's side of her pedigree, but she is by Galileo and was strong at the finish over a mile in testing ground at Newmarket last backend, so I think she will get the trip and she is also open to improvement on quicker terrain.

Passion is nicely bred for the job, being a sister to Irish Derby and St Leger winner Capri. She stayed on well to win a hot maiden at Cork on her second start and her subsequent May Hill seventh is misleading as she was keeping on and likely going to be involved in the battle for the places when hampered, with Ryan Moore going easy on her afterwards. It wouldn't be a surprise to see her take a big step forward this term for a greater test of stamina.

Fancy Blue has an Oaks pedigree, being by Deep Impact out of a sister to High Chaparral, and she showed that stamina will be her game in staying on well to win both her starts last year. She is probably the pick of the horses previously trained by Aidan O'Brien who have been moved to his son Donnacha, who also has an unraced sister to Derby runner-up Cliffs Of Moher named **Lugnaquilla** in the yard.

Donnacha's older brother Joseph could well have a runner in **New York Girl**, who built on a promising debut fourth over a mile to take the Group 3 Park Stakes on her second start, finishing really strongly to lead close home on the drop to 7f. The heavy ground saw her stamina come into play but she should enjoy getting back on a sounder surface over further this term as she is by New Approach out of a Giant's Causeway mare who stayed beyond 1m2f.

John Gosden doesn't appear to have a top-tier contender at the moment but I'm sure that will change.

Miss Yoda won her first two starts in good fashion, giving weight and a beating to colts in the second of them at Sandown. She ran well again when second in the Zetland Stakes, especially as I doubt the soft ground was in her favour, and there is more to come from her back on a sound surface and over further.

Heiress was an authoritative winner on her debut over 7f at Newmarket in November. She is by Kingman, but her dam won the Oaks and her siblings include St Leger winner Sixties Icon and several others who stayed at least 1m4f. Robert Havlin, who rode her, said afterwards that she was on the weak side and mentioned 1m2f as her likely trip this year. It wouldn't be a shock if she got a bit further and she clearly has plenty of improvement in her.

Tiempo Vuela overcame greenness to finish well on top over a mile on her debut at Newcastle in October. By Lope De Vega out of a mare who won in Listed company over 1m5f, she will stay all right.

Star Spirit is unraced but has the right credentials on paper, being by Deep Impact and the first foal of Gosden's French Oaks winner Star Of Seville.

The last Gosden filly to discuss is **Frankly Darling**, second in a fillies' novice at Yarmouth last October which is often informative – two divisions in 2018 were won by Frankellina and Mehdaayih, who won Oaks trials and were sixth and seventh at Epsom. There were just nine runners last year and the first three all look contenders, including Frankly Darling, who travelled well for a long way but was seen off by a stronger stayer. She shaped with plenty of promise and, being by Frankel out of a Cheshire Oaks winner, should be well suited by the trip.

Roger Varian's **Cabaletta** stayed on strongest and it's easy to see why judged by her breeding as her dam won at up to 2m and she's a sister to a 2m winner as well. If anything the Oaks trip might prove on the short side for her.

Back in third was **Combine**, who stayed on from the rear. She is by Zoffany out of a Sadler's Wells mare and her trainer Hugo

Palmer sent out Architecture, another daughter of Zoffany, to finish second in the Oaks four years ago. There is enough stamina on the dam's side of her pedigree to give encouragement she will get the trip as well.

Sir Michael Stoute's **Soffika** is another daughter of Zoffany. She won over 6f on her debut but has the stamina in her pedigree (dam stayed 1m6f) to suggest the Oaks trip might well be fine for her.

White Moonlight, trained by Saeed bin Suroor, easily defied a penalty when beating colts second time out at Newmarket. She is bred to appreciate the trip, but she spent the winter in Dubai and in general that hasn't been a positive in recent times.

Ralph Beckett often has a runner in the Oaks and his most likely contender is **Trefoil**, who won first time up at Newmarket last backend. She is a sister to a 1m2f winner who stayed 1m4f so there is a good chance she will get the trip.

Delta's Royalty won at odds-on first time out at Kempton in December despite being so green the bare form underrates her considerably. She is bred to be high-class, being by Galileo and the only offspring of multiple Grade 1 dirt winner Royal Delta, who sadly died from the foaling. She could take a big leap forward.

Recommended bets

2,000 Guineas

Earthlight 2pts 8-1
(generally available)

Al Madhar 1pt 33-1
(Betfred, Paddy Power)

1,000 Guineas

Tropbeau 3pts 33-1
(Paddy Power)

Powerful Breeze 1pt 10-1
(bet365, Hills, Skybet)

Derby

Waldkonig 2pts 20-1
(Paddy Power, Skybet)

Brentford Hope 1pt 33-1
(generally available)

Oaks

Domino Darling 2pts 20-1
(Hills)

Oaks

Epsom, 5 June

	Bet365	*Betfred*	*Betway*	*Coral*	*Hills*	*Lads*	*PPower*	*SkyBet*
Quadrilateral	8	8	8	7	**10**	8	8	**10**
Powerful Breeze	12	-	-	-	-	-	**16**	-
Love	14	16	16	16	12	**20**	14	-
Born With Pride	16	-	16	16	16	14	**20**	12
Domino Darling	16	16	14	16	**20**	16	-	16
Cayenne Pepper	**25**	**25**	20	20	20	16	20	16
Fancy Blue	20	-	22	**25**	**25**	**25**	-	20
Peaceful	**25**	-	-	**25**	**25**	**25**	-	-
Albigna	**25**	-	22	-	**25**	-	-	16
Passion	25	**33**	**33**	**33**	25	**33**	-	**33**
Alpine Star	**33**	**33**	**33**	-	25	-	**33**	25
Delta's Royalty	25	-	25	25	**40**	25	33	-
Miss Yoda	33	-	33	**40**	33	**40**	33	33

each-way 1/5 odds, 1-2-3

Others on application, prices correct at time of going to press

RACING & FOOTBALL **outlook**

Nick Watts's horses to follow

AGITARE 3 ch c
Teofilo – Sway Me Now (Speightstown)
22433-

A maiden he might be, but Agitare showed a high level of form in his juvenile season and could still become a very good three-year-old. Some of his runs last year were excellent – he was beaten only a length by Sinawann at the Curragh in August and was placed behind Mogul in a Group 2 at Leopardstown after that. All bar one of his runs came over a mile and he is likely to be suited by middle distances this season. He has entries in the Irish 2,000 Guineas and Derby.

Jim Bolger, Co Carlow

ALBIGNA 3 ch f
Zoffany – Freedonia (Selkirk)
11614-

Although Albigna disappointed on her final start of the season in the Breeders' Cup in America, any horse is worth forgiving what can be an arduous trip at the end of a long season. She had looked electric prior to that when landing the Group 1 Prix Marcel Boussac in easy fashion and should be well up to a Guineas shot in the early part of the season. It would be no surprise if she stayed further, however, so an Oaks bid may not be out of the question. Her trainer certainly knows a good filly when she sees one having had Alpha Centauri for the same connections.

Jessica Harrington, Co Kildare

AUCKLAND LODGE 3 ch f
Dandy Man – Proud Maria (Medicean)
5144114-

Auckland Lodge made great progress as a juvenile last season, winning three times – twice at juicy odds of 15-2 and 6-1. All of her runs came over the minimum trip but, accoring to her breeding, six furlongs shouldn't be an issue. She also struck up a great rapport with claiming jockey Harrison Shaw, who was on board for every win. Her current mark of 77 still gives her a bit of scope and it would be no surprise if she improved well past that mark this summer. Good to firm ground suits well.

Ben Haslam, Middleham

BAYROOT 4 b c

Exceed And Excel – Alwarga (Street Sense)

32372-

This talented colt has only one win to his name – and that came in a Kempton maiden back in 2018. It's high time he improved on that and, based on his solid, if winless, campaign in 2019 he should have no problem in doing so. Bayroot's best effort last season came in a mile handicap at Doncaster's St Leger meeting, where he was beaten just a head by Qaysar in a race that turned into a bit of a dash. A mile appears to be his best trip and he seems to handle different ground types so is versatile in that regard.

Roger Varian, Newmarket

BUHTURI 3 ch g

Raven's Pass – Moon's Whisper (Storm Cat)

21563-

Not a stable star on last season's evidence, but Buhturi did show plenty of ability nonetheless and may improve for being gelded over the winter. His season began well with a close second behind Wild Thunder over 6f before he got off the mark at the next time of asking at Haydock over the same trip. That was the only success he managed, but he also ran well at Yarmouth on his final start of the campaign when beaten a length by Tiger Crusade. Six furlongs is his trip.

Charlie Hills, Lambourn

CAPE BYRON 6 ch g

Shamardal – Reem Three (Mark Of Esteem)

110310-

Group 1 company proved too much on Cape Byron's final start of last season, but that might have been down to the heavy ground as much as anything else and a top-level triumph might still be possible this season. It may come at his beloved Ascot where his course figures read 1027110 – and that includes a Victoria Cup/ Wokingham double last season. Six furlongs is his best trip and a Diamond Jubilee bid could be a viable option for him. Newmarket is the only other track he has won at, although he has performed creditably at Goodwood in the past.

Roger Varian, Newmarket

CHICAGO DOLL 4 oh f

Cityscape – Crooked Wood (Woodman)

351212-

Alan King has made a great play in recent seasons of having a strong Flat team and he enjoyed a great 2019. That was helped in no small part by Chicago Doll, who was very consistent on the turf and all-weather – winning one race on either, at Leicester in July and Wolverhampton in August. She was gradually upped in trip, starting off over a mile before finishing up over a mile and a half when a good runner-up at Kempton. Her mark of 83 still gives her some scope and she may even stay a bit further now she has turned four.

Alan King, Barbury Castle

CRESSIDA 3 b f

Dansili – Modern Look (Zamindar)

1-

John Gosden has a wide array of female talent in his yard and might have another good one on his hands in the shape of the Dansili filly Cressida. She won on her only start last season at Kempton, beating stablemate Wasaayef much more comfortably than a neck winning margin suggests. The way she came up mid-track to take the lead was impressive and she just idled close home with the race won. It was a maiden won by Billesdon Brook a few years ago and, with the runner-up having won on her next start, the form looks useful. She will stay a mile.

John Gosden, Newmarket

DOMINO DARLING 3 b f

Golden Horn – Disco Volante (Sadler's Wells)

1-

A well-bred filly closely related to Namibian and Westwood Hoe, Domino Darling could be one for an Oaks trial early in the season, possibly something like the Pretty Polly at Newmarket. She went off at 10-1 for a maiden at Doncaster last October, so maybe surprised connections by winning the race, beating 6-4 favourite Gold Wand by a neck with a good gap back to the third. The heavy ground didn't really suit her so the performance can be marked up and owner Anthony Oppenheimer would dearly love a good one from his Derby winner Golden Horn.

William Haggas, Newmarket

EAGLES BY DAY 4 bb c

Sea The Stars – Missunited (Golan)

21638-

Eagles By Day is all about stamina and it would be no shock if he improved massively when stepped up to two miles and beyond – possibly even putting himself in line for a crack at the Ascot Gold Cup. He didn't do badly as a three-year-old, winning his Salisbury maiden by seven lengths and finishing third at Royal Ascot behind Japan in the King Edward VII. He disappointed in the Bahrain Trophy on his final start of the campaign, but that shouldn't stop him progressing this season and his dam, Missunited didn't really come to the fore until she got older.

Michael Bell, Newmarket

HIGHEST GROUND 3 b c

Frankel – Celestial Lagoon (Sunday Silence)

1-

There were persistent whispers about this horse over the winter and it will be fascinating to see how high he can go in his Classic season. Racecourse evidence is brief, with a single outing at Leicester in September all we can call upon, but it should be said that what he did was very good. He thrashed Macho Boy by two and three-quarter lengths with the odds-on favourite, Godolphin's Law Of Peace, well held in fourth. It was even more impressive as he blew the start completely. He has all the right entries and could go all the way.

Sir Michael Stoute, Newmarket

IBERIA 3 b c

Galileo – Beauty Bright (Danehill)

17532-

Often one can make the impression that a Ballydoyle inmate is exposed – and one could certainly think that with Iberia as he won only once from five starts as a juvenile. However, horses from this yard can suddenly take off and show form which they had never seemed capable of and this could be just such a horse. He couldn't strike again after his debut win at the Curragh last July, but he ran good races in the Royal Lodge and Killavullan later in the season and might take off when sent over middle distances this spring.

Aidan O'Brien, Ballydoyle

INNISFREE 3 bb c

Galileo – Palace (Fastnet Rock)

2112-

As the winner of last season's Beresford Stakes, Innisfree is of automatic interest. It doesn't necessarily translate that he will be a top-class three-year-old, but the race has a fantastic roll of honour. On his latest start he was outpointed by Kameko in the Vertem Futurity Trophy, but who knows how much he was disrupted by the race being cancelled at Doncaster and transferred to the Tapeta of Newcastle? It doesn't alter the fact he is another fine middle-distance prospect and it would be no surprise if he did the Ballysax/Derrinstown double in the spring.

Aidan O'Brien, Ballydoyle

JUAN ELCANO 3 ch c

Frankel – Whatami (Daylami)

123-

It was very much a breakthrough year for Frankel as a sire last summer with British Classic successes coming his way via Anapurna and Logician. In Juan Elcano, he may have an outside chance of another. He did well to win on his debut at Haydock, pulling the race out of the fire late, and he wasn't disgraced in two subsequent starts in the Superlative and Champagne Stakes. All his runs came over 7f, but Frankel's progeny do stay very well, so he may get 1m2f/1m4f in time. He has a potent turn of foot and should be in for a good season.

Kevin Ryan, Hambleton

KHAADEM 4 br c

Dark Angel – White Daffodil (Footstepsinthesand)

172100-

Charlie Hills has proved so adept with sprinters in the last few years that it makes perfect sense to keep Khaadem firmly on the radar. He couldn't emulate Muharaar by winning the Commonwealth Cup, but he did emulate Magical Memory by hosing up in the Stewards' Cup at Goodwood. His last two runs both came in Group 1 company and he was below par in both, but neither race was a reflection of his true ability and he is much better than he showed in both. With a clean slate going into this season, Group-class sprints should be well within his remit.

Charlie Hills, Lambourn

LAND OF OZ 4 ch c

Australia – Madame Defarge (Motivator)

411113110-

As with most horses from this yard, Land Of Oz started off from modest beginnings, failing to get anywhere near in a trio of maidens all around the mile mark. Lo and behold, when upped to trips more in keeping with his breeding the following season, he blossomed, winning six races and finishing a good third in a hot-looking Melrose at York in August. On his final start of the season he finished nearer last than first in the Cesarewitch, but that was one run too many for him and it is best forgotten. A strong stayer, he could make his mark in Group company.

Sir Mark Prescott, Newmarket

LOGICIAN 4 ro c

Frankel – Scuffle (Daylami)

11111-

You can't do much more than go unbeaten for a whole season – five runs, five wins and five times as market leader. Logician may seem too obvious to put in the 30 but he was so impressive over a range of trips that it's madness to leave him out – he could really be anything connections want him to be. He could be kept to middle-distances bringing in races like the King George and Arc, but he didn't look to be stopping at the end of his Leger win so I wonder whether he would even stay an extreme trip as well.

John Gosden, Newmarket

NATIVE TRIBE 3 b c

Farhh – Anything Goes (Nayef)

21-

Native Tribe has no fancy entries as yet but he didn't do much wrong as a juvenile, finishing second at Newbury on his debut in July before going one place better at Sandown over a mile shortly afterwards. His future very much looks as though it will be over further, though, with his sire, Farhh, and damsire, Nayef, both positives for stamina. Indeed, his dam was a 1m4f winner in France and the 1998 Irish Oaks winner, Winona, also appears on the dam's side of her pedigree. He's not a name on everyone's radar just yet but do keep him on your side.

Charlie Appleby, Newmarket

OUTBOX 5 b g

Frankel – Emirates Queen (Street Cry)

26233-

Outbox's two seasons in training couldn't have been more contrasting. As a three-year-old he won three races from as many starts. However, last season he didn't win a single race, although on two separate occasions he was beaten a head and a neck. In one of those races he was done by the smallest of margins by prolific winner King's Advice in a red-hot Goodwood handicap and, although he wasn't as good in two subsequent outings in cheekpieces, he still retains potential for this season from 1m4f upwards.

Simon Crisford, Newmarket

QUADRILATERAL 3 ch f

Frankel – Nimble Thimble (Mizzen Mast)

111-

Frankel's progeny have tended to stay very well, but he does have a Group 1 mile winner to his name in Veracious, proving he can get speedier types, and in the unbeaten Quadrilateral he has a genuine chances of getting a Guineas winner. This filly showed a good all-round game last season. Two of her three wins were achieved by a neck and a head respectively, while at Newbury on her second start she also showed style in winning by nine lengths. There was more in the tank when she took the Fillies' Mile and she can win the 1,000 Guineas.

Roger Charlton, Beckhampton

QUE AMORO 4 b f

Es Que Love – Onomatomania (Mr Greeley)

034112-

Some of this trainer's greatest successes in recent years have come with sprinting fillies and, while Que Amoro has a long way to emulate the likes of Mabs Cross and Mecca's Angel, she is good and getting better. She rose in the handicap last year from a mark of 81 in June to 98 in September, winning two handicaps at York along the way including one by seven lengths. Just beaten in a Listed race at Ayr on her final start of the season, she could be up to Group level this season and is in the best hands to realise her full potential.

Michael Dods, Co Durham

QUINTADA 4 b f

Leroidesanimaux – Quiza Quiza Quiza (Golden Snake)

33105318-

Quintada isn't the most consistent, but when does that bother a horse from this yard? They run a lot and just when you think they may have reached a plateau they go again. This is essentially what happened to this filly last season. She started off with a win at Catterick in July before being well beaten in her next two starts. But then she regrouped, got her act together again and went in at Newmarket in September in a 1m4f handicap. An all-weather run to round off the season was unsuccessful, but she could easily have more in her off a mark of 82.

Mark Johnston, Middleham

SANGARIUS 4 b c

Kingman – Trojan Queen (Empire Maker)

114/31-

Sangarius was a noticeable disappointment in the 2018 Dewhurst, finishing only fourth. However, when you consider the first three were Too Darn Hot, Advertise and Anthony Van Dyck it puts it in some sort of perspective and he bounced back last season to win the Hampton Court Stakes easily – beating the useful Fox Chairman by more than two lengths. He wasn't seen after that and probably hasn't been the easiest to train, but Stoute is renowned for his patience and he could be Group 1 level as a four-year-old now.

Sir Michael Stoute, Newmarket

SINAWANN 3 b c

Kingman – Simawa (Anabaa)

512-

Every now and then Mick Halford unearths a good one – like Casamento – and Sinawann comes from a very good Aga Khan family. The dam's side of his pedigree traces back to the great Sinndar and, while that is more stamina-based, the influence of his more speedy sire Kingman could make for the perfect middle-distance horse. He won his maiden at the Curragh in August, beating Agitare, and then went for a Group 2 at Leopardstown, where he wasn't disgraced behind Mogul. He should improve enormously this season over further.

Mick Halford, Co Kildare

THREAT 3 ch c

Footstepsinthesand – Flare Of Firelight (Birdstone)

122115-

Threat gave a very early indication that he was in for a good season when winning on his debut at Newmarket in May at odds of 10-1. He backed that up with great seconds in the Coventry and Richmond before returning to winning ways in the Gimcrack and Richmond – both Group 2s. Although only fifth on his final start in the Middle Park, the drop back to six furlongs probably found him out and he will be much better this season when stretched out to a mile. By a 2,000 Guineas winner, he will probably try to emulate him in 2020.

Richard Hannon, East Everleigh

TRUESHAN 4 b g

Planteur – Shao Line (General Holme)

11211-

Another from the King yard to make the list, Trueshan is owned by the fantastically successful Barbury Lions syndicate. He had a fantastic campaign last year, winning four of his five races, including a heritage handicap at Newmarket and a conditions race at Newbury, where he edged out the useful Hamish by a neck. That success came on officially heavy ground, so he obviously doesn't mind it deep, but earlier on he had also scored on good and good to soft ground so he is versatile. Effective from 1m4f-1m6f, he can win a Listed or a Group 3 easily.

Alan King, Barbury Castle

VICTOR LUDORUM 3 b c

Shamardal – Antiquities (Kaldounevees)

111-

In what turned out to be a stellar season for the sire, Shamardal, Victor Ludorum turned out to be one of his best, winning all three starts last year. He was a late developer as he didn't make his debut until September 1, but he quickly made up for lost time and in a little over five weeks he had progressed into a Group 1 winner – taking the Jean-Luc Lagardere by three-quarters of a length over Alson. He goes on any ground and his trainer expects him to stay 1m2f so maybe the French Derby could be his big aim.

Andre Fabre, Chantilly

WASAAYEF 3 b f

Kingman – Seagull (Sea The Stars)

212-

Although winning only one of her three starts last season, she actually came very close to going unbeaten. Her two defeats, either side of a win at Newmarket, were by tiny margins – two necks respectively. On her final start of the season in September, in a novice race at Newmarket over a mile, she was just done by the Roger Varian-trained Queen Daenerys, who took her chance (and ran quite well) in the Fillies' Mile subsequently. That was her first start over a mile, which she seemed to stay very well, and further may well suit this term.

John Gosden, Newmarket

WEEKENDER 6 b g

Frankel – Very Good News (Empire Maker)

6140137-

Weekender has been around for a few years now, but he continues to hold his form very well and notched his fifth career win at Salisbury last September when edging out King's Advice by a neck over 1m6f. Subsequent to that he was placed in a Listed race at Newmarket back down to 1m4f and he can easily be forgiven a rare flop on the all-weather at Kempton in December. He made no show in the Ebor last season, but he finished second in it two years ago and it would be no surprise to see him back there for a third crack this August.

John Gosden, Newmarket

WENTWORTH FALLS 8 gr g

Dansili – Strawberry Morn (Travelling Victor)

52265305-

An ex-Godolphin gelding, Wentworth Falls hasn't won for a while, but having been rated as high as 96 a few years ago he is starting to slide back down the ratings and some of his efforts last season indicate that the ability still lurks within. His best effort came at Doncaster last May when a neck second to Sir Maximilian in a 6f handicap off a mark of 93 – 3lb higher than the rating he kicks off this season with. Although campaigned solely on turf in 2019, he is effective on the all-weather too, so his options are plentiful.

Geoff Harker, Thirkleby

Top ten horses

Albigna	Khaadem
Bayroot	Logician
Cape Byron	Threat
Highest Ground	Trueshan
Juan Elcano	Wasaayef

LOGICIAN: has overcome peritonitis and will be seen later in the season

Newmarket by Aborigine

JOHN GOSDEN won back-to-back trainers' titles for the first time in 2019 when his older team provided most of the ammunition behind a record haul of 192 winners.

The Clarehaven Stables handler breached £8 million in prize-money for the second successive year in landing his fourth domestic crown and it could be argued he has an even stronger array of senior stars to go to war with in 2020.

Top contributor last year was obviously **Enable**, who was the centre of attention even after her defeat in the Arc in October when it was announced she would stay in training as a six-year-old.

Prior to her Paris reversal, Enable had looked on top of her game when winning the Eclipse, King George and Yorkshire Oaks and all roads will again lead to another shot at a record-breaking third Arc win.

She is unlikely to appear until Royal Ascot in June and will have another second-half-of-the-season campaign.

Logician is likely to be out even later than Enable after an eventful winter during which he suffered from a bout of life-threatening peritonitis.

Last year's St Leger winner has been recovering in the spring and should be worth the wait as he is another top-class prospect for Group 1 middle-distance races.

Fellow Classic winner **Star Catcher** is a bit more forward than that pair and did have an entry in the Sheema Classic in Dubai, although that was expected to come too soon at the time of writing.

The daughter of Sea The Stars should be a big player in all the fillies' Group 1 contests around Europe this summer and could even wind up at the Breeders' Cup.

Others on the team of older horses include three-time Group 2 winner **Enbihaar**, Cambridgeshire hero **Lord North** and **King Of Comedy**.

Of the Classic generation, **Waldkonig** looked an exciting colt when scoring by nine lengths on his debut at Wolverhampton in December and will have Derby aspirations, while **Palace Pier** has overcome a setback and could be a 2,000 Guineas horse.

Talking of the first Classic of the year, *CHARLIE APPLEBY* holds all the aces with the unbeaten **Pinatubo**, who has wintered well at Moulton Paddocks by all accounts.

Last seen when landing the odds in the Group 1 Dewhurst Stakes at Newmarket in October, the son of Shamardal is expected to head straight to post on May 2 via a racecourse gallop at the Craven meeting.

He will be very hard to beat as he bids to give Appleby his second domestic Classic after Masar's triumph in the Derby two years ago.

Of his older team, **Ghaiyyath** looks sure to be in the mix in top middle-distance races in Europe this summer after kicking off in Dubai, while **Space Blues**, **Cross Counter** and **Old Persian** are also capable of making their mark at the highest level.

Over at the rival Godolphin base of *SAEED BIN SUROOR* on the Bury Road, most of the older team and nicer three-year-olds have wintered in Dubai, but one notable exception is the classy **Military March**.

The son of New Approach was unbeaten in both juvenile starts, most notably

PALACE PIER: has had a setback but is over it and goes for the Guineas

POWERFUL BREEZE: ran a cracker behind Equilateral at Newmarket

when overcoming Al Suhail in the Group 3 Autumn Stakes at Newmarket in October.

Obviously at home on the Rowley Mile, Military March has done very well over winter and will be trained for the 2,000 Guineas, but a crack at the Derby looks a strong possibility after that judged on his pedigree and the longer trip could see him come into his own.

Other promising three-year-olds to remain at HQ over winter include the unraced pair **Untold Story** (colt by Teofilio) and the filly **Beautiful Scenery** (by Shamardal), who holds an Irish Oaks entry.

HUGO PALMER is another Newmarket trainer with serious Classic aspirations.

Palmer would appear to have his best chance of winning a Classic since Galileo Gold handed him a breakthrough success in the 2,000 Guineas in 2016 with **Powerful Breeze**, who went down fighting when second when last seen in the Group 1 Fillies' Mile in October.

The daughter of Iffraaj has wintered very well and spent a six-week break at Barton Stud near Bury St Edmunds, the very place where she was conceived in 2017.

Powerful Breeze had run out a game winner of the Group 2 May Hill Stakes at Doncaster in September prior to her narrow Newmarket reversal and is to plot a similar course to the Classic as her predecessor Galileo Gold.

Palmer told Aborigine: "Powerful Breeze is cantering away nicely and the plan is to take her to the Craven meeting for a racecourse gallop in April before heading for the 1,000 Guineas. It's something that we did with Galileo Gold to good effect and it makes sense to do it again."

ROGER VARIAN registered his best ever season numerically with 116 winners and over £2.6 million in prize-money in 2019 and has plenty of talent tucked away at

SANGARIUS: back for more at the yard of Sir Michael Stoute

Carlberg Stakes on the Bury Road to better that in 2020.

Like those adjacent to him, Varian has plenty of older bullets to fire again but also some nice three-year-olds, including **Pierre Lapin**, who landed the Group 2 Mill Reef Stakes when last seen at Newbury last September.

Other classy types include **Molatham**, who was on a roll until turned over in the Group 3 Autumn Stakes at Newmarket, where he may well have been undone by the undulations and soft ground.

Varian also went mighty close to winning again at the Breeders' Cup last November when **Daahyeh** was just touched off in the Juvenile Fillies Turf and she could well be a major player In the 1,000 Guineas.

Varian's neighbour *SIR MICHAEL STOUTE* is still a force to be reckoned with, especially with his older horses, and the likes of **Veracious**, **Regal Reality**, **Mustashry**, **Sangarius** and **Sextant** are still to be found at Freemason Lodge and Beech Hurst.

Apart from the claims of those old stagers, Stoute could have a Derby hope on his hands in **Highest Ground**, who was a most impressive winner of his sole start at Leicester last backend.

Judging by his recent work, Highest Ground has wintered exceptionally well and the son of Frankel can be expected to take in a Derby trial this spring.

Highest Ground is owned by the Niarchos family, who have a similar type on their hands in Law Of One.

A brother to Group 1 winner Cloth Of Stars, Law Of One ran an eyecatching debut when fourth at Chelmsford before Christmas and could be anything.

Just along the Bury Road at Bedford House Stables, *CHARLIE FELLOWES* is fancied to make a splash in his second season at Luca Cumani's former base with the likes of Derby hope **King Carney**.

The son of Australia was most progressive last backend when winning twice, most notably landing the Listed Silver Tankard Stakes at Pontefract, and he should get a mile and a half.

Across town on Racecourse Side, *DAVID SIMCOCK* seems to have more horses than ever and has a strong old guard, including **Spanish Mission**, who may kick off his season at the Dubai Carnival but has the Melbourne Cup as a long-term goal.

Smart handicapper **Durston**, a winner at Doncaster and Chester last summer, should also pay his way.

Down the road at Gainsborough Stables, **A'Ali** failed to give *SIMON CRISFORD* a first win at the Breeders' Cup last November when well fancied, but the dual Group 2 winner may well emerge as a leading contender for the Group 1 Commonwealth Cup at Royal Ascot come June.

Crisford has his team well forward as he was crossing Newmarket to use Warren Hill most days in February, ensuring his team won't lack for fitness in the early stages of the turf season.

Similar remarks apply to *JAMES TATE*, who has recently expanded to more than 100 horses and has bought Alan Bailey's former yard across the road as an overflow. Tate often makes the trek across town to use Warren Hill, a ploy that paid dividends last year when the stable had its best ever tally with 74 winners.

Among Tate's ammunition is the promising filly **Melodic Charm**.

This daughter of Exceed and Excel confirmed the promise of some smart homework when scoring on her debut over 6f at Wolverhampton last August before finishing fourth to Streamline in the Group 3 Sirenia Stakes the following month. She has wintered well at Jamesfield Stables.

Also worth noting is the colt **Sky Commander**, who looks an exciting prospect.

The Saeed Manana-owned son of War Command found things happening a bit quick for him when he finishing only eighth on his debut over 6f at Leicester in May, but it was a different story when he resurfaced after five months out over an extra furlong at Kempton before Christmas.Given a patient ride by James Doyle, Sky Commander went right away from some streetwise types to score by seven lengths.

Tate has the Listed Burradon Stakes at Newcastle on April 10 in mind for his promising type.

Last but not least, *GEORGE MARGARSON* deserves a mention as the veteran trainer can always be relied upon to turn up a diamond of some sorts and has another in **Ropey Guest**, a serial loser but one with some high-class placed form to his name.

The son of Cable Bay reached the frame in five of his ten starts last year, most notably when second to Kenzai Warrior in the rescheduled Group 3 Horris Hill at Newmarket in November, and earned a mark of 101 despite not getting his head in front.

Margarson is eyeing a return trip to the Rowley Mile for the Free Handicap in April for his stable star, who could then head to the 2,000 Guineas. He is just the type who could manage a place at a massive price.

Hot off the Heath

Logician
Powerful Breeze
Ropey Guest

A'ALI: a definite contender for the Commonwealth Cup at Royal Ascot

Ireland by Jerry M

THERE was a somewhat more egalitarian look about the Irish juvenile rankings at the end of last season.

As ever, though, *AIDAN O'BRIEN'S* Ballydoyle operation had far more juveniles rated 100-plus than anyone else and it is the logical place to start.

Among the colts, everything really hinges on how well Pinatubo trains on, so far was he in front of the rest of the two-year-old crop, and Irish racegoers were privileged to see him put up the best performance by a juvenile in many years in the National Stakes at the Curragh in September.

ARIZONA: goes for the Guineas

The top-rated Irish two-year-old was O'Brien's **Arizona**. His victory in the Coventry Stakes in June gave portents of possibly a stellar season to come, but it was his last success.

However, he lost little in defeat against Pinatubo in the Dewhurst and when unlucky in running in the Breeders' Cup Juvenile Turf and he looks the most realistic one to put it up to Pinatubo in the 2,000 Guineas.

Wichita ran below his best in the Dewhurst but had been a very impressive winner of the Tattersalls Stakes at Newmarket a couple of weeks previously and could add some depth to the Ballydoyle challenge.

Armory finished a remote second to Pinatubo at the Curragh and is also a likely representative at Newmarket. He stepped up on that when a close third in the Prix Jean-Luc Lagardere but clearly needs to improve a great deal.

O'Brien is likely to hold a much stronger hand over middle distances.

Innisfree ended up with a mark of 111 and is bred to stay a mile and a half. He also showed a really good attitude to just prevail in a heavy-ground Beresford Stakes in September and, while he didn't have the pace to go with Kameko in the Vertem Futurity Trophy at Newcastle, it was probably his best performance of the season.

There should not be much between him and **Mogul**, not far behind Innisfree at Newcastle and a colt who improved through the season.

Royal Dornoch will probably get a chance to prove himself over a mile and a quarter early in the year rather than sticking at a mile for long. His narrow defeat of Kameko in the Royal Lodge Stakes makes

KEW GARDENS (left): will have the Gold Cup on his agenda

very good reading now after the latter's performance in the Vertem Futurity.

Easily the best of last year's Ballydoyle fillies would appear to be **Love**.

She enjoyed a very good campaign last season and turned up everywhere, winning the Moyglare Stud Stakes and arguably putting up a better performance in defeat when a very solid third to Quadrilateral in the Fillies' Mile.

She will most likely start off over a mile and may get a chance to prove that she stays beyond that trip.

Among those likely to do well over sprint trips, a couple to stand out are **Monarch Of Egypt** and **Royal Lytham**.

Monarch Of Egypt came up short against Siskin a couple of times but held his form quite well, while Royal Lytham followed up his July Stakes win with a solid third in the Phoenix Stakes with a slipped saddle.

With the Classic generation possibly lacking the strength in depth of previous seasons, it is good news for Ballydoyle that plenty of their good older horses are set to stay in training this year.

Magical enjoyed a fine campaign last season, culminating in deserved victories in the Irish Champion Stakes and the Ascot equivalent, and helps to give the stable a powerful hand in the big middle-distance contests if O'Brien succeeds in persuades in talking 'the lads' into reversing last year's retirement decision.

That O'Brien was so keen for her to stay in training after seeing how well she had wintered speaks volumes.

Allied to that is the return of Prix de l'Arc de Triomphe fourth **Japan**, last season's joint top-rated three-year-old. He has been partially bought by Japanese interests with the Arc as his main target.

Derby winners **Anthony Van Dyck** and **Sovereign** both remain in training, while other middle-distance performers such as **Lancaster House**, **Broome**, **Mount Everest** and **Sir Dragonet** all return this year.

Kew Gardens will get his chance to stake a claim as the leading stayer in the business, claims initially laid by his battling defeat of Stradivarius in the Long Distance Cup at Ascot in October.

Leading miler **Circus Maximus** will return this year after a three-year-old campaign highlighted by victories in the St James Palace Stakes and a controversial win in the Prix du Moulin.

BUCKHURST: should continue to progress this year for Joseph O'Brien

JOSEPH O'BRIEN is once again likely to be the main competition to his father in terms of volume of winners. He doesn't have any obvious Classic contenders, but there are a number of three-year-olds of whom the best is yet to be seen.

Principal among those could well be Killavullan Stakes winner **Degraves**, likely to be prepared for an Irish Derby bid.

Alligator Alley could make up into a useful sprinter. He created a good impression when a ready winner of the Roses Stakes at York and was not disgraced in the Breeders' Cup Juvenile Sprint Turf.

The very promising **New York Girl** holds an entry in the Irish Oaks, although she might get the chance to see what she can do over a mile first. She broke her maiden tag in the Group 3 Park Stakes at the Curragh from stablemate **A New Dawn**, who is entered in both the Irish 1,000 Guineas and Irish Oaks.

Undoubtedly, though, the strength of the O'Brien charge will be among his older horses. Breeders' Cup winner Iridessa won't be back, nor will Group 2-winning mare Red Tea, but plenty of others will.

Master Of Reality went down by only a length to Stradivarius in the Ascot Gold Cup and was later beaten a head in a driving finish to the Melbourne Cup. He will be vowing for top staying honours.

Despite being more soundly beaten at Flemington, the 2018 Irish Derby winner **Latrobe** also looks likely to go more down the staying route this season than he did in 2019, which should suit.

Buckhurst was progressive throughout last season and looked like he stayed a mile and a half well when second in a Group 3 at Leopardstown on Champions Weekend. He could well progress enough to at least contemplate giving him a crack at the highest level.

Speak In Colours will continue to be an effective sort over 6f, although 7f looks now as though it might be her optimum trip.

The story of last season was *JESSICA HARRINGTON* and the amazing run of success she had with her juvenile fillies.

On official ratings, she has the two best fillies in her care in Millisle and Albigna and it does not stop there.

From the humble beginnings of a Bellewstown maiden, **Millisle** progressed and ended up recording a battling success in the Cheveley Park Stakes at Newmarket. The way she won demonstrated that she has every chance of staying a mile.

Albigna was one of those fillies who really stood out at the end of a race. She handled any ground last year, bolting up in the mud in the Prix Marcel Boussac and an unlucky fourth on fast ground in the Breeders' Cup Juvenile Fillies Turf. She will stay middle distances but is likely to get a chance over a mile before that.

If there is an Oaks filly in the yard, it is **Cayenne Pepper**. She enjoyed an almost unblemished campaign last season, winning her first three starts, but arguably a lot more was learned by her strong-staying fourth to Quadrilateral in the Fillies' Mile at Newmarket. Middle distances look very likely to be her strength.

GER LYONS finally broke his duck in domestic Group 1s with the victory of the unbeaten **Siskin** in the Keeneland Phoenix Stakes in August, a victory achieved on unsuitably soft ground.

He didn't get the chance to back that up after it all went wrong at the start in the Middle Park and his achievements were a little overshadowed, particularly by the brilliant Pinatubo, but he is a fascinating player this season.

The chances are that he might be at his best at around 6f, but expect Lyons to at least give him the chance to prove himself over 7f and see what happens.

Lyons had a pretty good bunch of juveniles last season overall. **Nurse Barbara** was beaten in the last stride in a Leopardstown Listed event before running respectably in the Cheveley Park and her best days are ahead of her, while the useful-looking **Auxilia** has an Irish Oaks entry but will probably be given a chance to prove herself in a Guineas trial.

SISKIN: a fascinating player this year

DERMOT WELD's best three-year-old might not even have seen the light of day yet, but his best juvenile from last season is the 107-rated **Shekhem**.

He progressed throughout the season, ending with a very narrow defeat by Innisfree in the Beresford Stakes. He holds entries in the Derby and the Irish Derby and his early campaign is likely to be with those races in mind.

Weld has a strong looking hand among his older horses, the best of whom will be middle-distance and staying horses.

Tarnawa was a progressive filly and it is hoped that she will be able to make the breakthrough at Group 1 level over 1m2f-1m4f.

Irish St Leger winner **Search For A Song** and rapidly improving handicapper **Kastasa**, who made the breakthrough at Group 3 level in September, will be campaigned in a staying division which could be the hottest it has been for some years. Add into the mix the exciting **Falcon Eight** and Weld will be able to campaign those assets far and wide.

Last year's top older miler **Romanised** will be returning for another year. Trainer *KEN CONDON* is likely to start him off in the Lockinge and will be aimed at all of the top mile races once again.

No horse improved more last season than the *DENIS HOGAN*-trained sprinter **Make A Challenge**. He only emptied in the last half-furlong of the Group 1 Champions Sprint at Ascot in October and could do very well over the minimum trip this season.

Just in front of him that day was the *AIDAN FOGARTY*-trained **Forever In Dreams**. She had earlier been second in the Commonwealth Cup and there could easily be a Group 1 sprint to be won with her this season.

Invincible Irish

Buckhurst

Royal Dornoch

Siskin

Berkshire by Downsman

NOT for the first time, the most exciting horse in Lambourn last year was **Battaash** and, having famously banished one hoodoo, the first half of the season will be all about trying to do the same with another.

The lightning-quick six-year-old has twice been beaten in the King's Stand at Royal Ascot, but that was also the case in the Nunthorpe before his bewitching display at York last summer.

He is hard to beat at his brilliant best and was far more consistent last season as he settled down with age. His sole flop came in the Prix de l'Abbaye, in which trainer *CHARLIE HILLS* thinks the ground and draw were against his stable star.

Hills, who will start Battaash in the Temple, is brilliant with sprinters and Stewards' Cup winner **Khaadem**, who has thrived during the winter, is another who should do well. The Diamond Jubilee is a big plan for him.

Other speedsters to note from the yard are the highly regarded **Equilateral**, who has been gelded, and **Garrus**, who will be tried over 6f.

Royal Hunt Cup winner **Afaak** will be aimed at that race again but should also get a mile and a quarter, while **Brushwork** is a scopey horse capable of making his mark in decent handicaps.

Persuasion, **Cable Speed**, **Royal Commando** and **Tommy De Vito** are three-year-olds to keen on your side, while **Badrah** is a promising filly who might take in a Classic trial.

That is also what *CLIVE COX* is thinking of for the exciting **Positive**, who will stick to a sound surface after his Dewhurst no-show. Cox is thrilled with how his Solario Stakes winner – in a red-hot renewal of that Group 3 – has done over the winter.

Golden Horde has also strengthened up again despite being a strong juvenile last term. He is seen as a sprinting type and the Commonwealth Cup is his goal.

BATTAASH: a third crack at the King's Stand beckons for him at Royal Ascot

ENGLISH KING: is in the Derby and owner Bjorn Nielsen is keen on him

Like Hills, Cox excels with sprinters and **Snazzy Jazzy** (on easy ground), **Tis Marvellous** and **Shades Of Blue** are reliable types who should continue to be profitable, as should **Hand On My Heart**, while **Wise Counsel**, **Dance Fever** and **Notforalongtime** are thought capable of improvement.

Getchagetchagetcha should also develop into a solid stayer, especially with cut in the ground.

ED WALKER'S globetrotting stalwart **Stormy Antarctic** should continue to perform with credit, while **Caradoc**'s ability has not levelled out yet.

Royal Intervention ought to be at home in classy Group sprints and **Tonyx** is another four-year-old filly open to progress, albeit over middle distances.

Owner Bjorn Nielsen is said to be quite keen on **English King**, who is in the Derby, in which **Bright Eyed Eagle**, who can win a race before too long, is also entered.

OWEN BURROWS could be in for a productive campaign with his older horses and **Habub**, effective on the all-weather and round a bend, can translate that form to turf on good ground over a mile.

The useful **Shabaaby** will be minded when it comes to ground, so could be out if there is juice around in the early part of the season.

Tabdeed has been gelded, which might make him easier to train, while **Alfarqad** is unexposed and has always been well thought of. He likes the all-weather but should perform on turf and has speed, so a stiff 6f is not out of the question.

Dawaam is another fine prospect, although he is slightly tricky to handle and his lack of experience might force him into Pattern company – rather than big handicaps – with the Earl of Sefton a likely starting slot.

Of the three-year-olds, **Hukum** and **Thumur**, once he wins a maiden or novice, could go for Classic trials and are a lovely pair.

It's been 17 years since *PAUL COLE* last trained a Group 1 winner – Mr Dinos in the Gold Cup if you were wondering – but he could be back in the big time with Lockinge hope **Duke Of Hazzard**, who is in tip-top form and is now clear of the seedy toe that affected him last season.

He "couldn't be better and has everything a trainer wants in a horse" according to Cole, who also thinks **Majestic Dawn** was unlucky in 2019 and might have a nice prize in him.

Celtic Art disappointed a bit last season after being green from the stalls but is rated highly and going well, although he might not be out until conditions become quick. A Classic trial is not off the agenda for him or the up-and-coming **Highland Chief**, who has been treated for ulcers and has never looked better.

Atlantic Crossing could be another three-year-old colt for the tracker and **Glengowan**, too free last time, is talented. She has done well over the winter.

Classic aspirations also exist for the *RICHARD HUGHES*-trained **Brentford Hope**, who earned a favourable mention from official handicappers at January's world rankings ceremony, while stablemates **Queen Of All**, **Punting**, **So I Told You** and **Lady Lynetta** are three-year-old fillies who struck at two.

Kenzai Warrior, a big scopey colt in brilliant condition, goes straight for the 2,000 Guineas for *ROGER TEAL*, who nearly caused a huge shock in Newmarket's best race two years ago when Tip Two Win was second. He is back in light training and will go for a Listed or conditions race over 7f.

The July Cup is the ambition for **Oxted** and not a completely unrealistic one.

The hunky **Bear Force One** is another four-year-old Teal is looking forward to if strengthening again and smart bumper horse **Ocean Wind** could also shine back on the Flat.

Whelans Way and **Spirit Of May** will win more races and "always get you out of trouble" and Tip Two Win's half-sister **The Gurkha Girl** is a juvenile said to be shaping up pleasingly.

WILLIAM MUIR has the Melbourne Cup as the ultimate dream for **Just Hubert**, who should improve for being gelded and might still be well handicapped for an Ebor along the way.

Muir is purring about his Listed winner **Pyledriver**, who is in great order and has put on loads of condition. Described as looking beautiful, he has the Craven, Feilden Stakes and Sandown's Classic Trial as options and Muir, who could not be happier, is thinking big.

Natty Night, ahead of Just Hubert when they were beaten by St Leger winner Logician, can also develop after a gelding operation, while **Data Protection** is now a big, strapping horse.

Jack's Point, Muir admits, has been disappointing, but he is more than good enough to win off 91.

Final Option will improve with age, being from the family of The Tin Man and Deacon Blues. She has also prospered during the off season.

JOE TUITE expects **Surrey Pride** – versatile with regard to ground – to stay a mile and a half and deems him "quite nice", while **Bythebay** – "a big baby" – is also worth remembering.

Of Tuite's older horses, the gelded **Pesto** is an interesting recruit with a decent race in him, something that **Kimifive** can also achieve when things fall right.

Dunkerron, who bled last time but had never done so before, should provide some fun on good ground if that was just a one-off.

ARCHIE WATSON continues to make training winners looks as easy as shelling peas and he should get the best out of **Band Practice**, **The Perfect Crown** and **Higher Kingdom**, who – whisper it quietly – could be special.

Second-season trainer *TOM WARD* is optimistic of making headlines with **Vintage Rascal**, who is likely to start in the Newbury conditions race in April in which Enable was beaten three years ago.

A leggy sort, he has filled into an impos-

HIGHLAND CHIEF (far side): should give Paul Cole some fun this year

ing type and that should tell connections where to head, but he will win races.

So should **Dirty Rascal**, who has improved more from three to four than from two to three. The Victoria and Bunbury Cup route is for him, but there is also hope he can compete at Listed level.

Star Of Wells is a winter arrival with a decent pedigree and thought open to improvement.

Knight To Behold has left *HARRY DUNLOP* for the US, but stable hopes rest with his half-brother **Angel On High** – a nice, staying horse who could run in the Lingfield Derby Trial, which his sibling won two years ago. He needs improvement to reach that level but is immature, so could excel when the penny drops.

The French-bred **Pride Of America**, who is highly rated, will cross the Channel for the Prix Greffulhe.

HUGHIE MORRISON insists **Telecaster** is worth another chance. He could return in Sandown's Gordon Richards Stakes.

The trainer will aim high with three-year-olds **With Respect** and **Starcat**, who may not take loads of racing, and do not forget **Kipps**.

Not So Sleepy, who has starred over hurdles, might also have races in him back on the Flat in the autumn.

Speaking of hurdling, *NICKY HENDERSON*'s **Verdana Blue** is one to note on rapid ground and her stablemate **Gunnery** is another who will be interesting switched back to the summer code.

DOMINIC FFRENCH DAVIS believes good days lie ahead in black-type races over a mle and a quarter on easy ground for **Indeed**, although mile events in desperate conditions could come into the reckoning, as may high-class handicaps. He is reported to be flying, while **Thematic** could be an unexposed stayer.

Sweet Reward will not be winning any major races but is reckoned up to winning something by *JONATHAN PORTMAN*.

Berkshire's best

Battaash

Habub

Indeed

The North by Borderer

THE conveyor belt of top-notch sprinters from the Hambleton yard of *KEVIN RYAN* continued to roll last season, with the trainer celebrating Group 1 victories from Hello Youmzain and Glass Slippers, and Ryan has got more than just that pair to look forward to this year.

Hello Youmzain won the Sprint Cup at Haydock in September and there should be more to come from this lightly raced four-year-old, who can be a serious force in all the top 6f sprints.

Glass Slippers proved to be a revelation in France in the second half of the campaign, winning the Prix de l'Abbaye by three lengths at Longchamp on Arc day, and she will be an interesting contender in 5f Group 1 contests such as the Nunthorpe, in which the emphasis is on speed.

The hugely admirable **Brando** had just a Hamilton conditions win to his name for his 2019 endeavours but there were several other fine runs, including a close second in the Group 1 Prix Maurice de Gheest at Deauville.

The eight-year-old won that race in 2017 and should be back for more this term, while he is fancied to regain his crown in the Group 3 Abernant Stakes having been denied a hat-trick of wins in that Newmarket contest last April.

The next Group 1 winner for the Ryan stable could well be **Bielsa**, who, like Brando earlier in his career, has been highly progressive in the handicap ranks.

The five-year-old bolted up at Doncaster in October and, having won four of his five starts, is just the type of sprinter his trainer excels with. He is an exciting horse for the season ahead.

Juan Elcano and **Repartee**, both

HELLO YOUMZAIN: should be a serious force in all 6f Group 1 races

FOREST RANGER: a hat-trick in the Huxley Stakes is on his agenda

owned by Sheikh Mohammed Obaid, are a pair of three-year-olds to look forward to. Both had a light juvenile campaign with the future in mind and Juan Elcano in particular has the potential to evolve into a top performer.

The County Durham stable of *MICHAEL DODS* is another top northern sprinting yard and he has several speedy sorts who should land some nice prizes this season.

His sprinters tend to progress well with age and **Dakota Gold**, who won five times during last season's five-year-old campaign, is a prime example. The front-runner can continue to improve this term and should be capable of winning Group races.

Sprinting fillies and mares have also been a speciality for Dods, notably Mecca's Angel and Mabs Cross, and **Que Amoro** could be the next to take up the mantle for the yard. She was highly progressive last season and this four-year-old should thrive this term.

Queens Gift is another mare who could go to the next level this season, while Qatar Racing have bought Group 3 winner **Good Vibes** out of David Evans' yard and the three-year-old filly is an exciting recruit for Dods.

Prolific juvenile **Troubador** is another three-year-old to follow for Dods, while things started to click for **Pendleton** in the autumn and he could evolve into a leading sprint handicapper.

RICHARD FAHEY struck at Royal Ascot last year with **Space Traveller** in the Jersey Stakes and he proved it was no fluke when he added the Group 2 Boomerang Stakes at Leopardstown in September. He is unexposed over a mile and this hold-up horse is at his most effective when getting a strong pace.

Stablemate **Forest Ranger** won the Group 2 Huxley Stakes at Chester for the second consecutive season last May and a popular hat-trick will be on the cards this spring after a bid to repeat his 2018 win in the Earl of Sefton at Newmarket in April.

The 2018 Group 1 Champions Sprint winner **Sands Of Mali** had a campaign interrupted by injury last season but, granted a clear run for the five-year-old, he could well recapture his former glories.

Eva Maria was highly progressive over a mile and a quarter in the later stages of the season and remains one to be interested in despite her all-weather flop at Lingfield in November, with the step up to a mile and a half a possible source of further improvement.

Ventura Rebel has been off since finishing fourth in the Super Sprint in July but this Royal Ascot runner-up retains

VENTURA REBEL: has potential

significant potential, especially when he goes beyond 5f for the first time.

The retirement of multiple Group 1 winner Laurens has left a hole in the ranks at Spigot Lodge, the Middleham stable of *KARL BURKE*, but one of his promising three-year-olds may be capable of striking at the top level.

Living In The Past and **Lord Of The Lodge** were the pick of last year's juveniles, the first-named making all in the Group 2 Lowther Stakes at York in August and the latter finishing second in the Group 2 Gimcrack Stakes at the same meeting. They are nice types for the season ahead, as is prolific nursery winner **Ainsdale**.

Fellow three-year-olds **Classy Moon** and **Yes Always** are somewhat darker horses, but Classy Moon remains one to be interested in judged on the promise of her debut win at Carlisle last June and Yes Always was seriously impressive on her sole two-year-old outing at Newcastle in October.

Lady In France, now four, made her debut only last May but quickly made up for lost time and was a Listed winner at Ayr in September. She remains unexposed and should be placed to good effect by Burke in Listed and Group races.

Lord Glitters posted a deserved first Group 1 win at his beloved Ascot for *DAVID O'MEARA* in the Queen Anne Stakes last June and the seven-year-old will be a strong candidate in the same race at this year's royal meeting. Ascot brings out the best in him and he went close in the Queen Anne in 2018.

O'Meara's skills have been seen to excellent effect with **Escobar**, a Listed winner as a juvenile who was brought back to his best, and more, by the Helmsley trainer at the age of five last year. His season concluded with a big handicap win at Ascot in November and he should be set for another solid campaign.

Gulliver is another six-year-old who races in the same colours as Escobar and, likewise, has been better than ever on his last few starts. Sprinters are hard to knock off a roll when they get on one and there could be some nice early-season prizes for him.

There are plenty of *MARK JOHNSTON*-trained stable stalwarts who contributed to last year's record-breaking British tally of 249 winners and the likes of **Elarqam** and **King's Advice** should enjoy further success this year.

However, the fun bit at this stage of the year is to look beyond the more obvious Johnston horses to find the next middle-distance or staying stars.

Two three-year-olds to keep a close eye on are **Zabeel Champion**, who is out of a Galileo mare and should relish being stepped up in trip, and **Salamanca School**, who can build on the promise he showed last autumn.

Having had several promising juvenile winners last season, 2020 could be a big year for *TOM DASCOMBE*.

Prestige Stakes winner **Boomer** could be the pick of the bunch, although **Brad The Brief** has won three of his four starts and can take higher rank still.

Stablemates **Dr Simpson** and **Sir Boris** showed strong form in Ireland, while **Morisco** kept on well for fifth in the Group 3 Acomb Stakes over 7f at York and could have untapped potential.

When *TIM EASTERBY* has a first-time-out two-year-old winner it is worth sitting up to take note and **Lampang** could be a star for the Great Habton trainer this season, despite disappointing in the Rockingham at York on his final juvenile outing.

Aberama Gold won that Listed contest for *KEITH DALGLEISH* but arguably a more interesting three-year-old for the yard is **Volatile Analyst**, who was a good fourth in the Group 2 Richmond Stakes at Glorious Goodwood on just his second start.

Older horses **What's The Story** and **Alright Sunshine** were other 2019 success stories for the Scottish stable and the latter in particularly has unfinished business in terms of how far he can go.

The *JOHN QUINN*-trained pair **Liberty Beach** and **Safe Voyage** can continue to win races, while *JEDD O'KEEFFE* had by far and away his best ever Flat season last year and **Air Raid**, who scored three times, remains one to follow in 2020, as does **Starcaster** when he returns to the track.

Angels of the north

Boomer

Dakota Gold

Hello Youmzain

BOOMER: she could be the star of Tom Dascombe's yard this season

The West by Hastings

MANY moons have waned since the historic Beckhampton Stables in Wiltshire sent out winners of the Oaks, but all that may change in the first week of June as *ROGER CHARLTON*'s **Quadrilateral** looks tailor-made for the second fillies' Classic of the 2020 British turf season.

Back in the 1970s Charlton's mentor, the legendary Jeremy Tree, was the previous incumbent at the yard and he saddled Juliette Marny to take the prize in 1975, followed later in the decade by Scintillate in 1979. But things have been pretty quiet since then.

Quadrilateral went into winter quarters unbeaten after three visits to the racecourse, culminating in success in the Group 1 Fillies' Mile at Newmarket where she proved too good for Powerful Breeze despite finding the tacky underfoot conditions not to her liking.

The runner-up had previously landed the Group 2 May Hill at Doncaster so the form has a solid look about it and, as it looks like Quadrilateral has trained on based on the evidence at home, there is every reason to believe she will continue to thrive this year.

There is a chance that Charlton and connections may well decide to let her take her chance in the 1,000 Guineas at Newmarket, for which she was made antepost favourite last autumn.

However, her participation in that race very much hinges on the weather as a wet or cold spring wouldn't be in her favour, so a decision as to whether she makes the trek from Beckhampton to Newmarket will

QUADRILATERAL (far side): has the Oaks and possibly the Guineas to go for

THREAT (left): had a very good season for Richard Hannon as a juvenile

be made much closer to the time.

Another Khalid Abdullah-owned filly worth following is **It's A Given**, who overcame greenness on her belated debut back in November and gave the distinct impression there was plenty more to come in her second season as she will have come on plenty for the run.

She was friendless in the market at the Essex circuit but still came from an unpromising position at halfway in the 6f contest to win with a bit more in hand than the official margin suggests. Another bonus is that many of the horses she beat have franked the form since.

Charlton is a dab hand at placing this type of unexposed filly through the spring and summer and it would be no surprise to see her lining up at one of the marquee meetings such as Ascot or Goodwood.

She could end up being right out of the top drawer if several good judges at the yard are correct.

Since *RICHARD HANNON* took over the reins from his legendary father Richard back in 2014, the emphasis at the yard has changed slightly as sharp two-year-olds are no longer top of the priority pile, Hannon now favouring horses who could have a little more longevity.

However, that certainly does not mean that he has lost his touch with classy juveniles, as was perfectly illustrated by the highly regarded **Threat**.

He finished last season with a below-par effort when only fifth in the Group 1 Middle Park Stakes at Newmarket, but his form up to that point in all the top juvenile contests had been exemplary and he was possibly feeling the effects of a busy summer and

KING OF CHANGE: will be a contender in some big races this year

autumn. It's probably fair to say that it was one race too many for the youngster, who still remains open to more progress and is certain to pay his way again this term.

One of Threat's big wins last season came in the Gimcrack at York's Ebor meeting, where **Mums Tipple** also announced himself as a force to be reckoned with by running away with the big sales race by a whopping 11 lengths.

He was subsequently beaten when raised in grade next time, but he finished lame that day and there is more to come with another year on his back as he will be more the finished article.

Al Madhar, a 200,000 guineas yearling, caught the eye when winning a very competitive Newmarket maiden in July, going into many notebooks as he gave the impression he still had plenty to learn and looked as if the race would only do him good in the preliminaries.

Like many in the same race, Al Madhar did not reappear as the decision was taken that he was a horse with a definite future and there was no point in rushing him at that stage of his career. He is another three-year-old to follow this season.

King Of Change finished an honourable runner-up in the 2,000 Guineas at 66-1 and the result was not a surprise to many at the Hannon yard as he had been working like a good horse going into the Newmarket Group 1.

He returned from a midsummer break to score convincingly in Listed company at Sandown before going on the land an overdue Group 1 in the Queen Elizabeth II Stakes on Champions Day at Ascot, albeit on very testing going that was officially heavy.

However, the Hannon camp don't consider him to be ground-dependent and some sound judges think he is just as good in decent underfoot conditions.

He remains a horse on the up and can play a leading role in some of the major races over the summer.

This year is bound to be deeply important for *MARTYN MEADE* as the trainer has now settled into Manton after moving to Wiltshire from Newmarket last year and **Ebury** could get him off to a flyer when taking the first big handicap of the new term, the Lincoln at Doncaster at the end of March.

He seems at home on most types of ground and took a huge leap forward when switched to turf last autumn as his previous three outings had been on the all-weather.

He has had just five career runs to date and can only go one way this season as he remains a potentially smart horse at a mile and a bit further.

The dream for **Technician**, who signed off last year with success in the Group 1 Prix Royal-Oak at Longchamp last October, is the Ascot Gold Cup and that will be the four-year-old's main early season target at the royal meeting in mid-June.

Meade's charge kept progressing last year and not even a minor bug which hit the yard at a critical point of the summer could prevent him from finishing on a high. The Manton team are confident he will stay the Gold Cup trip and he looks a leading player in the Ascot marathon come June.

ALAN KING successfully mixes training jumpers and Flat horses and he looks to have a star staying handicapper on his hands in **Trueshan**, who went from strength to strength last summer and he has not finished improving yet.

The four-year-old looks an ideal type for King to aim at the Ebor at York's festival showpiece meeting in August as he will undoubtedly get a decent pace to aim at and there are no question marks about him getting the 1m6f trip.

Trueshan made giant strides in just a handful of runs last year and finished like he started with victories at Newmarket and Newbury. Although the trainer is wary of running his stable star on fast ground, he can operate on most surfaces having won on good and heavy going.

Western wonders

It's A Given

King Of Change

Trueshan

TECHNICIAN: the Gold Cup is his big target for the season

The South by Southerner

R*ALPH BECKETT* had a roller-coaster 2019 but has every reason to hope that his strong finish to the year will continue as he builds up for the turf season with a well-balanced strength of established stars and promising three-year-olds.

There are justifiable expectations of remaining on the up, not least because three of his four winners at Newmarket on a remarkable day on October 12 are among the returning stars.

Feliciana De Vega beat the colts in the Group 3 Darley Stakes to cap the day and Beckett will not be afraid to repeat that with a filly who is open to any amount of improvement having had only five races. The Group 2 Prix d'Harcourt is a possible first start.

Max Vega, impressive winner of the Group 3 Zetland Stakes, has the Irish Derby entry and will be tested for Epsom first in one of the traditional Derby trials.

Tomfre, who won the nursery on the card, has wintered well but, rated 95 after four juvenile wins, is going to be harder to place.

Beckett is again strong in the fillies' department, with **Hereby**, daughter of his Oaks winner Look Here, back for another year after four wins in a row, culminating in Listed success, and with her liking for Chester she could contest the Ormonde at the May meeting.

Manuela De Vega, who could start at York, and **Antonia De Vega**, who has the Daisy Warwick at Goodwood as a possible starting point, have also stayed in training looking for more black type.

Among the younger fillies, **Trefoil**, who beat the colts on debut over a mile on soft ground at Newmarket later in October, is being aimed at an Oaks trial.

Beckett has welcomed back the classy **Aloe Vera**, who has recovered from a bad overreach, along with stable favourite and soft-ground lover **Air Pilot**, who is back at the age of 11.

Other older horses to look out for are **Sam Cooke**, recovered from injury, and **Moon King**, who could be contenders for the Chester Cup consolation after an amazing 2019.

Three-year-olds who look on the up include **Mascat**, who could start in the Feilden Stakes, **Heart Reef**, who was backward last year but has wintered well, and **Jacksonian**, who has had his ailments but is well regarded and showed talent in his only run last July.

Kinross, fifth in the Vertem Futurity Trophy, has had a hold-up which could rule him out of an early return but will also be worth watching in the second half of the season.

ANDREW BALDING has a genuine Classic contender in the Vertem Futurity winner **Kameko**, who is not only seen as a Qipco 2,000 Guineas contender but also an Investec Derby candidate.

He heads another exciting bunch of three-year-olds, which has been the Kingsclere trainer's strongest suit in recent years and helped him to a personal-best season in Britain last year, both in winners and prize-money.

Khalifa Sat, who won his maiden over 1m2f at Goodwood on his second start, is another colt with top potential and a Derby entry after wintering well.

The Queen's **King's Lynn**, who won a big sales race over 6½f at Doncaster, remains an exciting prospect along with the likes of **Berkshire Rocco**, **Bronze River**, who has been gelded, and **Fox Duty Free**.

Grove Ferry, injured at Epsom in July, is another with potential who could go as far as a mile, while **Symbolize** is an out-and-out sprinter on the way back after picking up an injury following good efforts in the

KAMEKO: covers both bases of the 2,000 Guineas and Derby

Windsor Castle and Richmond Stakes.

Kalsara is an interesting filly. She chased home the Qipco 1,000 Guineas favourite Quadrilateral at Newbury on her third start after winning at Kempton.

Balding is not short of classy older horses as most of last year's successful three-year-olds are back.

The possible headline act is **Bangkok**. He disappointed in the Derby last year after winning the Sandown Classic Trial but has been back in winning form on the all-weather, albeit beaten in the Winter Derby.

Fellow King Power four-year-olds **Good Birthday**, a good third in the Cambridgeshire, **Fox Tal**, not disgraced when supplemented for the Champion Stakes on only his sixth start, **Fox Chairman** and **Fox Premier** should all contribute to the Kingsclere total.

Shine So Bright, who did not quite see out the mile in the 2,000 Guineas, could have a good year as a specialist 7f performer.

There is also plenty of staying power in the ranks. Queen's Vase winner **Dashing Willoughby**, who has been gelded and had a long break, and **Ranch Hand**, the beaten favourite in the Cesarewitch, are two to watch.

Dioclesian has Chester Cup pretensions and Cumberland Lodge winner **Morando** has strong form in the book to suggest another good year.

Balding's Queen Alexandra winner **Cleonte** has suffered an early setback but could be back for the second half of the season.

Among the fillies, Balding is hoping for a drier year for **Look Around**, who was put away when the autumn rain came. The likes of **Be More**, **Tribal Craft** and **Chil Chil**, a half-sister to the stable's late, lamented Beat The Bank, are also expected to earn black type this year.

Shailene has turned five and this Listed winner in Italy is another back for another year in search of Group-race glory along with sprinter **Foxtrot Lady**, whom Balding is hoping will follow family habits of improving with age.

DAVID MENUISIER had a memorable 2019, remaining on an upward curve both in terms of winners and stable numbers and registering a first Group 1 success in only his fourth year training.

His top performer Danceteria and Group 2 winner Chief Ironside have moved on in Australia, but he still has old ally **Thundering Blue**, who races on at the age of seven and will have a season geared around the second half.

Migration is seen as another flagbearer, with the trainer feeling the four-year-old

HISTORY WRITER: might go abroad

was unlucky not to win his last two races.

He was gelded before his winter holiday and has the makings of a top handicapper with his rating already in the 90s, although he will not run at Epsom, where the City and Suburban would have been the sort of handicap to suit but the track would not.

A Listed win in France for **History Writer** last November sees his sights raised to Group races this year, but he must have cut in the ground so might race more in France and Germany.

Menuisier has welcomed two new exciting recruits in **Dean Street Doll** from Ireland and **Kaloor** from Brian Meehan.

Dean Street Doll was fifth to Hermosa in the Irish 1,000 Guineas last year after finishing second in the Derrinstown Stud trial before her form tailed off. The Oasis Dream filly is pleasing Menuisier, who plans to start her off over a mile but could step her up in trip later.

Kaloor is another four-year-old. He has not won since his juvenile win over a mile at Salisbury but contested some hot 1m4f handicaps last year.

The Pulborough man has high hopes for three-year-old colts **Into Faith** and **Luigi Vampa**, who ended last year finishing first and third in a big sales races at Longchamp in October.

Into Faith could start in a Classic trial wlth thoughts of the German or even French 2,000 Guineas, but Luigi Vampa will come into his own over slightly further and will have the French Derby entry.

Two three-year-old fillies worth looking out for are the lightly raced pair **Gypsy Whisper** and **Wonderful Tonight**.

Gypsy Whisper is a big filly who has done well over the winter after being put away following her Newbury nursery fourth to a filly who subsequently was not disgraced in Group races.

Wonderful Tonight confirmed the promise of her Doncaster debut third when winning a 1m2f maiden in France four weeks later and can pay to follow.

Dragons Voice might be tried over further to try to thwart the handicapper and **Nuits St Georges**, a successful stayer who wants soft ground, is reaching his physical peak at five.

GARY MOORE continues to prove a man for all seasons, with more than 30 winners on the Flat last year alongside his jumping exploits.

One horse he is hoping will span the two is his smart hurdler **Goshen**, who officially improved 24lb to a rating of 88 in three wins after going handicapping. Moore has high hopes of a big handicap win with him in the summer.

Southern stars

Kameko

Manuela De Vega

Migration

Midlands by John Bull

CROPTHORNE trainer *TONY CARROLL* enjoyed his best year in 2019 and has set his sights on saddling 100 winners across both codes for the first time this year, with star sprinters Recon Mission and Kondratiev Wave among his "strongest team".

Carroll has a full yard of 70 horses with new recruits and talented types among his armour for an exciting 2020.

A blistering start to the year bodes well for Carroll hitting three figures come the end of the campaign and the former jump jockey has high hopes.

Carroll said: "We've had our best start to the year and we're normally quite good in the summer but the key to hitting 100 winners will be to make sure we don't fade away at the backend, which we have in the past when the handicapper has caught up with us and you have a few tired legs.

"We've been very lucky and been inundated with horses and new blood. This is our strongest team so we'll be giving it our best shot."

High-profile handicap success at York showcased the talent of **Recon Mission** last year and Carroll believes there is more to come from his stable star this term.

The speedy colt ended last season contesting the Abbaye, in which he finished down the field, but Carroll believes his final couple of runs can be discarded in a campaign in which the four-year-old's rating rose from 93 to 102.

Carroll said: "He's had a nice break, which he needed as his form was very good last year but his last two runs weren't his true showing. His main gig was at York and he took that in his stride and won well in a competitive handicap.

"He's a very good sprinter and there's more to come from him. We may tiptoe around the route we went last year with him but there are many opportunities for a horse of his calibre."

Another smart speedster is **Kondratiev**

TONY CARROLL: could be set for his winningmost season in 2020

Wave, who has made a positive start to life in Britain over the winter, and Carroll believes the three-year-old will be better on turf.

Carroll said: "He's very talented and a nice horse to have in the yard as he's young, good-looking and progressive.

"I've always thought he'd be better on turf than the all-weather so hopefully he can progress through the year."

A three-figure turf mark means big handicaps await the lightly raced seven-year-old **Silent Attack**.

He appears a bargain buy for £10,000 from Godolphin after a successful all-weather stint and a Royal Ascot assignment could beckon in June.

Carroll said: "He's done exceptionally well so far and settled in nicely for us. He's got a good level of form and certainly could go to the big venues as he's off a mark that gets him in there. He's fairly lightly raced for his age and could be a Royal Hunt Cup horse."

Owner-breeder Lady Whent has opted to keep the progressive **Rose Hip** in training this year and connections would love to seal some black type for the likeable mare.

The daughter of Acclamation out of Poppy Seed won four of her six starts last campaign and Carroll said: "She's a lovely mare and it's great she stays in training this year.

"She's done everything right, crept her way up the ladder nicely and we'd love to get some black type for her before she goes to the paddocks."

DE VEGAS KID (left): likes Brighton

Second Collection was a four-time winner from ten starts last year and the Windsor sprint series could once again be her aim, while **De Vegas Kid**, described as "an incredible horse" by Carroll, may take a similar path to 2019 when he landed the Brighton Mile Challenge Trophy.

The unexposed **Awesome Gary**, who finished second on his final two starts last year, and handicapper **Sir Titan** were nominated as dark horses to follow by Carroll.

He said: "Awesome Gary is a nice horse. He didn't win last year – I still can't believe I took him to Brighton twice and he didn't win! He has ability, while I'd like to think I can land a big handicap with Sir Titan."

Oakham trainer *MICK APPLEBY* enjoyed his best year in 2019 and was just one victory short of training 100 winners.

In a similar vein to Carroll, Appleby has made a fast start to 2020 and veteran sprinters **Danzeno** and **Caspian Prince** will fly the flag for the trainer in big handicaps.

Kasbaan, **Merryweather** and **Ayr Harbour** have proved revelations since joining the yard and are worth following on the turf after fruitful all-weather campaigns.

Sprinters **Free Love** and **Fantasy Keeper** enjoyed good seasons last year and are also worth noting, particularly at Nottingham, where they boast winning form.

IVAN FURTADO moved to his new Averham base in 2019 and is confident of building on last year's tally of 24 winners this season.

Furtado, whose Munhamek shone for the yard prior to being sold to Hong Kong, said: "It was our first season at a new yard and we had a reasonable year but too many seconds! It was a promising start at lovely facilities and I'm hopeful there's more to come.

"We want to beat our best tally of 33 winners this year and keep improving the quality we have."

Furtado has some nice three-year-olds at his disposal, with **Noble Dawn** – nominated by the trainer as a horse to follow – catching the eye when a ready winner at Wolverhampton in December.

THE GRAND VISIR (left): won the Ascot Stakes last season for Ian Williams

He said: "She's a big filly, improved with each start and hasn't run a bad race. She should stay further and is very progressive."

Healing Power, a debut winner at Chelmsford, and progressive sprinter **Last Date** are other three-year-olds to note, while new recruit **Teston** has plenty of form in France and Furtado hopes the €57,000 buy can be a Saturday horse for connections.

"He's a lovely horse, has proven form and the big mile handicaps will be on his agenda," Furtado said.

"He should be a nice Saturday horse for his owners and galloping tracks like Doncaster and Newbury would suit as he's got good form at Longchamp. He doesn't mind cut in the ground and could be out early in the season."

Big handicaps also await **Medahim** following a winter stint in Dubai, while the doughty **Sparklealot** is one for the tracker and rarely runs a bad race.

Furtado said: "Sparklealot is very consistent and loves quirky courses like Catterick, Chester and Goodwood where he can dominate. He doesn't mind cut in the ground so we aim to have him out early.

"He's off a tough mark but he's a proper trier and should win another race or two this season."

Kings Highway, described as "a lovely prospect" by the trainer, made a successful yard debut at Kempton in June but a bout of colic prevented a crack at the London Mile final.

He should be back in action in the summer, while new purchases **Alminoor** and **Jungle Speed** are others to note.

Alvechurch trainer *IAN WILLIAMS* enjoyed a first Royal Ascot success last year and his Ascot Stakes hero **The Grand Visir**, progressive handicapper **Cardano** and Lincoln entry **Mustarrid** are worth following from the dual-purpose yard.

Midlands magic

De Vegas Kid
Fantasy Keeper
Noble Dawn

Tipping Point Tom Collins

Haggas trio are key to my Flat punting fortunes

HAS anyone got over the fact that Enable and Stradivarius suffered shock defeats on their final outings of the 2019 Flat season in the Arc and Long Distance Cup? I'm still convinced I was dreaming.

John Gosden's powerhouses were cooking perfect seasons for the second year in a row, but narrow runner-up efforts meant that their winning streaks of 12 and ten came to end in unceremonious fashion.

Nevertheless, both had another phenomenal year and it was music to the ears to hear that they will be returning to the fray this year alongside Gosden's new star Logician, who is sure to dominate headlines.

Add in Charlie Appleby's star colt Pinatubo, who took the juvenile division by storm with six consecutive successes over sprint trips, and 2020 is rated one of the most hotly anticipated Flat seasons for some time. And that's without even mentioning the trainer and jockey titles.

Gosden and Aidan O'Brien will likely fight out the former championship once again having dominated since 2015 – my money is on Gosden this time around.

Oisin Murphy and Danny Tudhope's tussle in the rider ranks last year marked a changing of the guard. They will both go for the title once again but could be joined by the likes of Tom Marquand and all-weather supremo Ben Curtis in a thrilling battle.

Let's get back to the equine athletes, though, and aside from the superstars already mentioned here are six horses who may have gone under the radar and are worth keeping a close eye on this campaign.

Accountability 4yo gelding
0/21- (Ger Lyons)

A well-bred son of Dubawi out of Oaks fourth Vow, Accountability was bought by Godolphin in October 2017 for a pricey 240,000gns.

However, it clearly wasn't plain sailing for his powerful connections as he made only one start for them, finishing 11th of 12 in a Newmarket novice event a year later when appearing as if he hadn't a clue what he was doing on the racetrack.

Subsequently gelded and sold for just 14,000gns last year to Ger Lyons, he caught the eye with a strong-staying effort on his debut for the yard in a Leopardstown maiden in August, beating all bar subsequent Listed winner Silk Forest (rated 106) when giving away 5lb.

He needed only a similar performance to win when stepped up to a mile on his final outing last term in a weaker race, but the second that day has the potential to be useful and he hit the line takingly.

Accountability has been given an opening mark of 80 and can rack up several successes this season in handicap company, especially when stepped up in trip.

Born With Pride **3yo filly**
1- (William Haggas)

William Haggas doesn't often run a two-year-old filly in a Listed race first time out, but that was the route chosen for Born With Pride and she rewarded his optimism with an impressive 20-1 strike.

Outsider of the seven-strong field, which was justified given she was taking on six previous winners, Born With Pride travelled powerfully on heavy ground and picked up takingly under a hands-and-heels ride to fend off the Aidan O'Brien-trained Peaceful.

Judging on her pedigree, she will prefer better conditions, so you can mark up the performance on that basis and a longer trip will certainly suit as she is related to Raheen House.

She has an entry in the Irish Oaks in July and it wouldn't be surprising to see her emulate Sea Of Class, who represented the same connections when winning the race in 2018.

Hamish **4yo gelding**
213112- (William Haggas)

Hamish is a scopey son of Motivator who improved through the ranks in fine style last season, notching victories in a couple of competitive York handicaps along the way.

He won only once in three novice starts before that – a seven-length score in a

HAMISH: could be in line for a tilt at the Ebor Handicap at York in August

1m2f Windsor event – but you can put that down to quick ground and inadequate trips.

Once stepped up in trip to 1m6f and entered in handicap company, Hamish came into his own, winning the Melrose off a mark of 92 before following up off a 6lb higher mark when giving lumps of weight away to a decent field.

Maureen Haggas, wife of trainer William, said after that victory that Hamish would probably be done for the season and that would have been wise in hindsight as he suffered a shock defeat to the talented Trueshan at Newbury, albeit in a thrilling finish when they drew clear of their rivals.

He is my idea of the Ebor winner this year given rain-softened going.

King's Lynn 3yo colt
21- (William Haggas)

King's Lynn, who is owned by the Queen, produced one of the most eyecatching debut efforts of 2019 when seemingly engaging an extra turbo engine close home to finish a narrow second at Windsor.

The gorgeous son of Cable Bay looked clueless for the first three-quarters of the race but realised his job once given a reminder by rider Oisin Murphy and went into plenty of notebooks as a result.

He was set a tough task on his only other outing in the £300,000 sales race at Doncaster in September but proved his quality and professionalism when getting up close home to land the huge prize fund for connections.

King's Lynn beat the 101-rated Repartee into second that day, so we have a small clue as to how good he could be, and further progress is almost guaranteed this year. Look for him in the big sprints.

VICTORY DAY: one for the sprints

Palace Pier 3yo colt
11- (John Gosden)

An expensive purchase by John Gosden in October 2018, Palace Pier had a highly promising two-year-old campaign when landing a couple of Sandown 7f maiden/novice victories under Frankie Dettori.

The big-striding son of Kingman bolted up on both occasions, quickening clear having travelled strongly throughout to beat some useful-looking rivals by comprehensive margins.

Palace Pier was described by Gosden as still being "very green" after the second of his successes and he should have matured physically and mentally over the winter.

It will be interesting to see how much he has grown when he makes his seasonal reappearance and Group races look on the agenda this year.

Victory Day 4yo gelding
54/121- (William Haggas)

Victory Day is a lightly raced sprinter who proved much better for a gelding operation last winter when hacking up on his seasonal reappearance by three and three-quarter lengths at Ripon in May.

He was then the subject of strong market support before making his handicap debut off a mark of 90 at York, resulting in him being sent off at just 4-1 for a 22-runner contest. He travelled like the winner throughout that race but set a tough task from the back of the pack and eventually went down fighting in second to another well-treated rival.

He proved he was firmly on the upgrade when winning on his final outing at Ascot off 6lb higher and he looks one for the big sprints at that venue this summer.

RACING & FOOTBALL outlook

Richard Birch

Read Richard every week in the RFO

I've got the Derby nailed already – that's not bad at this stage

THE most taking performance I saw from any horse on the Flat last year was **Highest Ground's** debut success at Leicester in September.

After missing his break, the Sir Michael Stoute-trained two-year-old lengthened his stride in the style of a future Group 1 winner to slam Macho Boy by two and three-quarter lengths.

Racing pundits tend to use the word 'quicken' far too liberally, but in this case it was thoroughly justified. When Ryan Moore asked him to accelerate, Highest Ground went 'whoosh'.

The son of Frankel is bred to excel at up to a mile and a half and already holds entries in the Irish 2,000 Guineas, Derby and Irish Derby.

I don't usually include Group-bound performers in a list of ten horses to follow but will make an exception for Highest Ground. He looks very special.

I can't tell you how excited I am about the prospects of winning more money this season from the David Barron-trained **Mr Coco Bean**.

Winner of five handicaps in 2019, Mr Coco Bean showed a particular affinity for Redcar and was successful at the Cleveland track three times.

He simply toyed with his rivals in a 1m2f handicap there in July, scoring without coming off the bridle, and I believe he can make further progress as a six-year-old.

Best on fast terrain in a strongly run 1m2f at Redcar, he is tailor-made for the one-time prestigious Zetland Gold Cup on May 25.

That is by no means as competitive or valuable a race as it was during its halcyon days and I will be amazed if Barron isn't thinking along similar lines.

Another Redcar hero, **Give It Some Teddy**, will be in new ownership this season having been sold for 25,000gns at Tattersalls last October.

The five-time course scorer improved again last term, proving himself to be more versatile in terms of ground conditions than had previously been the case.

He has won the Redcar Straight-Mile Series Handicap Final in the last two years and, while it would seem logical that he'll be campaigned with the hat-trick bid firmly in mind, I still think Give It Some Teddy has untapped potential off 85 in some of the better mile handicaps throughout the season.

When fully on-song, Give It Some Teddy possesses a turn of foot which could take him into the 90-plus territory this season. If it does, my bookmaker won't be happy.

Brighton legend **Roy Rocket** drew a blank in seven starts at the seaside track last season but shaped on more than one occasion as though retaining plenty of ability.

As a result of that series of defeats, the 54-rated grey can begin 2020 off a mark 13lb lower than when he competed at Brighton last April.

He has won three times off a mark of 67 and I'll be amazed if he doesn't register at least two 1m2f-1m4f Brighton handicaps this summer.

His best efforts have been achieved in Class 6 company on very firm ground and he seems to thrive on hot days. Let's hope for a scorching summer.

Pour La Victoire, who narrowly holds the modern-day record for winningmost Brighton horse, will need to be on his guard to retain that honour with Roy Rocket competitively handicapped once more.

Boudica Bay is a low-rated sprinter who goes particularly well at Musselburgh.

Eric Alston's mare landed three Class 6 handicaps at the Scottish track in 2019, and soft ground may not have suited her ideally when she was beaten on her last two visits.

Currently rated 61, her high cruising speed and turn of foot renders it likely she could develop into a 70-plus handicapper this campaign when granted her favoured conditions.

I am banking on her proving to be a Musselburgh money-spinner at 5f on good or faster ground once again.

There was lots to like about **Springwood Drive's** first campaign.

After three quick runs in June/July, Tim Easterby's daughter of Mayson was given a mark of 62 and duly rattled off two victories in sprint handicaps at Haydock and Pontefract. The four-year-old won those races with more in hand than the victory margins suggest and looks just the type to make further improvement this term.

She was put away after that Pontefract success in August and should return a stronger and more mature mare in 2020.

I think she could well progress into a smart sprint handicapper and end up in races like the Ayr Gold Cup. I can't wait for her reappearance.

The Mick Easterby-trained **Art Of Diplo-**

BOUDICA BAY: Eric Alston's mare goes particularly well at Musselburgh

DREAMWEAVER: can take his form to another level when upped in trip

macy is another late-maturing type who could enjoy a rewarding 2020.

Art Of Diplomacy belied market weakness to land a 1m4f soft-ground Hamilton handicap in September off an opening mark of 65.

Despite not enjoying the smoothest of passages, the son of Archipenko was firmly on top at the finish and he ought to improve again as a four-year-old.

He has also shown an aptitude for hurdling over the winter and rates a very interesting dual-purpose performer for 2020.

Dreamweaver is from a family which improves with age and I reckon he'll land a valuable handicap or two over 1m4f or beyond at the big Saturday meetings this season.

Ed Walker's four-year-old won three handicaps last term – at Goodwood, Haydock and Newcastle – and begins his campaign with a rating of 80.

He is just the type to take his form to another level when he steps up in trip – the furthest he has raced over so far is 1m4f – at a track with a long straight.

Dreamweaver takes time to engage top gear, but he was deadly at Haydock and Newcastle when he moved into overdrive and I firmly believe that the best is yet to come.

Keep **Langholm** firmly on side for 1m2f handicaps at Beverley. His front-running style is ideally suited to that track and he retains plenty of scope off 65.

Where's Jeff, winner of last year's Cumberland Plate, is another to follow closely. His tendency to idle in front means the handicapper struggles to get a proper grip on him.

I fancy him to win a valuable 1m4f handicap at a major meeting this summer.

Time Test speed ratings

Figures put peerless Pinatubo in a league of his own

PINATUBO swept all before him on the two-year-old front in 2019 and his Time Test figures prove there was a huge amount of substance along with the style.

Godolphin's budding superstar peaked with a figure of 92 for his nine-length demolition job in the National Stakes when he stormed away from Aidan O'Brien's smart pair Arizona and Armory.

Such is Pinatubo's dominance that he also achieved the second and third best figures among the juveniles last year, with his Dewhurst success – a thoroughly professional performance on ground softer than he would prefer – coming next on the clock followed by his five-length romp in the Vintage Stakes.

That means the son of Shamardal is 12 points ahead of his nearest challenger coming into the new season and it is hard to argue with his status as a short-priced favourite for the 2,000 Guineas.

Earthlight is Pinatubo's main rival according to the betting but looks a solid rather than spectacular opponent. He twice ran to a figure of 75 last season when winning the Prix Morny and the Middle Park, proving himself equally effective on good and heavy ground, but he has an awful lot of ground to make up on the favourite and doesn't look to have such great scope for improvement.

According to the figures Pinatubo might have more to fear from Middle Park also-ran **Mums Tipple** (80), whose runaway win in a valuable sales race at York was every bit as good as it looked despite his subsequent flop at Newmarket. Indeed, that was the best two-year-old performance of the season bar Pinatubo, so he looks more than capable of bouncing back at the top level in 2020.

There were other eyecatchingly wide-margin victories in good races last season from the likes of **Wichita** (73) and **Kameko** (69) but neither got the clock ticking in quite the same way.

Indeed, Wichita's subsequent third in the Dewhurst looks about the limit of his ability, with stablemate **Arizona** (78) surpassing him as Aidan O'Brien's best two-year-old of last year, while the horse to take from the Vertem Futurity Trophy, despite Kameko's easy victory, might well

MUMS TIPPLE: the second best two-year-old of last season after Pinatubo

be beaten favourite **Kinross** (70). He was only fifth that day but perhaps the switch to the all-weather was against him and the big, competitive field on just his second run was too much. He had clocked a stunning debut time at Newmarket when winning by eight lengths and is worth another chance.

The most significant trial for the Derby at this early stage looks to have been the Autumn Stakes run over a mile at Newmarket on the same day as the Dewhurst. It was won by **Military March** (77), who made the running at a strong gallop and did really well to battle back when headed by another high-class Godolphin horse in **Al Suhail**. The pair pulled seven lengths clear and the clock suggests the form is strong.

In stark contrast to the colts, there was very little to separate the two-year-old fillies last season and no standout performer among them, but **Millisle** (73) finished top of the pile thanks to her victory in the Cheveley Park.

Being delivered late in such a strongly run race was clearly the right tactics and front-running second **Raffle Prize** didn't quite match the level of her victory in the Duchess of Cambridge Stakes earlier in the season, which earned a mark of 71 and was the second best performance by a two-year-old filly on the clock.

The other top races were the Fillies' Mile and the Rockfel Stakes, although the strength of the Fillies' Mile might have been overplayed given the dominance of the first and second, **Quadrilateral** (69) and **Powerful Breeze** (68), in the Classic markets is at odds with their positions lower down the Time Test table. The Rockfel, on the other hand, seems to have been largely overlooked, but **Daahyeh** (70), **Stylistique** (68), **Cloak Of Spirits** (67)

LOGICIAN: already proven against the clock and should be a force in top races

and **Under The Stars** (66) have all proved themselves to be very smart fillies.

Much of the season's focus will be on **Enable**'s bid for a third Prix de l'Arc de Triomphe after she was unlucky to be denied the landmark by Waldgeist's late surge in the 2019 renewal – unlucky in that she bumped into a top-class and hugely underrated winner who produced a truly stunning late burst off punishing fractions in the conditions, worthy of a Time Test figure of 92.

Enable ran right up to her best in second, the remarkably consistent mare having now run to marks between 84 and 87 six times, including in all three cracks at the Arc. With Waldgeist now retired, she will set a tough standard again in 2020.

Interestingly, the standout Arc horses among last year's three-year-olds are also in the John Gosden camp.

Logician (84) won all five of his races last season, producing two outstanding performances against the clock in the Great Voltigeur and the St Leger. While the Doncaster Classic was his Group 1 breakthrough, his comfortable victory in the Great Voltigeur was only a fraction below that level and suggests he can be a force in top 1m4f races when he returns.

Stablemate **Star Catcher** (81) also won five times last year, with just a single defeat at Newbury before she hit back to win three Group 1 races as well as the Ribblesdale. Her best performance came when getting up to beat **Delphinia** (80) in a red-hot Champions Fillies & Mares Stakes.

Gosden also holds a strong hand in the staying division again with **Stradivarius** going for his third successive Ascot Gold Cup.

However, the five-year-old has never

Top two-year-old colts of 2019

	Horse	Speed rating	Distance in furlongs	Going	Track	Date achieved
1	**Pinatubo**	**92**	**7**	**SFT**	**Newmarket**	**Oct 12**
2	Mums Tipple	80	6	GD	York	Aug 22
3	Arizona	78	7	SFT	Newmarket	Oct 12
4	Military March	77	8	SFT	Newmarket	Oct 12
5	Al Suhail	75	8	SFT	Newmarket	Oct 12
5	Earthlight	75	6	HY	Deauville	Aug 18
7	Golden Horde	74	6	GD	Newmarket	Sep 28
8	Wichita	73	7	GD	Newmarket	Sep 26
9	Kenzai Warrior	71	7	HY	Newmarket	Nov 2
9	Mystery Power	71	7	GF	Newmarket	Jul 13

Top two-year-old fillies of 2019

	Horse	Speed rating	Distance in furlongs	Going	Track	Date achieved
1	**Millisle**	**73**	**6**	**GD**	**Newmarket**	**Sep 28**
2	Raffle Prize	71	6	GF	Newmarket	Jul 12
3	Daahyeh	70	7	GD	Newmarket	Sep 27
4	Quadrilateral	69	8	SFT	Newmarket	Oct 11
5	Powerful Breeze	68	8	SFT	Newmarket	Oct 11
5	Stylistique	68	7	GD	Newmarket	Sep 27
7	Cloak Of Spirits	67	7	GD	Newmarket	Sep 27
8	Summer Romance	66	6	GF	Newmarket	Jun 29
8	Under The Stars	66	7	GD	Newmarket	Sep 27
10	Rose Of Kildare	65	7	SFT	Newmarket	Oct 11

clocked an outstanding Time Test figure and his best last season was just 66, coming for the second year in a row in the Lonsdale Cup at York.

His defeat by **Kew Gardens** in the Long Distance Cup is perhaps a sign of the changing of the guard, that horse having had the class to go close in the Coronation Cup (matching his best figure of 78) before stepping up in trip.

As for the sprinters, it's all about **Battaash** (93) over the minimum trip. Charlie Hills's speedster achieved the best Time Test figure of any horse in 2019 with his stunning victory in the Nunthorpe Stakes at York and it was far from a one-off as he was also rated 93 after his Prix de l'Abbaye win in 2017 and was the leading sprinter of 2018 on the strength of his King George Stakes victory. He is close to unbeatable on his day.

The two best performances outside the juvenile division over 6f last season came from horses who have now been retired in Advertise and Donjuan Triumphant. The old guard like **Brando** (80) will again be out in force, while **Hello Youmzain** (79) will be in contention, but this looks ripe for a three-year-old to make a mark. Perhaps it could be Mums Tipple.

Group 1 review by Dylan Hill

1 Qipco 2,000 Guineas (1m) Newmarket May 4 (Good)

1 **Magna Grecia** 3-9-0 Donnacha O'Brien
2 **King Of Change** 3-9-0 Sean Levey
3 **Skardu** 3-9-0 James Doyle
11/2, 66/1, 8/1. 2½l, 1¾l. 19 ran. 1:36
(A P O'Brien).

An odd and slightly unsatisfying renewal saw a small group of three on the stands' side prove utterly dominant, led by **Magna Grecia**, although he was probably much the best horse on the day anyway. Magna Grecia tracked the pace set by **Shine So Bright** before drawing clear for a convincing victory and, while injury held him back subsequently, he was chased home on that side by **King Of Change**, who franked the form by winning the QEII later in the year, while the non-staying Shine So Bright also progressed well over 7f. **Skardu** was best of those on the far side, just holding off **Madhmoon**, while **Ten Sovereigns** failed to get home in fifth. Another future sprinter, **Advertise**, was beaten far more comprehensively.

2 Qipco 1,000 Guineas (Fillies) (1m) Newmarket May 5 (Good)

1 **Hermosa** 3-9-0 Wayne Lordan
2 **Lady Kaya** 3-9-0 Robbie Colgan
3 **Qabala** 3-9-0 David Egan
14/1, 11/1, 7/2F. 1l, nk. 15 ran. 1:36
(A P O'Brien).

A gutsy win from **Hermosa**, who perhaps didn't get the credit she deserved at the time. Just below the best as a juvenile, Hermosa had clearly improved in the meantime and made all the running, gamely holding off **Lady Kaya**. With Lady Kaya also ridden prominently, there was an initial feeling that those up with the pace had been favoured, but Hermosa would go on to prove it was no fluke and Lady Kaya might well have done likewise but for her sad death. **Qabala** did best of those held up in third, with **Angel's Hideaway** next ahead of **Fairyland** and **Just Wonderful**, while **Iridessa** was only eighth.

3 Al Shaqab Lockinge Stakes (1m) Newbury May 18 (Good)

1 **Mustashry** 6-9-0 Jim Crowley
2 **Laurens** 4-8-11 P J McDonald
3 **Accidental Agent** 5-9-0 Charles Bishop
9/1, 5/1J, 33/1. 2½l, ½l. 14 ran. 1:35
(Sir Michael Stoute).

While few trainers can improve older horses like Sir Michael Stoute, the sight of a six-year-old making a Group 1 breakthrough would generally raise eyebrows and that was probably still justified in this case, with **Mustashry** a moderate winner. Mustashry was the only horse among the first four to have had a prior run and that perhaps proved critical, with runner-up **Laurens** reported to have needed the outing and **Romanised** leaving this form behind after finishing fourth. **Accidental Agent** split that pair in third, while Queen Anne one-two **Lord Glitters** and **Beat The Bank** were well below their best.

4 Tattersalls Irish 2,000 Guineas (1m) Curragh (IRE) May 25 (Good To Firm)

1 **Phoenix Of Spain** 3-9-0 Jamie Spencer
2 **Too Darn Hot** 3-9-0 Frankie Dettori
3 **Decrypt** 3-9-0 W J Lee

16/1, 6/4J, 20/1. 3l, ½l. 14 ran. 1:36 (Charles Hills).

The build-up to this race was all about **Too Darn Hot**, quickly dropping back to a mile after finishing second on his belated reappearance in the Dante, but he was below his best in second to open the door to **Phoenix Of Spain**. Also held up in the spring, Phoenix Of Spain comfortably made all the running on his first run of the year, although subsequent events would suggest he dropped lucky in a poor race and was favoured by having the run of the race in front. **Decrypt** was third ahead of the disappointing **Skardu** and **Magna Grecia**, who suffered a hamstring injury that kept him out until the QEII.

5 Tattersalls Irish 1,000 Guineas (Fillies) (1m)

Curragh (IRE) May 26 (Good To Firm)

1 **Hermosa** 3-9-0 Ryan Moore
2 **Pretty Pollyanna** 3-9-0 Frankie Dettori
3 **Foxtrot Liv** 3-9-0 W J Lee
5/2F, 9/1, 25/1. 4l, 1½l. 10 ran. 1:35 (A P O'Brien).

A Classic double for **Hermosa**, who made all the running in even more comprehensive fashion than she had managed at Newmarket. Hermosa again set a good gallop and stayed on strongly in a race that seemed to bring stamina more to the fore, with her rivals left trailing. **Pretty Pollyanna** was second ahead of **Foxtrot Liv**, with **Iridessa** staying on from the rear in fourth. **Fairyland** was only sixth to prompt her successful return to sprinting, while **Just Wonderful** was seventh and **Qabala** scoped badly after coming ninth.

6 Tattersalls Gold Cup (1m2f110y)

Curragh (IRE) May 26 (Good To Firm)

1 **Magical** 4-9-0 Ryan Moore
2 **Flag Of Honour** 4-9-3 Donnacha O'Brien
3 **Mustajeer** 6-9-3 Colin Keane
2/7F, 4/1, 16/1. 7l, 4¾l. 5 ran. 2:13 (A P O'Brien).

One of the most uncompetitive Group 1 races in recent history provided an open goal for **Magical**, who duly hacked up at odds of 2-7. Magical toyed with front-running stablemate **Flag Of Honour**, whose best performances have all come over 1m6f, while another stayer, the subsequent Ebor winner **Mustajeer**, won the battle for a remote third.

7 Investec Oaks (Fillies) (1m4f6y)

Epsom May 31 (Good)

1 **Anapurna** 3-9-0 Frankie Dettori

ANAPURNA: won a poor Oaks

2 **Pink Dogwood** 3-9-0 Ryan Moore
3 **Fleeting** 3-9-0 Wayne Lordan
8/1, 3/1, 25/1. nk, 1¼l. 14 ran. 2:36 (John Gosden).

A thrilling finish and a wonderful story as **Anapurna** became a first British Classic winner for Frankel, albeit in a poor race. Anapurna lacked the speed to get competitive in other Group 1 races over this trip, although she did win the Prix de Royallieu on very soft ground over 1m6f and that stamina held her in good stead here as she ran down **Pink Dogwood**. However, **Fleeting** looked the best horse in the race, running out of road to chase down the first two after she couldn't get a clear run, while **Manuela De Vega** was fourth ahead of **Delphinia** and **Frankellina**. **Mehdaayih**, favourite on the strength of a runaway win in the Cheshire Oaks, never got the chance to land a blow having been repeatedly stopped in the straight.

8 Investec Coronation Cup (1m4f6y)

Epsom May 31 (Good)

1 **Defoe** 5-9-0 Andrea Atzeni
2 **Kew Gardens** 4-9-0 Ryan Moore
3 **Salouen** 5-9-0 Oisin Murphy
11/1, 100/30, 10/1. ½l, 5l. 9 ran. 2:33 (Roger Varian).

A first Group 1 win for **Defoe**, who had been 0-5 at the top level previously and probably didn't achieve as much as it appeared at the time in breaking his duck this time. Having been held up, Defoe produced a powerful late charge to run down **Kew Gardens**, who had been expected to have a big season having won the St Leger in 2018 but would need a much stiffer test of stamina on Champions Day before living up to his billing when he edged out Stradivarius in an epic over 2m. **Old Persian**, the only Group 1 winner in the field, was well below his best in seventh.

9 Investec Derby (1m4f6y) Epsom June 1 (Good To Firm)

1 **Anthony Van Dyck** 3-9-0 S Heffernan
2 **Madhmoon** 3-9-0 Chris Hayes
3 **Japan** 3-9-0 Wayne Lordan
13/2, 10/1, 20/1. ½l, nse. 13 ran. 2:33
(A P O'Brien).

A thrilling Derby with the first five separated by just ¾l, **Anthony Van Dyck** the best of them on the day. Stablemate **Japan** would prove the class act in the field, but he was still short of peak form in third – an interrupted spring had barely seen him make his trial in the Dante when only fourth – and runner-up **Madhmoon** didn't quite get this trip, meaning Anthony Van Dyck's storming run from an unpromising position at the top of the straight was good enough. **Broome** and **Sir Dragonet** were also involved in a blanket finish for the places, pulling 4½l clear of **Circus Maximus**, who ran out of stamina but still completed a clean sweep of the first six for Irish trainers. **Humanitarian** was best of the home team, with trial winners **Bangkok** and **Telecaster** the main disappointments. Subsequent Irish Derby winner **Sovereign** faded into a poor tenth after making the running.

10 Queen Anne Stakes (1m) Ascot June 18 (Good)

1 **Lord Glitters** 6-9-0 Daniel Tudhope
2 **Beat The Bank** 5-9-0 Silvestre De Sousa
3 **One Master** 5-8-11 Pierre-Charles Boudot
14/1, 20/1, 20/1. nk, ¾l. 16 ran. 1:37
(David O'Meara).

The lack of a standout older miler gave this a wide-open look and **Lord Glitters** improved on his 2018 second in a thrilling finish. An Ascot specialist at his best when delivered late off a fast pace, Lord Glitters had everything in his favour and made the most of it as he just pipped **Beat The Bank**, with the strong-travelling mare **One Master** overhauled close home. **Romanised** would prove the best horse in the race, winning the Prix Jacques le Marois, but he had no luck in running and had to settle for fourth ahead of **Le Brivido** and **Laurens**, who was best of those ridden close to the overly strong pace. **Mustashry** and the favourite **Barney Roy**, back in training after proving a flop at stud, were next.

11 King's Stand Stakes (5f) Ascot June 18 (Good)

1 **Blue Point** 5-9-4 James Doyle
2 **Battaash** 5-9-4 Jim Crowley
3 **Soldier's Call** 3-8-12 Daniel Tudhope
5/2, 2/1F, 16/1. 1¼l, 1½l. 12 ran. 0:58
(Charlie Appleby).

A second successive King's Stand for **Blue Point**, who again proved too strong for the speedier **Battaash** over this stiff 5f. Battaash was less keen than he had been when second in 2018, but being drawn on the opposite side to Blue Point did him no favours and he was well held despite making good ground. In a really strong race, **Soldier's Call**, second to Battaash in the Nunthorpe later in the year, ran another cracker in third ahead of **Mabs Cross** and the subsequent Flying Five heroine **Fairyland**, with those five pulling 1¾l clear of the rest.

12 St James's Palace Stakes (1m) Ascot June 18 (Good)

1 **Circus Maximus** 3-9-0 Ryan Moore
2 **King Of Comedy** 3-9-0 Adam Kirby
3 **Too Darn Hot** 3-9-0 Frankie Dettori
10/1, 4/1, 2/1F. nk, ¾l. 11 ran. 1:39
(A P O'Brien).

Conditions were much more testing than the official going description – amid heavy rain, the going was changed to good to soft after the race and soft after just one more – and that helped **Circus Maximus** to come out on top. Down in trip after the Derby, Circus Maximus stayed on well in the final furlong, whereas **Too Darn Hot** found little after looming up ominously. **King Of Comedy** finished strongly to split the pair and looked a shade unlucky having been forced to switch at a key stage, with **Skardu** also close up in fourth. It was 2l back to French Guineas runner-up **Shaman** and the disappointing **Phoenix Of Spain**.

13 Prince of Wales's Stakes (1m2f) Ascot June 19 (Soft)

1 **Crystal Ocean** 5-9-0 Frankie Dettori
2 **Magical** 4-8-11 Ryan Moore
3 **Waldgeist** 5-9-0 Pierre-Charles Boudot
3/1, 13/8F, 4/1. 1¼l, 3¼l. 8 ran. 2:10
(Sir Michael Stoute).

Crystal Ocean had come up short in three previous attempts at the top level, but he was much improved last season and made

CIRCUS MAXIMUS (second right): appreciated the emphasis on stamina

his Group 1 breakthrough even over a trip short of his best. Soft ground helped to negate the threat of arguably a speedier rival in **Magical**, while an uneven gallop also favoured those racing handily, with Crystal Ocean always in the ideal position and able to strike for home early. Magical stuck on well for a fine second and had the rest of the field well strung out, with **Waldgeist** given too much to do but staying on for third ahead of **Hunting Horn**, the ill-fated **Sea Of Class** and the Japanese raider **Deirdre**.

14 Gold Cup (2m4f) Ascot June 20 (Soft)

1 **Stradivarius** 5-9-2 Frankie Dettori
2 **Dee Ex Bee** 4-9-1 Silvestre De Sousa
3 **Master Of Reality** 4-9-1 Wayne Lordan
EvensF, 7/2, 66/1. 1l, nse. 11 ran. 4:30
(John Gosden).

Stradivarius earned the £1 million stayers' bonus for the second successive year, the crowning glory coming with this second successive Gold Cup. Stamina remains a potential issue over this marathon trip, but for the second year in a row it wasn't seriously tested in a steadily run affair and Stradivarius had far too much speed for his rivals. **Dee Ex Bee** tried all sorts of different tactics to unsettle Stradivarius over the season and nothing worked for him, but connections might have been left to regret not riding him more forcefully on this occasion given he proved his stamina by rallying strongly once done for toe, regaining second from **Master Of Reality**. **Cross Counter** finished a good fourth, pulling 5l clear of **Flag Of Honour** and the bitterly disappointing **Capri**.

15 Commonwealth Cup (6f) Ascot June 21 (Good To Soft)

1 **Advertise** 3-9-3 Frankie Dettori
2 **Forever In Dreams** 3-9-0 Oisin Murphy
3 **Hello Youmzain** 3-9-3 Kevin Stott
8/1, 20/1, 6/1. 1½l, hd. 9 ran. 1:11
(Martyn Meade).

With three of these horses going on to win three of the four all-aged 6f-6½f Group 1 races in Europe later in the year between them, this race had a really strong line-up, though subsequent Prix de Maurice Gheest winner **Advertise** perhaps benefited from a couple of his main rivals running below form. **Hello Youmzain** blew the start and had to use up too much energy to get back into contention, with his run flattening out late on, though he still fared better than **Ten Sovereigns**, who ran an oddly flat race in fourth. Nevertheless, Advertise produced a high-class effort to beat the Irish filly **Forever In Dreams**, who would prove herself an Ascot specialist with a close third on Champions Day, and the first four pulled 6l clear of the rest, including Stewards' Cup winner **Khaadem**.

16 Coronation Stakes (Fillies) (1m) Ascot June 21 (Good)

1 **Watch Me** 3-9-0 Pierre-Charles Boudot
2 **Hermosa** 3-9-0 Ryan Moore
3 **Jubiloso** 3-9-0 James McDonald
20/1, EvensF, 9/2. 1½l, 1l. 9 ran. 1:39
(F-H Graffard).

A surprise result as **Watch Me**, not even rated

the best of the French fillies in the market, had too much toe for hot favourite **Hermosa**. Watch Me hadn't got much of a run when sixth in the French Guineas and put that misfortune behind her in style, quickening up smartly whereas Longchamp winner **Castle Lady** disappointed in fifth. A wide draw went against Hermosa, who was unable to get to the front and ran slightly below her best, with **Pretty Pollyanna** instead driven up to lead but fading into seventh to prompt a return to sprinting. Inexperienced fillies **Jubiloso** and **Twist 'N' Shake** ran well in third and fourth, though neither did much subsequently.

17 Diamond Jubilee Stakes (6f) Ascot June 22 (Good To Firm)

1 **Blue Point** 5-9-3 James Doyle
2 **Dream Of Dreams** 5-9-3 Daniel Tudhope
3 **Kachy** 6-9-3 Richard Kingscote
6/4F, 12/1, 33/1. hd, 2½l. 17 ran. 1:11
(Charlie Appleby).

Blue Point went out in a blaze of glory as he completed a stunning Royal Ascot double and was immediately retired to stud. Blue Point travelled supremely well and looked set to win comfortably for much of the race, but **Dream Of Dreams** made it close at the end, running well above the rest of his form as he flashed home late. The pair were 2½l clear of the all-weather king **Kachy**, who couldn't quite last home to prompt his turf campaign to be drawn to a halt, although he still took third ahead of **Speak In Colours** and **Le Brivido. The Tin Man** struggled to get a clear run and was sixth, with **Invincible Army** next.

18 Juddmonte Pretty Polly Stakes (Fillies & Mares) (1m2f)

Curragh (IRE) June 28 (Good)
1 **Iridessa** 3-8-12 Wayne Lordan
2 **Magic Wand** 4-9-10 Donnacha O'Brien
3 **Pink Dogwood** 3-8-12 Ryan Moore
8/1, 9/2, 11/10F. 2¼l, 1¼l. 5 ran. 2:06
(Joseph Patrick O'Brien).

Iridessa has run several fine races over a mile, even winning the Matron Stakes, but this intermediate trip saw her in her element, as she would underline when adding the Breeders' Cup Filly & Mare Turf. Iridessa comfortably beat a rock-solid yardstick in **Magic Wand**, who would later finish second at the top level for a sixth time in the Irish Champion Stakes before finally breaking her duck in Australia, while **Pink Dogwood** and **Wild Illusion**, the last two Oaks runners-up, completed a high-quality first four.

19 Dubai Duty Free Irish Derby (1m4f)

Curragh (IRE) June 29 (Good)
1 **Sovereign** 3-9-0 P B Beggy
2 **Anthony Van Dyck** 3-9-0 Ryan Moore
3 **Norway** 3-9-0 Seamie Heffernan
33/1, 5/4F, 16/1. 6l, 2½l. 8 ran. 2:31
(A P O'Brien).

One of the most remarkable races of the season as **Sovereign**, ridden like a pacemaker, never came back to the field and eased home at 33-1 ahead of Derby winner **Anthony Van Dyck**. With no sectional times available and Sovereign missing the rest of the season, it remains a hard performance to assess, but

SOVEREIGN (left): barely saw another horse in a bizarre Irish Derby

the temptation to write off the winner might be wide of the mark as he set what looked a decent gallop and kept it up much better than fellow front-runner **Norway**, while the test of stamina even proved too much for the non-staying **Madhmoon** in fourth. That said, Epsom hero Anthony Van Dyck clearly suffered from a misjudged ride, finishing best of all into a clear second without ever being given a chance of hauling back Sovereign. **Broome** was well below form in sixth.

20 Coral-Eclipse (1m2f) Sandown July 6 (Good To Firm)

1 **Enable** 5-9-4 Frankie Dettori
2 **Magical** 4-9-4 Ryan Moore
3 **Regal Reality** 4-9-7 Kerrin McEvoy
4/6F, 11/4, 17/2. ¾l, 2l. 8 ran. 2:04
(John Gosden).

Enable probably had less in her favour than at any stage during her long winning run, dropping back to 1m2f for the only time since suffering her only previous defeat in 2017 and without the benefit of a prep run, but she proved she was as good as ever with a terrific victory. Displaying more than enough speed for the shorter distance, Enable travelled better than her big rival **Magical** and quickened into a decisive lead before holding on comfortably. Apart from Magical, the rest of the field disappointingly wasn't up to much, with sole three-year-old **Telecaster** faring little better than in the Derby. Instead **Regal Reality** was the only other horse to land any sort of blow, finishing a clear third as **Danceteria** plugged on into fourth ahead of **Mustashry** and **Hunting Horn**.

21 Tattersalls Falmouth Stakes (Fillies & Mares) (1m) Newmarket (July) July 12 (Good To Firm)

1 **Veracious** 4-9-7 Oisin Murphy
2 **One Master** 5-9-7 James Doyle
3 **I Can Fly** 4-9-7 Ryan Moore
6/1, 100/30, 5/2F. nk, 2¾l. 6 ran. 1:35
(Sir Michael Stoute).

Lightning-quick conditions saw six course records fall in seven races on the card, yet **Veracious** was allowed an easy lead despite setting a fairly steady pace in the circumstances – the time was worthy of a Time Test figure of just 43 – and was flattered by her maiden Group 1 victory. Dual Prix de la Foret winner **One Master** certainly looked the best horse in the race, producing a mighty effort to go close having been held up in the last pair as she pulled 2¾l clear of **I Can Fly**, with **Qabala** disappointing behind.

22 Darley July Cup (6f) Newmarket (July) July 13 (Good To Firm)

1 **Ten Sovereigns** 3-9-0 Ryan Moore
2 **Advertise** 3-9-0 Frankie Dettori
3 **Fairyland** 3-8-11 Seamie Heffernan
9/2, 3/1F, 10/1. 2¾l, ¾l. 12 ran. 1:09
(A P O'Brien).

Ten Sovereigns had a strange season, often struggling to live up to lofty expectations, but this blistering performance justified all the hype. Favoured by quick ground, Ten Sovereigns relished being given his head in front and was never headed by those in his group on the far side, easily seeing off old rival **Advertise**, who ran another solid race in second. Three-year-olds filled the first five places, with **Fairyland** next ahead of fellow fillies **Pretty Pollyanna** and **So Perfect**, while **Brando**. **Dream Of Dreams** and Wokingham winner **Cape Byron** were all well beaten.

23 Kerrygold Irish Oaks (Fillies) (1m4f) Curragh (IRE) July 20 (Good)

1 **Star Catcher** 3-9-0 Frankie Dettori
2 **Fleeting** 3-9-0 Donnacha O'Brien
3 **Pink Dogwood** 3-9-0 Ryan Moore
7/2, 9/2, 5/2F. ½l, 4½l. 8 ran. 2:34
(John Gosden).

John Gosden had Oaks winner Anapurna and beaten favourite Mehdaayih in his yard, but **Star Catcher** had still emerged as his leading middle-distance filly with victory in the Ribblesdale Stakes at Royal Ascot and underlined the point in fine style. Benefiting from a terrific front-running ride, Star Catcher quickened into a decisive lead and was always holding off **Fleeting** despite a strong late challenge from the Oaks third. There was a 4½l gap back to **Pink Dogwood**, who ran close to Epsom form with **Manuela De Vega**, while subsequent Irish St Leger winner **Search For A Song**, still very much a work in progress at this stage, did all her best work at the finish to split that pair in fourth. **Iridessa** was a non-stayer in seventh.

24 King George VI and Queen Elizabeth Qipco Stakes (1m4f) Ascot July 27 (Good To Soft)

1 **Enable** 5-9-4 Frankie Dettori
2 **Crystal Ocean** 5-9-7 James Doyle
3 **Waldgeist** 5-9-7 Pierre-Charles Boudot
8/15F, 7/2, 12/1. nk, 1¾l. 11 ran. 2:32
(John Gosden).

One of the races of the season as **Enable** won a thrilling battle against **Crystal Ocean**, again proving she could do it the hard way. Unusually held up having been drawn widest of all, Enable made up plenty of ground to strike for home early in the straight and did really well to maintain the gallop as she went head to head with the more prominently ridden Crystal Ocean. Crystal Ocean produced probably a career-best performance in defeat, with **Waldgeist** also running a huge race as he stayed on into a clear third. It was 7l back to **Salouen** and **Hunting Horn**, while **Defoe** and **Anthony Van Dyck** were both big disappointments behind.

25 Qatar Goodwood Cup (2m) Goodwood July 30 (Good)

1 **Stradivarius** 5-9-9 Frankie Dettori
2 **Dee Ex Bee** 4-9-9 Silvestre De Sousa
3 **Cross Counter** 4-9-9 James Doyle
4/5F, 11/2, 3/1. nk, 1¾l. 8 ran. 3:29
(John Gosden).

A Goodwood Cup hat-trick for **Stradivarius**, who is perhaps ideally suited by this sort of test on good ground and recorded his highest seasonal Racing Post Rating in this race for the second successive year. **Dee Ex Bee** and **Cross Counter** had first run on the champion stayer, but Stradivarius always had them in his sights and produced a typically telling turn of foot to win with far more in hand than the margin suggests, with Frankie Dettori able to celebrate early. Dee Ex Bee rallied strongly for second as the first three pulled 7l clear of **Southern France** and the leading three-year-old **Dashing Willoughby**.

STRADIVARIUS: best at Goodwood

26 Qatar Sussex Stakes (1m) Goodwood July 31 (Good)

1 **Too Darn Hot** 3-9-0 Frankie Dettori
2 **Circus Maximus** 3-9-0 Ryan Moore
3 **I Can Fly** 4-9-5 Donnacha O'Brien
EvensF, 9/2, 14/1. ½l, 1¼l. 8 ran. 1:38
(John Gosden).

Too Darn Hot finally got his Group 1 mile win after coming up short in the Irish 2,000 Guineas and the St James's Palace, seeing off old rival **Circus Maximus** in what would sadly prove to be his final race due to injury. Quicker ground proved the key to turning around that Royal Ascot form, with Too Darn Hot able to find the decisive turn of foot that he had rediscovered when winning the Prix Jean Prat over 7f, underlining the fact he was much more of an out-and-out speed horse than many had previously realised. The older challenge was weak and **I Can Fly** proved best of them in third, with **Lord Glitters** unsuited by the smaller field in fifth, while **Phoenix Of Spain** was a disappointing sixth.

27 Qatar Nassau Stakes (Fillies & Mares) (1m2f) Goodwood August 1 (Good)

1 **Deirdre** 5-9-7 Oisin Murphy
2 **Mehdaayih** 3-8-13 Frankie Dettori
3 **Rawdaa** 4-9-7 Daniel Tudhope
20/1, 3/1, 6/1. 1¼l, 1¼l. 9 ran. 2:02
(Mitsuru Hashida).

Deserved reward for an ambitious plan by connections of **Deirdre**, the Japanese filly whose European campaign brought this Group 1 success to go with several more good efforts at the top level. Deirdre probably wasn't the best horse on the day, but she produced a powerful late finish to make the most of **Mehdaayih**'s late collapse, getting up in the final 50 yards. Mehdaayih had been too keen as she set an overly strong gallop but still finished second ahead of **Rawdaa** before a 2½l gap back to **Sun Maiden** and **Just Wonderful. Hermosa**, expected to be suited by the step up in trip, was a big letdown and was beaten before stamina became an issue.

28 Juddmonte International Stakes (1m2f56y) York August 21 (Good)

1 **Japan** 3-8-13 Ryan Moore
2 **Crystal Ocean** 5-9-6 James Doyle

3 **Elarqam** 4-9-6 Jim Crowley
5/1, 11/10F, 8/1. hd, 1l. 9 ran. 2:07
(A P O'Brien).

Japan had already progressed from his Derby third to win the Grand Prix de Paris but took a bigger leap forward by showing enough speed to excel over this shorter trip as he proved too good for **Crystal Ocean**. Japan stayed on relentlessly to run down Crystal Ocean, who looked a likely winner when hitting the front two furlongs out but couldn't put the race to bed. Just 2l covered the first four, with the 2018 Guineas fourth **Elarqam** third having been coaxed back to form at a lower level while **King Of Comedy** didn't quite see out the trip strongly enough in fourth. **Regal Reality** was next ahead of **Lord Glitters** and **Circus Maximus**, who didn't seem to stay having made the running.

29 Darley Yorkshire Oaks (Fillies & Mares) (1m4f)

York August 22 (Good)

1 **Enable** 5-9-7 Frankie Dettori
2 **Magical** 4-9-7 Ryan Moore
3 **Lah Ti Dar** 4-9-7 William Buick
1/4F, 4/1, 11/1. 2¾l, 10l. 4 ran. 2:29
(John Gosden).

Yet another instalment in the **Enable**-**Magical** rivalry and, given Magical hadn't quite been able to lower Enable's colours when she had plenty in her favour in the Eclipse, this latest verdict in favour of the dual Arc winner followed a somewhat inevitable pattern as Enable made all the running, coasting to a comfortable victory. The pair pulled 10l clear of **Lah Ti Dar**, who was totally outpaced by two top-class rivals.

30 Coolmore Nunthorpe Stakes (5f) York August 23 (Good To Firm)

1 **Battaash** 5-9-11 Jim Crowley
2 **Soldier's Call** 3-9-9 Daniel Tudhope
3 **So Perfect** 3-9-6 Wayne Lordan
7/4, 20/1, 25/1. 3¾l, 1l. 11 ran. 0:55
(Charles Hills).

Well below his best in this race in the previous two years, **Battaash** put his York hoodoo to bed in breathtaking fashion with arguably his best ever performance. A far more mature performer in 2019, Battaash was simply brilliant when making it third time lucky, racing prominently and quickening away from his rivals in the final furlong. **Soldier's Call** was the only horse to briefly threaten and stayed on for a fine second ahead of **So Perfect** and **Mabs Cross**, who was reported to find the ground too quick. **Ten Sovereigns** was a big disappointment in sixth and perhaps found it all happening too quickly on this drop in trip, as did **Fairyland**.

31 Betfair Sprint Cup (6f) Haydock September 7 (Soft)

1 **Hello Youmzain** 3-9-1 James Doyle
2 **The Tin Man** 7-9-3 Oisin Murphy
3 **Waldpfad** 5-9-3 Andrea Atzeni
9/2C, 7/1, 9/1. ½l, 2l. 11 ran. 1:12
(Kevin Ryan).

With Advertise (bad scope) and Ten Sovereigns (ground) non-runners, it was another three-year-old who stepped forward to fill the void, with **Hello Youmzain** seeing off the 2018 winner **The Tin Man** in a slightly disappointing renewal. Fresh after a break since Royal Ascot, Hello Youmzain made all the running and comfortably held off The Tin Man, who was nonetheless perhaps a shade unlucky having stumbled badly leaving the stalls. **Brando** was another standing dish to run well in fourth, splitting German raider **Waldpfad** and **Invincible Army**, but there were several below-par efforts behind, with **Fairyland** only sixth and **Dream Of Dreams**, **So Perfect**, **Forever In Dreams** and **Khaadem** filling the final four places.

32 William Hill St Leger Stakes (1m6f115y)

Doncaster September 14 (Good To Firm)

1 **Logician** 3-9-1 Frankie Dettori
2 **Sir Ron Priestley** 3-9-1 Franny Norton
3 **Nayef Road** 3-9-1 Andrea Atzeni
5/6F, 7/1, 40/1. 2¼l, hd. 8 ran. 3:00
(John Gosden).

Far from a vintage edition of the season's final British Classic, with four of the first five in handicaps earlier in the season, but **Logician** proved that is not always an impediment in becoming a top-class horse as he maintained his unbeaten record. Having continued his rise through the ranks by winning the Great Voltigeur at York, Logician was a warm favourite and easily lived up to his billing, travelling smoothly in rear and quickening away from **Sir Ron Priestley** and **Nayef Road**. **Sir Dragonet** held every chance but came up short in the final furlong, finishing only fourth ahead of **Il Paradiso**, with **Technician** and **Dashing Willoughby** behind.

33 Qipco Irish Champion Stakes (1m2f)

Leopardstown (IRE) September 14 (Good)

1 **Magical** 4-9-4 Ryan Moore
2 **Magic Wand** 4-9-4 Seamie Heffernan
3 **Anthony Van Dyck** 3-9-1 Wayne Lordan

11/10F, 20/1, 12/1. 2¼l, hd. 8 ran. 2:06 (A P O'Brien).

Magical set the standard in the absence of old foes Enable and Crystal Ocean and duly ran out an emphatic winner under a positive ride, comfortably beating **Magic Wand**. While she was clearly the best horse in the race, those behind were unlucky not to get closer, with **Deirdre** getting no run before finishing strongly in fourth and **Headman** having to do too much to make up his ground after an awkward start left him well off the pace in rear. Instead Magic Wand and **Anthony Van Dyck**, back on song over an inadequate trip, filled the places, while **Madhmoon** and **Elarqam** were notable disappointments behind.

34 Coolmore "Fastnet Rock" Matron Stakes (Fillies & Mares) (1m)

Leopardstown (IRE) September 14 (Good)

1 **Iridessa** 3-9-0 Wayne Lordan
2 **Hermosa** 3-9-0 Ryan Moore
3 **Just Wonderful** 3-9-0 Oisin Murphy
10/1, 7/2, 12/1. ¾l, hd. 7 ran. 1:38 (Joseph Patrick O'Brien).

Iridessa had been well beaten twice by **Hermosa** earlier in the season, but this race played out perfectly for her as she picked up the pieces late on. With top-class form over 1m2f, Iridessa was always likely to be finishing strongly and that swept her to victory after Hermosa and **Laurens** had softened each other up in front. Hermosa ran a fine race in the circumstances, holding on for second ahead of the fast-finishing **Just Wonderful**, who was flattered by the way the race panned out, with Laurens fourth and the disappointing **I Can Fly** back in fifth.

35 Comer Group International Irish St Leger (1m6f)

Curragh (IRE) September 15 (Good To Firm)

1 **Search For A Song** 3-8-11 Chris Hayes
2 **Kew Gardens** 4-9-9 Ryan Moore
3 **Southern France** 4-9-9 Seamie Heffernan
10/1, 7/2, 9/1. 2¼l, 1½l. 10 ran. 3:03 (D K Weld).

A bold tactical move from Chris Hayes on **Search For A Song** proved a race-winning one as the lightly raced filly comfortably pulled off a surprise win that, for all her progressive profile, might just prove to have flattered her given the run of the race. Keen early, Search For A Song was sent to the front a mile from home and granted an easy lead, pulling out plenty as those held up found it impossible to make up significant ground off a steady gallop. Big guns **Kew Gardens** and **Cross Counter** were among those caught flat-footed before staying on again, Kew Gardens finishing best in second ahead of **Southern France** with Cross Counter just pipping **Master Of Reality** for fourth. **Salouen** and **Capri** brought up the rear.

36 Derrinstown Stud Flying Five Stakes (5f)

Curragh (IRE) September 15 (Good)

1 **Fairyland** 3-9-0 Ryan Moore
2 **So Perfect** 3-9-0 Donnacha O'Brien
3 **Invincible Army** 4-9-4 P J McDonald
12/1, 12/1, 12/1. shd, 1½l. 11 ran. 0:57 (A P O'Brien).

This looked wide-open beforehand and became even more so with several of the leading contenders underperforming, handing a golden opportunity to **Fairyland**, who just pipped fellow Ballydoyle filly **So Perfect** with **Invincible Army** back in third. **Soldier's Call** had the beating of the first two on his placed efforts at Royal Ascot and York but ran a slightly flat race in fourth ahead of **Soffia**, who was sent off favourite having easily won a course-and-distance Group 2 on his previous start but broke a blood vessel, and the below-par **Mabs Cross**.

37 Kingdom of Bahrain Sun Chariot Stakes (Fillies & Mares) (1m)

Newmarket October 5 (Good To Soft)

1 **Billesdon Brook** 4-9-3 Sean Levey
2 **Veracious** 4-9-3 Oisin Murphy
3 **Iridessa** 3-9-0 Donnacha O'Brien
16/1, 10/1, 4/1. 1½l, ½l. 9 ran. 1:38 (Richard Hannon).

This became a far more winnable race with **Hermosa** and **Laurens** both bombing out and **Billesdon Brook**, clearly ideally suited by a strongly run mile on this course, duly repeated her victory in the 2018 1,000 Guineas. Billesdon Brook came from off the pace with a powerful late run and won going away from **Veracious**, with **Iridessa** a close third ahead of **Lavender's Blue**, who had been stopped in her run. It was 2l back to **I Can Fly**, with Hermosa and Laurens behind.

38 Qatar Prix de l'Arc de Triomphe (1m4f)

Longchamp (FR) October 6 (Very Soft)

1 **Waldgeist** 5-9-5 Pierre-Charles Boudot
2 **Enable** 5-9-2 Frankie Dettori
3 **Sottsass** 3-8-13 Cristian Demuro
131/10, 1/2F, 66/10. 1¾l, 1¾l. 12 ran. 2:31 (A Fabre).

Agony for **Enable**'s army of supporters as the mighty mare was denied a record-breaking third successive win in the race in dramatic circumstances, with **Waldgeist** getting up in the final 50 yards. The race seemed to have gone perfectly for Enable when she quickened clear in the straight, but for the second year in a row she was treading water close home and, while she had hung on 12 months earlier, she couldn't get away with it as even more testing conditions and a strong gallop perhaps found out her stamina. In contrast, Waldgeist powered home from off the pace, while leading three-year-olds **Sottsass** and **Japan** fought a tight battle for third. There were huge gaps behind, with 6l back to **Magical**, who looked a patent non-stayer despite being a Group 1 winner at the trip, and the rest well strung out, notably **Ghaiyyath**.

39 Qipco British Champions Sprint (6f)

Ascot October 19 (Heavy)

1 **Donjuan Triumphant** 6-9-2 S De Sousa
2 **One Master** 5-8-13 Pierre-Charles Boudot
3 **Forever In Dreams** 3-8-12 Jamie Spencer
33/1, 4/1J, 66/1. 1l, nk. 17 ran. 1:16
(Andrew Balding).

Desperate ground on the straight course at Ascot – much worse than on the round course – was ideal for **Donjuan Triumphant**, who finished his career with a first Group 1 win at the ninth attempt. Donjuan Triumphant had looked below this level throughout that time, but his best form had come on heavy ground and he proved in his element as he beat **One Master**, another horse effective in the conditions whose stamina was brought to the fore. Commonwealth Cup second **Forever In Dreams** bounced back to form on her favourite track in third ahead of **Brando**, but the more fancied three-year-olds, **Advertise** and **Hello Youmzain**, were well below their best.

40 Qipco British Champions Fillies & Mares Stakes (1m4f133y)

Ascot October 19 (Soft)

1 **Star Catcher** 3-8-13 Frankie Dettori
2 **Delphinia** 3-8-13 Seamie Heffernan
3 **Sun Maiden** 4-9-5 Jim Crowley
7/4F, 20/1, 25/1. shd, 1l. 12 ran. 2:28
(John Gosden).

With the best older horses in the division contesting the Champion Stakes, this was all about the three-year-olds and **Star Catcher** confirmed herself the best of that generation with a third Group 1 win. Again allowed an easy lead when adding the Prix Vermeille to her Irish Oaks win, Star Catcher had to come from behind this time and just about scraped past the front-running **Delphinia**, who had been steadily progressive since her Oaks fifth. **Sun Maiden** was third ahead of **Fleeting**, who was unlucky in running.

41 Queen Elizabeth II Stakes (1m) Ascot October 19 (Heavy)

1 **King Of Change** 3-9-1 Sean Levey
2 **The Revenant** 4-9-4 P-C Boudot
3 **Safe Voyage** 6-9-4 Jamie Spencer
12/1, 4/1, 40/1. 1¼l, 1½l. 16 ran. 1:44
(Richard Hannon).

A big field was strung out down the track as several failed to run close to form in the conditions, but **King Of Change** still produced a smart performance in victory to back up his 2,000 Guineas second. Restricted to just one run since that Newmarket effort, King Of Change showed a smart turn of foot to beat a couple of limited but proven mudlarks in **The Revenant** and **Safe Voyage**, who had run just once at this level between them (Safe Voyage fourth in the Prix de la Foret). **Veracious** was fourth ahead of **Mohaather**, who ran well on his first outing since winning the Greenham, while **Lord Glitters**, **Phoenix Of Spain** and **King Of Comedy** were well beaten but still fared much better than **Magna Grecia**, who was tailed off on his first run since the Irish 2,000 Guineas.

42 Qipco Champion Stakes (1m2f) Ascot October 19 (Soft)

1 **Magical** 4-9-2 Donnacha O'Brien
2 **Addeybb** 5-9-5 James Doyle
3 **Deirdre** 5-9-2 Oisin Murphy
EvensF, 5/1, 10/1. ¾l, 2¼l. 9 ran. 2:08
(A P O'Brien).

A slightly disappointing renewal with Crystal Ocean having departed the scene and the only three-year-old colts sent off 20-1 and 33-1, but **Magical** again confirmed herself a wonderful mare without the shadow of Enable hanging over her. Finishing an exhausted fifth in the Arc must have inevitably left some sort of mark, but Magical showed her toughness and durability to hold off **Addeybb**, who relished the ground and ran much better than on his two previous runs at Group 1 level. **Deirdre** was unsuited by the conditions but ran on well to take third from **Fox Tal**, who ran a fine race on just his second run of the year, and **Mehdaayih**, who switched to hold-up tactics but struggled to pick up on ground much softer than ideal. **Coronet**, **I Can Fly** and **Regal Reality** were all well beaten.

Group 1 index

All horses placed or commented on in our Group 1 review section, with race numbers

FAIRYLAND (centre): Flying Five winner was a standing dish in the top sprints

LORD GLITTERS: finally gained a Group 1 victory in the Queen Anne

Two-year-old review by Dylan Hill

1 Coventry Stakes (Group 2) (6f) Ascot June 18 (Good)

1 **Arizona** 2-9-1 Ryan Moore
2 **Threat** 2-9-1 Tom Marquand
3 **Guildsman** 2-9-1 Oisin Murphy
15/8F, 4/1, 6/1. ½l, nk. 17 ran. 1:13
(A P O'Brien).

The ground was much worse than the official description of 'good' – persistent rain had turned it soft by the end of the card – and that helped **Arizona** to wear down **Threat**. Going nowhere at halfway, Arizona just got up and would prove himself a smart juvenile with his second to Pinatubo on soft ground in the Dewhurst, whereas Threat's two subsequent Group 2 wins came on good to firm. **Guildsman** ran a cracker in third and was another to benefit from cut in the ground, while **Fort Myers** was fourth ahead of **Golden Horde**, who hung left as his rider briefly lost his irons, **Ropey Guest**, **Royal Lytham** and **Maxi Boy**.

2 Queen Mary Stakes (Group 2) (Fillies) (5f) Ascot June 19 (Good To Soft)

1 **Raffle Prize** 2-9-0 Frankie Dettori
2 **Kimari** 2-9-0 John R Velazquez
3 **Final Song** 2-9-0 Christophe Soumillon
18/1, 13/2, 6/1F. hd, 1l. 25 ran. 1:01
(Mark Johnston).

A really strong race won by **Raffle Prize**, who battled gamely to see off US raider **Kimari** in a thriller before going on to prove herself a top-class filly over further. The favourite **Final Song** and subsequent Molecomb winner **Liberty Beach** made up a classy first four, the latter perhaps unlucky not to finish closer having done best on those on the seemingly unfavoured far side. There was plenty more quality just behind, led by **Al Raya**, who also went on to win a Group 3 at Chantilly, while precocious pair **Mighty Spirit** and **Flippa The Strippa** – second and first in Listed races earlier in the season – were split by Flying Childers fourth **Flaming Princess** with Cheveley Park fourth **Tango** completing the top nine. **Shadn** and **Isabeau** were well beaten.

3 Windsor Castle Stakes (Listed) (5f) Ascot June 19 (Soft)

1 **Southern Hills** 2-9-3 Ryan Moore
2 **Platinum Star** 2-9-3 Christophe Soumillon
3 **Glasvegas** 2-9-3 Paul Mulrennan
7/1, 8/1, 25/1. ½l, hd. 21 ran. 1:03
(A P O'Brien).

Southern Hills missed the rest of the season but proved himself a useful colt with this game victory as he won going away. Southern Hills came from the highest stall and was chased home by the two drawn immediately next to him, but there was no question of the draw favouring them as runner up **Platinum Star** did most for the form with his second in the July Stakes. **Glasvegas** finished strongly in third ahead of **Symbolize**, while **Summer Sands** was sixth with that group separated by just 2l. **Rayong** would also have been close but for being badly hampered.

4 Norfolk Stakes (Group 2) (5f) Ascot June 20 (Soft)

1 **A'Ali** 2-9-1 Frankie Dettori
2 **Ventura Rebel** 2-9-1 Paul Hanagan
3 **Dubai Station** 2-9-1 Jamie Spencer
5/1, 16/1, 14/1. nk, 2¾l. 14 ran. 1:01

(Simon Crisford).

A'Ali would prove the best juvenile 5f sprinter over the season and gave an early indication of his prowess as he cosily held off the fast-finishing **Ventura Rebel**. The first two pulled nicely clear, making the runner-up worth bearing in mind despite just one below-par subsequent run when a beaten favourite in the Super Sprint, especially as the form of those behind generally stood up well, with **Strive For Glory** winning a decent Listed race at Fairyhouse after taking fourth ahead of **Emten** and **King Neptune**. **Sunday Sovereign** was sent off favourite but managed only eighth, with **Mount Fuji** also disappointing, while **Air Force Jet** wasn't suited by the soft ground.

5 Albany Stakes (Group 3) (Fillies) (6f) Ascot June 21 (Good To Soft)

1 **Daahyeh** 2-9-0 David Egan
2 **Celtic Beauty** 2-9-0 W J Lee
3 **Aroha** 2-9-0 Harry Bentley
4/1F, 25/1, 100/1. 1½l, 1l. 25 ran. 1:14
(Roger Varian).

Despite the big field, this lacked great quality and **Daahyeh** proved much the best filly. Daahyeh was always going well enough and stayed on strongly to forge clear of Irish raider **Celtic Beauty**. **Aroha**, a revelation at 100-1 and seemingly much better at Ascot than anywhere else on the balance of her form, might have proved a bigger danger but for what looked a significant draw bias as she did much the best of a small group on the far side, with subsequent Group 2 runner-up **Precious Moments** in turn well clear of the rest. **Alabama Whitman** was fourth overall, pulling clear of **Lil Grey**.

6 Chesham Stakes (Listed) (7f) Ascot June 22 (Good)

1 **Pinatubo** 2-9-3 James Doyle
2 **Lope Y Fernandez** 2-9-3 Ryan Moore
3 **Highland Chief** 2-9-3 Raul Da Silva
3/1, 5/4F, 14/1. 3¼l, 1¼l. 14 ran. 1:25
(Charlie Appleby).

The first sign of **Pinatubo**'s brilliance as he destroyed what had looked a strong field. Having already won the Woodcote Stakes at Epsom, Pinatubo relished going up in trip as he drew clear of favourite **Lope Y Fernandez**, who would prove a non-stayer over this distance. **Highland Chief** ran a good race in third as the first three pulled 2¼l clear of **Sun Power** and **Harpocrates**, who would prove fair yardsticks in this sort of grade.

A'ALI: dominant at the minimum trip

7 Airlie Stud Stakes (Group 2) (Fillies) (6f) Curragh (IRE) June 28 (Good)

1 **Albigna** 2-9-0 Shane Foley
2 **Precious Moments** 2-9-0 Ryan Moore
3 **Peace Charter** 2-9-0 Colin Keane
5/2F, 5/1, 4/1. ½l, 1½l. 10 ran. 1:12
(Mrs John Harrington).

The decision to upgrade this race to a Group 2 for the first time was justified by **Albigna** going on to win a Group 1, although that isn't necessarily any endorsement of this contest as the Prix Marcel Boussac heroine managed to get up over a trip clearly short of her best having been scrubbed along in rear. **Precious Moments** and **Peace Charter** pulled clear of the rest as they filled the places but proved flattered to finish so close to such a high-class filly. **Tango** and **Blissful** were well beaten.

8 Randox Health Empress Fillies' Stakes (Listed) (6f) Newmarket (July) June 29 (Good To Firm)

1 **Summer Romance** 2-9-0 James Doyle
2 **Ursulina** 2-9-0 Richard Kingscote
3 **Companion** 2-9-0 Frankie Dettori
5/6F, 14/1, 10/1. 6l, 1¾l. 7 ran. 1:12
(Charlie Appleby).

One of the most misleading performances of the season as **Summer Romance** was catapulted into Guineas favouritism by this runaway victory only to twice flop at short prices in a higher grade. Summer Romance proved

SISKIN: produced perhaps the best 6f juvenile performance of the season

herself a much better filly than that as she stormed clear despite failing to settle early, seemingly relishing a quicker surface than she would face later, though the opposition also proved a moderate bunch.

9 GAIN Railway Stakes (Group 2) (6f) Curragh (IRE) June 29 (Good)

1 **Siskin** 2-9-3 Colin Keane
2 **Monarch Of Egypt** 2-9-3 Ryan Moore
3 **Fort Myers** 2-9-3 Donnacha O'Brien
4/6F, 7/2, 7/2. 2½l, 2¼l. 5 ran. 1:13
(G M Lyons).

A terrific performance from **Siskin**, who finished the season unbeaten in four runs after being withdrawn from the Middle Park with this being probably the best performance of the lot – arguably the best over this trip by any juvenile all season. Siskin produced an impressive turn of foot as he pulled clear of **Monarch Of Egypt** with another gap back to **Fort Myers**, who was beaten much further than when fourth in the Coventry and the Champagne Stakes.

10 Coolmore US Navy Flag Tipperary Stakes (Listed) (5f) Tipperary (IRE) July 4 (Good To Firm)

1 **Strive For Glory** 2-9-3 W J Lee
2 **Air Force Jet** 2-9-3 Donnacha O'Brien
3 **Isabeau** 2-8-12 Leigh Roche
9/4F, 7/2, 6/1. ¾l, ½l. 7 ran. 0:57
(Robert Cowell).

A decent Listed race won in good style by Norfolk fourth **Strive For Glory**, who beat a solid yardstricks **Air Force Jet** and **Isabeau**. Air Force Jet struggled to see out many of his races but very nearly lasted home on quick ground – his only subsequent win in a premier nursery also came on good to firm – and Strive To Glory had to stay on well to run him down. Isabeau was a good third on ground perhaps faster than ideal, with the first three pulling 2½l clear of the rest.

11 Chasemore Farm Dragon Stakes (Listed) (5f10y) Sandown July 5 (Good To Firm)

1 **Liberty Beach** 2-8-11 Jason Hart
2 **Dream Shot** 2-9-2 Jamie Spencer
3 **Rayong** 2-9-2 Oisin Murphy
9/4F, 12/1, 7/1. 3¼l, nk. 10 ran. 1:00
(John Quinn).

An outstanding performance from **Liberty Beach**, who had perhaps been beaten by the draw at Royal Ascot but left that form well behind anyway on a much quicker surface. Liberty Beach destroyed a solid field for the grade, with subsequent Flying Childers runner-up **Dream Shot** a distant second ahead of **Rayong** and **Al Raya**.

12 Tattersalls July Stakes (Group 2) (6f) Newmarket (July) July 11 (Good To Firm)

1 **Royal Lytham** 2-9-0 Wayne Lordan
2 **Platinum Star** 2-9-0 Harry Bentley
3 **Visinari** 2-9-0 Frankie Dettori
11/1, 10/1, 4/6F. shd, hd. 7 ran. 1:11
(A P O'Brien).

An ordinary running of this Group 2, with **Platinum Star**'s win in a weak Two-Year-Old

Trophy at Ripon in August the only subsequent win from any of the seven runners all year, but there was still a thrilling finish fought out between three useful juveniles. **Royal Lytham** just got the verdict, edging out fellow fast finisher Platinum Star as the pair stormed past **Visinari**, the odds-on favourite much better than he showed in two disappointing subsequent runs. **Guildsman** was nowhere near the level of his Coventry third, seemingly struggling to cope with a much quicker surface in fourth, with **King Neptune** next.

13 Duchess of Cambridge Stakes (Group 2) (Fillies) (6f)

Newmarket (July) July 12 (Good To Firm)

1 **Raffle Prize** 2-9-3 Frankie Dettori
2 **Daahyeh** 2-9-0 David Egan
3 **Final Song** 2-9-0 Ryan Moore
9/2, 5/4F, 100/30. 1¾l, hd. 7 ran. 1:09
(Mark Johnston).

An intriguing clash between two Royal Ascot winners didn't really live up to its billing as **Raffle Prize** was always well in command against **Daahyeh**. Raffle Prize was definitely favoured by the draw and her running style as she moved quickly into the lead from her berth against the rails, which was very much the place to be on this day, although it was still no mean feat to win so decisively under a 3lb penalty. Daahyeh stayed on well to take second from Queen Mary third **Final Song**, who ran another solid race to fill the same spot, with those three pulling 2¼l clear of the rest. **Celtic Beauty** was a big disappointment, finishing last of the seven runners.

14 bet365 Superlative Stakes (Group 2) (7f)

Newmarket (July) July 13 (Good To Firm)

1 **Mystery Power** 2-9-1 Oisin Murphy
2 **Juan Elcano** 2-9-1 Andrea Atzeni
3 **Maxi Boy** 2-9-1 Frankie Dettori
7/1, 6/1, 7/1. 1l, 3¼l. 8 ran. 1:23
(Richard Hannon).

Not much depth to this Group 2, but the first two were at least much too good for the rest with **Mystery Power** edging out **Juan Elcano**. Mystery Power stayed on well to win and, while he would twice disappoint behind the mighty Pinatubo, he was favoured by this quick surface and it still looks decent form with runner-up Juan Elcano going on to finish a close third in the Champagne Stakes. The pair pulled 3¼l clear of **Maxi Boy** and the rest were well strung out, with further gaps back to **Ropey Guest** and **Year Of The Tiger**.

15 Jebel Ali Racecourse And Stables Anglesey Stakes (Group 3) (6f63y)

Curragh (IRE) July 20 (Good)

1 **Roman Turbo** 2-9-3 Ronan Whelan
2 **Lil Grey** 2-9-0 Robbie Colgan
3 **Soul Search** 2-9-0 Colin Keane
6/1, 4/1, 5/1. ¾l, hd. 7 ran. 1:16
(M Halford).

A modest race for the grade and just 1½l covered the first five, with **Roman Turbo** just outstaying **Lil Grey**, whose limitations were exposed several times during the season. **Soul Search** would prove the best of these in time but seemed green on his second run before finishing strongly in third, while Aidan O'Brien's pair **Mount Fuji** and **Pistoletto** proved a long way down the Ballydoyle pecking order despite heading the market.

16 Jockey Club Of Turkey Silver Flash Stakes (Group 3) (Fillies) (7f20y)

Leopardstown (IRE) July 25 (Good)

1 **Love** 2-9-0 Seamie Heffernan
2 **Unforgetable** 2-9-0 Donnacha O'Brien
3 **So Wonderful** 2-9-0 Wayne Lordan
8/1, 7/1, 14/1. 3¼l, 1l. 8 ran. 1:30
(A P O'Brien).

Love needed three runs to get off the mark but this was suddenly a big step forward for the subsequent Moyglare winner as she hacked up from the front. Love was much too good for **Unforgetable** and **So Wonderful**, with **Precious Moments** back in fourth and **Isabeau** well below her best in seventh.

17 Princess Margaret Keeneland Stakes (Group 3) (Fillies) (6f)

Ascot July 27 (Good To Soft)

1 **Under The Stars** 2-9-0 P J McDonald
2 **Aroha** 2-9-0 Oisin Murphy
3 **Living In The Past** 2-9-0 Frankie Dettori
25/1, 16/1, 12/1. ½l, hd. 9 ran. 1:17
(James Tate).

A really strong Group 3 in which **Under The Stars** quickened up smartly to claim some notable scalps, with three subsequent Group winners behind her. Under The Stars would also go on to run consistently well at a higher level, although subsequent Lowther winner **Living In The Past** wasn't ideally suited by this ground and **Good Vibes** was much too keen on her first attempt at 6f, with **Dark Lady** splitting that pair having struggled to get a clear run. The subsequently disappointing **Aroha** finished ahead of that trio in second, running her second fine race at Ascot as she clearly relished the track, but odds-on shot **Summer Romance** was a poor sixth.

18 **Qatar Vintage Stakes (Group 2) (7f)**
Goodwood July 30 (Good)
1 **Pinatubo** 2-9-1 James Doyle
2 **Positive** 2-9-1 Adam Kirby
3 **Lope Y Fernandez** 2-9-1 Ryan Moore
6/4F, 12/1, 9/2. 5l, 5l. 7 ran. 1:27
(Charlie Appleby).

A stunning performance from **Pinatubo**, who absolutely routed a quality field. **Visinari** ensured a true test and that enabled Pinatubo to fully demonstrate his prowess for the first time as he stormed clear with his rivals well strung out, only **Positive**, who would go on to win a high-class Solario Stakes, finishing within less than 10l as he ran a tremendous race in second. **Lope Y Fernandez**'s lack of stamina was exposed in third as he was beaten far more comprehensively by the winner than at Royal Ascot, while Visinari dropped out to finish a disappointing fourth ahead of **Platinum Star** and **Mystery Power**.

19 **Markel Insurance Molecomb Stakes (Group 3) (5f)**
Goodwood July 31 (Good)
1 **Liberty Beach** 2-8-12 Jason Hart
2 **Alligator Alley** 2-9-1 Donnacha O'Brien
3 **Show Me Show Me** 2-9-1 Paddy Mathers
11/8F, 8/1, 25/1. 1l, 1l. 13 ran. 0:58
(John Quinn).

Although it seemed unlikely for much of the contest, class came to the fore in the nick of time as **Liberty Beach** and **Alligator Alley** claimed first and second despite problems in running, both looking much better than the bare form. Building on her Sandown win, Liberty Beach stormed home having had to be switched for a gap, while Alligator Alley also finished strongly having been badly hampered. The rest weren't up to much, with **Show Me Show Me** just the best of them. **Wheels On Fire** was fifth with **Air Force Jet** and **Dr Simpson** among those further back.

20 **Qatar Richmond Stakes (Group 2) (6f)**
Goodwood August 1 (Good)
1 **Golden Horde** 2-9-0 Adam Kirby
2 **Threat** 2-9-0 Tom Marquand
3 **Royal Dornoch** 2-9-0 Wayne Lordan
15/2, 11/8F, 25/1. ¾l, 3l. 13 ran. 1:11
(Clive Cox).

The Coventry form dominated but **Threat** still came up just short again as **Golden Horde** stepped up on his fifth at Royal Ascot with a terrific performance. Looking much wiser for that experience, Golden Horde knuckled down well and was well on top in the final 100 yards as the pair pulled 3l clear of **Royal Dornoch**, who stayed on past the likes of **Symbolize** and **Misty Grey** close home and would prove much better when stepped up in trip. **Guildsman**, bumped at the start, was always in rear and never got a run.

21 **Keeneland Phoenix Stakes (Group 1) (6f)**
Curragh (IRE) August 9 (Soft)
1 **Siskin** 2-9-3 Colin Keane
2 **Monarch Of Egypt** 2-9-3 Ryan Moore
3 **Royal Lytham** 2-9-3 Donnacha O'Brien
10/11F, 6/4, 9/2. ¾l, hd. 5 ran. 1:17
(G M Lyons).

Siskin was no doubt a worthy Group 1 winner as he stretched his unbeaten record to four, but he didn't have to run to his best as he saw off **Monarch Of Egypt** and **Royal Lytham** in much more workmanlike fashion. Seemingly unsuited by the soft ground, Siskin struggled to gain the upper hand but picked up in time and was going away from old rival Monarch Of Egypt at the line. Royal Lytham also finished close up in third, keeping on well, and it was 7l back to **Mount Fuji**.

22 **german-thoroughbred.com Sweet Solera Stakes (Group 3) (Fillies) (7f)**
Newmarket (July) August 10 (Good To Firm)
1 **West End Girl** 2-9-0 Franny Norton
2 **Soffika** 2-9-0 James Doyle
3 **Dark Lady** 2-9-0 Pat Dobbs
11/2, 9/2, 8/1. 1¼l, ½l. 8 ran. 1:25
(Mark Johnston).

Bitterly disappointing twice at a higher level after this win, **West End Girl** nonetheless proved herself a smart filly as she won what looked a decent race for the grade. Unlucky in running when fifth in a Listed race at Sandown in July, West End Girl reversed form with two of those in front of her that day as she made virtually all for a comfortable victory. **Soffika** finished strongly from the rear to pip **Dark Lady** for second, while **Ananya** blew the start, losing many lengths, before coming home fifth.

23 **Coolmore Caravaggio Stakes (Listed) (7f115y)**
Tipperary (IRE) August 11 (Soft To Heavy)
1 **Justifier** 2-9-3 Colin Keane
2 **Harpocrates** 2-9-3 Seamie Heffernan
3 **Rebel Tale** 2-9-3 Oisin Orr
6/4, 5/4F, 10/1. 1½l, 3¾l. 5 ran. 1:39
(G M Lyons).

A good win for **Justifier**, who comfortably saw off a decent yardstick in **Harpocrates**. Showing plenty of stamina in testing conditions, Justifier was strongest at the finish and well on top by the line. **Rebel Tale** was a big improver subsequently but didn't cope with the ground in third.

24 Ryans Cleaning Event Specialist Curragh Stakes (Listed) (5f)

Curragh (IRE) August 16 (Soft)

1 **Millisle** 2-8-12 Shane Foley
2 **Isabeau** 2-8-12 Leigh Roche
3 **Lil Grey** 2-8-12 Robbie Colgan

11/2, 13/2, 11/8F. ½l, 2½l. 6 ran. 1:01 (Mrs John Harrington).

A dramatic win for subsequent Cheveley Park heroine **Millisle**, who got up on the line to beat **Isabeau**. Seemingly not quite as effective over the minimum trip, Millisle just about got away with it as her stamina kicked in, denying the unfortunate Isabeau, who left the rest of her form behind as she dropped back in trip and ran on soft ground for the first time. It was 2½l back to **Lil Grey** in third, while **King Neptune** was a below-par fifth and **Air Force Jet** didn't appreciate the conditions.

25 Denford Stakes (Listed) (formerly Washington Singer Stakes) (7f)

Newbury August 17 (Soft)

1 **Thunderous** 2-9-1 Franny Norton
2 **Sesame Birah** 2-8-10 Tom Marquand
3 **Sun Power** 2-9-1 Silvestre De Sousa

11/8F, 16/1, 15/8. 1l, nk. 5 ran. 1:30 (Mark Johnston).

A workmanlike victory for **Thunderous**, who did enough to finish his two-year-old campaign unbeaten in three runs. Thunderous battled hard to hold off the filly **Sesame Birah**, whose form was generally below this level, while form horse **Sun Power** was too keen and hung left in third. **Pyledriver** was another who seemed to run below his best, the subsequent Listed winner looking green on his second run as he drifted left and made no impression in fourth.

26 Darley Prix Morny (Group 1) (6f)

Deauville (FR) August 18 (Heavy)

1 **Earthlight** 2-9-0 Mickael Barzalona
2 **Raffle Prize** 2-8-10 Frankie Dettori
3 **Golden Horde** 2-9-0 Adam Kirby

12/5, 19/10F, 13/1. nk, 2½l. 8 ran. 1:12 (A Fabre).

Albeit without the outstanding Pinatubo, this was probably the strongest juvenile race of the season in terms of depth, with a strong field largely running to form and **Earthlight** proving himself a top-class colt. Earthlight wasn't expected to be suited by heavy ground, but conditions didn't seem to affect many and he powered through it to wear down the long-time leader **Raffle Prize**, who ran another terrific race from the front. The pair pulled 2½l clear of **Golden Horde** and **Arizona**, who seemed just below his best but

LIBERTY BEACH: got herself out of trouble in the Molecomb

still took a good fourth ahead of **A'Ali**, **Aroha** and **Royal Dornoch**.

27 Tattersalls Acomb Stakes (Group 3) (7f)

York August 21 (Good)

1 **Valdermoro** 2-9-1 Tony Hamilton
2 **Harpocrates** 2-9-1 Ryan Moore
3 **Ropey Guest** 2-9-1 Tom Queally
9/2, 7/1, 25/1. nk, 2½l. 9 ran. 1:24
(Richard Fahey).

The victorious **Valdermoro** was due to be sold to Hong Kong after this race, further minimising the likely impact of what looked a modest race for the grade. Valdermoro stayed on well to see off **Harpocrates**, who came a good deal closer to winning than he had in three attempts in Listed races previously, while **Ropey Guest** was third and the favourite **Persuasion** a disappointing sixth.

28 Goffs UK Premier Yearling Stakes (6f)

York August 22 (Good)

1 **Mums Tipple** 2-9-5 Ryan Moore
2 **Rayong** 2-9-0 Silvestre De Sousa
3 **Klopp Of The Kop** 2-9-0 Adam Kirby
7/2F, 10/1, 20/1. 11l, nk. 21 ran. 1:09
(Richard Hannon).

One of the most astonishing performances of the season as **Mums Tipple** turned a 21-runner sales race into a procession, storming home by 11l as he made all the running and quickened clear off the front. While his subsequent failure at Newmarket, albeit with a valid excuse, left questions about the reliability of the form, there was plenty of quality at the head of the chasing pack as **Rayong** got up for second ahead of **Klopp Of The Kop**, subsequent Listed winner **Piece Of Paradise** and another next-time-out winner in **National League**, while a quick time earned the second best juvenile Time Test figure of the year.

29 Sky Bet Lowther Stakes (Group 2) (Fillies) (6f)

York August 22 (Good)

1 **Living In The Past** 2-9-0 Daniel Tudhope
2 **Liberty Beach** 2-9-0 Jason Hart
3 **Good Vibes** 2-9-0 Harry Bentley
12/1, 15/8F, 20/1. ¾l, 1l. 10 ran. 1:10
(K R Burke).

An all-the-way win for **Living In The Past**, who benefited from a well-judged ride and better ground than when third in the Princess Margaret. The subsequent Cheveley Park fifth had opened up a decisive lead by the time **Liberty Beach** had hit her stride and held on by a narrowing margin. Liberty Beach, shaping like the best filly in the race, saw out the extra furlong well and was a clear second ahead of **Good Vibes**, while **Under The Stars**, who had beaten the first and third at Ascot, was just short of pace on this quicker surface, finishing fourth to prompt a step up to 7f. **Wejdan** was fifth ahead of **Precious Moments** and **Celtic Beauty**.

30 Al Basti Equiworld Dubai Gimcrack Stakes (Group 2) (6f)

York August 23 (Good To Firm)

1 **Threat** 2-9-0 Oisin Murphy
2 **Lord Of The Lodge** 2-9-0 Ben Curtis
3 **Repartee** 2-9-0 Andrea Atzeni
11/10F, 16/1, 11/2. 1¼l, 2¾l. 12 ran. 1:09
(Richard Hannon).

Threat set a clear form standard having just been pipped by two smart horses in Arizona and Golden Horde at this level and he comfortably made the most of a softer race for the grade. Always to the fore, Threat stayed on powerfully to beat **Lord Of The Lodge**, who ran a big race in second as he pulled clear of the rest. **Repartee** was third ahead of **Malotru**, **Summer Sands** and **Pistoletto**.

31 Longines Irish Champions Weekend EBF Stonehenge Stakes (Listed) (1m)

Salisbury August 23 (Good)

1 **Mohican Heights** 2-9-1 Jamie Spencer
2 **Subjectivist** 2-9-1 Jack Mitchell
3 **Berlin Tango** 2-9-1 Oisin Murphy
6/1, 11/2, 7/2. 2l, ¾l. 6 ran. 1:42
(David Simcock).

A weak Listed race but a decisive win for big-money purchase **Mohican Heights**, who signed off for the year by making a winning start for new connections. Mohican Heights was always well in command as he saw off **Subjectivist**, who was beaten much further in two other runs in this grade. **Berlin Tango** did most for the form after taking third but was probably flattered to fill the same spot in a slowly run Flying Scotsman at Doncaster.

32 Galileo Irish EBF Futurity Stakes (Group 2) (7f)

Curragh (IRE) August 23 (Yielding)

1 **Armory** 2-9-3 Ryan Moore
2 **Rebel Tale** 2-9-3 Ben Coen
3 **Geometrical** 2-9-3 Kevin Manning
4/6F, 50/1, 14/1. ¾l, 1l. 8 ran. 1:28
(A P O'Brien).

Armory had won the Tyros Stakes at 2-5 on his previous start and had it easy in another

ALPINE STAR (far side, left): Debutante Stakes win looks like red-hot form

poor race here, completing a hat-trick without having to be near his best. Armory was always doing enough in front, but the form didn't work out with placed horses **Rebel Tale** and **Geometrical** coming up well short several times between them subsequently. **Roman Turbo** was a close fourth ahead of the below-par **Justifier**.

33 Debutante Stakes (Group 2) (Fillies) (7f)

Curragh (IRE) August 23 (Yielding)

1 **Alpine Star** 2-9-0 Shane Foley
2 **Petite Mustique** 2-9-0 Donnacha O'Brien
3 **Soul Search** 2-9-0 Colin Keane
2/1, 9/1, 10/1. shd, ¾l. 9 ran. 1:27
(Mrs John Harrington).

Outpaced and going nowhere at one stage, **Alpine Star** came home really strongly to beat **Petite Mustique** in a thriller and, even with the pair not running again, it looks red-hot form after the race threw up three of the first four in the Moyglare. The winner that day, **Love**, was below her best in fifth here behind two seemingly much-improved fillies in **Soul Search** and **So Wonderful**, who both backed up their progressive profiles while **Tango** and **Know It All** also franked this form after finishing sixth and seventh.

34 Ladbrokes Prestige Stakes (Group 3) (Fillies) (7f)

Goodwood August 24 (Good)

1 **Boomer** 2-9-0 Richard Kingscote
2 **Dark Lady** 2-9-0 Pat Dobbs
3 **Shadn** 2-9-0 Oisin Murphy
5/2F, 5/1, 3/1. nk, ¾l. 7 ran. 1:26
(Tom Dascombe).

A really competitive Group 3 won more easily than the margin suggests by **Boomer**. Shaken up to lead, Boomer just had to be nudged out with mainly hands and heels to win a shade cosily from **Dark Lady** and **Shadn**, both of whom went on to win Group races themselves later in the campaign, while **Stylistique** was second in the Rockfel after completing a quality foursome in front. It was 2¼l back to the rest.

35 Julia Graves Roses Stakes (Listed) (5f)

York August 24 (Good To Firm)

1 **Alligator Alley** 2-9-0 Donnacha O'Brien
2 **Dr Simpson** 2-8-9 Paul Hanagan
3 **Streamline** 2-9-0 Hector Crouch
11/8F, 16/1, 25/1. 1l, shd. 12 ran. 0:57
(Joseph Patrick O'Brien).

An impressive win from **Alligator Alley**, who had plenty go wrong but still won cosily. Hampered early, Alligator Alley produced a terrific turn of foot despite being forced off his true line and was going away at the line as the winning margin underestimated his superiority. It was still a good run in second from **Dr Simpson**, who beat older horses in a Group 3 at Dundalk later in the year, while **Streamline** came home strongly to take third and **Dream Shot** was unlucky not to finish much closer after getting badly bumped. **Kemble** did best of those ridden prominently.

36 Flame of Tara Irish EBF Stakes (Group 3) (Fillies) (1m)

Curragh (IRE) August 30 (Good To Yielding)
1 **Cayenne Pepper** 2-9-0 Shane Foley
2 **So Wonderful** 2-9-0 Ryan Moore
3 **A New Dawn** 2-9-0 Wayne Lordan
6/4F, 7/2, 12/1. 2½l, 2¾l. 6 ran. 1:39
(Mrs John Harrington).

A terrific performance from **Cayenne Pepper**, who put a couple of useful rivals firmly in their place. Setting a decent enough clip that the field finishing well strung out, Cayenne Pepper quickened smartly and comfortably saw off the progressive **So Wonderful**, who was third in the Moyglare on her next run, with another gap back to the subsequent Park Stakes runner-up **A New Dawn**. Market rival **Brook On Fifth** sat closest to Cayenne Pepper but was ultimately beaten 8¾l in fourth.

37 Round Tower Stakes (Group 3) (6f)

Curragh (IRE) August 30 (Good To Yielding)
1 **Lope Y Fernandez** 2-9-3 Ryan Moore
2 **Guildsman** 2-9-3 Oisin Murphy
3 **Fort Myers** 2-9-3 Donnacha O'Brien
11/8F, 5/1, 6/1. 1½l, shd. 12 ran. 1:12
(A P O'Brien).

This was a strong race dominated by three horses with decent form against top opposition, with **Lope Y Fernandez** proving the best of them. Benefiting from a drop in trip, Lope Y Fernandez stayed on strongly for a clearcut win over Coventry runner-up **Guildsman**, who bounced back to form when faced with some cut in the ground again as he just held off **Fort Myers** for second. **Zarzyni** was fourth ahead of **Ventura Lightning**.

38 Betway Solario Stakes (Group 3) (7f)

Sandown August 31 (Good To Firm)
1 **Positive** 2-9-1 Adam Kirby
2 **Kameko** 2-9-1 Oisin Murphy
3 **Al Suhail** 2-9-1 William Buick
4/5F, 14/1, 7/4. nse, 1l. 6 ran. 1:27
(Clive Cox).

A quality edition of what tends to be a strong Group 3 anyway, with **Positive** just pipping subsequent Vertem Futurity Trophy winner **Kameko**. While Kameko was very much a work in progress at this point, looking notably green when asked to pick up before storming home in the final furlong, it was still a terrific effort from Positive to rally again close home and hang on to win, especially with third-placed **Al Suhail** also franking the form with a near miss in the Autumn Stakes and a 5l gap back to the rest.

39 Shadwell Dick Poole Fillies' Stakes (Group 3) (6f)

Salisbury September 5 (Good)
1 **Dark Lady** 2-9-0 Pat Dobbs
2 **Millisle** 2-9-0 Shane Foley
3 **Summer Romance** 2-9-0 William Buick
13/2, 9/2, 6/4F. shd, 4½l. 10 ran. 1:14
(Richard Hannon).

A strange result in retrospect with **Millisle** turned over by **Dark Lady** before going on to win the Cheveley Park, but it was later reported that she had been upset by having a blood sample taken beforehand, perhaps explaining her defeat. Even so, it was still a fine effort from the useful and progressive Dark Lady to land a Group 3 win at the fourth attempt, pipping the front-running Millisle as she put her stamina to good use on this drop in trip. The pair were 4½l clear of **Summer Romance**, with **Jouska**, **Good Vibes** and **Dr Simpson** among those further back.

40 Sun Racing Sirenia Stakes (Group 3) (6f)

Kempton (AW) September 7 (Standard To Slow)
1 **Streamline** 2-9-1 Hector Crouch
2 **Oh Purple Reign** 2-9-1 Sean Levey
3 **Huraiz** 2-9-1 Joe Fanning
9/2, 11/4, 9/1. 1l, nk. 7 ran. 1:11
(Clive Cox).

A weak Group 3 with the principals well beaten in Listed races before and since, although **Streamline** probably improved over this extra furlong compared to her strong-finishing third in the Roses Stakes. Streamline was too good for **Oh Purple Reign** and **Huraiz**, while **Sun Power** was a disappointing fifth.

41 Read Ryan Moore Exclusively At betfair.com Ascendant Stakes (Listed) (1m37y)

Haydock September 7 (Soft)
1 **Pyledriver** 2-9-2 P J McDonald
2 **Sound Of Cannons** 2-9-2 Oisin Murphy
3 **Tammani** 2-9-2 James Doyle
14/1, 11/2, 5/2F. 1¼l, 1¼l. 8 ran. 1:45
(William Muir).

A strange result on tacky ground, which probably led to several of the form horses running below their best, with **Pyledriver** flattered to win so decisively. Pyledriver saw out his race much the best and is clearly much better than he showed in the Royal Lodge, although runner-up **Sound Of Cannons**'s fifth place at Newmarket also pointed to the shortcomings of this form. Favourite **Tammani** was third ahead of **Subjectivist** and **Sesame Birah**.

42 William Hill May Hill Stakes (Group 2) (Fillies) (1m)

Doncaster September 12 (Good To Firm)
1 **Powerful Breeze** 2-9-0 James Doyle
2 **Boomer** 2-9-0 Richard Kingscote
3 **Alpen Rose** 2-9-0 William Buick
6/1, 8/1, 10/1. 1l, nk. 9 ran. 1:39
(Hugo Palmer).

A fiercely competitive race won by a very smart filly in subsequent Fillies' Mile runner-up **Powerful Breeze**, who beat a classy opponent in **Boomer** with a bit in hand. Powerful Breeze looked green as she drifted in front but was never in danger of being caught by Boomer, who held off **Alpen Rose** and **Run Wild** for second with the first four covered by less than 2l. **Passion** would have been in the mix as well but for being badly hampered, so instead **Ananya**, who was much better at the start than when fifth in the Sweet Solera, filled the same spot ahead of the disappointing favourite **Cloak Of Spirits**, with **West End Girl** another to run below her best in eighth.

43 Wainwright Flying Childers Stakes (Group 2) (5f)

Doncaster September 13 (Good To Firm)
1 **A'Ali** 2-9-1 Frankie Dettori
2 **Dream Shot** 2-9-1 P J McDonald
3 **Wheels On Fire** 2-9-1 Daniel Tudhope
6/4, 20/1, 12/1. 1l, nse. 7 ran. 0:59
(Simon Crisford).

The 5f juvenile championship saw **A'Ali** confirm the superiority he had carried since Royal Ascot, albeit in an unusually small field and uncompetitive race. Market rival **Alligator Alley** was the only other horse sent off at single-figure odds and, as he ran well below form in rear, A'Ali had a straightforward task as he won a shade cosily. With **Wheels On Fire** dictating a steady gallop and perhaps flattered by his third place, it was a good effort from **Dream Shot** to come through into second. **Flaming Princess** was fourth ahead of **Emten**, who had disappointed since his Norfolk fifth but ran to the pound with A'Ali.

44 Weatherbys Global Stallions App Flying Scotsman Stakes (Listed) (7f)

Doncaster September 13 (Good To Firm)
1 **Molatham** 2-9-0 Jim Crowley

MOLATHAM: won a tactical race at Doncaster, with the form questionable

2 **Wichita** 2-9-0 Ryan Moore
3 **Berlin Tango** 2-9-0 Oisin Murphy
EvensF, 11/4, 14/1. ½l, ¾l. 5 ran. 1:25
(Roger Varian).

A fascinating small-field affair which became somewhat tactical, perhaps rendering the form questionable, although **Molatham** was still an impressive winner. Held up in last off the steady gallop, Molatham showed a tremendous turn of foot to power home from **Wichita**, whose subsequent Tattersalls Stakes romp suggested he would have been much better suited by a truer test. **Berlin Tango** was a close third, running some way above the rest of his form, but **Visinari** was again disappointing, fading into fourth having been allowed an easy lead.

45 Pommery Champagne Stakes (Group 2) (7f)

Doncaster September 14 (Good To Firm)
1 **Threat** 2-9-3 Pat Dobbs
2 **Royal Crusade** 2-9-0 William Buick
3 **Juan Elcano** 2-9-0 Andrea Atzeni
6/5F, 9/4, 4/1. nk, ¾l. 5 ran. 1:25
(Richard Hannon).

An excellent performance from **Threat**, who defied a 3lb penalty for his Gimcrack win and looked an improved horse over the extra furlong. Threat kept on well to run down his market rival **Royal Crusade**, with Superlative runner-up **Juan Elcano** and **Fort Myers**, who also seemed to improve for the longer trip, close behind. **Royal Dornoch** was unsuited by the steady pace and completed the five runners before going on to win the Royal Lodge when faced with a stiffer stamina test.

46 KPMG Champions Juvenile Stakes (Group 2) (1m)

Leopardstown (IRE) September 14 (Good)

1 **Mogul** 2-9-3 Ryan Moore
2 **Sinawann** 2-9-3 Ronan Whelan
3 **Agitare** 2-9-3 Kevin Manning
1/2F, 5/1, 14/1. 1¼l, 1¾l. 7 ran. 1:42
(A P O'Brien).

Anyone who took odds of 1-2 about **Mogul** rarely had a moment of worry, but nonetheless he made hard enough work of landing a desperately uncompetitive race for the grade and would come unstuck when up in grade at Newcastle. Mogul had to be driven out to beat **Sinawann**, who was having his only run outside maiden company, and **Agitare**, who failed to win in four runs at that level last year. **Rebel Tale** was the most solid yardstick in the race and finished fourth.

47 Ballylinch Stud Irish EBF Ingabelle Stakes (Listed) (Fillies) (7f)

Leopardstown (IRE) September 14 (Good)

1 **Blissful** 2-9-0 Ryan Moore
2 **Nurse Barbara** 2-9-0 Colin Keane
3 **Pronouncement** 2-9-0 Chris Hayes
13/2, 7/2, 11/2. nse, ¾l. 9 ran. 1:29
(A P O'Brien).

A fair race for the grade, although the best filly was perhaps beaten as **Nurse Barbara** was reeled in by **Blissful**. Nurse Barbara had made all over 6f first time out and tried similar tactics over the longer trip, but she couldn't quite last home and would revert to sprinting when a good sixth in the Cheveley Park. **Punita Arora** was below her best in fifth.

48 Goffs Vincent O'Brien National Stakes (Group 1) (7f)

Curragh (IRE) September 15 (Good)

1 **Pinatubo** 2-9-3 William Buick
2 **Armory** 2-9-3 Ryan Moore
3 **Arizona** 2-9-3 Donnacha O'Brien
1/3F, 100/30, 5/1. 9l, nk. 8 ran. 1:21
(Charlie Appleby).

Another astonishing win from **Pinatubo**, who remarkably surpassed his Vintage Stakes rout with the best two-year-old performance of the last 25 years according to Racing Post Ratings. There was plenty to back up such a superlative figure as Pinatubo showed a stunning turn of foot and stormed clear of **Armory**, who kept on to pip below-par stablemate **Arizona** for second. **Monoski** took a fair fourth ahead of **Iberia**, **Geometrical** and **Roman Turbo**.

49 Moyglare Stud Stakes (Group 1) (Fillies) (7f)

Curragh (IRE) September 15 (Good)

1 **Love** 2-9-0 Ryan Moore
2 **Daahyeh** 2-9-0 William Buick
3 **So Wonderful** 2-9-0 Seamie Heffernan
6/1, 13/8F, 16/1. ¾l, ¾l. 9 ran. 1:24
(A P O'Brien).

Below her best in the Debutante, **Love** put that behind her to come out on top in a tight contest in which less than 3l covered the first seven. Love certainly benefited from not hav-

WICHITA: won in terrific fashion at Newmarket, albeit against weak opposition

ing to reoppose the Debutante one-two Alpine Star and Petite Mustique in what was left as a slightly sub-standard renewal, but she stayed on strongly to put more distance into **Soul Search** than that pair had managed. **Daahyeh** also finished well in second ahead of **So Wonderful**, whose 0-6 record at Group level holds down the form, while Soul Search was fourth ahead of **Under The Stars**, the disappointing **Albigna** and **Tango**.

50 Dubai Duty Free Mill Reef Stakes (Group 2) (6f)

Newbury September 21 (Good To Firm)

1 **Pierre Lapin** 2-9-1 Andrea Atzeni
2 **Mystery Power** 2-9-4 Ryan Moore
3 **Shadn** 2-8-12 Jim Crowley
9/4J, 9/4J, 8/1. 1½l, ½l. 8 ran. 1:10
(Roger Varian).

Only an ordinary race for the grade but it was won in taking fashion by **Pierre Lapin**. On only his second run, Pierre Lapin readily saw off **Mystery Power**, who returned to form on this quick ground though would perhaps have preferred an extra furlong. **Shadn**, who would go on to win a Group 2 at Maisons-Laffitte next time, progressed again in third, with **Malotru** among those behind.

51 William Hill Firth of Clyde Stakes (Group 3) (Fillies) (6f)

Ayr September 21 (Good)

1 **Rose Of Kildare** 2-9-0 Joe Fanning
2 **Graceful Magic** 2-9-0 Richard Kingscote
3 **Endless Joy** 2-9-0 Daniel Tudhope
8/1, 5/1, 20/1. ½l, ½l. 9 ran. 1:10
(Mark Johnston).

This didn't look strong form at the time with the principals all coming via nurseries and **Rose Of Kildare** beaten in her last two, but she was still improving and ran out a gutsy winner before following up in the Oh So Sharp. **Graceful Magic**, who had beaten subsequent Rockfel runner-up Stylistique in her latest nursery, and **Endless Joy** built on their last-time-out wins to fill the places, while Listed winner **Orlaith** was fourth.

52 Ballyhane Blenheim Stakes (Listed) (6f)

Fairyhouse (IRE) September 23 (Yielding To Soft)

1 **Sir Boris** 2-9-3 Declan McDonogh
2 **Soul Search** 2-8-12 Colin Keane
3 **Zarzyni** 2-9-3 Ronan Whelan
14/1, 5/4F, 3/1. 1½l, 4½l. 5 ran. 1:17
(Tom Dascombe).

Tom Dascombe made a late decision to send **Sir Boris** across the Irish Sea once he discovered the forecast rain and the move paid off as his horse relished the conditions to turn the formbook on its head. Two out of two on soft ground but well beaten when stepped up to this level on quicker, Sir Boris was in his element as conditions worsened all day and also benefited from being the only front-runner in the field, dictating a steady gallop before seeing off **Soul Search**. **Zarzyni** and **Pistoletto** were well below their best behind.

53 Tattersalls Stakes (Group 3) (7f)

Newmarket September 26 (Good)

1 **Wichita** 2-9-0 Ryan Moore
2 **Persuasion** 2-9-0 James Doyle
3 **Ropey Guest** 2-9-0 Tom Queally
10/11F, 6/1, 20/1. 7l, 1¼l. 6 ran. 1:23
(A P O'Brien).

A devastating performance from **Wichita**, who stormed away from his rivals in a manner that inevitably pointed the way to Group 1 races later in the year when soft ground perhaps went against him in the Dewhurst. The opposition was fairly weak, with a thrice-raced maiden in **Manigordo** sent off second favourite on his first run above Class 2 level and **Persuasion** taking second despite being beaten a similar distance in the Acomb, though solid yardstick **Ropey Guest** suffered his heaviest defeat in seven runs at Group/Listed level through the year and was still ahead of **Monoski** and Manigordo in third.

54 Shadwell Rockfel Stakes (Group 2) (Fillies) (7f)

Newmarket September 27 (Good)

1 **Daahyeh** 2-9-0 William Buick
2 **Stylistique** 2-9-0 Frankie Dettori
3 **Cloak Of Spirits** 2-9-0 Andrea Atzeni
11/8F, 14/1, 4/1. ½l, shd. 8 ran. 1:24
(Roger Varian).

Albany winner **Daahyeh** set the standard on her seconds behind Raffle Prize and Love and duly got the job done in determined fashion without setting the world alight. In front soon enough, Daahyeh got the better of a sustained battle with **Cloak Of Spirits** and **Under The Stars**, while **Stylistique** caught the eye as she came from much further back than the rest of the first four to snatch second on the line. That quartet pulled 7l clear of the rest, including the disappointing **Blissful** and **Alabama Whitman**.

55 Juddmonte Cheveley Park Stakes (Group 1) (Fillies) (6f)

Newmarket September 28 (Good)

1 **Millisle** 2-9-0 Shane Foley

2 **Raffle Prize** 2-9-0 Frankie Dettori
3 **Tropbeau** 2-9-0 Mickael Barzalona
16/1, 10/11F, 9/2. 1¾l, ½l. 11 ran. 1:09
(Mrs John Harrington).

A surprise win for **Millisle**, who proved her Salisbury defeat all wrong as she beat **Raffle Prize** in what looked a strong race. Outpaced at halfway, Millisle found her stride as she hit the rising ground and produced a storming run nearest the rail to win going away. Raffle Prize was perhaps just below her best as she got away slowly, failing to make the most of a tailwind that should have suited her front-running, and instead ended up doing too much in a battle up front with **Tango** and **Living In The Past**, who finished in a photo for fourth 2½l behind her, the progressive Tango franking the form with a 6l Listed win two weeks later. French raider **Tropbeau** was another to come through from the rear having been pushed along early, giving further substance to the form having easily beaten subsequent Prix Marcel Boussac runner-up Marieta at Deauville. **Nurse Barbara** was sixth ahead of the disappointing **Dark Lady** and **Etoile**, with **Lil Grey** among those further back.

56 Juddmonte Middle Park Stakes (Group 1) (6f)

Newmarket September 28 (Good)
1 **Earthlight** 2-9-0 Mickael Barzalona
2 **Golden Horde** 2-9-0 Adam Kirby
3 **Summer Sands** 2-9-0 Barry McHugh
11/4F, 16/1, 100/1. nk, 1¾l. 8 ran. 1:09
(A Fabre).

This looked like one of the races of the season beforehand, but it proved a bit of a damp squib as the first two were the only principals to run close to form, with **Earthlight** maintaining his unbeaten record by beating **Golden Horde**. Earthlight probably wasn't quite at the level of his Prix Morny victory as Golden Horde got much closer this time, though he looked a fairly snug winner and challenged away from the favoured near rail, which was fast all day and helped Golden Horde to produce a career-best. **Summer Sands** and **King Neptune** were surely flattered to get so close as they ran a long way above the rest of their form – even Summer Sands's subsequent win in the Two-Year-Old Trophy at Redcar saw her run 20lb worse on Racing Post Ratings – with Summer Sands running against the rail and King Neptune making the running alone in the centre with a strong tailwind behind. **Threat** was outpaced coming down in trip but stuck on into fifth ahead of **Lope Y Fernandez**, while **Mums Tipple** finished lame and **Monarch Of Egypt** was a major disappointment.

57 Juddmonte Royal Lodge Stakes (Group 2) (1m)

Newmarket September 28 (Good)
1 **Royal Dornoch** 2-9-0 Wayne Lordan
2 **Kameko** 2-9-0 Oisin Murphy
3 **Iberia** 2-9-0 Donnacha O'Brien
16/1, 6/5F, 9/1. nk, 1½l. 7 ran. 1:35
(A P O'Brien).

Kameko looked the best horse in the race and would prove the point with his runaway Vertem Futurity Trophy win, but greenness seemed to catch him out for the second time after his near miss in the Solario as he was run down in another close finish by **Royal Dornoch**, who improved for the step up in trip without doing anything to suggest he was a strong winner for the grade. **Iberia** was third ahead of **Year Of The Tiger**, who was returning from a two-and-a-half-month break and didn't run to the level he would reach in the Dewhurst and the Vertem Futurity Trophy. **Sound Of Cannons** was fifth, with **Highland Chief** and **Pyledriver** tailed off behind.

58 Beresford Stakes (Group 2) (1m)

Curragh (IRE) September 29 (Heavy)
1 **Innisfree** 2-9-3 Donnacha O'Brien
2 **Shekhem** 2-9-3 Chris Hayes
3 **Gold Maze** 2-9-3 Shane Foley
4/6F, 11/4, 9/1. nk, 3¾l. 5 ran. 1:50
(A P O'Brien).

Heavy ground contributed to a disappointingly uncompetitive race, with a couple of withdrawals meaning nothing in the field had run in anything more than a maiden, but two smart colts came to the fore, with the subsequent Vertem Futurity Trophy runner-up **Innisfree** just beating **Shekhem** in a sustained duel. Shekhem had needed four attempts to win a maiden, but one of his defeats had been a neck second to Innisfree and he again showed plenty of quality as the pair left the rest well strung out.

59 Weld Park Stakes (Group 3) (Fillies) (7f)

Curragh (IRE) September 29 (Heavy)
1 **New York Girl** 2-9-0 Shane Crosse
2 **A New Dawn** 2-9-0 Wayne Lordan
3 **Know It All** 2-9-0 Ronan Whelan
12/1, 6/1, 9/2. nk, ½l. 9 ran. 1:30
(Joseph Patrick O'Brien).

New York Girl had shown little when beaten

four lengths on her only previous run, but she took a massive step forward to win a good Group 3. Waited with and short of room when making her move, New York Girl stormed home to nail **A New Dawn** and **Know It All**, who looked to have opened up a decisive lead but fell in a hole close home. The first three pulled 4½l clear of **Shehreen**, who was a length fourth in a Listed race next time, and **Nope**, who got even closer than that in the Oh So Sharp.

60 BoyleSports Irish EBF Star Appeal Stakes (Listed) (7f)

Dundalk (AW) (IRE) October 4 (Standard)

1 **Fort Myers** 2-9-3 Donnacha O'Brien
2 **Justifier** 2-9-6 Colin Keane
3 **Punita Arora** 2-8-12 Shane Foley
EvensF, 9/2, 10/1. 1l, hd. 6 ran. 1:25
(A P O'Brien).

Fort Myers had run with distinction in Group races in his previous four runs and made the most of this easier opportunity, confirming the improvement over 7f he had shown in the Champagne Stakes as he stayed on strongly to win. **Justifier** ran a fine race in second under a penalty, taking a narrow second ahead of the fillies **Punita Arora** and **Unforgetable**.

61 Qatar Prix Marcel Boussac – Criterium des Pouliches (Group 1) (Fillies) (1m)

Longchamp (FR) October 6 (Very Soft)

1 **Albigna** 2-8-11 Shane Foley
2 **Marieta** 2-8-11 Tony Piccone
3 **Flighty Lady** 2-8-11 Maxime Guyon
42/10, 58/10, 9/1. 2½l, ½l. 9 ran. 1:41
(Mrs John Harrington).

There was only one horse trained outside France in the field and Jessica Harrington's **Albigna** duly put a modest home team in their place with a comprehensive triumph. Staying on much the best in a serious test of stamina, Albigna pulled clear as the front-running **Marieta**, no match for Cheveley Park third Tropbeau on her previous start, ran out of steam, the fact she was still the best of the French suggesting this probably wasn't a strong Group 1. **Flighty Lady** ran on for third yet had filled the same spot on her previous start behind **Savarin**, who was a disappointing favourite as she trailed home seventh.

62 Qatar Prix Jean-Luc Lagardere (Group 1) (1m)

Longchamp (FR) October 6 (Very Soft)

1 **Victor Ludorum** 2-9-0 Mickael Barzalona
2 **Alson** 2-9-0 Frankie Dettori
3 **Armory** 2-9-0 Ryan Moore
9/5F, 87/10, 11/5. ¾l, snk. 7 ran. 1:44
(A Fabre).

A moderate pace led to the first five finishing in a heap, covered by just 1¼l, but **Victor Ludorum** won quite readily in the circumstances to suggest he might prove a cut above. Taking his unbeaten record to three, Victor Ludorum quickened up smartly and was well on top as the front-running **Alson** proved impossible for anything else to pass, with **Armory** third ahead of **Ecrivain** and **Helter Skelter**, who was much the best of those held up.

63 bet365 Fillies' Mile (Group 1) (1m)

Newmarket October 11 (Good To Soft)

1 **Quadrilateral** 2-9-0 Jason Watson

ROYAL DORNOCH (right): stamina saw him run down the green Kameko

ROSE OF KILDARE (left): won two Group 3 races in quick succession

2 **Powerful Breeze** 2-9-0 James Doyle
3 **Love** 2-9-0 Ryan Moore
9/4F, 7/1, 4/1. hd, 1½l. 9 ran. 1:37
(Roger Charlton).

Quadrilateral had surged to the head of the 1,000 Guineas market with a runaway win at Newbury on her previous start and justified that billing as she coped with a sharp step up in class to beat **Powerful Breeze** and **Love**. Quadrilateral came under pressure early but stayed on strongly once switched to the rail and got up to beat Powerful Breeze, who ran a remarkable race in second having got loose in the paddock and raced keenly early on. **Cayenne Pepper**, the shortest price of the Irish fillies and entitled to finish in front of Love on a line through So Wonderful, seemed below her best on the track, hitting her stride only once meeting the rising ground as she powered home in fourth ahead of **Boomer**, who didn't quite get home in the conditions. **Ananya** and **West End Girl** were among those well strung out behind.

64 Newmarket Academy Godolphin Beacon Project Cornwallis Stakes (Group 3) (5f)

Newmarket October 11 (Good To Soft)
1 **Good Vibes** 2-8-12 Richard Kingscote
2 **Pistoletto** 2-9-1 Ryan Moore
3 **Jouska** 2-8-12 Shane Foley
12/1, 12/1, 20/1. nk, ½l. 12 ran. 0:59
(David Evans).

A somewhat disappointing race with all the fancied runners below their best, helping **Good Vibes** to come out on top. Good Vibes had been inconsistent since winning a Listed race over this trip in May, but the form of her Lowther third stood out compared to those who finished closest to her and she was a worthy winner ahead of **Pistoletto**, who ran a career-best dropping back in trip, **Jouska** and **Kemble**. **Flaming Princess** was sixth ahead of **Platinum Star**, who failed to cope with the drop in trip.

65 Godolphin Lifetime Care Oh So Sharp Stakes (Group 3) (Fillies) (7f)

Newmarket October 11 (Good To Soft)
1 **Rose Of Kildare** 2-9-3 Joe Fanning
2 **Valeria Messalina** 2-9-0 Shane Foley
3 **Separate** 2-9-0 Sean Levey
12/1, 9/1, 8/1. nk, nk. 9 ran. 1:25
(Mark Johnston)

A moderate race with **Rose Of Kildare** able to defy a 3lb penalty for her Ayr win, proving herself a typically hardy Mark Johnston type as she won a tight battle in which the first four were covered by just ¾l. Still improving on her 12th run of the season, Rose Of Kildare fought off **Valeria Messalina**, **Separate** and **Nope** in a thriller, though the form still looks questionable with Separate, having her 11th run, beaten off 88 the time before and Nope only fifth in a Group 3 at the Curragh. **Final**

Song, **Stylistique** and **Wejdan** were all well below their best.

66 Darley Dewhurst Stakes (Group 1) (7f)

Newmarket October 12 (Soft)

1 **Pinatubo** 2-9-1 William Buick
2 **Arizona** 2-9-1 Seamie Heffernan
3 **Wichita** 2-9-1 Ryan Moore
1/3F, 14/1, 7/2. 2l, 2¾l. 9 ran. 1:26
(Charlie Appleby).

Pinatubo couldn't hit the same heights as at the Curragh but still signed off his incredible two-year-old campaign with another Group 1 win. Soft ground perhaps blunted Pinatubo's brilliance as he failed to quicken in his trademark manner, but he still hit the front inside the final furlong and stayed on well. **Wichita** was much the strongest of Aidan O'Brien's team in the market, but he was encountering soft ground for the first time and also seemed to run below his best in third, whereas the return to easier terrain brought a better performance from **Arizona**, who made the running and kept Pinatubo honest throughout. **Year Of The Tiger** and **Monarch Of Egypt** also filled the next two spots for O'Brien ahead of the below-par **Positive** and **Mystery Power**, who both seemed to hate the conditions.

67 Dubai Autumn Stakes (Group 3) (1m)

Newmarket October 12 (Soft)

1 **Military March** 2-9-1 Oisin Murphy
2 **Al Suhail** 2-9-1 William Buick
3 **Ropey Guest** 2-9-1 Shane Kelly
4/1, 4/1, 33/1. ½l, 7l. 8 ran. 1:40
(Saeed bin Suroor).

A terrific clash between two smart colts as **Military March** just saw off fellow Godolphin hope **Al Suhail** with the pair well clear of the rest. Having only his second run, Military March knuckled down well to rally past the Solario third **Al Suhail**, who had looked likely to win when heading the front-running winner but was just outstayed. It was 7l back to **Ropey Guest**, while the favourite **Molatham** struggled in vastly different conditions to those which had seen him win at Doncaster and was a tame fourth ahead of **Persia**.

68 Godolphin Flying Start Zetland Stakes (Group 3) (1m2f)

Newmarket October 12 (Soft)

1 **Max Vega** 2-9-2 Harry Bentley
2 **Miss Yoda** 2-8-13 Frankie Dettori
3 **Berkshire Rocco** 2-9-2 Oisin Murphy
7/1, 9/2, 16/1. 3l, ¾l. 8 ran. 2:09
(Ralph Beckett).

Little proven form but plenty of potential on show, the first six having all won their most recent outing, and it looked a useful performance from **Max Vega** to run out a convincing winner. In a real test of stamina on soft ground, Max Vega drew clear of **Miss Yoda** and **Berkshire Royal**. It was 2¾l back to subsequent Group 1 third **Mythical**, who was in turn clear of Haynes, Hanson and Clark Stakes winner **Tritonic** and **Subjectivist**.

69 coral.co.uk Rockingham Stakes (Listed) (6f)

York October 12 (Soft)

1 **Aberama Gold** 2-9-1 Shane Gray
2 **Ventura Lightning** 2-9-1 Tony Hamilton
3 **Orlaith** 2-8-13 Paul Mulrennan
10/1, 12/1, 12/1. ¾l, 2l. 12 ran. 1:16
(Keith Dalgleish).

While **Lampang**, seemingly the only potential star in the field, was a major disappointment, this was still a fairly solid race for the grade, making **Aberama Gold**'s victory all the harder to work out. Aberama Gold seemed fairly exposed after seven runs yet ran more than a stone above his previous best according to Racing Post Ratings, relishing the soft ground and helped by making most of the running at a moderate gallop as **Ventura Lightning**, perhaps the moral winner as he finished fast in second, was given too much to do. It was 2l back to **Orlaith** and **Huraiz**, two proven performers at this sort of level, but Lampang lost his unbeaten record in eighth.

70 Staffordstown Stud Stakes (Listed) (Fillies) (1m)

Curragh (IRE) October 13 (Soft)

1 **Fancy Blue** 2-9-0 Seamie Heffernan
2 **A New Dawn** 2-9-0 Donnacha O'Brien
3 **Auxilia** 2-9-0 Colin Keane
4/1, 15/8F, 5/2. hd, ½l. 7 ran. 1:53
(A P O'Brien).

An eyecatching win from **Fancy Blue**, who came from last to first off a moderate gallop to win what looked a decent Listed race despite still appearing green on just her second run. Fancy Blue ran around a bit when asked to pick up but finished strongly to nail Park Stakes runner-up **A New Dawn**. **Shehreen** got much closer to the runner-up than she had that day in a close fourth but was probably helped by setting such a steady pace.

71 Killavullan Stakes (Group 3) (7f) Leopardstown (IRE) October 19

(Soft To Heavy)

1 **Stela Star** 2-9-0 Colin Keane
2 **Iberia** 2-9-3 Wayne Lordan

3 **Katiba** 2-9-0 Oisin Orr
33/1, 6/4F, 3/1. 1½l, hd. 5 ran. 1:37
(Thomas Mullins).

A big upset as **Stela Star** took a massive step forward from her maiden form to beat Royal Lodge third **Iberia**, who was made to look decidedly one-paced over this shorter trip. While that suggests this was probably a weak race for the grade, Stela Star clearly relished the most testing conditions she had encountered. **Geometrical** was a major disappointment, finishing last of five.

72 ebfstallions.com Silver Tankard Stakes (Listed) (1m)

Pontefract October 21 (Soft)
1 **King Carney** 2-9-3 Daniel Tudhope
2 **Wyclif** 2-9-3 Harry Bentley
3 **Grand Rock** 2-9-3 James Doyle
7/2, 15/8F, 7/2. ¾l, ½l. 6 ran. 1:50
(Charlie Fellowes).

An interesting race which saw the three market principals, all last-time-out winners at a lower level, pull a remarkable 15l clear of their three rivals, with **King Carney** leading the way. Off the mark at the third attempt when running on soft ground for the first time on his previous start, King Carney again enjoyed the conditions as he made all the running and gamely saw off **Wyclif** and **Grand Rock**.

73 Bet With The Tote At Leopardstown Eyrefield Stakes (Group 3) (1m1f)

Leopardstown (IRE) October 26 (Soft To Heavy)
1 **Degraves** 2-9-3 Shane Crosse
2 **Persia** 2-9-3 Seamie Heffernan
3 **Justifier** 2-9-3 Colin Keane
7/2, 4/1, 7/4F. ½l, ½l. 5 ran. 2:09
(Joseph Patrick O'Brien).

Probably not the strongest form for the grade with favourite **Justifier** appearing to run a bit flat, although he certainly didn't fail through lack of stamina over this longer trip, plugging on after **Degraves** had shown a potent turn of foot to put the race to bed. Degraves even looked a bit green when he hit the front and was arguably value for more than the winning margin, with **Persia** improving on his disappointing Autumn Stakes run in second.

74 Criterium de Saint-Cloud (Group 1) 1m2f

Saint-Cloud (FR) October 26 (Heavy)
1 **Mkfancy** 2-9-0 Theo Bachelet
2 **Arthur's Kingdom** 2-9-0 Olivier Peslier
3 **Mythical** 2-9-0 Mickael Barzalona
53/10, 36/5, 48/10. 3l, ½l. 8 ran. 2:20
(Mme Pia Brandt).

A desperately weak Group 1, with **The Summit** sent off favourite despite finishing only third at 14-1 on his previous start and Aidan O'Brien's preferred runner in the market, **Mythical**, not among the leading lights at Ballydoyle judged on his Zetland fourth, but it was still a good win from **Mkfancy**. The French colt made all the running and stayed on strongly to beat O'Brien's **Arthur's Kingdom**, who just beat stablemate Mythical into second, with **Sound Of Cannons** fourth ahead of The Summit.

75 Criterium International (Group 1) (7f)

Longchamp (FR) October 27 (Heavy)
1 **Alson** 2-9-0 Frankie Dettori
2 **Armory** 2-9-0 Donnacha O'Brien
1/2F, 9/5. 20l. 2 ran. 1:28
(Jean-Pierre Carvalho).

Something of a farce as two non-runners left a field of just two, one of whom failed to run his race at all, making it impossible to know what to make of **Alson**'s runaway victory. Alson always looked like confirming Lagardere superiority over **Armory**, who was quickly beaten and trailed home a dismal second.

76 Vertem Futurity Trophy Stakes (Group 1) (1m)

Newcastle (AW) November 1 (Standard)
1 **Kameko** 2-9-1 Oisin Murphy
2 **Innisfree** 2-9-1 Seamie Heffernan
3 **Year Of The Tiger** 2-9-1 P B Beggy
11/2, 11/1, 16/1. 3¼l, nk. 11 ran. 1:36
(Andrew Balding).

Kameko finally got things right as he made up for a couple of narrow defeats at a lower level with a runaway victory. Switched to Newcastle to become the first Group 1 ever run on the all-weather in Britain after Doncaster was abandoned, the race saw Kameko prove much too good for a strong numerical challenge from Aidan O'Brien's yard, quickening well clear of **Innisfree**, who just saw off stablemates **Year Of The Tiger** and **Mogul** in a tight battle for second, Year Of The Tiger finishing much closer than he had in the Dewhurst. It was 2½l back to **Kinross**, who was made favourite on the strength of a wide-margin debut win but looked green in fifth, with bigger gaps back to the likes of **Tammani** and **Geometrical**.

77 Irish Stallion Farms EBF "Bosra Sham" Fillies' Stakes (Listed) (6f)

Newmarket November 1 (Soft)

KAMEKO (left): finally got things right with a runaway win at Newcastle

1 **Mild Illusion** 2-9-0 Josephine Gordon
2 **Magical Journey** 2-9-0 P J McDonald
3 **Lady Light** 2-9-0 Hayley Turner
10/1, 14/1, 10/1. ¾l, ¾l. 16 ran. 1:15
(Jonathan Portman).

A big field went in pursuit of some late-season black type but very few could land a blow in the face of a significant draw bias, with **Mild Illusion** flourishing under a forceful ride that made the most of her favourable berth. Drawn highest of all in a race that saw the first five emerge from the eight top stalls, Mild Illusion still took a big step forward, continuing her busy but progressive campaign as she beat a pair of once-raced winners in **Magical Journey** and **Lady Light**. **Orlaith** was best of those drawn low in sixth, with **Precious Moments** a big disappointment behind.

78 Heath Court Hotel Horris Hill Stakes (Group 3) (7f)

Newmarket November 2 (Heavy)

1 **Kenzai Warrior** 2-9-0 Jack Mitchell
2 **Ropey Guest** 2-9-0 Tom Queally
3 **Impressor** 2-9-0 Martin Dwyer
13/2, 8/1, 16/1. ½l, ¾l. 11 ran. 1:28
(Roger Teal).

Switched from Newbury, this race very nearly saw **Ropey Guest** finally shake off his maiden tag, but he was nailed close home by **Kenzai Warrior**, who came home strongly having been stopped in his run when initially trying to make his ground. While Kenzai Warrior was therefore perhaps value for more, the fact that Ropey Guest came much closer than he had in six previous runs at Group/Listed level says plenty about the quality of the race overall. While the first three came 3¼l clear of the rest, the fourth and fifth were both rated much lower than this level and plenty of others failed to cope with heavy ground.

79 British Stallion Studs EBF Montrose Fillies' Stakes (Listed) (1m)

Newmarket November 2 (Heavy)

1 **Born With Pride** 2-9-0 Tom Marquand
2 **Peaceful** 2-9-1 Donnacha O'Brien
3 **Run Wild** 2-9-0 Harry Bentley
20/1, 3/1F, 4/1. nk, 1¼l. 7 ran. 1:43
(William Haggas).

A stunning effort from **Born With Pride**, who achieved the rare distinction of winning a Listed race first time out – and a pretty strong one to boot. Soon sent to the front, Born With Pride was always travelling well and stayed on strongly to beat the favourite **Peaceful**, who had won a maiden by 7l, and May Hill fourth **Run Wild**. It was 2¾l back to the rest, including the disappointing **Alpen Rose** and **Separate**.

Two-year-old index

All horses placed or commented on in our two-year-old review section, with race numbers

Trainer Statistics

Mark Johnston

By month - 2019

	Overall			Two-year-olds			Three-year-olds			Older horses		
	W-R	%	£1	W-R	%	£1	W-R	%	£1	W-R	%	£1
January	7-34	21	+10.85	0-0	-	+0.00	3-23	13	-11.63	4-11	36	+22.48
February	11-33	33	+22.53	0-0	-	+0.00	8-23	35	+21.78	3-10	30	+0.75
March	11-62	18	-12.90	0-0	-	+0.00	7-34	21	+5.50	4-28	14	-18.40
April	21-135	16	-58.65	3-13	23	-2.56	9-76	12	-42.36	9-46	20	-13.73
May	34-200	17	-40.70	7-31	23	-3.11	11-100	11	-52.29	16-69	23	+14.71
June	36-197	18	-12.07	14-53	26	+23.57	13-87	15	-10.38	9-57	16	-25.26
July	50-215	23	-34.26	20-66	30	-5.42	23-108	21	-40.45	7-41	17	+11.60
August	32-195	16	-54.02	20-74	27	+3.52	11-85	13	-26.04	1-36	3	-31.50
September	25-151	17	-50.21	15-78	19	-14.48	9-63	14	-27.40	1-10	10	-8.33
October	13-130	10	-41.10	6-81	7	-38.40	7-44	16	+2.30	0-5	-	-5.00
November	8-58	14	-31.72	7-46	15	-21.25	1-11	9	-9.47	0-1	-	-1.00
December	1-49	2	-44.67	1-32	3	-27.67	0-12	-	-12.00	0-5	-	-5.00

By month - 2018

	Overall			Two-year-olds			Three-year-olds			Older horses		
	W-R	%	£1	W-R	%	£1	W-R	%	£1	W-R	%	£1
January	6-29	21	-5.65	0-0	-	+0.00	3-20	15	-10.90	3-9	33	+5.25
February	7-32	22	+4.88	0-0	-	+0.00	1-18	6	-14.75	6-14	43	+19.63
March	11-80	14	-27.13	0-3	-	-3.00	9-47	19	-3.63	2-30	7	-20.50
April	10-73	14	-19.15	3-13	23	-3.00	4-40	10	-16.15	3-20	15	+0.00
May	38-200	19	-18.78	13-41	32	+5.95	17-104	16	-13.47	8-55	15	-11.25
June	44-232	19	-53.57	18-63	29	-5.53	19-116	16	-24.77	7-53	13	-23.27
July	42-207	20	-16.81	16-61	26	-1.51	22-116	19	-14.05	4-30	13	-1.25
August	24-181	13	-50.15	12-66	18	-15.65	8-78	10	-40.50	4-37	11	+6.00
September	13-108	12	-34.72	7-55	13	-18.59	6-40	15	-3.13	0-13	-	-13.00
October	11-131	8	-40.47	4-71	6	-49.27	7-44	16	+24.80	0-16	-	-16.00
November	6-57	11	-17.50	2-33	6	-16.25	2-17	12	-5.00	2-7	29	+3.75
December	6-30	20	-12.18	3-12	25	-1.50	3-12	25	-4.68	0-6	-	-6.00

By month - 2017

	Overall			Two-year-olds			Three-year-olds			Older horses		
	W-R	%	£1	W-R	%	£1	W-R	%	£1	W-R	%	£1
January	8-51	16	-18.45	0-0	-	+0.00	4-34	12	-18.86	4-17	24	+0.41
February	8-47	17	-13.60	0-0	-	+0.00	4-28	14	-9.43	4-19	21	-4.17
March	12-44	27	+12.80	0-0	-	+0.00	5-21	24	+5.05	7-23	30	+7.75
April	12-81	15	-23.50	1-9	11	-7.56	7-45	16	-10.04	4-27	15	-5.90
May	24-172	14	-58.28	7-36	19	-15.36	14-92	15	-13.17	3-44	7	-29.75
June	37-213	17	-42.26	15-62	24	+15.14	17-119	14	-60.65	5-32	16	+3.25
July	38-203	19	-15.92	22-63	35	+40.16	13-112	12	-52.08	3-28	11	-4.00
August	33-196	17	-23.05	16-66	24	+18.58	13-103	13	-38.63	4-27	15	-3.00
September	17-156	11	-79.09	9-71	13	-41.97	7-64	11	-28.13	1-21	5	-9.00
October	19-133	14	+82.21	7-64	11	+28.83	10-52	19	+49.38	2-17	12	+4.00
November	6-46	13	-11.65	4-31	13	-16.65	1-9	11	+4.00	1-6	17	+1.00
December	0-21	-	-21.00	0-13	-	-13.00	0-2	-	-2.00	0-6	-	-6.00

By race type - 2019

	Overall			Two-year-olds			Three-year-olds			Older horses		
	W-R	%	£1	W-R	%	£1	W-R	%	£1	W-R	%	£1
Group	12-80	15	+21.95	5-24	21	+29.00	2-18	11	-6.00	5-38	13	-1.05
Handicap	136-851	16	-220.17	18-95	19	+1.45	77-506	15	-166.09	41-250	16	-55.53
Maiden	17-111	15	-48.79	14-88	16	-39.63	2-21	10	-16.16	1-2	50	+7.00

By race type - 2018

	Overall			Two-year-olds			Three-year-olds			Older horses		
	W-R	%	£1	W-R	%	£1	W-R	%	£1	W-R	%	£1
Group	4-52	8	-30.92	4-19	21	+2.08	0-27	-	-27.00	0-6	-	-6.00
Handicap	123-858	14	-170.47	10-101	10	-55.54	77-495	16	-76.16	36-262	14	-38.77
Maiden	15-89	17	-2.29	10-59	17	-1.59	5-29	17	+0.30	0-1	-	-1.00

By race type - 2017

	Overall			Two-year-olds			Three-year-olds			Older horses		
	W-R	%	£1	W-R	%	£1	W-R	%	£1	W-R	%	£1
Group	7-49	14	-2.13	4-27	15	-7.13	3-20	15	+7.00	0-2	-	-2.00
Handicap	127-911	14	-230.55	17-107	16	+2.53	75-552	14	-185.17	35-252	14	-47.91
Maiden	17-116	15	-28.59	9-44	20	+13.83	8-72	11	-42.42	0-0	-	+0.00

By jockey - 2019

	Overall			Two-year-olds			Three-year-olds			Older horses		
	W-R	%	£1	W-R	%	£1	W-R	%	£1	W-R	%	£1
Joe Fanning	81-391	21	-23.30	26-114	23	-11.43	33-194	17	-26.23	22-83	27	+14.36
Franny Norton	54-370	15	-157.92	17-132	13	-76.28	24-154	16	-61.28	13-84	15	-20.37
P J McDonald	20-139	14	-44.20	7-43	16	-17.23	11-61	18	-0.08	2-35	6	-26.90
S De Sousa	18-87	21	+4.17	5-25	20	-10.23	7-35	20	+2.58	6-27	22	+11.82
Jason Hart	14-69	20	-10.89	9-31	29	+11.70	4-26	15	-15.59	1-12	8	-7.00
Ryan Moore	7-32	22	-1.51	3-12	25	+6.70	2-11	18	-5.38	2-9	22	-2.83
Frankie Dettori	6-28	21	+11.75	5-15	33	+17.25	0-5	-	-5.00	1-8	13	-0.50
James Doyle	6-28	21	-6.77	2-10	20	+0.20	4-17	24	-5.97	0-1	-	-1.00
Dane O'Neill	5-12	42	+8.69	3-8	38	+0.94	0-2	-	-2.00	2-2	100	+9.75
C Y Ho	4-12	33	+11.50	2-4	50	+6.50	2-8	25	+5.00	0-0	-	+0.00
Connor Beasley	4-17	24	-1.50	2-2	100	+3.00	2-15	13	-4.50	0-0	-	+0.00
Adam Kirby	4-22	18	-12.38	3-10	30	-2.75	1-7	14	-4.63	0-5	-	-5.00

By jockey - 2018

	Overall			Two-year-olds			Three-year-olds			Older horses		
	W-R	%	£1	W-R	%	£1	W-R	%	£1	W-R	%	£1
Joe Fanning	53-345	15	-105.68	11-74	15	-28.40	31-205	15	-68.41	11-66	17	-8.88
Franny Norton	47-295	16	-76.99	20-108	19	-24.94	21-139	15	-27.55	6-48	13	-24.50
P J McDonald	34-206	17	-45.99	13-74	18	-22.67	17-88	19	+4.68	4-44	9	-28.00
S De Sousa	24-121	20	-8.61	12-58	21	-1.53	11-52	21	+2.19	1-11	9	-9.27
James Doyle	8-32	25	-2.74	7-18	39	+7.51	1-12	8	-8.25	0-2	-	-2.00
O Stammers	6-45	13	+3.25	0-1	-	-1.00	0-11	-	-11.00	6-33	18	+15.25
Adam Kirby	5-20	25	+0.55	0-5	-	-5.00	2-4	50	+1.30	3-11	27	+4.25
William Buick	5-32	16	-14.00	3-14	21	-4.25	2-15	13	-6.75	0-3	-	-3.00
Andrew Breslin	5-38	13	-2.00	0-4	-	-4.00	3-20	15	+4.00	2-14	14	-2.00

By jockey - 2017

	Overall			Two-year-olds			Three-year-olds			Older horses		
	W-R	%	£1	W-R	%	£1	W-R	%	£1	W-R	%	£1
Joe Fanning	64-392	16	-50.66	17-96	18	-49.44	27-192	14	-7.21	20-104	19	+5.99
Franny Norton	41-294	14	-74.62	17-97	18	-6.03	19-147	13	-38.44	5-50	10	-30.15
P J McDonald	35-204	17	+25.44	16-74	22	+67.50	19-108	18	-20.06	0-22	-	-22.00
S De Sousa	21-79	27	+7.97	14-34	41	+23.28	6-32	19	-14.32	1-13	8	-1.00
Jim Crowley	9-32	28	+8.75	3-9	33	+0.25	4-17	24	+2.00	2-6	33	+6.50
James Doyle	6-51	12	-15.00	3-24	13	-6.50	2-23	9	-17.50	1-4	25	+9.00
Ryan Moore	4-13	31	-2.64	2-4	50	+0.62	2-7	29	-1.25	0-2	-	-2.00
Dane O'Neill	4-21	19	-4.09	1-4	25	-2.09	2-11	18	-2.50	1-6	17	+0.50
Richard Oliver	4-30	13	-10.25	0-0	-	+0.00	4-21	19	-1.25	0-9	-	-9.00

By course - 2016-2019

	Overall			Two-year-olds			Three-year-olds			Older horses		
	W-R	%	£1	W-R	%	£1	W-R	%	£1	W-R	%	£1
Ascot	20-210	10	-87.75	10-51	20	+3.88	6-113	5	-71.00	4-46	9	-20.63
Ayr	15-110	14	-51.25	9-39	23	-7.83	5-46	11	-31.42	1-25	4	-12.00
Bath	19-80	24	-21.09	6-25	24	-3.94	11-42	26	-7.37	2-13	15	-9.77
Beverley	38-208	18	-60.08	20-75	27	-16.99	15-107	14	-27.09	3-26	12	-16.00
Brighton	15-91	16	-40.15	8-33	24	-10.10	6-45	13	-18.67	1-13	8	-11.39
Carlisle	18-99	18	-31.52	6-37	16	-15.85	8-46	17	-15.25	4-16	25	-0.42
Catterick	19-119	16	-54.44	11-53	21	-13.83	7-52	13	-30.36	1-14	7	-10.25
Chelmsf'd (AW)	60-394	15	-119.39	26-133	20	-36.52	24-179	13	-38.88	10-82	12	-44.00
Chepstow	7-38	18	-11.61	3-13	23	-3.58	4-20	20	-3.02	0-5	-	-5.00
Chester	28-190	15	-28.09	10-53	19	-2.47	12-94	13	-34.13	6-43	14	+8.50
Doncaster	22-148	15	-25.29	10-62	16	+5.80	11-63	17	-17.09	1-23	4	-14.00
Epsom	18-105	17	-24.45	11-23	48	+15.70	4-46	9	-23.75	3-36	8	-16.40
Ffos Las	0-10	-	-10.00	0-4	-	-4.00	0-6	-	-6.00	0-0	-	+0.00
Goodwood	40-253	16	-5.01	15-76	20	+15.08	15-117	13	-17.50	10-60	17	-2.59
Hamilton	29-165	18	-36.15	13-58	22	+3.84	14-82	17	-21.99	2-25	8	-18.00
Haydock	37-201	18	-18.97	15-63	24	+4.16	17-96	18	-17.13	5-42	12	-6.00
Kempton (AW)	33-245	13	-75.47	17-97	18	-30.07	8-93	9	-32.26	8-55	15	-13.15
Leicester	19-107	18	-28.99	6-37	16	-18.56	10-54	19	-17.18	3-16	19	+6.75
Lingfield	8-46	17	-19.92	0-11	-	-11.00	6-25	24	-7.17	2-10	20	-1.75
Lingfield (AW)	55-267	21	+7.46	7-46	15	-2.20	25-133	19	-31.19	23-88	26	+40.85
Musselburgh	35-177	20	-2.53	12-61	20	-24.57	18-84	21	+34.07	5-32	16	-12.03
Newbury	12-75	16	-9.15	5-24	21	-4.03	6-35	17	+4.88	1-16	6	-10.00
N'castle (AW)	34-330	10	-95.42	13-141	9	-85.54	15-125	12	+22.46	6-64	9	-32.34
Newmarket	23-218	11	-30.06	11-88	13	+25.82	8-87	9	-39.63	4-43	9	-16.25
Newmarket (J)	39-176	22	+32.90	12-47	26	+9.79	15-89	17	-11.15	12-40	30	+34.25
Nottingham	13-114	11	-64.18	8-55	15	-19.75	4-46	9	-34.18	1-13	8	-10.25
Pontefract	35-165	21	-39.45	13-49	27	-13.98	15-86	17	-26.13	7-30	23	+0.66
Redcar	19-105	18	-11.32	6-37	16	-19.16	9-51	18	-6.67	4-17	24	+14.50
Ripon	28-182	15	-29.62	11-48	23	-9.63	14-90	16	+16.86	3-44	7	-36.85
Salisbury	6-35	17	+0.98	4-19	21	+10.48	2-13	15	-6.50	0-3	-	-3.00
Sandown	12-103	12	-54.17	6-32	19	-4.59	4-52	8	-34.25	2-19	11	-15.33
S'well (AW)	16-96	17	-28.08	4-22	18	-8.17	9-51	18	-13.42	3-23	13	-6.50
Thirsk	6-59	10	-38.30	2-28	7	-18.50	3-24	13	-15.00	1-7	14	-4.80
Wetherby	2-19	11	+4.00	0-4	-	-4.00	2-14	14	+9.00	0-1	-	-1.00
Windsor	16-59	27	+5.72	10-20	50	+14.35	2-27	7	-16.25	4-12	33	+7.63
Wolves (AW)	49-389	13	-129.67	13-120	11	-50.13	23-188	12	-85.29	13-81	16	+5.75
Yarmouth	18-76	24	+48.40	8-25	32	+57.95	7-42	17	-16.72	3-9	33	+7.17
York	22-227	10	-44.74	11-81	14	+4.01	7-86	8	-32.75	4-60	7	-16.00

Ten-year summary

	Wins	Runs	%	Win prize-money	Total prize-money	£1
2019	249	1459	17	£3,174,442.66	£5,399,661.26	-346.92
2018	226	1440	16	£2,357,973.8	£4,330,786.44	-339.17
2017	215	1379	16	£2,409,999.47	£3,555,120.04	-223.79
2016	195	1413	14	£1,553,727.94	£2,726,246.11	-316.95
2015	204	1208	17	£1,806,254.46	£2,749,132.37	-111.80
2014	207	1344	15	£1,985,940.54	£2,992,111.823	-283.07
2013	216	1557	14	£1,826,629.78	£2,743,581.49	-396.21
2012	215	1344	16	£1,545,130.29	£2,284,275.755	-148.88
2011	179	1311	14	£927,711.46	£1,550,631.62	-270.94
2010	211	1458	14	£1,657,512.68	£2,419,718.15	-377.04

KING'S ADVICE: contributed eight of Mark Johnston's record haul of 249

John Gosden

By month - 2019

	Overall			Two-year-olds			Three-year-olds			Older horses		
	W-R	%	£1	W-R	%	£1	W-R	%	£1	W-R	%	£1
January	7-20	35	-0.11	0-0	-	+0.00	4-15	27	-1.84	3-5	60	+1.73
February	8-19	42	-2.57	0-0	-	+0.00	5-13	38	-1.35	3-6	50	-1.22
March	6-19	32	-7.73	0-0	-	+0.00	6-18	33	-6.73	0-1	-	-1.00
April	13-59	22	-31.11	0-0	-	+0.00	13-53	25	-25.11	0-6	-	-6.00
May	24-97	25	+6.05	1-6	17	-0.50	16-77	21	+0.80	7-14	50	+5.75
June	15-70	21	-10.14	0-6	-	-6.00	13-54	24	-8.14	2-10	20	+4.00
July	21-72	29	-0.71	4-18	22	-1.05	13-42	31	+3.84	4-12	33	-3.50
August	26-89	29	-9.49	6-19	32	-0.14	16-57	28	-5.64	4-13	31	-3.71
September	32-86	37	+2.29	10-30	33	-2.79	18-48	38	-0.24	4-8	50	+5.31
October	18-87	21	-27.29	7-42	17	-17.39	11-41	27	-5.90	0-4	-	-4.00
November	13-60	22	-3.91	6-42	14	-9.42	6-16	38	+4.26	1-2	50	+1.25
December	9-36	25	-11.62	6-25	24	-7.00	3-8	38	-1.62	0-3	-	-3.00

By month - 2018

	Overall			Two-year-olds			Three-year-olds			Older horses		
	W-R	%	£1	W-R	%	£1	W-R	%	£1	W-R	%	£1
January	6-25	24	-4.78	0-0	-	+0.00	6-24	25	-3.78	0-1	-	-1.00
February	5-13	38	+11.03	0-0	-	+0.00	4-11	36	+7.03	1-2	50	+4.00
March	3-22	14	-15.58	0-0	-	+0.00	3-17	18	-10.58	0-5	-	-5.00
April	20-55	36	+25.60	0-0	-	+0.00	17-50	34	+18.40	3-5	60	+7.20
May	28-96	29	-0.33	1-4	25	-1.00	20-72	28	+1.80	7-20	35	-1.13
June	18-85	21	-28.46	4-10	40	+1.23	11-57	19	-24.73	3-18	17	-4.96
July	17-68	25	-23.91	7-22	32	-2.02	9-39	23	-16.68	1-7	14	-5.20
August	17-62	27	-2.98	5-19	26	-3.59	10-37	27	-6.76	2-6	33	+7.36
September	11-54	20	+6.32	5-27	19	-0.80	6-23	26	+11.13	0-4	-	-4.00
October	17-85	20	-19.62	8-48	17	-17.30	7-28	25	+2.85	2-9	22	-5.17
November	13-58	22	+3.00	9-40	23	+0.28	3-15	20	-4.27	1-3	33	+7.00
December	10-31	32	+7.37	7-26	27	+5.82	3-5	60	+1.55	0-0	-	+0.00

By month - 2017

	Overall			Two-year-olds			Three-year-olds			Older horses		
	W-R	%	£1	W-R	%	£1	W-R	%	£1	W-R	%	£1
January	4-19	21	-5.14	0-0	-	+0.00	4-19	21	-5.14	0-0	-	+0.00
February	4-17	24	-9.18	0-0	-	+0.00	4-17	24	-9.18	0-0	-	+0.00
March	3-18	17	-8.25	0-0	-	+0.00	3-18	17	-8.25	0-0	-	+0.00
April	19-68	28	+30.42	0-0	-	+0.00	17-56	30	+34.04	2-12	17	-3.63
May	17-80	21	-24.70	1-7	14	-5.47	14-59	24	-13.73	2-14	14	-5.50
June	13-81	16	+0.21	0-11	-	-11.00	12-56	21	+23.41	1-14	7	-12.20
July	11-68	16	-37.99	1-14	7	-12.20	9-38	24	-13.79	1-16	6	-12.00
August	13-55	24	+4.42	5-27	19	-5.75	6-20	30	+4.67	2-8	25	+5.50
September	17-70	24	+9.07	10-30	33	+12.41	5-27	19	-4.58	2-13	15	+1.25
October	18-98	18	-3.76	10-48	21	+2.24	7-36	19	-1.00	1-14	7	-5.00
November	11-65	17	-13.52	9-49	18	-6.52	2-14	14	-5.00	0-2	-	-2.00
December	4-36	11	-24.56	4-30	13	-18.56	0-6	-	-6.00	0-0	-	+0.00

By race type - 2019

	Overall			Two-year-olds			Three-year-olds			Older horses		
	W-R	%	£1	W-R	%	£1	W-R	%	£1	W-R	%	£1
Group	23-88	26	-24.49	0-7	-	-7.00	9-51	18	-19.87	14-30	47	+2.38
Handicap	42-187	22	-33.63	0-10	-	-10.00	35-149	23	-25.98	7-28	25	+2.35
Maiden	28-103	27	-6.34	10-47	21	-9.37	18-56	32	+3.03	0-0	-	+0.00

By race type - 2018

	Overall			Two-year-olds			Three-year-olds			Older horses		
	W-R	%	£1	W-R	%	£1	W-R	%	£1	W-R	%	£1
Group	21-80	26	-13.23	5-20	25	-5.55	7-35	20	-2.13	9-25	36	-5.55
Handicap	37-175	21	-23.57	4-17	24	+0.58	26-122	21	-29.94	7-36	19	+5.78
Maiden	15-86	17	-19.50	5-38	13	-21.05	10-47	21	+2.55	0-1	-	-1.00

By race type - 2017

	Overall			Two-year-olds			Three-year-olds			Older horses		
	W-R	%	£1	W-R	%	£1	W-R	%	£1	W-R	%	£1
Group	21-80	26	-13.23	5-20	25	-5.55	7-35	20	-2.13	9-25	36	-5.55
Handicap	32-191	17	-27.63	3-12	25	+6.63	26-147	18	-23.63	3-32	9	-10.63
Maiden	40-168	24	-28.34	5-47	11	-34.30	35-121	29	+5.96	0-0	-	+0.00

By jockey - 2019

	Overall			Two-year-olds			Three-year-olds			Older horses		
	W-R	%	£1	W-R	%	£1	W-R	%	£1	W-R	%	£1
Robert Havlin	74-297	25	-64.73	21-85	25	-13.10	48-187	26	-43.36	5-25	20	-8.27
Frankie Dettori	49-156	31	-26.99	4-21	19	-11.13	31-101	31	-9.45	14-34	41	-6.41
Kieran O'Neill	18-79	23	-9.84	2-25	8	-14.50	15-50	30	+6.66	1-4	25	-2.00
Nicky Mackay	16-62	26	+6.22	3-17	18	+2.75	11-43	26	-8.53	2-2	100	+12.00
Jim Crowley	15-33	45	+8.97	3-10	30	+0.38	8-16	50	+3.55	4-7	57	+5.05
Oisin Murphy	8-24	33	+3.87	4-10	40	+3.87	4-13	31	+1.00	0-1	-	-1.00
Dane O'Neill	4-13	31	-1.05	0-2	-	-2.00	2-5	40	-0.30	2-6	33	+1.25
David Egan	3-5	60	+11.83	1-2	50	-0.17	2-3	67	+12.00	0-0	-	+0.00
P J McDonald	2-4	50	+7.00	1-1	100	+3.00	1-3	33	+4.00	0-0	-	+0.00
Cieren Fallon	1-4	25	-1.25	0-3	-	-3.00	1-1	100	+1.75	0-0	-	+0.00
Harry Bentley	1-4	25	+1.00	0-2	-	-2.00	1-2	50	+3.00	0-0	-	+0.00
Ryan Moore	1-4	25	-2.39	1-1	100	+0.62	0-3	-	-3.00	0-0	-	+0.00

By jockey - 2018

	Overall			Two-year-olds			Three-year-olds			Older horses		
	W-R	%	£1	W-R	%	£1	W-R	%	£1	W-R	%	£1
Robert Havlin	84-286	29	+5.11	27-95	28	+1.51	52-169	31	+1.77	5-22	23	+1.83
Frankie Dettori	36-123	29	-5.46	6-28	21	-14.24	20-77	26	-2.79	10-18	56	+11.57
Nicky Mackay	12-78	15	-9.87	4-25	16	-5.92	8-50	16	-0.95	0-3	-	-3.00
Oisin Murphy	8-19	42	+7.17	3-8	38	+2.75	5-11	45	+4.42	0-0	-	+0.00
Kieran O'Neill	8-44	18	+8.00	3-16	19	+11.00	4-25	16	-4.00	1-3	33	+1.00
Jim Crowley	6-33	18	-9.25	1-12	8	-8.50	4-14	29	-5.75	1-7	14	+5.00
James Doyle	5-22	23	-6.99	0-1	-	-1.00	3-8	38	-0.90	2-13	15	-5.09
William Buick	2-12	17	-3.75	1-2	50	+3.00	1-5	20	-1.75	0-5	-	-5.00
Adam Kirby	1-1	100	+2.00	1-1	100	+2.00	0-0	-	+0.00	0-0	-	+0.00

By jockey - 2017

	Overall			Two-year-olds			Three-year-olds			Older horses		
	W-R	%	£1	W-R	%	£1	W-R	%	£1	W-R	%	£1
Frankie Dettori	37-131	28	+44.96	8-25	32	+14.70	27-84	32	+38.76	2-22	9	-8.50
Robert Tart	19-80	24	+7.30	4-28	14	-12.20	13-48	27	+12.00	2-4	50	+7.50
Robert Havlin	15-106	14	-47.14	12-66	18	-19.14	3-31	10	-19.00	0-9	-	-9.00
James Doyle	10-43	23	-7.27	1-9	11	-7.71	7-22	32	+4.65	2-12	17	-4.20
Nicky Mackay	10-55	18	-17.56	2-24	8	-8.50	8-31	26	-9.06	0-0	-	+0.00
Jim Crowley	9-41	22	-12.40	3-10	30	-2.06	4-19	21	-7.09	2-12	17	-3.25
K Shoemark	7-32	22	-0.09	2-12	17	-1.50	4-16	25	-5.59	1-4	25	+7.00
Andrea Atzeni	5-27	19	-6.72	1-3	33	-0.50	4-20	20	-2.22	0-4	-	-4.00
Jimmy Fortune	4-12	33	+7.38	1-1	100	+7.00	2-8	25	-0.63	1-3	33	+1.00

By course - 2016-2019

	Overall			Two-year-olds			Three-year-olds			Older horses		
	W-R	%	£1	W-R	%	£1	W-R	%	£1	W-R	%	£1
Ascot	40-234	17	-21.18	9-23	39	+33.08	19-134	14	-36.29	12-77	16	-17.98
Ayr	1-2	50	-0.92	0-0	-	+0.00	1-1	100	+0.08	0-1	-	-1.00
Bath	0-6	-	-6.00	0-2	-	-2.00	0-4	-	-4.00	0-0	-	+0.00
Beverley	1-6	17	-2.75	0-0	-	+0.00	1-6	17	-2.75	0-0	-	+0.00
Brighton	3-9	33	-3.37	0-3	-	-3.00	2-5	40	-2.25	1-1	100	+1.88
Carlisle	0-1	-	-1.00	0-0	-	+0.00	0-1	-	-1.00	0-0	-	+0.00
Catterick	1-1	100	+0.83	0-0	-	+0.00	1-1	100	+0.83	0-0	-	+0.00
Chelmsf'd (AW)	53-222	24	-53.53	13-81	16	-30.18	36-129	28	-19.50	4-12	33	-3.84
Chepstow	5-6	83	+4.47	0-0	-	+0.00	5-6	83	+4.47	0-0	-	+0.00
Chester	6-25	24	-6.58	0-1	-	-1.00	5-19	26	-5.08	1-5	20	-0.50
Doncaster	21-109	19	-34.88	7-34	21	-7.76	11-57	19	-22.43	3-18	17	-4.69
Epsom	9-43	21	-5.25	0-6	-	-6.00	6-28	21	+0.67	3-9	33	+0.09
Goodwood	23-100	23	-15.70	3-16	19	-11.37	13-65	20	-14.18	7-19	37	+9.85
Hamilton	0-1	-	-1.00	0-0	-	+0.00	0-1	-	-1.00	0-0	-	+0.00
Haydock	20-83	24	+9.84	6-23	26	-0.44	11-43	26	+17.78	3-17	18	-7.50
Kempton (AW)	67-259	26	+9.85	23-125	18	-23.57	39-115	34	+37.04	5-19	26	-3.62
Leicester	7-44	16	-8.62	3-16	19	-8.62	2-25	8	-17.25	2-3	67	+17.25
Lingfield	4-14	29	+3.75	0-1	-	-1.00	4-13	31	+4.75	0-0	-	+0.00
Lingfield (AW)	50-167	30	+4.71	8-38	21	-7.81	36-104	35	+18.75	6-25	24	-6.24
Newbury	35-144	24	+16.70	15-46	33	+11.22	16-77	21	-0.02	4-21	19	+5.50
N'castle (AW)	42-110	38	+8.93	19-42	45	+13.36	22-61	36	-9.43	1-7	14	+5.00
Newmarket	51-269	19	+1.66	19-93	20	+21.16	29-143	20	+3.54	3-33	9	-23.04
Newmarket (J)	31-184	17	-58.50	11-73	15	-31.75	19-93	20	-14.75	1-18	6	-12.00
Nottingham	18-94	19	-7.40	9-44	20	+5.94	9-45	20	-8.33	0-5	-	-5.00
Pontefract	1-9	11	-7.20	0-0	-	+0.00	1-7	14	-5.20	0-2	-	-2.00
Redcar	2-7	29	-0.59	1-4	25	+0.50	1-3	33	-1.09	0-0	-	+0.00
Ripon	1-2	50	-0.50	0-1	-	-1.00	1-1	100	+0.50	0-0	-	+0.00
Salisbury	10-39	26	-2.28	1-6	17	-3.50	8-30	27	+1.22	1-3	33	0.00
Sandown	27-120	23	-15.98	9-35	26	-10.40	16-67	24	-6.25	2-18	11	+0.67
S'well (AW)	8-20	40	-2.72	1-3	33	-1.17	5-15	33	-3.65	2-2	100	+2.10
Thirsk	1-6	17	-4.20	1-3	33	-1.20	0-3	-	-3.00	0-0	-	+0.00
Wetherby	4-9	44	-0.21	0-0	-	+0.00	4-9	44	-0.21	0-0	-	+0.00
Windsor	13-62	21	-29.67	1-6	17	-4.27	12-52	23	-21.39	0-4	-	-4.00
Wolves (AW)	43-152	28	-20.55	15-62	24	-11.73	26-86	30	-8.52	2-4	50	-0.30
Yarmouth	28-79	35	+27.13	11-43	26	+0.73	17-35	49	+27.40	0-1	-	-1.00
York	24-84	29	+2.47	1-5	20	+1.50	13-47	28	-0.64	10-32	31	+1.61

Ten-year summary

	Wins	*Runs*	*%*	*Win prize-money*	*Total prize-money*	*£1*
2019	192	714	27	£6,282,133.51	£8,000,228.12	-96.35
2018	178	705	25	£6,634,850.85	£8,516,013.67	-49.66
2017	138	690	20	£4,558,363.75	£6,185,144.275	-81.86
2016	142	613	23	£1,997,426.28	£3,487,430.77	+7.64
2015	133	577	23	£3,094,711.38	£5,277,650.54	-17.52
2014	132	613	22	£2,876,012.06	£4,241,990.89	-24.63
2013	108	525	21	£1,263,914.58	£2,033,077.64	-24.83
2012	119	629	19	£2,150,284.26	£3,739,407.23	-60.64
2011	99	553	18	£1,828,265.33	£2,529,369.21	-14.31
2010	105	518	20	£1,101,277.72	£1,714,237.43	-28.71

ENBIHAAR (right): won four times for John Gosden during a stellar 2019

Richard Fahey

By month - 2019

	Overall			Two-year-olds			Three-year-olds			Older horses		
	W-R	%	£1	W-R	%	£1	W-R	%	£1	W-R	%	£1
January	6-46	13	-15.00	0-0	-	+0.00	4-22	18	-7.50	2-24	8	-7.50
February	4-23	17	-6.77	0-0	-	+0.00	1-12	8	-10.27	3-11	27	+3.50
March	3-41	7	-21.25	1-2	50	+1.75	0-10	-	-10.00	2-29	7	-13.00
April	11-119	9	-7.75	2-16	13	+2.75	7-49	14	+12.50	2-54	4	-23.00
May	28-194	14	-2.90	6-43	14	+7.80	10-63	16	+1.85	12-88	14	-12.55
June	25-242	10	-47.75	9-66	14	-4.75	10-90	11	-12.25	6-86	7	-30.75
July	23-234	10	-21.55	9-78	12	-36.30	6-80	8	+22.00	8-76	11	-7.25
August	30-223	13	-25.78	12-77	16	-0.88	10-74	14	-18.15	8-72	11	-6.75
September	22-197	11	-49.80	10-73	14	-3.02	8-59	14	-15.77	4-65	6	-31.00
October	17-127	13	-15.78	5-55	9	-31.53	7-36	19	+4.75	5-36	14	+11.00
November	4-41	10	+6.50	0-18	-	-18.00	1-10	10	+1.00	3-13	23	+23.50
December	5-27	19	+7.50	0-13	-	-13.00	2-6	33	+5.75	3-8	38	+14.75

By month - 2018

	Overall			Two-year-olds			Three-year-olds			Older horses		
	W-R	%	£1	W-R	%	£1	W-R	%	£1	W-R	%	£1
January	2-40	5	-31.75	0-0	-	+0.00	1-17	6	-12.50	1-23	4	-19.25
February	3-38	8	-10.00	0-0	-	+0.00	2-16	13	+3.00	1-22	5	-13.00
March	8-56	14	+7.00	0-2	-	-2.00	3-24	13	+1.00	5-30	17	+8.00
April	17-98	17	+13.75	2-14	14	-0.50	7-40	18	-1.50	8-44	18	+15.75
May	28-198	14	-39.70	9-44	20	+8.88	11-75	15	-18.37	8-79	10	-30.21
June	34-232	15	+40.41	8-60	13	-9.34	14-84	17	+49.63	12-88	14	+0.13
July	36-232	16	-25.13	12-82	15	-17.58	15-82	18	-1.80	9-68	13	-5.75
August	27-215	13	-26.88	12-90	13	-13.51	9-73	12	-25.59	6-52	12	+12.23
September	6-147	4	-67.25	1-55	2	-46.00	3-48	6	-7.00	2-44	5	-14.25
October	14-154	9	-30.38	6-60	10	-32.38	5-50	10	+21.00	3-44	7	-19.00
November	4-66	6	-34.50	1-30	3	-25.50	2-22	9	-6.00	1-14	7	-3.00
December	5-31	16	+1.50	2-17	12	-1.00	3-12	25	+4.50	0-2	-	-2.00

By month - 2017

	Overall			Two-year-olds			Three-year-olds			Older horses		
	W-R	%	£1	W-R	%	£1	W-R	%	£1	W-R	%	£1
January	6-61	10	-27.00	0-0	-	+0.00	4-25	16	-7.00	2-36	6	-20.00
February	8-38	21	+1.38	0-0	-	+0.00	1-14	7	-10.50	7-24	29	+11.88
March	5-35	14	-7.00	0-0	-	+0.00	0-10	-	-10.00	5-25	20	+3.00
April	19-122	16	+14.88	6-17	35	+13.00	4-34	12	+21.00	9-71	13	-19.13
May	27-198	14	-61.18	6-43	14	-22.88	6-70	9	-38.40	15-85	18	+0.10
June	29-232	13	-83.14	13-67	19	+8.16	7-64	11	-31.13	9-101	9	-60.17
July	21-259	8	-85.66	7-93	8	-57.74	10-77	13	-5.17	4-89	4	-22.75
August	18-235	8	-141.06	11-108	10	-37.56	5-53	9	-36.25	2-74	3	-67.25
September	29-233	12	-1.00	12-108	11	-33.08	10-44	23	+37.25	7-81	9	-5.17
October	20-188	11	-81.86	10-83	12	-31.02	6-45	13	-12.00	4-60	7	-38.84
November	5-61	8	-18.13	3-20	15	+8.38	0-15	-	-15.00	2-26	8	-11.50
December	6-43	14	-14.00	1-17	6	-12.50	1-9	11	-3.50	4-17	24	+2.00

By race type - 2019

	Overall			Two-year-olds			Three-year-olds			Older horses		
	W-R	%	£1	W-R	%	£1	W-R	%	£1	W-R	%	£1
Group	3-34	9	+3.00	1-18	6	-12.50	1-4	25	+22.00	1-12	8	-6.50
Handicap	118-1028	11	-143.49	8-94	9	-43.25	55-411	13	-22.69	55-523	11	-77.55
Maiden	18-95	19	-8.14	16-77	21	+0.11	2-18	11	-8.25	0-0	-	0

By race type - 2018

	Overall			Two-year-olds			Three-year-olds			Older horses		
	W-R	%	£1	W-R	%	£1	W-R	%	£1	W-R	%	£1
Group	5-40	13	+13.08	0-17	-	-17.00	2-7	29	+26.33	3-16	19	+3.75
Handicap	115-1025	11	-156.76	10-126	8	-75.13	61-449	14	+0.07	44-450	10	-81.71
Maiden	5-46	11	-23.95	2-31	6	-23.75	3-15	20	-0.20	0-0	-	+0.00

By race type - 2017

	Overall			Two-year-olds			Three-year-olds			Older horses		
	W-R	%	£1	W-R	%	£1	W-R	%	£1	W-R	%	£1
Group	3-52	6	-32.15	1-14	7	+1.00	0-10	-	-10.00	2-28	7	-23.15
Handicap	106-1128	9	-350.03	13-150	9	-54.25	40-370	11	-93.71	53-608	9	-202.07
Maiden	16-92	17	-10.73	6-36	17	+8.75	10-55	18	-18.48	0-1	-	-1.00

By jockey - 2019

	Overall			Two-year-olds			Three-year-olds			Older horses		
	W-R	%	£1	W-R	%	£1	W-R	%	£1	W-R	%	£1
Paul Hanagan	41-311	13	-32.60	10-101	10	-23.00	18-92	20	+10.45	13-118	11	-20.05
Tony Hamilton	38-330	12	-76.82	24-134	18	+14.20	10-101	10	-32.02	4-95	4	-59.00
Sean Davis	30-325	9	-56.07	5-74	7	-51.32	12-120	10	-3.75	13-131	10	-1.00
Barry McHugh	19-97	20	+36.25	7-37	19	-1.25	7-37	19	+3.75	5-23	22	+33.75
Paddy Mathers	12-95	13	-14.88	4-27	15	+5.75	5-40	13	-7.63	3-28	11	-13.00
Connor Murtagh	8-99	8	-13.75	1-16	6	+1.00	3-28	11	-9.75	4-55	7	-5.00
Sebastian Woods	5-17	29	+16.75	0-1	-	-1.00	0-2	-	-2.00	5-14	36	+19.75
P J McDonald	5-31	16	-2.40	2-12	17	-4.90	2-14	14	-7.50	1-5	20	+10.00
Megan Nicholls	4-13	31	+1.00	0-2	-	-2.00	2-4	50	+2.75	2-7	29	+0.25
David Nolan	3-31	10	-16.42	1-9	11	-4.67	0-9	-	-9.00	2-13	15	-2.75
Mrs Carol Bartley	2-3	67	+32.00	0-0	-	+0.00	2-3	67	+32.00	0-0	-	+0.00
Paul Mulrennan	2-3	67	+10.00	0-1	-	-1.00	1-1	100	+6.50	1-1	100	+4.50

By jockey - 2018

	Overall			Two-year-olds			Three-year-olds			Older horses		
	W-R	%	£1	W-R	%	£1	W-R	%	£1	W-R	%	£1
Paul Hanagan	70-525	13	-25.61	18-146	12	-47.08	33-201	16	+47.20	19-178	11	-25.73
Tony Hamilton	28-299	9	-66.63	12-111	11	-31.25	8-103	8	-33.63	8-85	9	-1.75
David Nolan	12-52	23	+16.42	5-26	19	-0.71	2-11	18	+2.75	5-15	33	+14.38
C Murtagh	11-90	12	-24.25	2-18	11	-5.00	5-31	16	-1.00	4-41	10	-18.25
Barry McHugh	8-37	22	+36.25	3-18	17	+32.00	4-13	31	+7.00	1-6	17	-2.75
Jack Garritty	8-67	12	-7.84	2-23	9	-18.84	3-22	14	+17.50	3-22	14	-6.50
Paddy Mathers	8-120	7	-83.77	4-43	9	-28.18	4-48	8	-26.59	0-29	-	-29.00
S Woods	6-66	9	-13.50	0-5	-	-5.00	2-17	12	+5.00	4-44	9	-13.50
P J McDonald	4-20	20	+5.50	2-7	29	+7.00	2-12	17	-0.50	0-1	-	-1.00

By jockey - 2017

	Overall			Two-year-olds			Three-year-olds			Older horses		
	W-R	%	£1	W-R	%	£1	W-R	%	£1	W-R	%	£1
Paul Hanagan	68-453	15	-29.76	28-148	19	+3.59	10-123	8	-66.07	30-182	16	+32.72
Tony Hamilton	36-383	9	-155.58	16-144	11	-55.50	11-116	9	-28.58	9-123	7	-71.50
A McNamara	22-160	14	-34.50	7-49	14	-7.58	10-32	31	+22.83	5-79	6	-49.75
C Murtagh	12-104	12	-38.52	1-6	17	-3.50	6-35	17	-4.13	5-63	8	-30.90
Jack Garritty	10-114	9	-64.71	5-57	9	-33.13	3-28	11	-11.25	2-29	7	-20.33
Barry McHugh	9-61	15	+2.13	4-31	13	+4.38	3-21	14	-7.25	2-9	22	+5.00
S Woods	6-42	14	+0.50	0-1	-	-1.00	2-10	20	+1.00	4-31	13	+0.50
Sammy Jo Bell	6-77	8	-30.50	1-20	5	-16.00	3-21	14	+14.00	2-36	6	-28.50
William Buick	3-8	38	+0.85	1-1	100	+3.00	0-2	-	-2.00	2-5	40	-0.15

By course - 2016-2019

	Overall			Two-year-olds			Three-year-olds			Older horses		
	W-R	%	£1	W-R	%	£1	W-R	%	£1	W-R	%	£1
Ascot	6-134	4	+3.10	1-34	3	-13.00	3-28	11	+35.00	2-72	3	-18.90
Ayr	24-280	9	-130.95	6-69	9	-46.20	10-88	11	-16.50	8-123	7	-68.25
Bath	1-10	10	-6.00	0-0	-	+0.00	1-4	25	0.00	0-6	-	-6.00
Beverley	44-323	14	-96.44	18-115	16	-35.82	14-116	12	-27.97	12-92	13	-32.65
Brighton	1-2	50	+2.00	0-0	-	+0.00	1-1	100	+3.00	0-1	-	-1.00
Carlisle	26-202	13	-47.29	11-80	14	-15.04	10-71	14	-27.00	5-51	10	-5.25
Catterick	34-189	18	+2.35	12-72	17	-27.15	9-59	15	-14.50	13-58	22	+44.00
Chelmsf'd (AW)	13-147	9	-38.33	3-33	9	-22.25	4-49	8	-20.08	6-65	9	+4.00
Chepstow	1-4	25	-1.90	0-1	-	-1.00	1-3	33	-0.90	0-0	-	+0.00
Chester	54-438	12	-27.80	8-85	9	-29.51	21-111	19	+50.08	25-242	10	-48.38
Doncaster	29-343	8	-127.18	10-92	11	-30.13	7-103	7	-26.00	12-148	8	-71.05
Epsom	7-82	9	-16.75	1-13	8	-2.00	2-23	9	-11.00	4-46	9	-3.75
Ffos Las	1-2	50	+0.50	1-2	50	+0.50	0-0	-	+0.00	0-0	-	+0.00
Goodwood	4-114	4	-91.50	1-22	5	-17.00	2-32	6	-18.00	1-60	2	-56.50
Hamilton	32-238	13	-70.38	11-81	14	-19.70	14-74	19	-8.79	7-83	8	-41.89
Haydock	21-270	8	-130.60	8-74	11	-13.68	7-91	8	-34.17	6-105	6	-82.75
Kempton (AW)	2-52	4	-33.00	0-10	-	-10.00	1-15	7	-4.00	1-27	4	-19.00
Leicester	25-138	18	+4.64	10-53	19	-6.65	11-53	21	-0.22	4-32	13	+11.50
Lingfield	2-12	17	-6.13	1-7	14	-4.38	1-5	20	-1.75	0-0	-	+0.00
Lingfield (AW)	15-167	9	-88.25	1-20	5	-15.50	4-53	8	-37.25	10-94	11	-35.50
Musselburgh	34-207	16	+21.05	8-50	16	-2.65	15-77	19	+34.20	11-80	14	-10.50
Newbury	5-55	9	-9.50	2-27	7	-1.00	0-11	-	-11.00	3-17	18	+2.50
N'castle (AW)	63-514	12	-27.63	17-163	10	-37.63	26-162	16	+34.00	20-189	11	-24.00
Newmarket	6-125	5	-72.25	0-36	-	-36.00	3-48	6	-19.00	3-41	7	-17.25
Newmarket (J)	7-98	7	-39.00	2-30	7	-20.00	4-34	12	+10.50	1-34	3	-29.50
Nottingham	30-190	16	+16.81	11-72	15	-8.29	9-72	13	-15.90	10-46	22	+41.00
Pontefract	39-277	14	-3.79	19-85	22	+36.33	11-90	12	-25.55	9-102	9	-14.57
Redcar	38-271	14	-14.86	16-114	14	-8.65	10-89	11	-39.08	12-68	18	+32.88
Ripon	37-270	14	-64.61	13-87	15	-33.88	15-83	18	+22.13	9-100	9	-52.86
Salisbury	1-6	17	-1.50	0-0	-	+0.00	0-2	-	-2.00	1-4	25	+0.50
Sandown	1-17	6	-12.00	1-4	25	+1.00	0-5	-	-5.00	0-8	-	-8.00
S'well (AW)	28-151	19	+5.91	5-31	16	-3.88	11-66	17	-3.14	12-54	22	+12.92
Thirsk	41-257	16	+11.12	17-100	17	+20.99	15-84	18	+11.88	9-73	12	-21.75
Wetherby	8-34	24	+27.75	2-9	22	-3.25	5-15	33	+33.00	1-10	10	-2.00
Windsor	7-40	18	+2.91	0-3	-	-3.00	3-18	17	0.00	4-19	21	+5.91
Wolves (AW)	42-403	10	-121.54	9-118	8	-75.55	15-135	11	+4.98	18-150	12	-50.96
Yarmouth	2-25	8	-13.50	1-7	14	0.00	0-10	-	-10.00	1-8	13	-3.50
York	36-514	7	-156.63	13-172	8	-28.00	11-114	10	-30.13	12-228	5	-98.50

Ten-year summary

	Wins	Runs	%	Win prize-money	Total prize-money	£1
2019	178	1514	12	£1,391,189.13	£2,545,525.43	-200.33
2018	190	1599	12	£2,067,729.32	£3,377,934.94	-249.92
2017	200	1748	11	£2,467,394.29	£4,239,127.44	-506.07
2016	198	1739	11	£1,555,029.70	£3,162,107.98	-397.84
2015	235	1691	14	£2,394,305.99	£3,846,973.63	-227.69
2014	192	1502	13	£1,882,767.02	£2,882,652.01	-119.24
2013	164	1287	13	£1,588,826.54	£2,455,584.17	-236.90
2012	142	1294	11	£1,213,826.13	£1,982,267.62	-294.66
2011	151	1224	12	£980,328.63	£1,650,127.14	-260.88
2010	181	1356	13	£1,325,389.94	£2,075,925.435	-273.54

SPACE TRAVELLER (second right): a Royal Ascot winner for Richard Fahey

Richard Hannon

By month - 2019

	Overall			Two-year-olds			Three-year-olds			Older horses		
	W-R	%	£1	W-R	%	£1	W-R	%	£1	W-R	%	£1
January	2-27	7	-10.50	0-0	-	+0.00	2-20	10	-3.50	0-7	-	-7.00
February	1-9	11	-6.00	0-0	-	+0.00	0-3	-	-3.00	1-6	17	-3.00
March	7-39	18	-17.92	0-0	-	+0.00	4-27	15	-16.92	3-12	25	-1.00
April	15-130	12	-22.92	1-16	6	-12.25	11-90	12	-11.67	3-24	13	+1.00
May	16-164	10	-44.50	5-31	16	+12.50	7-94	7	-39.00	4-39	10	-18.00
June	24-170	14	-63.93	8-62	13	-34.75	12-76	16	-17.93	4-32	13	-11.25
July	25-202	12	-54.00	12-97	12	-42.83	11-80	14	+7.33	2-25	8	-18.50
August	25-195	13	-49.44	13-109	12	-65.94	6-58	10	-16.25	6-28	21	+32.75
September	21-167	13	+6.97	11-100	11	+25.20	6-51	12	-14.08	4-16	25	-4.15
October	13-107	12	+11.25	6-69	9	-29.50	4-28	14	+5.75	3-10	30	+35.00
November	1-44	2	-36.00	1-27	4	-19.00	0-13	-	-13.00	0-4	-	-4.00
December	3-32	9	-13.75	1-25	4	-16.00	1-6	17	-0.50	1-1	100	+2.75

By month - 2018

	Overall			Two-year-olds			Three-year-olds			Older horses		
	W-R	%	£1	W-R	%	£1	W-R	%	£1	W-R	%	£1
January	1-28	4	-24.50	0-0	-	+0.00	1-18	6	-14.50	0-10	-	-10.00
February	3-16	19	-7.25	0-0	-	+0.00	2-11	18	-6.00	1-5	20	-1.25
March	6-23	26	+1.83	0-0	-	+0.00	2-12	17	-6.50	4-11	36	+8.33
April	14-84	17	+47.88	2-8	25	-2.13	8-53	15	+38.50	4-23	17	+11.50
May	25-187	13	-7.66	7-42	17	-8.80	13-107	12	+14.31	5-38	13	-13.17
June	19-202	9	-74.22	9-72	13	-12.84	8-96	8	-57.38	2-34	6	-4.00
July	29-176	16	-17.27	14-88	16	-13.69	13-66	20	+8.92	2-22	9	-12.50
August	35-234	15	-55.23	18-122	15	-41.69	14-85	16	-14.53	3-27	11	+1.00
September	9-108	8	-67.92	7-73	10	-37.03	0-24	-	-24.00	2-11	18	-6.90
October	12-148	8	-82.27	9-104	9	-55.77	0-28	-	-28.00	3-16	19	+1.50
November	5-51	10	-19.75	5-35	14	-3.75	0-11	-	-11.00	0-5	-	-5.00
December	2-43	5	-15.00	2-31	6	-3.00	0-9	-	-9.00	0-3	-	-3.00

By month - 2017

	Overall			Two-year-olds			Three-year-olds			Older horses		
	W-R	%	£1	W-R	%	£1	W-R	%	£1	W-R	%	£1
January	4-28	14	+19.88	0-0	-	+0.00	2-20	10	-13.13	2-8	25	+33.00
February	4-17	24	+6.57	0-0	-	+0.00	4-14	29	+9.57	0-3	-	-3.00
March	5-31	16	+13.98	0-0	-	+0.00	5-29	17	+15.98	0-2	-	-2.00
April	20-125	16	-7.84	1-12	8	-9.25	14-87	16	-14.59	5-26	19	+16.00
May	30-173	17	-29.49	10-38	26	-1.32	12-113	11	-45.13	8-22	36	+16.95
June	19-167	11	-56.47	8-58	14	-23.97	10-89	11	-17.50	1-20	5	-15.00
July	27-206	13	+20.63	15-101	15	+38.63	11-91	12	-15.00	1-14	7	-3.00
August	32-198	16	-32.41	18-101	18	-6.72	13-82	16	-14.69	1-15	7	-11.00
September	18-160	11	+2.99	9-88	10	+22.91	7-57	12	-15.92	2-15	13	-4.00
October	17-152	11	-5.98	10-98	10	-9.90	5-41	12	+5.55	2-13	15	-1.63
November	7-49	14	-20.09	6-38	16	-11.97	1-10	10	-7.13	0-1	-	-1.00
December	6-29	21	-1.13	6-21	29	+6.88	0-7	-	-7.00	0-1	-	-1.00

By race type - 2019

	Overall			Two-year-olds			Three-year-olds			Older horses		
	W-R	%	£1	W-R	%	£1	W-R	%	£1	W-R	%	£1
Group	8-73	11	-4.70	4-31	13	-11.20	1-22	5	-9.00	3-20	15	+15.50
Handicap	76-665	11	-129.92	9-127	7	-65.75	49-389	13	-51.30	18-149	12	-12.87
Maiden	12-109	11	+5.25	11-86	13	+2.25	1-23	4	+3.00	0-0	-	+0.00

By race type - 2018

	Overall			Two-year-olds			Three-year-olds			Older horses		
	W-R	%	£1	W-R	%	£1	W-R	%	£1	W-R	%	£1
Group	4-65	6	+25.50	0-22	-	-22.00	3-23	13	+60.00	1-20	5	-12.50
Handicap	71-643	11	-212.18	15-135	11	-46.99	39-361	11	-134.27	17-147	12	-30.92
Maiden	13-96	14	-13.17	9-75	12	-18.67	4-20	20	+6.50	0-1	-	-1.00

By race type - 2017

	Overall			Two-year-olds			Three-year-olds			Older horses		
	W-R	%	£1	W-R	%	£1	W-R	%	£1	W-R	%	£1
Group	7-54	13	+30.00	3-24	13	+33.00	2-13	15	-6.00	2-17	12	+3.00
Handicap	83-700	12	-129.34	16-124	13	-14.04	53-474	11	-125.50	14-102	14	+10.20
Maiden	22-178	12	-24.44	8-73	11	+15.41	14-105	13	-39.85	0-0	-	+0.00

By jockey - 2019

	Overall			Two-year-olds			Three-year-olds			Older horses		
	W-R	%	£1	W-R	%	£1	W-R	%	£1	W-R	%	£1
Sean Levey	42-302	14	-48.61	16-130	12	-52.28	14-125	11	-60.83	12-47	26	+64.50
Tom Marquand	21-176	12	-38.48	7-58	12	-14.92	8-81	10	-21.07	6-37	16	-2.50
Pat Dobbs	16-106	15	+21.99	5-48	10	+2.45	10-40	25	+34.92	1-18	6	-15.38
Rossa Ryan	15-168	9	-88.67	6-72	8	-42.13	9-77	12	-27.54	0-19	-	-19.00
Jim Crowley	8-28	29	+20.48	3-10	30	+12.50	4-14	29	+10.25	1-4	25	-2.27
Ryan Moore	7-45	16	-5.15	2-15	13	-8.40	3-22	14	+0.75	2-8	25	+2.50
S De Sousa	7-54	13	-27.65	4-28	14	-16.40	3-26	12	-11.25	0-0	-	+0.00
James Doyle	6-17	35	+26.25	3-9	33	+18.50	1-4	25	+1.50	2-4	50	+6.25
Oisin Murphy	6-36	17	-2.90	4-26	15	-7.90	1-7	14	0.00	1-3	33	+5.00
T H Hansen	6-76	8	-26.25	3-30	10	+4.50	2-34	6	-22.50	1-12	8	-8.25
Seamus Cronin	5-27	19	+9.25	1-8	13	-5.50	2-9	22	+19.00	2-10	20	-4.25
Andrea Atzeni	3-33	9	-10.50	2-26	8	-7.00	0-5	-	-5.00	1-2	50	+1.50

By jockey - 2018

	Overall			Two-year-olds			Three-year-olds			Older horses		
	W-R	%	£1	W-R	%	£1	W-R	%	£1	W-R	%	£1
Tom Marquand	47-367	13	-101.43	23-175	13	-48.57	20-151	13	-41.86	4-41	10	-11.00
Sean Levey	17-180	9	+7.49	7-67	10	-17.14	8-84	10	+40.13	2-29	7	-15.50
Rossa Ryan	15-139	11	-65.42	9-64	14	-15.15	3-41	7	-32.50	3-34	9	-17.77
S De Sousa	11-30	37	+17.49	5-17	29	+1.62	5-10	50	+15.37	1-3	33	+0.50
T H Hansen	7-40	18	+6.85	1-16	6	-9.00	5-23	22	+9.85	1-1	100	+6.00
Jim Crowley	7-43	16	-14.61	4-18	22	-3.56	2-17	12	-7.39	1-8	13	-3.67
Pat Dobbs	6-43	14	+2.88	2-20	10	-10.63	4-18	22	+18.50	0-5	-	-5.00
Ryan Moore	6-58	10	-31.93	4-29	14	-13.31	0-17	-	-17.00	2-12	17	-1.63
Hollie Doyle	6-83	7	-28.00	1-22	5	-1.00	0-39	-	-39.00	5-22	23	+12.00

By jockey - 2017

	Overall			Two-year-olds			Three-year-olds			Older horses		
	W-R	%	£1	W-R	%	£1	W-R	%	£1	W-R	%	£1
Sean Levey	54-368	15	-23.19	26-174	15	-8.51	24-157	15	-2.18	4-37	11	-12.50
Tom Marquand	33-275	12	-18.55	18-130	14	+28.60	13-125	10	-32.77	2-20	10	-14.38
Hollie Doyle	20-124	16	+12.04	6-47	13	-12.29	11-64	17	+12.33	3-13	23	+12.00
Jim Crowley	12-46	26	+3.39	4-15	27	+4.67	6-24	25	-4.78	2-7	29	+3.50
Dane O'Neill	10-35	29	+53.43	7-21	33	+35.92	3-14	21	+17.50	0-0	-	+0.00
Ryan Moore	10-73	14	-30.81	4-38	11	-27.81	4-25	16	-9.00	2-10	20	+6.00
Rossa Ryan	9-61	15	+14.33	2-16	13	-5.00	4-36	11	+8.63	3-9	33	+10.70
Pat Dobbs	7-79	9	-42.80	1-14	7	-12.39	4-53	8	-33.42	2-12	17	+3.00
S De Sousa	6-17	35	+3.22	2-6	33	+2.30	4-10	40	+1.92	0-1	-	-1.00

By course - 2016-2019

	Overall			Two-year-olds			Three-year-olds			Older horses		
	W-R	%	£1	W-R	%	£1	W-R	%	£1	W-R	%	£1
Ascot	18-257	7	-107.75	9-88	10	-21.00	7-102	7	-33.25	2-67	3	-53.50
Ayr	0-14	-	-14.00	0-8	-	-8.00	0-4	-	-4.00	0-2	-	-2.00
Bath	21-150	14	-56.30	10-61	16	-29.47	8-78	10	-29.83	3-11	27	+3.00
Beverley	5-17	29	+2.54	3-8	38	+4.17	2-8	25	-0.63	0-1	-	-1.00
Brighton	33-136	24	+53.41	14-58	24	+19.00	19-71	27	+41.41	0-7	-	-7.00
Carlisle	0-2	-	-2.00	0-1	-	-1.00	0-1	-	-1.00	0-0	-	+0.00
Catterick	0-7	-	-7.00	0-4	-	-4.00	0-3	-	-3.00	0-0	-	+0.00
Chelmsf'd (AW)	31-288	11	-87.49	13-118	11	-23.65	14-130	11	-65.84	4-40	10	+2.00
Chepstow	17-121	14	-30.73	10-50	20	+7.78	7-64	11	-31.50	0-7	-	-7.00
Chester	13-65	20	+3.41	8-29	28	+7.91	2-25	8	-7.50	3-11	27	+3.00
Doncaster	26-244	11	-52.78	10-108	9	-52.12	10-96	10	-1.67	6-40	15	+1.00
Epsom	5-67	7	-43.25	4-27	15	-8.75	0-28	-	-28.00	1-12	8	-6.50
Ffos Las	3-43	7	-32.25	2-35	6	-28.25	1-8	13	-4.00	0-0	-	+0.00
Goodwood	23-254	9	-71.28	11-116	9	-34.28	10-90	11	-10.00	2-48	4	-27.00
Hamilton	2-4	50	+7.75	0-1	-	-1.00	2-3	67	+8.75	0-0	-	+0.00
Haydock	16-142	11	-51.42	4-55	7	-18.00	8-61	13	-22.00	4-26	15	-11.42
Kempton (AW)	60-532	11	-120.73	27-239	11	-65.19	25-233	11	-93.37	8-60	13	+37.83
Leicester	23-157	15	-33.85	14-74	19	+1.85	9-69	13	-21.70	0-14	-	-14.00
Lingfield	24-131	18	-9.84	7-46	15	-3.85	12-70	17	-11.24	5-15	33	+5.25
Lingfield (AW)	55-316	17	+40.42	17-90	19	-9.32	26-179	15	+28.51	12-47	26	+21.23
Musselburgh	2-4	50	+22.50	0-1	-	-1.00	1-1	100	+4.50	1-2	50	+19.00
Newbury	46-397	12	-19.61	26-224	12	-15.19	15-120	13	+20.85	5-53	9	-25.27
N'castle (AW)	6-19	32	+29.08	3-8	38	+13.33	1-9	11	-1.00	2-2	100	+16.75
Newmarket	23-294	8	-31.63	8-131	6	-75.75	10-124	8	+36.63	5-39	13	+7.50
Newmarket (J)	42-295	14	-28.53	18-143	13	-34.58	19-123	15	+5.31	5-29	17	+0.75
Nottingham	21-141	15	-30.37	7-65	11	-23.06	12-59	20	-0.80	2-17	12	-6.50
Pontefract	2-16	13	-8.75	0-6	-	-6.00	2-5	40	+2.25	0-5	-	-5.00
Redcar	5-25	20	+26.00	1-10	10	+16.00	2-12	17	+3.00	2-3	67	+7.00
Ripon	6-28	21	-7.06	2-7	29	+2.50	4-17	24	-5.56	0-4	-	-4.00
Salisbury	28-297	9	-98.30	15-147	10	-24.02	11-131	8	-64.65	2-19	11	-9.63
Sandown	29-209	14	-9.02	12-80	15	+1.53	15-99	15	+6.94	2-30	7	-17.50
S'well (AW)	5-29	17	-8.25	0-3	-	-3.00	4-19	21	-3.25	1-7	14	-2.00
Thirsk	3-6	50	+3.41	2-4	50	+3.41	0-0	-	+0.00	1-2	50	0.00
Wetherby	1-6	17	-2.50	0-0	-	+0.00	0-3	-	-3.00	1-3	33	+0.50
Windsor	48-286	17	-38.55	25-122	20	-27.38	17-121	14	-2.88	6-43	14	-8.30
Wolves (AW)	36-264	14	-93.11	16-119	13	-25.18	17-124	14	-66.19	3-21	14	-1.75
Yarmouth	2-27	7	-13.50	2-18	11	-4.50	0-8	-	-8.00	0-1	-	-1.00
York	11-108	10	-16.10	9-56	16	+1.90	1-34	3	-13.00	1-18	6	-5.00

Ten-year summary

	Wins	Runs	%	Win prize-money	Total prize-money	£1
2019	153	1286	12	£2,732,962.93	£4,012,258.68	-300.75
2018	172	1401	12	£1,859,205.70	£3,188,245.42	-345.26
2017	194	1354	14	£1,850,403.13	£3,000,248.20	-79.49
2016	172	1357	13	£1,562,891.35	£2,809,779.05	-211.92
2015	195	1382	14	£2,050,242.78	£3,606,069.97	-348.38
2014	206	1404	15	£2,729,648.95	£4,749,469.60	-366.41
2013*	235	1412	17	£3,137,720.00	£4,532,464.69	-306.32
2012*	218	1367	16	£1,767,369.39	£2,821,469.49	-165.90
2011*	218	1408	15	£2,283,589.58	£3,726,396.80	-46.12
2010*	210	1341	16	£2,054,058.90	£3,218,574.92	-203.61

*Richard Hannon Sr training

KING OF CHANGE: Richard Hannon's highest-profile winner of the year by far

William Haggas

By month - 2019

	Overall			Two-year-olds			Three-year-olds			Older horses		
	W-R	%	£1	W-R	%	£1	W-R	%	£1	W-R	%	£1
January	8-18	44	+0.86	0-0	-	+0.00	5-13	38	-3.47	3-5	60	+4.33
February	1-2	50	-0.27	0-0	-	+0.00	1-2	50	-0.27	0-0	-	+0.00
March	2-15	13	-11.48	0-0	-	+0.00	2-10	20	-6.48	0-5	-	-5.00
April	6-40	15	-23.15	0-0	-	+0.00	6-35	17	-18.15	0-5	-	-5.00
May	16-79	20	-12.83	0-3	-	-3.00	12-59	20	-9.95	4-17	24	+0.13
June	33-113	29	+10.59	5-11	45	+6.94	24-79	30	-1.86	4-23	17	+5.50
July	24-96	25	-18.25	5-21	24	-8.29	15-53	28	-7.96	4-22	18	-2.00
August	24-96	25	-15.38	6-24	25	-0.95	15-52	29	-0.03	3-20	15	-14.40
September	8-49	16	-27.05	3-25	12	-18.64	5-17	29	-1.42	0-7	-	-7.00
October	5-69	7	-48.43	4-34	12	-16.05	1-24	4	-21.38	0-11	-	-11.00
November	10-49	20	+27.83	6-35	17	+24.00	3-12	25	+0.83	1-2	50	+3.00
December	5-20	25	+0.95	3-16	19	-5.55	1-2	50	+3.50	1-2	50	+3.00

By month - 2018

	Overall			Two-year-olds			Three-year-olds			Older horses		
	W-R	%	£1	W-R	%	£1	W-R	%	£1	W-R	%	£1
January	3-16	19	-9.60	0-0	-	+0.00	2-13	15	-8.00	1-3	33	-1.60
February	1-7	14	-3.50	0-0	-	+0.00	1-6	17	-2.50	0-1	-	-1.00
March	7-14	50	+7.43	0-0	-	+0.00	2-6	33	-2.33	5-8	63	+9.76
April	8-29	28	-8.93	1-3	33	+0.25	6-23	26	-8.68	1-3	33	-0.50
May	22-84	26	+4.02	2-9	22	-5.23	14-46	30	+8.88	6-29	21	+0.38
June	13-92	14	-49.40	2-11	18	-5.15	6-56	11	-40.00	5-25	20	-4.25
July	23-87	26	-1.51	2-16	13	-9.13	18-51	35	+11.62	3-20	15	-4.00
August	17-91	19	-31.80	3-23	13	-14.84	10-43	23	-11.96	4-25	16	-5.00
September	16-62	26	+32.95	6-30	20	+21.95	8-20	40	+14.50	2-12	17	-3.50
October	15-80	19	-29.42	10-43	23	-10.42	5-25	20	-7.00	0-12	-	-12.00
November	9-35	26	-7.46	5-20	25	-6.34	3-9	33	+2.00	1-6	17	-3.13
December	4-11	36	+8.00	2-6	33	+2.50	0-3	-	-3.00	2-2	100	+8.50

By month - 2017

	Overall			Two-year-olds			Three-year-olds			Older horses		
	W-R	%	£1	W-R	%	£1	W-R	%	£1	W-R	%	£1
January	6-10	60	+8.24	0-0	-	+0.00	6-10	60	+8.24	0-0	-	+0.00
February	2-3	67	+7.44	0-0	-	+0.00	1-1	100	+8.00	1-2	50	-0.56
March	4-7	57	+1.56	0-0	-	+0.00	3-5	60	+2.23	1-2	50	-0.67
April	10-32	31	+5.95	0-1	-	-1.00	5-21	24	+2.54	5-10	50	+4.41
May	18-70	26	+5.89	3-9	33	+3.80	9-42	21	-13.84	6-19	32	+15.93
June	18-85	21	-24.10	4-16	25	-4.49	11-53	21	-16.44	3-16	19	-3.17
July	29-92	32	+36.89	7-15	47	+2.59	16-55	29	+33.13	6-22	27	+1.17
August	17-86	20	+0.73	2-30	7	-8.50	13-41	32	+14.66	2-15	13	-5.43
September	18-80	23	-19.39	7-29	24	-5.04	8-34	24	-15.60	3-17	18	+1.25
October	19-72	26	+16.10	10-40	25	-6.50	6-20	30	+23.60	3-12	25	-1.00
November	12-35	34	+2.38	8-22	36	+1.06	2-8	25	-0.56	2-5	40	+1.88
December	3-10	30	+4.73	3-9	33	+5.73	0-1	-	-1.00	0-0	-	+0.00

By race type - 2019

	Overall			Two-year-olds			Three-year-olds			Older horses		
	W-R	%	£1	W-R	%	£1	W-R	%	£1	W-R	%	£1
Group	6-58	10	-26.52	0-6	-	-6.00	1-15	7	-11.00	5-37	14	-9.52
Handicap	51-246	21	-51.12	3-24	13	-10.80	41-170	24	-22.16	7-52	13	-18.16
Maiden	18-84	21	-27.14	8-42	19	-6.38	9-40	23	-22.51	1-2	50	+1.75

By race type - 2018

	Overall			Two-year-olds			Three-year-olds			Older horses		
	W-R	%	£1	W-R	%	£1	W-R	%	£1	W-R	%	£1
Group	8-48	17	-19.92	1-8	13	-2.50	6-14	43	+6.08	1-26	4	-23.50
Handicap	50-231	22	-16.62	3-25	12	-10.20	27-122	22	-20.67	20-84	24	+14.25
Maiden	21-87	24	+4.54	11-43	26	+17.22	10-43	23	-11.68	0-1	-	-1.00

By race type - 2017

	Overall			Two-year-olds			Three-year-olds			Older horses		
	W-R	%	£1	W-R	%	£1	W-R	%	£1	W-R	%	£1
Group	2-57	4	-40.43	0-12	-	-12.00	0-19	-	-19.00	2-26	8	-9.43
Handicap	59-238	25	+26.72	5-15	33	+20.70	35-152	23	+0.10	19-71	27	+5.92
Maiden	44-122	36	+30.19	7-29	24	-10.49	35-91	38	+39.14	2-2	100	+1.54

By jockey - 2019

	Overall			Two-year-olds			Three-year-olds			Older horses		
	W-R	%	£1	W-R	%	£1	W-R	%	£1	W-R	%	£1
Daniel Tudhope	26-63	41	+16.38	4-16	25	-9.15	17-33	52	+8.52	5-14	36	+17.00
Tom Marquand	24-102	24	+6.84	8-40	20	+10.61	14-45	31	+3.73	2-17	12	-7.50
James Doyle	21-136	15	-53.20	8-40	20	-11.43	10-66	15	-27.64	3-30	10	-14.13
Jim Crowley	9-43	21	-23.27	1-12	8	-9.38	8-26	31	-8.89	0-5	-	-5.00
Ben Curtis	7-16	44	+13.95	4-8	50	+9.12	3-8	38	+4.83	0-0	-	+0.00
Liam Jones	7-31	23	-3.08	2-5	40	-0.68	5-25	20	-1.40	0-1	-	-1.00
Georgia Cox	7-36	19	-2.21	1-10	10	-4.00	5-23	22	+3.39	1-3	33	-1.60
Paul Hanagan	6-20	30	-5.73	0-1	-	-1.00	6-18	33	-3.73	0-1	-	-1.00
R Kingscote	4-9	44	+2.18	0-1	-	-1.00	0-1	-	-1.00	4-7	57	+4.18
P J McDonald	3-7	43	+9.53	0-1	-	-1.00	2-5	40	+4.53	1-1	100	+6.00
Dane O'Neill	3-20	15	-10.45	0-2	-	-2.00	3-16	19	-6.45	0-2	-	-2.00
Ryan Moore	3-20	15	-10.25	0-3	-	-3.00	3-12	25	-2.25	0-5	-	-5.00

By jockey - 2018

	Overall			Two-year-olds			Three-year-olds			Older horses		
	W-R	%	£1	W-R	%	£1	W-R	%	£1	W-R	%	£1
James Doyle	49-164	30	+13.19	9-43	21	-18.04	31-78	40	+38.36	9-43	21	-7.13
Jim Crowley	13-47	28	+1.46	3-21	14	-13.79	5-11	45	+4.00	5-15	33	+11.25
Daniel Tudhope	10-51	20	-19.70	0-5	-	-5.00	8-31	26	-8.07	2-15	13	-6.63
Tom Marquand	9-38	24	-3.02	2-13	15	-4.50	5-19	26	-3.02	2-6	33	+4.50
Oisin Murphy	7-18	39	+9.28	3-8	38	+2.88	2-6	33	+5.50	2-4	50	+0.90
Ryan Moore	6-20	30	-2.50	2-6	33	-2.76	1-5	20	-3.96	3-9	33	+4.23
Liam Jones	5-29	17	-14.01	1-7	14	-5.64	4-22	18	-8.38	0-0	-	+0.00
Ben Curtis	4-11	36	+3.17	1-4	25	-2.33	1-5	20	-2.00	2-2	100	+7.50
Joe Fanning	4-13	31	+2.00	1-2	50	+3.50	3-10	30	-0.50	0-1	-	-1.00

By jockey - 2017

	Overall			Two-year-olds			Three-year-olds			Older horses		
	W-R	%	£1	W-R	%	£1	W-R	%	£1	W-R	%	£1
Pat Cosgrave	26-134	19	-36.76	8-36	22	-9.72	14-71	20	-17.78	4-27	15	-9.25
Ryan Moore	17-46	37	+16.70	4-13	31	-5.63	10-24	42	+16.08	3-9	33	+6.25
Jim Crowley	13-58	22	-8.16	5-18	28	-4.61	4-20	20	-8.40	4-20	20	+4.85
Georgia Cox	11-50	22	+6.28	2-13	15	-2.30	4-18	22	+2.75	5-19	26	+5.83
Daniel Tudhope	10-27	37	+0.36	6-16	38	+2.38	3-9	33	-1.58	1-2	50	-0.43
James Doyle	9-17	53	+9.45	3-7	43	+0.05	4-7	57	+6.78	2-3	67	+2.63
Martin Harley	8-25	32	+19.54	3-12	25	-3.55	4-11	36	+20.58	1-2	50	+2.50
Paul Hanagan	6-14	43	+8.78	0-0	-	+0.00	2-8	25	+0.00	4-6	67	+8.78
Joe Fanning	5-16	31	+3.38	1-5	20	-1.25	4-8	50	+7.63	0-3	-	-3.00

By course - 2016-2019

	Overall			Two-year-olds			Three-year-olds			Older horses		
	W-R	%	£1	W-R	%	£1	W-R	%	£1	W-R	%	£1
Ascot	19-154	12	-32.56	1-16	6	+1.00	9-70	13	-11.89	9-68	13	-21.68
Ayr	2-3	67	+4.07	1-1	100	+4.50	1-2	50	-0.43	0-0	-	+0.00
Bath	7-27	26	-7.73	2-5	40	-0.22	4-20	20	-7.42	1-2	50	-0.09
Beverley	6-21	29	-8.34	1-3	33	-1.56	5-17	29	-5.78	0-1	-	-1.00
Brighton	7-18	39	+2.02	1-3	33	-1.64	6-14	43	+4.66	0-1	-	-1.00
Carlisle	4-14	29	+2.25	0-0	-	+0.00	4-14	29	+2.25	0-0	-	+0.00
Catterick	4-10	40	-3.94	2-5	40	-2.39	2-5	40	-1.56	0-0	-	+0.00
Chelmsf'd (AW)	42-184	23	-34.85	10-47	21	-21.19	23-102	23	-17.82	9-35	26	+4.16
Chepstow	5-20	25	+3.70	0-5	-	-5.00	5-12	42	+11.70	0-3	-	-3.00
Chester	8-30	27	-6.68	2-4	50	+2.30	4-19	21	-7.32	2-7	29	-1.67
Doncaster	20-90	22	-3.97	8-29	28	+7.78	10-43	23	-1.85	2-18	11	-9.90
Epsom	3-23	13	-15.88	2-3	67	+1.63	1-13	8	-10.50	0-7	-	-7.00
Ffos Las	1-4	25	-1.63	0-0	-	+0.00	1-3	33	-0.63	0-1	-	-1.00
Goodwood	20-107	19	-9.93	3-15	20	-9.43	13-53	25	+13.75	4-39	10	-14.25
Hamilton	3-10	30	0.00	1-1	100	+3.50	2-9	22	-3.50	0-0	-	+0.00
Haydock	34-124	27	-4.53	3-24	13	-13.89	20-64	31	+1.84	11-36	31	+7.52
Kempton (AW)	31-152	20	-33.18	9-56	16	-28.29	16-73	22	-12.14	6-23	26	+7.25
Leicester	5-41	12	-27.70	2-13	15	-9.33	3-26	12	-16.38	0-2	-	-2.00
Lingfield	22-56	39	+30.13	11-19	58	+32.24	10-31	32	+1.01	1-6	17	-3.13
Lingfield (AW)	28-108	26	-6.62	8-26	31	+6.73	13-54	24	-11.22	7-28	25	-2.13
Musselburgh	7-24	29	+6.41	2-2	100	+1.28	4-19	21	+5.63	1-3	33	-0.50
Newbury	30-140	21	+1.34	9-60	15	-19.99	14-61	23	-3.17	7-19	37	+24.50
N'castle (AW)	31-86	36	+13.41	9-27	33	+7.03	18-46	39	+9.98	4-13	31	-3.60
Newmarket	20-156	13	-6.01	7-62	11	+24.74	10-68	15	-26.25	3-26	12	-4.50
Newmarket (J)	17-114	15	-41.04	1-22	5	-14.00	13-70	19	-27.54	3-22	14	+0.50
Nottingham	15-62	24	-10.93	5-24	21	-6.03	9-34	26	-2.31	1-4	25	-2.60
Pontefract	6-30	20	-16.81	1-8	13	-6.09	5-19	26	-7.72	0-3	-	-3.00
Redcar	16-34	47	+8.82	5-15	33	+0.35	10-18	56	+6.97	1-1	100	+1.50
Ripon	15-36	42	+1.95	1-5	20	-3.56	14-30	47	+6.50	0-1	-	-1.00
Salisbury	12-41	29	-1.21	2-14	14	-8.00	10-25	40	+8.79	0-2	-	-2.00
Sandown	12-65	18	-20.13	4-16	25	-1.13	5-34	15	-15.50	3-15	20	-3.50
S'well (AW)	4-7	57	+4.20	1-2	50	-0.33	2-4	50	+1.03	1-1	100	+3.50
Thirsk	9-36	25	-16.50	3-12	25	-6.08	5-23	22	-11.92	1-1	100	+1.50
Wetherby	2-8	25	+2.50	0-0	-	+0.00	1-6	17	-2.50	1-2	50	+5.00
Windsor	18-62	29	-11.01	4-18	22	-1.65	14-38	37	-3.36	0-6	-	-6.00
Wolves (AW)	39-114	34	+5.18	12-42	29	+4.36	20-55	36	-5.38	7-17	41	+6.21
Yarmouth	30-127	24	-14.26	12-57	21	-13.60	16-61	26	+0.84	2-9	22	-1.50
York	28-151	19	-15.56	7-40	18	-21.78	10-55	18	-9.46	11-56	20	+15.68

Ten-year summary

	Wins	Runs	%	Win prize-money	Total prize-money	£1
2019	142	646	22	£1,635,918.27	£3,125,480.95	-116.59
2018	145	657	22	£2,151,802.84	£3,060,943.05	-109.22
2017	158	590	27	£1,591,288.73	£2,702,577.98	+44.10
2016	137	596	23	£1,423,781.23	£2,127,308.68	-83.29
2015	113	533	21	£1,583,672.69	£2,364,888.31	-127.11
2014	113	520	22	£1,478,038.78	£2,281,869.22	+17.06
2013	107	503	21	£1,133,364.77	£1,896,067.18	-12.27
2012	83	448	19	£748,501.35	£1,257,840.26	-65.35
2011	76	423	18	£848,955.18	£1,228,089.25	-96.35
2010	59	361	16	£942,548.43	£1,181,417.91	-91.16

ONE MASTER: William Haggas's only Group 1 winner of 2019

Archie Watson

By month - 2019

	Overall			Two-year-olds			Three-year-olds			Older horses		
	W-R	%	£1	W-R	%	£1	W-R	%	£1	W-R	%	£1
January	7-49	14	-27.17	0-0	-	+0.00	3-20	15	-11.17	4-29	14	-16.00
February	5-38	13	-20.27	0-0	-	+0.00	1-15	7	-9.00	4-23	17	-11.27
March	3-39	8	-24.25	0-0	-	+0.00	2-14	14	-1.50	1-25	4	-22.75
April	16-66	24	-5.44	8-16	50	+7.36	5-25	20	-0.50	3-25	12	-12.30
May	17-81	21	+7.90	6-34	18	-13.88	10-35	29	+32.38	1-12	8	-10.60
June	12-93	13	-52.64	11-49	22	-11.39	1-33	3	-30.25	0-11	-	-11.00
July	20-105	19	-15.87	9-51	18	-11.30	8-35	23	+1.18	3-19	16	-5.75
August	23-107	21	-11.05	13-62	21	-18.75	6-32	19	+5.20	4-13	31	+2.50
September	12-87	14	-30.45	9-47	19	-11.86	3-24	13	-2.58	0-16	-	-16.00
October	9-46	20	-9.61	6-26	23	-8.11	1-13	8	-4.00	2-7	29	+2.50
November	4-32	13	-10.89	4-16	25	+5.12	0-8	-	-8.00	0-8	-	-8.00
December	5-33	15	-8.75	5-17	29	+7.25	0-9	-	-9.00	0-7	-	-7.00

By month - 2018

	Overall			Two-year-olds			Three-year-olds			Older horses		
	W-R	%	£1	W-R	%	£1	W-R	%	£1	W-R	%	£1
January	8-25	32	+34.13	0-0	-	+0.00	2-6	33	+17.00	6-19	32	+17.13
February	7-29	24	-5.18	0-0	-	+0.00	3-9	33	+0.35	4-20	20	-5.53
March	10-40	25	+4.98	0-1	-	-1.00	4-15	27	+0.85	6-24	25	+5.13
April	3-34	9	-27.71	0-7	-	-7.00	3-19	16	-12.71	0-8	-	-8.00
May	7-49	14	-23.24	3-15	20	-4.90	1-16	6	-12.50	3-18	17	-5.84
June	9-47	19	+3.78	8-22	36	+25.28	0-11	-	-11.00	1-14	7	-10.50
July	15-53	28	-8.55	10-25	40	+3.38	4-15	27	-1.43	1-13	8	-10.50
August	15-62	24	-14.28	15-43	35	+4.72	0-14	-	-14.00	0-5	-	-5.00
September	8-38	21	-8.76	6-23	26	-0.14	0-11	-	-11.00	2-4	50	+2.38
October	6-49	12	-10.50	3-35	9	-13.50	3-9	33	+8.00	0-5	-	-5.00
November	4-36	11	-16.25	2-18	11	-9.00	1-9	11	-5.25	1-9	11	-2.00
December	5-35	14	-4.00	1-15	7	-11.50	3-10	30	+10.00	1-10	10	-2.50

By month - 2017

	Overall			Two-year-olds			Three-year-olds			Older horses		
	W-R	%	£1	W-R	%	£1	W-R	%	£1	W-R	%	£1
January	3-11	27	+5.50	0-0	-	+0.00	0-3	-	-3.00	3-8	38	+8.50
February	2-12	17	-3.25	0-0	-	+0.00	1-2	50	+1.25	1-10	10	-4.50
March	2-15	13	-8.75	0-0	-	+0.00	0-2	-	-2.00	2-13	15	-6.75
April	2-10	20	-3.56	1-4	25	-2.56	0-2	-	-2.00	1-4	25	+1.00
May	3-23	13	-10.06	0-11	-	-11.00	2-8	25	+0.94	1-4	25	+0.00
June	4-34	12	-9.67	4-18	22	+6.33	0-10	-	-10.00	0-6	-	-6.00
July	7-29	24	+8.83	3-15	20	-0.17	3-9	33	+10.75	1-5	20	-1.75
August	10-33	30	+15.49	5-10	50	+13.61	2-15	13	-3.50	3-8	38	+5.38
September	7-27	26	+13.33	1-8	13	+4.00	2-9	22	+5.75	4-10	40	+3.58
October	4-22	18	-5.38	0-8	-	-8.00	3-11	27	+3.13	1-3	33	-0.50
November	4-25	16	-11.13	0-7	-	-7.00	3-12	25	-0.75	1-6	17	-3.38
December	7-32	22	+0.96	0-4	-	-4.00	5-18	28	+1.47	2-10	20	+3.50

By race type - 2019

	Overall			Two-year-olds			Three-year-olds			Older horses		
	W-R	%	£1	W-R	%	£1	W-R	%	£1	W-R	%	£1
Group	0-17	-	-17.00	0-11	-	-11.00	0-5	-	-5.00	0-1	-	-1.00
Handicap	54-396	14	-129.28	16-72	22	-9.74	25-169	15	-17.79	13-155	8	-101.75
Maiden	11-60	18	-6.59	6-40	15	-12.22	5-19	26	+6.63	0-1	-	-1.00

By race type - 2018

	Overall			Two-year-olds			Three-year-olds			Older horses		
	W-R	%	£1	W-R	%	£1	W-R	%	£1	W-R	%	£1
Group	1-13	8	-8.00	1-8	13	-3.00	0-1	-	-1.00	0-4	-	-4.00
Handicap	42-252	17	-40.01	12-44	27	+9.39	13-88	15	-20.38	17-120	14	-29.03
Maiden	6-35	17	+6.25	5-25	20	-4.75	1-9	11	+12.00	0-1	-	-1.00

By race type - 2017

	Overall			Two-year-olds			Three-year-olds			Older horses		
	W-R	%	£1	W-R	%	£1	W-R	%	£1	W-R	%	£1
Group	0-6	-	-6.00	0-4	-	-4.00	0-0	-	+0.00	0-2	-	-2.00
Handicap	31-164	19	-14.05	1-14	7	-6.00	13-74	18	-6.00	17-76	22	-2.05
Maiden	9-26	35	+30.41	2-4	50	+20.00	7-22	32	+10.41	0-0	-	+0.00

By jockey - 2019

	Overall			Two-year-olds			Three-year-olds			Older horses		
	W-R	%	£1	W-R	%	£1	W-R	%	£1	W-R	%	£1
Hollie Doyle	46-237	19	-74.92	29-105	28	-8.85	10-83	12	-40.68	7-49	14	-25.40
Oisin Murphy	22-77	29	+23.59	16-50	32	+0.12	6-18	33	+32.47	0-9	-	-9.00
Daniel Tudhope	12-37	32	+0.23	5-16	31	-1.90	5-15	33	-1.38	2-6	33	+3.50
Edward Greatrex	12-78	15	-26.91	3-19	16	-5.77	7-38	18	-4.87	2-21	10	-16.27
Miss B Hampson	7-31	23	-2.00	0-0	-	+0.00	0-0	-	+0.00	7-31	23	-2.00
Luke Morris	7-53	13	-28.47	5-27	19	-6.29	1-11	9	-9.43	1-15	7	-12.75
A McNamara	7-78	9	-42.00	3-46	7	-26.13	4-25	16	-8.88	0-7	-	-7.00
Paul Mulrennan	5-13	38	+22.00	2-6	33	+0.25	3-7	43	+21.75	0-0	-	+0.00
P-L Jamin	5-43	12	-4.50	2-6	33	+3.25	2-15	13	+9.25	1-22	5	-17.00
David Egan	4-8	50	+16.25	4-7	57	+17.25	0-1	-	-1.00	0-0	-	+0.00
Ben Curtis	3-17	18	+0.50	2-7	29	+1.50	1-9	11	0.00	0-1	-	-1.00
Kate Leahy	2-27	7	-17.25	0-2	-	-2.00	1-12	8	-5.50	1-13	8	-9.75

By jockey - 2018

	Overall			Two-year-olds			Three-year-olds			Older horses		
	W-R	%	£1	W-R	%	£1	W-R	%	£1	W-R	%	£1
E Greatrex	31-183	17	-37.27	14-79	18	-19.33	10-55	18	+1.83	7-49	14	-19.77
Oisin Murphy	18-76	24	-15.05	8-33	24	-4.83	4-20	20	-3.75	6-23	26	-6.46
Hollie Doyle	18-85	21	-21.07	15-49	31	+6.11	3-29	10	-20.18	0-7	-	-7.00
Daniel Tudhope	9-31	29	+11.43	7-19	37	+17.64	2-8	25	-2.21	0-4	-	-4.00
T Greatrex	4-13	31	+9.75	0-6	-	-6.00	3-4	75	+11.75	1-3	33	+4.00
Luke Morris	4-30	13	-0.38	0-2	-	-2.00	0-7	-	-7.00	4-21	19	+8.63
P-L Jamin	4-31	13	-8.25	0-1	-	-1.00	1-7	14	-0.50	3-23	13	-6.75
Mr S Walker	3-8	38	+1.13	0-0	-	+0.00	0-1	-	-1.00	3-7	43	+2.13
Ben Curtis	2-5	40	+1.41	2-5	40	+1.41	0-0	-	+0.00	0-0	-	+0.00

By jockey - 2017

	Overall			Two-year-olds			Three-year-olds			Older horses		
	W-R	%	£1	W-R	%	£1	W-R	%	£1	W-R	%	£1
E Greatrex	18-83	22	+4.54	4-20	20	+11.00	9-38	24	-4.96	5-25	20	-1.50
Luke Morris	11-52	21	-8.56	3-17	18	-8.80	1-8	13	-6.39	7-27	26	+6.63
Oisin Murphy	9-32	28	+5.07	3-14	21	-1.81	4-13	31	+3.63	2-5	40	+3.25
Andrew Mullen	5-9	56	+15.45	0-0	-	+0.00	2-5	40	+11.00	3-4	75	+4.45
Mr S Walker	3-8	38	+6.25	0-0	-	+0.00	2-3	67	+5.25	1-5	20	+1.00
Ben Curtis	3-14	21	-5.92	1-4	25	-2.17	0-6	-	-6.00	2-4	50	+2.25
Daniel Tudhope	2-6	33	+12.50	0-3	-	-3.00	2-3	67	+15.50	0-0	-	+0.00
Jimmy Quinn	1-2	50	+6.00	1-2	50	+6.00	0-0	-	+0.00	0-0	-	+0.00
Paul Mulrennan	1-3	33	+6.00	0-0	-	+0.00	1-3	33	+6.00	0-0	-	+0.00

By course - 2016-2019

	Overall			Two-year-olds			Three-year-olds			Older horses		
	W-R	%	£1	W-R	%	£1	W-R	%	£1	W-R	%	£1
Ascot	1-36	3	-23.00	1-20	5	-7.00	0-6	-	-6.00	0-10	-	-10.00
Ayr	1-14	7	-11.50	0-7	-	-7.00	0-2	-	-2.00	1-5	20	-2.50
Bath	9-46	20	-23.50	5-16	31	-4.55	3-19	16	-11.95	1-11	9	-7.00
Beverley	6-25	24	-5.75	4-15	27	-3.25	0-5	-	-5.00	2-5	40	+2.50
Brighton	9-40	23	-1.34	4-17	24	-3.45	5-14	36	+11.11	0-9	-	-9.00
Carlisle	3-18	17	-7.67	2-11	18	-3.67	1-5	20	-2.00	0-2	-	-2.00
Catterick	6-22	27	-2.92	3-10	30	-3.24	0-6	-	-6.00	3-6	50	+6.33
Chelmsf'd (AW)	23-164	14	-18.18	11-63	17	-11.03	9-54	17	+29.10	3-47	6	-36.25
Chepstow	5-33	15	-15.75	4-14	29	-0.50	1-12	8	-8.25	0-7	-	-7.00
Chester	3-19	16	-4.05	1-8	13	-5.80	1-7	14	+2.00	1-4	25	-0.25
Doncaster	2-21	10	-8.00	2-10	20	+3.00	0-6	-	-6.00	0-5	-	-5.00
Epsom	1-15	7	-11.25	0-5	-	-5.00	1-5	20	-1.25	0-5	-	-5.00
Ffos Las	8-24	33	+5.40	3-11	27	+4.00	4-12	33	+0.20	1-1	100	+1.20
Goodwood	2-24	8	-16.75	1-12	8	-8.00	0-5	-	-5.00	1-7	14	-3.75
Hamilton	6-18	33	+5.40	2-7	29	-0.67	4-9	44	+8.07	0-2	-	-2.00
Haydock	2-22	9	-13.97	2-10	20	-1.97	0-8	-	-8.00	0-4	-	-4.00
Kempton (AW)	38-172	22	-1.46	14-73	19	-23.01	14-59	24	+24.10	10-40	25	-2.55
Leicester	6-29	21	-5.75	2-13	15	-5.25	4-11	36	+4.50	0-5	-	-5.00
Lingfield	9-46	20	-0.90	6-24	25	+14.13	2-15	13	-10.53	1-7	14	-4.50
Lingfield (AW)	42-204	21	-7.70	12-40	30	+13.59	12-60	20	-17.13	18-104	17	-4.16
Musselburgh	10-20	50	+21.19	4-6	67	+6.49	1-4	25	+0.50	5-10	50	+14.20
Newbury	3-23	13	+8.60	2-14	14	-3.40	1-6	17	+15.00	0-3	-	-3.00
N'castle (AW)	11-64	17	-23.74	5-26	19	-10.59	4-26	15	-6.65	2-12	17	-6.50
Newmarket	0-17	-	-17.00	0-11	-	-11.00	0-2	-	-2.00	0-4	-	-4.00
Newmarket (J)	0-13	-	-13.00	0-10	-	-10.00	0-2	-	-2.00	0-1	-	-1.00
Nottingham	3-31	10	-16.70	2-15	13	-7.70	0-10	-	-10.00	1-6	17	+1.00
Pontefract	1-8	13	-2.50	0-3	-	-3.00	0-2	-	-2.00	1-3	33	+2.50
Redcar	11-35	31	+0.45	5-16	31	-3.03	4-12	33	+6.58	2-7	29	-3.10
Ripon	4-23	17	-13.55	2-10	20	-4.50	2-8	25	-4.05	0-5	-	-5.00
Salisbury	7-28	25	+8.25	5-14	36	+11.75	0-7	-	-7.00	2-7	29	+3.50
Sandown	3-13	23	+9.50	2-7	29	+10.50	1-4	25	+1.00	0-2	-	-2.00
S'well (AW)	11-61	18	-16.61	4-10	40	+8.08	6-35	17	-10.26	1-16	6	-14.43
Thirsk	2-14	14	-6.60	2-8	25	-0.60	0-5	-	-5.00	0-1	-	-1.00
Wetherby	1-6	17	-1.50	1-2	50	+2.50	0-4	-	-4.00	0-0	-	+0.00
Windsor	5-29	17	-7.16	5-16	31	+5.84	0-12	-	-12.00	0-1	-	-1.00
Wolves (AW)	39-186	21	-21.83	20-64	31	+6.30	8-57	14	-2.00	11-65	17	-26.13
Yarmouth	4-24	17	-11.81	3-12	25	-3.06	0-6	-	-6.00	1-6	17	-2.75
York	1-20	5	-16.50	1-12	8	-8.50	0-4	-	-4.00	0-4	-	-4.00

Ten-year summary

	Wins	Runs	%	Win prize-money	Total prize-money	£1
2019	133	776	17	£668,302.40	£1,270,046.25	-208.49
2018	105	528	20	£734,873.28	£1,108,646.34	-73.48
2017	56	274	20	£268,871.70	£458,985.29	-1.17
2016	4	29	14	£13,261.45	£32,685.67	-6.00

GUILDSMAN (right): highest-rated of Archie Watson's 71 two-year-old winners

David O'Meara

By month - 2019

	Overall			Two-year-olds			Three-year-olds			Older horses		
	W-R	%	£1	W-R	%	£1	W-R	%	£1	W-R	%	£1
January	5-40	13	-13.50	0-0	-	+0.00	1-12	8	-3.00	4-28	14	-10.50
February	4-25	16	-2.00	0-0	-	+0.00	0-7	-	-7.00	4-18	22	+5.00
March	4-28	14	+3.75	0-0	-	+0.00	0-5	-	-5.00	4-23	17	+8.75
April	9-89	10	-1.55	3-9	33	+33.00	2-25	8	-18.13	4-55	7	-16.43
May	20-123	16	+3.61	3-15	20	-1.75	7-36	19	-1.50	10-72	14	+6.86
June	22-124	18	+36.00	1-22	5	-16.50	6-35	17	-6.00	15-67	22	+58.50
July	20-138	14	-38.89	2-24	8	-14.63	9-39	23	-7.77	9-75	12	-16.50
August	17-131	13	-48.38	1-22	5	-17.67	5-39	13	-21.67	11-70	16	-9.04
September	14-98	14	-6.58	3-18	17	-4.40	5-28	18	-4.26	6-52	12	+2.08
October	8-85	9	-13.38	1-12	8	0.00	2-22	9	-9.38	5-51	10	-4.00
November	4-40	10	+6.00	1-12	8	-1.00	2-10	20	+2.00	1-18	6	+5.00
December	3-31	10	-15.38	0-8	-	-8.00	0-7	-	-7.00	3-16	19	-0.38

By month - 2018

	Overall			Two-year-olds			Three-year-olds			Older horses		
	W-R	%	£1	W-R	%	£1	W-R	%	£1	W-R	%	£1
January	0-34	-	-34.00	0-0	-	+0.00	0-1	-	-1.00	0-33	-	-33.00
February	0-23	-	-23.00	0-0	-	+0.00	0-2	-	-2.00	0-21	-	-21.00
March	1-31	3	-27.00	1-2	50	+2.00	0-7	-	-7.00	0-22	-	-22.00
April	9-56	16	+7.28	0-5	-	-5.00	3-16	19	+2.25	6-35	17	+10.03
May	14-130	11	-52.42	1-10	10	-2.00	3-34	9	-20.00	10-86	12	-30.42
June	16-158	10	-57.79	1-12	8	+5.00	4-39	10	-16.13	11-107	10	-46.67
July	29-146	20	+15.13	4-18	22	+10.88	6-37	16	-10.42	19-91	21	+14.67
August	15-126	12	-47.08	3-21	14	-9.50	5-34	15	+4.38	7-71	10	-41.96
September	9-87	10	+6.38	1-12	8	-9.63	2-22	9	-9.00	6-53	11	+25.00
October	7-102	7	-16.50	2-20	10	+0.00	4-24	17	+30.50	1-58	2	-47.00
November	5-71	7	-23.02	2-18	11	-3.47	0-8	-	-8.00	3-45	7	-11.56
December	1-51	2	-36.00	0-12	-	-12.00	1-6	17	+9.00	0-33	-	-33.00

By month - 2017

	Overall			Two-year-olds			Three-year-olds			Older horses		
	W-R	%	£1	W-R	%	£1	W-R	%	£1	W-R	%	£1
January	4-21	19	+9.25	0-0	-	+0.00	0-3	-	-3.00	4-18	22	+12.25
February	1-25	4	-20.50	0-0	-	+0.00	1-7	14	-2.50	0-18	-	-18.00
March	2-18	11	+10.10	0-0	-	+0.00	1-8	13	-5.90	1-10	10	+16.00
April	6-65	9	-7.63	0-1	-	-1.00	2-21	10	-12.13	4-43	9	+5.50
May	15-137	11	+23.91	1-10	10	-5.50	8-48	17	+62.41	6-79	8	-33.00
June	18-147	12	-5.24	4-19	21	+8.93	9-46	20	+10.58	5-82	6	-24.75
July	9-146	6	-77.48	1-16	6	-14.33	4-46	9	-29.15	4-84	5	-34.00
August	20-165	12	-61.05	1-21	5	-19.43	10-49	20	+5.88	9-95	9	-47.50
September	11-116	9	-40.13	2-21	10	-4.00	5-36	14	+6.75	4-59	7	-42.88
October	9-106	8	-46.88	1-13	8	+0.00	3-33	9	-17.00	5-60	8	-29.88
November	8-71	11	-27.50	1-7	14	-4.00	4-16	25	+8.00	3-48	6	-31.50
December	5-52	10	+0.00	0-9	-	-9.00	1-11	9	-6.00	4-32	13	+15.00

By race type - 2019

	Overall			Two-year-olds			Three-year-olds			Older horses		
	W-R	%	£1	W-R	%	£1	W-R	%	£1	W-R	%	£1
Group	2-20	10	+1.00	0-0	-	+0.00	0-4	-	-4.00	2-16	13	+5.00
Handicap	96-722	13	-69.22	6-41	15	-1.52	29-201	14	-58.97	61-480	13	-8.73
Maiden	5-41	12	-15.41	2-23	9	-14.91	2-16	13	-5.50	1-2	50	+5.00

By race type - 2018

	Overall			Two-year-olds			Three-year-olds			Older horses		
	W-R	%	£1	W-R	%	£1	W-R	%	£1	W-R	%	£1
Group	1-25	4	-22.00	0-1	-	-1.00	0-1	-	-1.00	1-23	4	-20.00
Handicap	74-768	10	-212.33	2-32	6	-9.00	21-177	12	-11.54	51-559	9	-191.79
Maiden	1-28	4	-26.00	0-15	-	-15.00	1-13	8	-11.00	0-0	-	+0.00

By race type - 2017

	Overall			Two-year-olds			Three-year-olds			Older horses		
	W-R	%	£1	W-R	%	£1	W-R	%	£1	W-R	%	£1
Group	0-26	-	-26.00	0-2	-	-2.00	0-1	-	-1.00	0-23	-	-23.00
Handicap	78-795	10	-197.17	1-28	4	-17.00	33-225	15	-1.17	44-542	8	-179.00
Maiden	13-97	13	+0.88	1-10	10	-4.00	12-84	14	+7.88	0-3	-	-3.00

By jockey - 2019

	Overall			Two-year-olds			Three-year-olds			Older horses		
	W-R	%	£1	W-R	%	£1	W-R	%	£1	W-R	%	£1
Daniel Tudhope	56-308	18	+16.42	9-48	19	+8.96	21-84	25	+4.32	26-176	15	+3.14
David Nolan	21-180	12	-70.47	1-26	4	-19.50	8-53	15	-20.68	12-101	12	-30.29
Shane Gray	9-58	16	+19.50	0-13	-	-13.00	1-16	6	-10.00	8-29	28	+42.50
Adam Kirby	8-52	15	+9.10	1-3	33	-0.90	1-9	11	0.00	6-40	15	+10.00
Harrison Shaw	5-18	28	+11.00	1-4	25	+7.00	1-9	11	-6.50	3-5	60	+10.50
Robbie Downey	4-40	10	-15.33	1-6	17	+1.50	1-12	8	-10.83	2-22	9	-6.00
C McGovern	4-54	7	-24.50	1-7	14	+8.00	2-21	10	-11.00	1-26	4	-21.50
David Probert	3-26	12	-7.75	0-3	-	-3.00	1-6	17	+1.00	2-17	12	-5.75
Cam Hardie	3-54	6	-12.50	0-15	-	-15.00	0-17	-	-17.00	3-22	14	+19.50
Jason Hart	2-4	50	+34.00	0-0	-	+0.00	0-1	-	-1.00	2-3	67	+35.00
S De Sousa	2-7	29	+2.00	0-0	-	+0.00	0-0	-	+0.00	2-7	29	+2.00
Harry Bentley	2-14	14	+7.00	0-2	-	-2.00	1-4	25	+4.00	1-8	13	+5.00

By jockey - 2018

	Overall			Two-year-olds			Three-year-olds			Older horses		
	W-R	%	£1	W-R	%	£1	W-R	%	£1	W-R	%	£1
Daniel Tudhope	36-274	13	-68.40	3-25	12	-10.00	9-57	16	-0.50	24-192	13	-57.90
David Nolan	27-172	16	-15.13	4-26	15	-16.72	7-42	17	+6.63	16-104	15	-5.04
C McGovern	11-119	9	-63.25	0-15	-	-15.00	5-37	14	-12.42	6-67	9	-35.83
Martin Harley	8-63	13	-6.38	1-6	17	+0.00	3-15	20	+0.88	4-42	10	-7.25
Shane Gray	5-59	8	+8.50	1-14	7	-1.00	2-18	11	+19.00	2-27	7	-9.50
Phillip Makin	3-30	10	-1.50	2-4	50	+15.50	0-3	-	-3.00	1-23	4	-14.00
Adam Kirby	3-37	8	+4.00	0-1	-	-1.00	1-3	33	+12.00	2-33	6	-7.00
Harry Bentley	2-21	10	-15.75	0-1	-	-1.00	0-4	-	-4.00	2-16	13	-10.75
Sam James	2-47	4	-23.50	1-11	9	+10.00	0-18	-	-18.00	1-18	6	-15.50

By jockey - 2017

	Overall			Two-year-olds			Three-year-olds			Older horses		
	W-R	%	£1	W-R	%	£1	W-R	%	£1	W-R	%	£1
Daniel Tudhope	54-389	14	+18.69	4-41	10	-20.15	26-115	23	+96.34	24-233	10	-57.50
Phillip Makin	11-108	10	-15.68	2-29	7	-16.43	7-43	16	-1.25	2-36	6	+2.00
David Nolan	6-73	8	-19.50	1-12	8	+1.00	1-18	6	-12.50	4-43	9	-8.00
Josh Doyle	5-99	5	-38.75	0-4	-	-4.00	2-36	6	-11.00	3-59	5	-23.75
K Shoemark	4-19	21	+4.00	0-1	-	-1.00	1-6	17	-2.00	3-12	25	+7.00
Martin Harley	4-34	12	-12.25	0-3	-	-3.00	1-8	13	-3.00	3-23	13	-6.25
Shelley Birkett	4-64	6	-25.50	0-0	-	+0.00	2-30	7	-9.00	2-34	6	-16.50
Patrick Vaughan	4-72	6	-19.75	0-1	-	-1.00	1-11	9	-8.25	3-60	5	-10.50
Adam Kirby	3-25	12	-11.25	0-0	-	+0.00	1-4	25	+0.50	2-21	10	-11.75

By course - 2016-2019

	Overall			Two-year-olds			Three-year-olds			Older horses		
	W-R	%	£1	W-R	%	£1	W-R	%	£1	W-R	%	£1
Ascot	5-128	4	-62.00	0-8	-	-8.00	0-11	-	-11.00	5-109	5	-43.00
Ayr	25-148	17	-1.67	1-16	6	-9.50	7-34	21	+1.00	17-98	17	+6.83
Bath	0-4	-	-4.00	0-0	-	+0.00	0-0	-	+0.00	0-4	-	-4.00
Beverley	37-219	17	+6.21	3-45	7	-4.00	15-58	26	+20.38	19-116	16	-10.17
Carlisle	5-64	8	-34.50	1-10	10	-3.00	2-27	7	-21.50	2-27	7	-10.00
Catterick	24-162	15	-81.13	8-41	20	-18.11	9-49	18	-14.52	7-72	10	-48.50
Chelmsf'd (AW)	16-189	8	-69.36	1-15	7	-12.50	2-42	5	-30.50	13-132	10	-26.36
Chepstow	0-1	-	-1.00	0-0	-	+0.00	0-1	-	-1.00	0-0	-	+0.00
Chester	5-53	9	-15.25	2-10	20	-1.75	2-15	13	-2.50	1-28	4	-11.00
Doncaster	16-194	8	-53.13	4-12	33	+12.13	2-43	5	-30.25	10-139	7	-35.00
Epsom	6-46	13	-2.00	0-0	-	+0.00	0-3	-	-3.00	6-43	14	+1.00
Goodwood	2-50	4	-18.00	0-1	-	-1.00	0-5	-	-5.00	2-44	5	-12.00
Hamilton	23-118	19	-10.63	1-15	7	-3.00	12-43	28	+11.88	10-60	17	-19.50
Haydock	20-173	12	+13.92	0-4	-	-4.00	6-35	17	+30.00	14-134	10	-12.08
Kempton (AW)	6-62	10	-13.50	0-3	-	-3.00	1-10	10	0.00	5-49	10	-10.50
Leicester	7-65	11	-35.50	0-8	-	-8.00	3-25	12	-14.50	4-32	13	-13.00
Lingfield	7-17	41	+5.37	1-4	25	+3.50	1-4	25	-1.80	5-9	56	+3.67
Lingfield (AW)	19-136	14	-20.15	1-5	20	-2.90	2-15	13	+5.00	16-116	14	-22.25
Musselburgh	13-108	12	-29.85	4-24	17	-6.68	2-28	7	-11.00	7-56	13	-12.17
Newbury	0-20	-	-20.00	0-4	-	-4.00	0-6	-	-6.00	0-10	-	-10.00
N'castle (AW)	26-314	8	-97.65	3-46	7	-6.00	11-103	11	-20.78	12-165	7	-70.88
Newmarket	6-53	11	-2.00	2-2	100	+14.00	2-8	25	+4.00	2-43	5	-20.00
Newmarket (J)	2-40	5	-33.38	0-4	-	-4.00	1-10	10	-6.00	1-26	4	-23.38
Nottingham	4-45	9	-26.38	1-5	20	-2.63	0-13	-	-13.00	3-27	11	-10.75
Pontefract	17-139	12	-52.25	0-18	-	-18.00	6-32	19	-7.38	11-89	12	-26.88
Redcar	27-207	13	-40.04	5-37	14	-6.00	8-65	12	+1.00	14-105	13	-35.04
Ripon	36-242	15	+28.33	8-34	24	+35.63	13-68	19	+14.08	15-140	11	-21.38
Salisbury	0-6	-	-6.00	0-0	-	+0.00	0-1	-	-1.00	0-5	-	-5.00
Sandown	2-20	10	-13.88	0-2	-	-2.00	1-6	17	-3.13	1-12	8	-8.75
S'well (AW)	8-80	10	-31.59	0-6	-	-6.00	3-24	13	-12.50	5-50	10	-13.09
Thirsk	24-210	11	-51.92	3-38	8	-25.33	9-63	14	-21.09	12-109	11	-5.50
Wetherby	4-28	14	+33.61	0-2	-	-2.00	2-11	18	+46.00	2-15	13	-10.39
Windsor	2-14	14	-4.00	0-0	-	+0.00	0-4	-	-4.00	2-10	20	0.00
Wolves (AW)	41-363	11	-71.43	5-51	10	-14.97	16-112	14	-15.29	20-200	10	-41.17
Yarmouth	4-28	14	-12.86	1-4	25	-2.33	2-10	20	-5.52	1-14	7	-5.00
York	16-333	5	-145.25	0-37	-	-37.00	2-45	4	-7.00	14-251	6	-101.25

Ten-year summary

	Wins	Runs	%	Win prize-money	Total prize-money	£1
2019	130	952	14	£1,555,135	£2,421,588.94	-90.28
2018	113	1074	11	£741,205.25	£1,912,467.15	-298.78
2017	109	1078	10	£1,010,206.34	£1,692,653.23	-247.14
2016	103	975	11	£767,371.55	£1,680,593.79	-336.62
2015	122	931	13	£1,024,052.53	£1,580,833.33	-176.30
2014	112	829	14	£1,257,328.64	£1,772,806.65	-101.16
2013	136	905	15	£777,659.87	£1,159,386.21	-121.29
2012	69	542	13	£517,175.66	£709,691.68	-34.43
2011	48	423	11	£297,865.68	£479,370.95	-149.06
2010	25	153	16	£87,754.32	£122,742.04	-29.60

ESCOBAR: won big handicaps at York and Ascot for David O'Meara last year

Andrew Balding

By month - 2019

	Overall			Two-year-olds			Three-year-olds			Older horses		
	W-R	%	£1	W-R	%	£1	W-R	%	£1	W-R	%	£1
January	6-40	15	-19.14	0-0	-	+0.00	5-21	24	-3.14	1-19	5	-16.00
February	2-25	8	-19.25	0-0	-	+0.00	1-11	9	-8.25	1-14	7	-11.00
March	12-33	36	+31.11	0-0	-	+0.00	9-19	47	+24.11	3-14	21	+7.00
April	15-81	19	-32.74	0-0	-	+0.00	12-57	21	-17.24	3-24	13	-15.50
May	20-143	14	-38.54	1-6	17	-1.50	12-81	15	-20.87	7-56	13	-16.17
June	14-111	13	-41.73	2-8	25	+4.80	8-65	12	-26.91	4-38	11	-19.63
July	15-98	15	-15.33	4-15	27	+11.00	7-53	13	-23.33	4-30	13	-3.00
August	14-115	12	-57.75	6-27	22	-4.20	7-56	13	-28.05	1-32	3	-25.50
September	18-102	18	+39.28	6-34	18	+35.04	7-37	19	+18.61	5-31	16	-14.38
October	9-75	12	+18.00	1-25	4	-20.50	5-35	14	+4.50	3-15	20	+34.00
November	1-18	6	-11.50	1-8	13	-1.50	0-9	-	-9.00	0-1	-	-1.00
December	0-11	-	-11.00	0-6	-	-6.00	0-2	-	-2.00	0-3	-	-3.00

By month - 2018

	Overall			Two-year-olds			Three-year-olds			Older horses		
	W-R	%	£1	W-R	%	£1	W-R	%	£1	W-R	%	£1
January	7-31	23	-10.74	0-0	-	+0.00	5-12	42	+3.96	2-19	11	-14.70
February	6-24	25	-3.68	0-0	-	+0.00	5-12	42	-1.68	1-12	8	-2.00
March	4-19	21	-9.04	0-0	-	+0.00	4-9	44	+0.96	0-10	-	-10.00
April	6-56	11	-31.25	0-0	-	+0.00	5-44	11	-20.75	1-12	8	-10.50
May	4-94	4	-74.25	0-8	-	-8.00	4-49	8	-29.25	0-37	-	-37.00
June	20-106	19	+13.10	1-14	7	-11.00	12-57	21	+20.73	7-35	20	+3.38
July	15-92	16	-32.79	5-20	25	+0.42	5-42	12	-20.88	5-30	17	-12.33
August	27-120	23	+59.45	8-44	18	+34.63	11-44	25	+18.66	8-32	25	+6.16
September	13-66	20	-6.56	3-24	13	-12.08	4-22	18	-6.10	6-20	30	+11.63
October	7-69	10	+48.25	5-32	16	+75.75	1-23	4	-18.00	1-14	7	-9.50
November	3-29	10	+13.50	1-12	8	+22.00	1-11	9	-5.50	1-6	17	-3.00
December	1-19	5	-15.25	0-7	-	-7.00	1-11	9	-7.25	0-1	-	-1.00

By month - 2017

	Overall			Two-year-olds			Three-year-olds			Older horses		
	W-R	%	£1	W-R	%	£1	W-R	%	£1	W-R	%	£1
January	4-31	13	-1.88	0-0	-	+0.00	0-8	-	-8.00	4-23	17	+6.13
February	7-35	20	-0.97	0-0	-	+0.00	2-10	20	-5.84	5-25	20	+4.88
March	5-25	20	-11.37	0-0	-	+0.00	3-8	38	-2.62	2-17	12	-8.75
April	6-52	12	-19.63	0-0	-	+0.00	4-27	15	-9.63	2-25	8	-10.00
May	13-85	15	+15.88	0-5	-	-5.00	8-45	18	-3.13	5-35	14	+24.00
June	10-74	14	-13.25	0-10	-	-10.00	6-46	13	-12.63	4-18	22	+9.38
July	10-83	12	+22.35	4-16	25	+5.75	4-48	8	-26.40	2-19	11	+43.00
August	13-89	15	+3.81	3-22	14	+2.06	8-43	19	-12.25	2-24	8	+14.00
September	16-87	18	-6.18	1-28	4	-23.00	7-33	21	-7.88	8-26	31	+24.70
October	6-66	9	-19.50	1-24	4	-11.00	4-28	14	-3.50	1-14	7	-5.00
November	3-35	9	-21.67	1-17	6	-13.00	1-10	10	-5.00	1-8	13	-3.67
December	0-10	-	-10.00	0-4	-	-4.00	0-4	-	-4.00	0-2	-	-2.00

By race type - 2019

	Overall			Two-year-olds			Three-year-olds			Older horses		
	W-R	%	£1	W-R	%	£1	W-R	%	£1	W-R	%	£1
Group	9-73	12	-3.84	1-8	13	-1.50	3-31	10	-15.09	5-34	15	+12.75
Handicap	53-451	12	-150.89	0-7	-	-7.00	32-247	13	-71.60	21-197	11	-72.29
Maiden	13-73	18	-15.48	4-36	11	-13.08	9-36	25	-1.40	0-1	-	-1.00

By race type - 2018

	Overall			Two-year-olds			Three-year-olds			Older horses		
	W-R	%	£1	W-R	%	£1	W-R	%	£1	W-R	%	£1
Group	6-56	11	-34.88	0-12	-	-12.00	1-9	11	-6.75	5-35	14	-16.13
Handicap	62-370	17	-42.35	1-19	5	-15.25	38-196	19	+8.45	23-155	15	-35.55
Maiden	9-71	13	-5.38	4-34	12	+5.63	5-37	14	-11.00	0-0	-	+0.00

By race type - 2017

	Overall			Two-year-olds			Three-year-olds			Older horses		
	W-R	%	£1	W-R	%	£1	W-R	%	£1	W-R	%	£1
Group	6-48	13	+14.13	0-7	-	-7.00	2-21	10	-15.88	4-20	20	+37.00
Handicap	50-376	13	-18.59	1-13	8	-8.00	24-184	13	-68.28	25-179	14	+57.68
Maiden	21-125	17	-61.77	2-28	7	-21.94	16-84	19	-36.21	3-13	23	-3.63

By jockey - 2019

	Overall			Two-year-olds			Three-year-olds			Older horses		
	W-R	%	£1	W-R	%	£1	W-R	%	£1	W-R	%	£1
Oisin Murphy	36-185	19	+10.61	10-39	26	+35.67	20-107	19	-5.81	6-39	15	-19.25
S De Sousa	25-114	22	-7.90	0-6	-	-6.00	17-59	29	-12.52	8-49	16	+10.63
David Probert	22-212	10	-55.83	6-44	14	+9.43	10-103	10	-37.59	6-65	9	-27.67
Joshua Bryan	10-53	19	-16.63	0-1	-	-1.00	7-26	27	-2.63	3-26	12	-13.00
William Carver	7-27	26	-1.22	1-3	33	+1.50	2-7	29	-2.09	4-17	24	-0.63
Rob Hornby	6-86	7	-52.76	2-14	14	-9.20	2-42	5	-34.56	2-30	7	-9.00
Martin Dwyer	3-27	11	+9.00	0-4	-	-4.00	2-20	10	-1.00	1-3	33	+14.00
Ben Curtis	2-4	50	+5.25	0-1	-	-1.00	2-3	67	+6.25	0-0	-	+0.00
James Doyle	2-10	20	-1.64	0-0	-	+0.00	2-6	33	+2.36	0-4	-	-4.00
J Gordon	2-12	17	+21.00	0-2	-	-2.00	2-8	25	+25.00	0-2	-	-2.00
William Cox	2-32	6	-21.50	1-3	33	+3.00	1-18	6	-13.50	0-11	-	-11.00
Filip Minarik	1-1	100	+5.50	0-0	-	+0.00	0-0	-	+0.00	1-1	100	+5.50

By jockey - 2018

	Overall			Two-year-olds			Three-year-olds			Older horses		
	W-R	%	£1	W-R	%	£1	W-R	%	£1	W-R	%	£1
Oisin Murphy	31-181	17	-33.50	5-39	13	+12.50	17-77	22	-11.51	9-65	14	-34.49
David Probert	22-157	14	+17.46	8-58	14	+51.67	9-69	13	-25.00	5-30	17	-9.21
Jason Watson	20-84	24	-12.94	1-10	10	-6.75	12-47	26	-7.89	7-27	26	+1.70
Rob Hornby	10-70	14	+7.85	2-18	11	+17.50	6-34	18	-4.15	2-18	11	-5.50
Joshua Bryan	8-52	15	-9.00	2-12	17	-6.25	4-23	17	+0.75	2-17	12	-3.50
William Cox	5-42	12	+1.45	1-3	33	+31.00	3-14	21	-8.30	1-25	4	-21.25
Graham Lee	3-10	30	+2.63	1-3	33	-0.38	2-3	67	+7.00	0-4	-	-4.00
Martin Dwyer	3-33	9	-18.33	1-5	20	-3.33	1-24	4	-21.00	1-4	25	+6.00
Franny Norton	2-6	33	+2.38	0-1	-	-1.00	1-2	50	+3.50	1-3	33	-0.13

By jockey - 2017

	Overall			Two-year-olds			Three-year-olds			Older horses		
	W-R	%	£1	W-R	%	£1	W-R	%	£1	W-R	%	£1
David Probert	30-213	14	-54.91	5-57	9	-33.94	15-86	17	-16.48	10-70	14	-4.50
Oisin Murphy	27-145	19	+8.59	3-25	12	+7.50	18-71	25	+0.24	6-49	12	+0.85
Joshua Bryan	8-41	20	-2.63	0-3	-	-3.00	3-15	20	+0.00	5-23	22	+0.38
Rob Hornby	8-75	11	-6.50	0-21	-	-21.00	5-38	13	-17.50	3-16	19	+32.00
William Cox	5-31	16	+0.58	1-4	25	-1.75	0-7	-	-7.00	4-20	20	+9.33
P J McDonald	3-8	38	+21.50	0-0	-	+0.00	0-3	-	-3.00	3-5	60	+24.50
Liam Keniry	3-40	8	-22.88	0-5	-	-5.00	3-23	13	-5.88	0-12	-	-12.00
Jim Crowley	2-5	40	+24.00	0-1	-	-1.00	1-2	50	+6.00	1-2	50	+19.00
Jimmy Quinn	2-23	9	-5.00	1-3	33	+7.00	0-13	-	-13.00	1-7	14	+1.00

By course - 2016-2019

	Overall			Two-year-olds			Three-year-olds			Older horses		
	W-R	%	£1	W-R	%	£1	W-R	%	£1	W-R	%	£1
Ascot	16-167	10	-54.00	0-17	-	-17.00	7-71	10	-35.25	9-79	11	-1.75
Ayr	3-14	21	+2.00	2-3	67	+7.50	1-3	33	+2.50	0-8	-	-8.00
Bath	9-69	13	-12.09	2-12	17	+11.25	3-42	7	-23.50	4-15	27	+0.16
Beverley	3-12	25	-2.38	0-1	-	-1.00	3-9	33	+0.63	0-2	-	-2.00
Brighton	11-58	19	-18.90	3-13	23	-5.77	4-27	15	-13.80	4-18	22	+0.67
Carlisle	4-12	33	+0.75	0-1	-	-1.00	4-10	40	+2.75	0-1	-	-1.00
Catterick	0-2	-	-2.00	0-0	-	+0.00	0-2	-	-2.00	0-0	-	+0.00
Chelmsf'd (AW)	30-194	15	-55.05	1-23	4	-18.50	21-97	22	+2.20	8-74	11	-38.75
Chepstow	10-70	14	-8.79	1-12	8	-5.50	4-42	10	-4.50	5-16	31	+1.21
Chester	37-168	22	+39.01	7-19	37	+5.29	16-85	19	-7.93	14-64	22	+41.65
Doncaster	12-67	18	+51.25	4-21	19	+23.75	6-21	29	+45.00	2-25	8	-17.50
Epsom	11-71	15	-10.04	1-8	13	-3.50	7-31	23	-1.04	3-32	9	-5.50
Ffos Las	11-46	24	+17.04	3-13	23	-5.33	7-24	29	+29.38	1-9	11	-7.00
Goodwood	19-154	12	-50.75	2-39	5	-27.25	13-59	22	+1.88	4-56	7	-25.38
Hamilton	3-13	23	-3.38	2-3	67	+2.13	1-7	14	-2.50	0-3	-	-3.00
Haydock	14-88	16	-14.35	3-8	38	+1.20	4-47	9	-16.50	7-33	21	+0.95
Kempton (AW)	38-268	14	-17.17	10-60	17	+58.50	17-127	13	-56.35	11-81	14	-19.33
Leicester	6-53	11	-28.40	0-8	-	-8.00	6-32	19	-7.40	0-13	-	-13.00
Lingfield	9-47	19	-12.56	1-7	14	-1.00	5-27	19	-14.56	3-13	23	+3.00
Lingfield (AW)	21-179	12	-92.88	0-8	-	-8.00	12-82	15	-35.88	9-89	10	-49.00
Musselburgh	0-3	-	-3.00	0-0	-	+0.00	0-2	-	-2.00	0-1	-	-1.00
Newbury	16-163	10	-20.55	5-56	9	+26.50	7-78	9	-57.05	4-29	14	+10.00
N'castle (AW)	7-38	18	-9.34	2-5	40	+5.50	3-14	21	-8.47	2-19	11	-6.38
Newmarket	15-142	11	-21.53	2-43	5	-1.50	10-56	18	+0.13	3-43	7	-20.15
Newmarket (J)	14-91	15	+4.29	3-20	15	+6.25	11-42	26	+27.04	0-29	-	-29.00
Nottingham	7-51	14	-18.94	3-17	18	-2.88	2-24	8	-19.40	2-10	20	+3.33
Pontefract	4-20	20	-5.04	2-5	40	+5.75	1-9	11	-7.17	1-6	17	-3.63
Redcar	2-18	11	-9.50	0-7	-	-7.00	2-9	22	-0.50	0-2	-	-2.00
Ripon	0-2	-	-2.00	0-0	-	+0.00	0-1	-	-1.00	0-1	-	-1.00
Salisbury	26-151	17	-10.14	11-48	23	+30.50	11-78	14	-34.23	4-25	16	-6.42
Sandown	16-124	13	+15.44	5-30	17	+15.75	6-60	10	-28.26	5-34	15	+27.95
S'well (AW)	18-90	20	-17.56	0-5	-	-5.00	11-47	23	-1.31	7-38	18	-11.25
Thirsk	3-11	27	+11.32	1-1	100	+0.57	2-10	20	+10.75	0-0	-	+0.00
Wetherby	0-7	-	-7.00	0-0	-	+0.00	0-5	-	-5.00	0-2	-	-2.00
Windsor	16-123	13	-44.31	4-24	17	-10.00	11-64	17	-1.31	1-35	3	-33.00
Wolves (AW)	23-131	18	-4.16	2-20	10	+7.80	14-69	20	-19.21	7-42	17	+7.25
Yarmouth	4-23	17	-8.25	1-2	50	+3.00	3-18	17	-8.25	0-3	-	-3.00
York	11-92	12	+35.20	0-18	-	-18.00	4-26	15	+4.20	7-48	15	+49.00

Ten-year summary

	Wins	*Runs*	*%*	*Win prize-money*	*Total prize-money*	*£1*
2019	126	852	15	£2,343,511.30	£3,601,158.03	-158.58
2018	123	772	16	£1,418,461.94	£2,601,152.21	-59.03
2017	93	677	14	£1,702,065.55	£2,565,904.52	-67.39
2016	107	731	15	£1,038,999.35	£1,672,623.97	-102.74
2015	95	755	13	£837,267.45	£1,548,715.65	-272.93
2014	119	659	18	£1,335,198.23	£2,035,497.26	-35.60
2013	99	713	14	£873,940.78	£1,356,742.43	-13.36
2012	93	712	13	£779,847.73	£1,365,377.42	-155.54
2011	70	543	13	£620,393.39	£971,676.62	-59.07
2010	78	511	15	£707,996.22	£1,116,809.38	-11.81

DONJUAN TRIUMPHANT: Andrew Balding's veteran won on Champions Day

Tim Easterby

By month - 2019

	Overall			Two-year-olds			Three-year-olds			Older horses		
	W-R	%	£1	W-R	%	£1	W-R	%	£1	W-R	%	£1
January	1-2	50	+6.50	0-0	-	+0.00	0-0	-	+0.00	1-2	50	+6.50
February	0-1	-	-1.00	0-0	-	+0.00	0-0	-	+0.00	0-1	-	-1.00
March	0-0	-	+0.00	0-0	-	+0.00	0-0	-	+0.00	0-0	-	+0.00
April	7-95	7	-12.78	1-14	7	-12.78	2-32	6	+13.50	4-49	8	-13.50
May	12-167	7	-46.00	0-23	-	-23.00	8-53	15	-2.00	4-91	4	-21.00
June	18-192	9	-48.04	1-22	5	-17.50	4-59	7	-36.92	13-111	12	+6.38
July	19-208	9	-93.13	1-36	3	-28.50	7-65	11	-16.25	11-107	10	-48.38
August	28-246	11	+6.60	5-57	9	-11.38	11-68	16	-6.40	12-121	10	+24.38
September	23-180	13	-33.83	2-55	4	-49.09	6-40	15	-17.92	15-85	18	+33.18
October	13-110	12	+36.50	3-25	12	+43.00	6-31	19	+25.88	4-54	7	-32.38
November	2-29	7	+13.00	0-10	-	-10.00	0-5	-	-5.00	2-14	14	+28.00
December	3-14	21	+17.00	0-3	-	-3.00	1-5	20	+10.00	2-6	33	+10.00

By month - 2018

	Overall			Two-year-olds			Three-year-olds			Older horses		
	W-R	%	£1	W-R	%	£1	W-R	%	£1	W-R	%	£1
January	2-6	33	+11.00	0-0	-	+0.00	0-0	-	+0.00	2-6	33	+11.00
February	0-2	-	-2.00	0-0	-	+0.00	0-0	-	+0.00	0-2	-	-2.00
March	0-2	-	-2.00	0-0	-	+0.00	0-2	-	-2.00	0-0	-	+0.00
April	2-71	3	-40.50	1-5	20	+21.00	1-29	3	-24.50	0-37	-	-37.00
May	17-130	13	-34.42	2-12	17	-4.75	7-48	15	-8.17	8-70	11	-21.50
June	27-153	18	+48.85	1-28	4	-23.00	5-39	13	-4.90	21-86	24	+76.75
July	22-172	13	+24.83	0-27	-	-27.00	10-67	15	+37.67	12-78	15	+14.16
August	17-161	11	-55.82	3-38	8	-27.00	8-51	16	+4.10	6-72	8	-32.92
September	9-116	8	-54.00	1-31	3	-27.60	3-25	12	-2.50	5-60	8	-23.90
October	13-133	10	-4.50	3-36	8	-8.00	4-24	17	+1.50	6-73	8	+2.00
November	3-33	9	-8.92	1-8	13	+9.00	0-3	-	-3.00	2-22	9	-14.92
December	0-2	-	-2.00	0-0	-	+0.00	0-0	-	+0.00	0-2	-	-2.00

By month - 2017

	Overall			Two-year-olds			Three-year-olds			Older horses		
	W-R	%	£1	W-R	%	£1	W-R	%	£1	W-R	%	£1
January	0-5	-	-5.00	0-0	-	+0.00	0-2	-	-2.00	0-3	-	-3.00
February	0-2	-	-2.00	0-0	-	+0.00	0-1	-	-1.00	0-1	-	-1.00
March	1-8	13	-4.75	0-0	-	+0.00	0-1	-	-1.00	1-7	14	-3.75
April	2-66	3	-54.00	0-6	-	-6.00	1-28	4	-22.00	1-32	3	-26.00
May	6-111	5	-74.50	0-13	-	-13.00	4-47	9	-20.50	2-51	4	-41.00
June	12-131	9	-18.05	1-18	6	-8.00	7-42	17	+14.45	4-71	6	-24.50
July	24-138	17	+88.00	3-26	12	+47.00	14-53	26	+21.00	7-59	12	+20.00
August	16-161	10	-35.50	2-45	4	-30.75	5-49	10	-26.75	9-67	13	+22.00
September	13-138	9	-46.00	2-46	4	-33.50	5-33	15	+0.00	6-59	10	-12.50
October	6-98	6	-60.25	2-28	7	-21.25	2-25	8	-12.50	2-45	4	-26.50
November	1-28	4	-17.00	0-10	-	-10.00	0-7	-	-7.00	1-11	9	+0.00
December	2-5	40	+2.50	0-0	-	+0.00	2-3	67	+4.50	0-2	-	-2.00

By race type - 2019

	Overall			Two-year-olds			Three-year-olds			Older horses		
	W-R	%	£1	W-R	%	£1	W-R	%	£1	W-R	%	£1
Group	0-5	-	-5.00	0-1	-	-1.00	0-0	-	+0.00	0-4	-	-4.00
Handicap	108-995	11	-54.16	2-63	3	-38.50	41-306	13	-10.60	65-626	10	-5.06
Maiden	5-71	7	-40.25	0-44	-	-44.00	5-24	21	+6.75	0-3	-	-3.00

By race type - 2018

	Overall			Two-year-olds			Three-year-olds			Older horses		
	W-R	%	£1	W-R	%	£1	W-R	%	£1	W-R	%	£1
Group	1-8	13	+0.00	0-3	-	-3.00	1-4	25	+4.00	0-1	-	-1.00
Handicap	96-787	12	-41.96	2-44	5	-25.00	33-245	13	+9.87	61-498	12	-26.83
Maiden	4-35	11	+4.50	1-14	7	+12.00	3-18	17	-4.50	0-3	-	-3.00

By race type - 2017

	Overall			Two-year-olds			Three-year-olds			Older horses		
	W-R	%	£1	W-R	%	£1	W-R	%	£1	W-R	%	£1
Group	1-10	10	+1.00	1-3	33	+8.00	0-0	-	+0.00	0-7	-	-7.00
Handicap	73-670	11	-121.55	3-49	6	-35.50	38-232	16	-0.80	32-389	8	-85.25
Maiden	2-78	3	-71.00	0-14	-	-14.00	2-58	3	-51.00	0-6	-	-6.00

By jockey - 2019

	Overall			Two-year-olds			Three-year-olds			Older horses		
	W-R	%	£1	W-R	%	£1	W-R	%	£1	W-R	%	£1
David Allan	58-442	13	-109.19	7-101	7	-68.74	22-135	16	-25.04	29-206	14	-15.40
D Fentiman	28-246	11	+114.46	6-63	10	+37.50	10-102	10	+47.50	12-81	15	+29.46
R Richardson	6-197	3	-145.63	0-35	-	-35.00	3-51	6	-32.13	3-111	3	-78.50
Nathan Evans	5-18	28	+7.75	0-2	-	-2.00	2-7	29	+4.88	3-9	33	+4.88
James Sullivan	5-37	14	-7.07	0-14	-	-14.00	2-10	20	-3.57	3-13	23	+10.50
D Redmond	4-52	8	-24.50	0-3	-	-3.00	1-7	14	-1.50	3-42	7	-20.00
Paul Mulrennan	3-13	23	+23.25	0-0	-	+0.00	0-1	-	-1.00	3-12	25	+24.25
Phil Dennis	3-24	13	+75.25	0-5	-	-5.00	1-6	17	-2.75	2-13	15	+83.00
Cam Hardie	3-27	11	+4.00	0-3	-	-3.00	0-9	-	-9.00	3-15	20	+16.00
Jason Hart	3-39	8	+11.50	0-4	-	-4.00	0-3	-	-3.00	3-32	9	+18.50
Daniel Tudhope	2-4	50	+8.00	0-1	-	-1.00	1-2	50	+3.50	1-1	100	+5.50
Mr W Easterby	2-8	25	+1.75	0-0	-	+0.00	1-2	50	+1.75	1-6	17	+0.00

By jockey - 2018

	Overall			Two-year-olds			Three-year-olds			Older horses		
	W-R	%	£1	W-R	%	£1	W-R	%	£1	W-R	%	£1
David Allan	46-362	13	-61.26	8-92	9	-20.35	14-99	14	-16.67	24-171	14	-24.24
R Richardson	17-221	8	-58.92	1-30	3	-24.00	5-63	8	-16.00	11-128	9	-18.92
Miss E Easterby	7-28	25	+2.42	0-0	-	+0.00	3-6	50	+3.92	4-22	18	-1.50
James Sullivan	7-48	15	+15.25	2-14	14	+2.75	3-21	14	-1.00	2-13	15	+13.50
Jason Hart	6-37	16	-10.50	0-3	-	-3.00	2-17	12	-8.00	4-17	24	+0.50
Duran Fentiman	6-100	6	-20.00	0-30	-	-30.00	2-33	6	+5.50	4-37	11	+4.50
R Dodsworth	4-30	13	+25.50	0-2	-	-2.00	2-12	17	+31.00	2-16	13	-3.50
Jamie Gormley	3-12	25	+6.00	0-0	-	+0.00	1-2	50	+6.00	2-10	20	+0.00
Nathan Evans	3-14	21	+18.00	0-4	-	-4.00	1-1	100	+4.00	2-9	22	+18.00

By jockey - 2017

	Overall			Two-year-olds			Three-year-olds			Older horses		
	W-R	%	£1	W-R	%	£1	W-R	%	£1	W-R	%	£1
David Allan	39-315	12	+34.58	6-79	8	+13.50	16-109	15	-12.43	17-127	13	+33.50
R Richardson	14-217	6	-93.25	0-40	-	-40.00	6-53	11	-18.00	8-124	6	-35.25
James Sullivan	7-45	16	-1.25	1-12	8	-8.75	6-26	23	+14.50	0-7	-	-7.00
Andrew Mullen	3-24	13	-7.13	1-4	25	+6.00	2-13	15	-6.13	0-7	-	-7.00
Duran Fentiman	3-88	3	-65.50	0-29	-	-29.00	2-30	7	-20.50	1-29	3	-16.00
Sammy Jo Bell	2-3	67	+11.50	0-0	-	+0.00	1-2	50	+8.00	1-1	100	+3.50
P J McDonald	2-4	50	+2.50	0-1	-	-1.00	1-1	100	+2.00	1-2	50	+1.50
Cam Hardie	2-27	7	-13.25	0-5	-	-5.00	2-11	18	+2.75	0-11	-	-11.00
Jason Hart	2-40	5	-32.75	1-7	14	-4.25	1-13	8	-8.50	0-20	-	-20.00

By course - 2016-2019

	Overall			Two-year-olds			Three-year-olds			Older horses		
	W-R	%	£1	W-R	%	£1	W-R	%	£1	W-R	%	£1
Ascot	3-26	12	+11.50	0-1	-	-1.00	2-6	33	+5.50	1-19	5	+7.00
Ayr	13-129	10	-1.59	0-11	-	-11.00	6-33	18	+28.00	7-85	8	-18.59
Beverley	38-333	11	-121.24	5-90	6	-67.78	18-123	15	-23.83	15-120	13	-29.63
Carlisle	28-252	11	-66.69	2-66	3	-59.40	12-68	18	+0.33	14-118	12	-7.63
Catterick	25-229	11	-61.40	3-49	6	-25.75	11-76	14	+1.23	11-104	11	-36.88
Chelmsf'd (AW)	1-19	5	-16.00	0-2	-	-2.00	1-5	20	-2.00	0-12	-	-12.00
Chester	18-126	14	+4.00	1-20	5	-15.00	4-20	20	+4.00	13-86	15	+15.00
Doncaster	12-206	6	-93.50	1-46	2	-36.00	3-41	7	-15.50	8-119	7	-42.00
Epsom	1-12	8	-7.50	0-0	-	+0.00	0-2	-	-2.00	1-10	10	-5.50
Goodwood	1-19	5	-14.00	0-2	-	-2.00	0-0	-	+0.00	1-17	6	-12.00
Hamilton	24-111	22	+22.65	3-9	33	+2.15	8-42	19	+0.25	13-60	22	+20.25
Haydock	18-201	9	-29.15	2-42	5	+12.25	7-57	12	-12.90	9-102	9	-28.50
Kempton (AW)	0-3	-	-3.00	0-1	-	-1.00	0-0	-	+0.00	0-2	-	-2.00
Leicester	4-49	8	-12.50	1-9	11	-3.00	2-19	11	+2.00	1-21	5	-11.50
Lingfield (AW)	0-2	-	-2.00	0-0	-	+0.00	0-0	-	+0.00	0-2	-	-2.00
Musselburgh	19-173	11	-45.80	4-26	15	-8.50	8-58	14	-2.80	7-89	8	-34.50
Newbury	0-7	-	-7.00	0-3	-	-3.00	0-0	-	+0.00	0-4	-	-4.00
N'castle (AW)	13-215	6	-78.13	2-60	3	-2.00	4-65	6	-44.13	7-90	8	-32.00
Newmarket	0-17	-	-17.00	0-3	-	-3.00	0-4	-	-4.00	0-10	-	-10.00
Newmarket (J)	4-22	18	-4.00	0-3	-	-3.00	3-13	23	+2.75	1-6	17	-3.75
Nottingham	6-83	7	-51.79	0-21	-	-21.00	3-18	17	+1.88	3-44	7	-32.67
Pontefract	23-194	12	-33.92	1-38	3	-30.50	10-66	15	-2.42	12-90	13	-1.00
Redcar	31-361	9	-91.84	2-93	2	-63.00	16-144	11	+3.98	13-124	10	-32.82
Ripon	42-381	11	-30.63	8-87	9	-35.72	13-116	11	+16.41	21-178	12	-11.32
Salisbury	1-1	100	+5.50	0-0	-	+0.00	0-0	-	+0.00	1-1	100	+5.50
Sandown	1-3	33	+1.50	1-1	100	+3.50	0-1	-	-1.00	0-1	-	-1.00
S'well (AW)	10-48	21	+51.13	1-4	25	+13.00	1-10	10	+5.00	8-34	24	+33.13
Thirsk	24-356	7	-124.15	3-94	3	-46.00	9-114	8	-49.65	12-148	8	-28.50
Wetherby	4-42	10	0.00	0-3	-	-3.00	2-27	7	-4.00	2-12	17	+7.00
Windsor	0-1	-	-1.00	0-0	-	+0.00	0-0	-	+0.00	0-1	-	-1.00
Wolves (AW)	13-109	12	+23.38	0-20	-	-20.00	7-43	16	-1.38	6-46	13	+44.75
Yarmouth	1-7	14	+0.50	0-2	-	-2.00	1-3	33	+4.50	0-2	-	-2.00
York	28-329	9	+12.00	5-57	9	-5.50	5-54	9	-21.50	18-218	8	+39.00

Trainer interviews start on page 6

Ten-year summary

	Wins	Runs	%	Win prize-money	Total prize-money	£1
2019	126	1244	10	£856,773.23	£1,392,889.70	-155.17
2018	118	1085	11	£944,580.92	£1,525,375.92	-174.87
2017	86	930	9	£800,912.96	£1,232,494.56	-238.55
2016	76	807	9	£472,565.89	£781,938.87	-213.08
2015	70	691	10	£354,477.64	£791,794.20	-202.16
2014	53	769	7	£346,857.09	£740,473.45	-293.98
2013	68	868	8	£470,015.75	£786,997.71	-381.88
2012	88	972	9	£687,967.28	£1,042,964.97	-344.13
2011	90	902	10	£481,298.69	£882,568.01	-81.31
2010	98	846	12	£551,995.88	£902,812.12	-200.59

COPPER KNIGHT: a Listed winner for Tim Easterby at York last year

Roger Varian

By month - 2019

	Overall			Two-year-olds			Three-year-olds			Older horses		
	W-R	%	£1	W-R	%	£1	W-R	%	£1	W-R	%	£1
January	1-9	11	+12.00	0-0	-	+0.00	1-8	13	+13.00	0-1	-	-1.00
February	1-6	17	-3.25	0-0	-	+0.00	1-4	25	-1.25	0-2	-	-2.00
March	3-11	27	-4.14	0-0	-	+0.00	2-7	29	-1.75	1-4	25	-2.39
April	17-59	29	+7.33	0-0	-	+0.00	10-41	24	-3.78	7-18	39	+11.12
May	18-96	19	+4.33	2-4	50	+2.00	9-68	13	-9.77	7-24	29	+12.10
June	17-86	20	-22.79	3-9	33	+3.38	10-51	20	-16.42	4-26	15	-9.75
July	8-64	13	-42.39	0-12	-	-12.00	8-42	19	-20.39	0-10	-	-10.00
August	15-81	19	-17.68	3-15	20	-2.38	10-49	20	-3.85	2-17	12	-11.45
September	16-85	19	-22.51	8-35	23	-13.59	8-38	21	+3.08	0-12	-	-12.00
October	14-60	23	-1.92	7-32	22	+6.70	5-23	22	-9.49	2-5	40	+0.88
November	5-32	16	-18.74	4-21	19	-12.74	1-10	10	-5.00	0-1	-	-1.00
December	1-13	8	-11.33	1-9	11	-7.33	0-3	-	-3.00	0-1	-	-1.00

By month - 2018

	Overall			Two-year-olds			Three-year-olds			Older horses		
	W-R	%	£1	W-R	%	£1	W-R	%	£1	W-R	%	£1
January	0-5	-	-5.00	0-0	-	+0.00	0-3	-	-3.00	0-2	-	-2.00
February	0-4	-	-4.00	0-0	-	+0.00	0-1	-	-1.00	0-3	-	-3.00
March	1-8	13	-6.09	0-0	-	+0.00	0-3	-	-3.00	1-5	20	-3.09
April	6-62	10	-44.75	0-0	-	+0.00	2-49	4	-44.25	4-13	31	-0.50
May	15-84	18	-3.30	0-1	-	-1.00	7-57	12	-4.38	8-26	31	+2.08
June	16-73	22	+0.90	1-7	14	-1.50	11-50	22	+10.56	4-16	25	-8.17
July	11-61	18	-24.29	2-8	25	-3.42	9-38	24	-5.87	0-15	-	-15.00
August	11-65	17	-32.42	1-16	6	-11.00	8-33	24	-11.43	2-16	13	-10.00
September	10-58	17	-12.99	3-20	15	-11.06	6-25	24	+7.57	1-13	8	-9.50
October	14-77	18	+14.03	8-39	21	+22.78	5-28	18	-7.75	1-10	10	-1.00
November	10-46	22	+4.91	6-34	18	-10.34	4-9	44	+18.25	0-3	-	-3.00
December	3-19	16	-7.93	2-15	13	-8.43	1-4	25	+0.50	0-0	-	+0.00

By month - 2017

	Overall			Two-year-olds			Three-year-olds			Older horses		
	W-R	%	£1	W-R	%	£1	W-R	%	£1	W-R	%	£1
January	0-7	-	-7.00	0-0	-	+0.00	0-1	-	-1.00	0-6	-	-6.00
February	0-0	-	+0.00	0-0	-	+0.00	0-0	-	+0.00	0-0	-	+0.00
March	1-1	100	+0.05	0-0	-	+0.00	0-0	-	+0.00	1-1	100	+0.05
April	15-41	37	+3.17	0-1	-	-1.00	11-27	41	+0.80	4-13	31	+3.38
May	17-68	25	-3.48	2-6	33	+1.13	9-37	24	-1.40	6-25	24	-3.20
June	14-78	18	-34.38	2-6	33	-0.75	9-50	18	-19.88	3-22	14	-13.75
July	19-83	23	-22.38	2-13	15	-6.04	10-45	22	-13.83	7-25	28	-2.51
August	10-94	11	-46.38	1-25	4	-22.25	7-49	14	-11.71	2-20	10	-12.42
September	12-74	16	-16.40	2-24	8	-7.25	8-37	22	-0.88	2-13	15	-8.27
October	13-72	18	+16.09	4-36	11	+2.73	8-27	30	+19.48	1-9	11	-6.13
November	6-30	20	-2.19	4-20	20	-4.94	0-4	-	-4.00	2-6	33	+6.75
December	2-7	29	-1.67	1-5	20	-1.50	1-1	100	+0.83	0-1	-	-1.00

By race type - 2019

	Overall			Two-year-olds			Three-year-olds			Older horses		
	W-R	%	£1	W-R	%	£1	W-R	%	£1	W-R	%	£1
Group	9-63	14	-9.16	3-10	30	+0.62	2-21	10	-1.66	4-32	13	-8.12
Handicap	46-263	17	-51.50	1-13	8	-1.00	30-188	16	-50.05	15-62	24	-0.45
Maiden	9-60	15	-39.50	5-35	14	-23.46	4-24	17	-15.04	0-1	-	-1.00

By race type - 2018

	Overall			Two-year-olds			Three-year-olds			Older horses		
	W-R	%	£1	W-R	%	£1	W-R	%	£1	W-R	%	£1
Group	5-31	16	-5.00	1-4	25	+9.00	1-15	7	-11.25	3-12	25	-2.75
Handicap	35-215	16	-73.42	2-7	29	+2.00	20-120	17	-37.17	13-88	15	-38.25
Maiden	10-69	14	-13.01	5-36	14	+2.24	5-32	16	-14.25	0-1	-	-1.00

By race type - 2017

	Overall			Two-year-olds			Three-year-olds			Older horses		
	W-R	%	£1	W-R	%	£1	W-R	%	£1	W-R	%	£1
Group	2-34	6	-5.38	1-6	17	+20.00	1-13	8	-10.38	0-15	-	-15.00
Handicap	49-228	21	-12.32	0-7	-	-7.00	29-132	22	+15.79	20-89	22	-21.11
Maiden	30-145	21	-70.62	2-35	6	-29.13	26-104	25	-38.92	2-6	33	-2.58

By jockey - 2019

	Overall			Two-year-olds			Three-year-olds			Older horses		
	W-R	%	£1	W-R	%	£1	W-R	%	£1	W-R	%	£1
Andrea Atzeni	42-203	21	-1.11	5-39	13	-14.89	21-106	20	-1.43	16-58	28	+15.21
Jack Mitchell	24-111	22	-0.27	7-28	25	-8.89	14-76	18	+6.75	3-7	43	+1.88
David Egan	21-148	14	-71.77	6-34	18	-7.75	14-89	16	-41.39	1-25	4	-22.63
Jim Crowley	13-29	45	+0.60	5-9	56	+2.60	7-16	44	-0.80	1-4	25	-1.20
Dane O'Neill	5-16	31	+6.75	1-2	50	+6.00	3-9	33	+1.75	1-5	20	-1.00
William Buick	2-7	29	-2.38	2-3	67	+1.63	0-2	-	-2.00	0-2	-	-2.00
Charlie Bennett	2-10	20	-3.50	0-1	-	-1.00	2-8	25	-1.50	0-1	-	-1.00
James Sullivan	1-1	100	+5.00	1-1	100	+5.00	0-0	-	+0.00	0-0	-	+0.00
Nicola Currie	1-1	100	+3.00	0-0	-	+0.00	1-1	100	+3.00	0-0	-	+0.00
S De Sousa	1-2	50	-0.67	1-2	50	-0.67	0-0	-	+0.00	0-0	-	+0.00
Daniel Tudhope	1-5	20	-2.75	0-0	-	+0.00	1-3	33	-0.75	0-2	-	-2.00
Rossa Ryan	1-5	20	+4.00	0-0	-	+0.00	1-4	25	+5.00	0-1	-	-1.00

By jockey - 2018

	Overall			Two-year-olds			Three-year-olds			Older horses		
	W-R	%	£1	W-R	%	£1	W-R	%	£1	W-R	%	£1
Andrea Atzeni	38-217	18	-88.93	5-41	12	-27.15	21-120	18	-39.10	12-56	21	-22.68
David Egan	22-121	18	+19.98	7-31	23	+21.53	14-69	20	+14.45	1-21	5	-16.00
Jack Mitchell	20-114	18	-15.44	6-43	14	-18.17	9-53	17	+8.48	5-18	28	-5.75
Jim Crowley	8-31	26	-8.71	2-7	29	-1.68	5-17	29	-3.78	1-7	14	-3.25
Tony Hamilton	1-1	100	+3.00	0-0	-	+0.00	1-1	100	+3.00	0-0	-	+0.00
James Doyle	1-2	50	+7.00	0-0	-	+0.00	0-0	-	+0.00	1-2	50	+7.00
Kieran Shoemark	1-2	50	+5.00	0-1	-	-1.00	1-1	100	+6.00	0-0	-	+0.00
William Buick	1-2	50	+11.00	1-2	50	+11.00	0-0	-	+0.00	0-0	-	+0.00
Daniel Tudhope	1-3	33	+0.75	1-2	50	+1.75	0-1	-	-1.00	0-0	-	+0.00

By jockey - 2017

	Overall			Two-year-olds			Three-year-olds			Older horses		
	W-R	%	£1	W-R	%	£1	W-R	%	£1	W-R	%	£1
Andrea Atzeni	51-218	23	-3.60	9-54	17	+12.44	29-101	29	+4.75	13-63	21	-20.79
S De Sousa	21-78	27	-5.03	2-16	13	-10.63	15-46	33	+10.74	4-16	25	-5.15
Jack Mitchell	18-93	19	-6.93	5-35	14	-16.44	10-37	27	+19.63	3-21	14	-10.13
Harry Bentley	6-52	12	-37.51	0-11	-	-11.00	4-29	14	-19.81	2-12	17	-6.70
Cameron Noble	3-12	25	-1.50	0-0	-	+0.00	1-5	20	-1.50	2-7	29	+0.00
Jim Crowley	3-25	12	-4.75	1-7	14	-3.25	1-15	7	-7.50	1-3	33	+6.00
Dane O'Neill	2-9	22	-4.90	1-5	20	-3.00	1-3	33	-0.90	0-1	-	-1.00
Daniel Tudhope	1-3	33	+0.75	0-0	-	+0.00	0-2	-	-2.00	1-1	100	+2.75
Ryan Moore	1-3	33	-1.09	0-0	-	+0.00	0-0	-	+0.00	1-3	33	-1.09

By course - 2016-2019

	Overall			Two-year-olds			Three-year-olds			Older horses		
	W-R	%	£1	W-R	%	£1	W-R	%	£1	W-R	%	£1
Ascot	16-124	13	-46.27	2-20	10	-10.00	5-43	12	-20.30	9-61	15	-15.97
Ayr	5-13	38	+3.43	0-1	-	-1.00	2-4	50	+7.00	3-8	38	-2.57
Bath	9-23	39	0.00	2-4	50	+0.38	4-15	27	-6.87	3-4	75	+6.50
Beverley	3-9	33	-1.69	2-3	67	+2.58	1-5	20	-3.27	0-1	-	-1.00
Brighton	2-17	12	-12.92	0-3	-	-3.00	2-13	15	-8.92	0-1	-	-1.00
Carlisle	1-9	11	-7.92	0-0	-	+0.00	0-7	-	-7.00	1-2	50	-0.92
Catterick	0-8	-	-8.00	0-1	-	-1.00	0-7	-	-7.00	0-0	-	+0.00
Chelmsf'd (AW)	14-118	12	-66.46	4-28	14	-11.02	8-65	12	-36.87	2-25	8	-18.57
Chepstow	2-11	18	-6.00	1-2	50	+0.75	1-8	13	-5.75	0-1	-	-1.00
Chester	4-30	13	-18.50	0-1	-	-1.00	4-20	20	-8.50	0-9	-	-9.00
Doncaster	32-129	25	-4.93	5-30	17	-6.25	16-63	25	-11.82	11-36	31	+13.14
Epsom	9-27	33	+17.38	0-2	-	-2.00	3-10	30	+6.90	6-15	40	+12.48
Ffos Las	2-5	40	-0.45	1-1	100	+0.30	0-3	-	-3.00	1-1	100	+2.25
Goodwood	10-83	12	-35.50	2-15	13	-5.00	5-37	14	-14.00	3-31	10	-16.50
Hamilton	4-13	31	-4.82	1-1	100	+0.36	3-10	30	-3.18	0-2	-	-2.00
Haydock	6-77	8	-59.66	2-16	13	-8.50	3-44	7	-35.73	1-17	6	-15.43
Kempton (AW)	51-219	23	+9.56	17-83	20	+5.80	28-112	25	+7.10	6-24	25	-3.34
Leicester	12-64	19	-21.38	2-18	11	-13.55	8-39	21	-6.45	2-7	29	-1.38
Lingfield	10-35	29	-2.25	2-7	29	+2.25	6-21	29	-5.37	2-7	29	+0.88
Lingfield (AW)	19-83	23	+11.84	4-17	24	+3.00	12-45	27	+18.54	3-21	14	-9.70
Musselburgh	0-4	-	-4.00	0-0	-	+0.00	0-2	-	-2.00	0-2	-	-2.00
Newbury	12-93	13	-24.00	5-33	15	-13.38	5-47	11	-8.88	2-13	15	-1.75
N'castle (AW)	27-120	23	-32.51	6-41	15	-25.12	16-54	30	+2.99	5-25	20	-10.38
Newmarket	29-184	16	-2.66	9-56	16	+36.13	16-88	18	-18.53	4-40	10	-20.25
Newmarket (J)	9-101	9	-49.75	0-23	-	-23.00	5-56	9	-22.00	4-22	18	-4.75
Nottingham	15-93	16	-19.13	5-33	15	-4.98	7-45	16	-10.13	3-15	20	-4.03
Pontefract	2-16	13	-8.00	0-2	-	-2.00	2-9	22	-1.00	0-5	-	-5.00
Redcar	7-28	25	-3.54	2-5	40	+4.00	5-18	28	-2.54	0-5	-	-5.00
Ripon	10-33	30	-4.21	1-3	33	-0.25	6-19	32	-1.01	3-11	27	-2.95
Salisbury	10-61	16	-5.53	4-19	21	-4.65	6-40	15	+1.11	0-2	-	-2.00
Sandown	12-66	18	-19.13	0-10	-	-10.00	10-42	24	-1.00	2-14	14	-8.13
S'well (AW)	2-12	17	-8.25	0-0	-	+0.00	2-9	22	-5.25	0-3	-	-3.00
Thirsk	3-22	14	-10.75	0-2	-	-2.00	3-18	17	-6.75	0-2	-	-2.00
Wetherby	1-4	25	-2.33	0-0	-	+0.00	0-3	-	-3.00	1-1	100	+0.67
Windsor	20-66	30	-2.91	0-6	-	-6.00	13-46	28	-7.82	7-14	50	+10.91
Wolves (AW)	27-133	20	-5.45	5-34	15	-15.09	18-80	23	+19.43	4-19	21	-9.79
Yarmouth	20-95	21	-17.27	7-38	18	-7.99	9-46	20	-9.00	4-11	36	-0.27
York	11-89	12	-33.50	2-11	18	-3.50	3-25	12	-0.50	6-53	11	-29.50

Ten-year summary

	Wins	Runs	%	Win prize-money	Total prize-money	£1
2019	116	602	19	£1,796,113.93	£2,662,806.36	-121.08
2018	106	603	18	£1,295,949.54	£2,034,904.77	-127.45
2017	109	558	20	£1,217,847.83	£1,913,778.74	-117.57
2016	97	554	18	£1,788,831.62	£2,394,852.99	-141.34
2015	100	474	21	£887,554.86	£1,541,464.56	-21.60
2014	78	471	17	£1,374,851.71	£2,252,219.09	-80.70
2013	89	402	22	£921,239.74	£1,332,296.98	+19.63
2012	72	398	18	£532,154.46	£877,983.27	-55.48
2011	53	272	19	£387,237.31	£702,386.72	+56.94

CAPE BYRON: part of a Saturday double at Royal Ascot for Roger Varian

Top trainers by winners (Turf)

All runs				First time out			Horses		
Won	Ran	%	Trainer	Won	Ran	%	Won	Ran	%
180	995	18	**Mark Johnston**	35	228	15	105	228	46
142	1204	12	**Richard Fahey**	31	251	12	106	251	42
110	932	12	**Richard Hannon**	23	230	10	75	230	33
108	1123	10	**Tim Easterby**	8	175	5	70	175	40
105	438	24	**John Gosden**	37	163	23	69	163	42
100	461	22	**William Haggas**	29	156	19	68	156	44
95	675	14	**David O'Meara**	9	126	7	54	126	43
82	585	14	**Andrew Balding**	22	163	13	65	163	40
73	408	18	**Roger Varian**	28	142	20	57	142	40
67	373	18	**Ralph Beckett**	14	114	12	40	114	35
67	402	17	**Archie Watson**	20	119	17	47	119	39
59	532	11	**Keith Dalgleish**	11	97	11	35	97	36
56	283	20	**Sir Michael Stoute**	19	101	19	40	101	40
56	430	13	**Kevin Ryan**	15	118	13	38	118	32
53	510	10	**Mick Channon**	4	99	4	37	99	37
51	208	25	**Charlie Appleby**	23	90	26	40	90	44
50	218	23	**Saeed bin Suroor**	17	90	19	39	90	43
49	352	14	**Tom Dascombe**	9	78	12	34	78	44
49	364	13	**Clive Cox**	12	104	12	39	104	38
45	339	13	**Charles Hills**	9	97	9	34	97	35
43	381	11	**Ian Williams**	6	83	7	31	83	37
41	337	12	**Stuart Williams**	5	67	7	28	67	42
41	353	12	**Tony Carroll**	6	84	7	27	84	32
39	380	10	**K R Burke**	12	107	11	31	107	29
39	385	10	**Roger Fell**	2	60	3	25	60	42
36	260	14	**Michael Bell**	5	81	6	24	81	30
34	312	11	**Nigel Tinkler**	2	46	4	17	46	37
34	383	9	**Michael Dods**	6	89	7	20	89	22
33	190	17	**Roger Charlton**	9	76	12	24	76	32
33	279	12	**Eve Johnson Houghton**	6	68	9	22	68	32
32	127	25	**James Tate**	15	48	31	21	48	44
32	282	11	**Paul Midgley**	3	44	7	22	44	50
31	250	12	**Ed Walker**	6	71	8	23	71	32
30	159	19	**Simon Crisford**	8	65	12	20	65	31
30	207	14	**Hugo Palmer**	4	73	5	20	73	27
29	210	14	**David Simcock**	7	82	9	23	82	28
29	332	9	**Michael Appleby**	7	85	8	18	85	21
27	264	10	**John Quinn**	5	58	9	18	58	31
26	157	17	**Jedd O'Keeffe**	5	36	14	15	36	42
26	271	10	**David Evans**	2	66	3	20	66	30
26	353	7	**Ruth Carr**	2	56	4	16	56	29
25	157	16	**James Fanshawe**	7	56	13	19	56	34
25	216	12	**Rod Millman**	2	38	5	17	38	45
24	237	10	**Iain Jardine**	6	50	12	15	50	30
22	208	11	**Gary Moore**	6	63	10	18	63	29
21	182	12	**Declan Carroll**	1	33	3	14	33	42
21	331	6	**Michael Easterby**	2	85	2	19	85	22

Top trainers by prize-money (Turf)

Total prize-money	Trainer	Win prize-money	Wins	Class 1-3 Won	Class 1-3 Ran	Class 1-3 %	Class 4-6 Won	Class 4-6 Ran	Class 4-6 %
£7,546,107	**A P O'Brien**	£4,351,897	20	19	197	10	1	6	17
£7,020,737	**John Gosden**	£5,547,063	105	55	258	21	50	180	28
£4,525,683	**Mark Johnston**	£2,575,913	180	77	505	15	103	490	21
£3,310,478	**Richard Hannon**	£2,215,417	110	45	379	12	65	553	12
£3,182,053	**Sir Michael Stoute**	£1,588,386	56	30	158	19	26	125	21
£3,092,220	**Andrew Balding**	£1,969,594	82	42	301	14	40	284	14
£2,613,653	**William Haggas**	£1,317,952	100	38	236	16	62	225	28
£2,302,561	**Roger Varian**	£1,584,395	73	37	227	16	36	181	20
£2,172,371	**Richard Fahey**	£1,182,712	142	31	430	7	111	774	14
£2,062,566	**David O'Meara**	£1,350,406	95	33	310	11	62	365	17
£2,045,767	**Charlie Appleby**	£1,599,691	51	22	135	16	29	73	40
£1,405,581	**Charles Hills**	£1,062,426	45	16	145	11	29	194	15
£1,268,376	**Tim Easterby**	£772,089	108	18	244	7	90	879	10
£1,100,052	**Ralph Beckett**	£688,719	67	26	153	17	41	220	19
£1,093,061	**Kevin Ryan**	£619,651	56	20	181	11	36	249	14
£1,004,939	**Clive Cox**	£558,490	49	14	130	11	35	234	15
£914,509	**K R Burke**	£452,550	39	10	111	9	29	269	11
£898,251	**Saeed bin Suroor**	£504,846	50	23	98	23	27	120	23
£876,158	**Tom Dascombe**	£503,238	49	15	158	9	34	194	18
£797,311	**Roger Charlton**	£612,671	33	7	61	11	26	129	20
£740,107	**Michael Dods**	£418,223	34	12	100	12	22	283	8
£730,525	**Archie Watson**	£294,734	67	4	89	4	63	313	20
£714,370	**Keith Dalgleish**	£418,453	59	11	116	9	48	416	12
£686,474	**Ian Williams**	£398,117	43	13	167	8	30	214	14
£685,777	**Martyn Meade**	£428,063	12	8	42	19	4	47	9
£668,664	**David Simcock**	£461,945	29	14	92	15	15	118	13
£611,414	**G M Lyons**	£602,782	2	1	8	13	1	2	50
£596,962	**James Tate**	£412,194	32	13	53	25	19	74	26
£585,689	**Mick Channon**	£294,097	53	9	147	6	44	363	12
£573,960	**John Quinn**	£279,613	27	7	64	11	20	200	10
£546,225	**Stuart Williams**	£339,690	41	15	134	11	26	203	13
£520,050	**F-H Graffard**	£283,550	1	1	3	33	0	0	-
£496,587	**Mitsuru Hashida**	£340,260	1	1	3	33	0	0	-
£495,115	**David Elsworth**	£294,320	6	4	43	9	2	51	4
£488,744	**Ed Walker**	£331,587	31	13	100	12	18	141	13
£482,543	**Roger Fell**	£276,600	39	4	93	4	35	292	12
£476,922	**Eve Johnson Houghton**	£244,437	33	7	80	9	26	199	13
£470,370	**Simon Crisford**	£327,163	30	10	69	14	20	90	22
£446,206	**Michael Appleby**	£245,414	29	9	90	10	20	242	8
£445,637	**Hughie Morrison**	£263,400	18	6	76	8	12	108	11
£429,656	**Alan King**	£253,563	19	6	57	11	13	97	13
£423,582	**Hugo Palmer**	£190,909	30	6	75	8	24	132	18
£413,018	**A Fabre**	£155,953	1	1	8	13	0	0	-
£397,045	**Nigel Tinkler**	£207,800	34	5	80	6	29	232	13
£393,220	**Michael Bell**	£208,970	36	6	83	7	30	177	17
£383,081	**Amanda Perrett**	£143,971	17	8	86	9	9	86	10
£377,448	**Kevin Prendergast**	£0	0	0	2	-	0	0	-

Top trainers by winners (AW)

All runs				First time out			Horses		
Won	Ran	%	Trainer	Won	Ran	%	Won	Ran	%
87	276	32	**John Gosden**	53	157	34	72	157	46
70	590	12	**Michael Appleby**	15	136	11	42	136	31
69	464	15	**Mark Johnston**	26	202	13	52	202	26
66	374	18	**Archie Watson**	26	128	20	47	128	37
44	267	16	**Andrew Balding**	23	116	20	38	116	33
43	194	22	**Roger Varian**	31	104	30	40	104	38
43	354	12	**Richard Hannon**	26	179	15	37	179	21
42	185	23	**William Haggas**	26	96	27	36	96	38
41	328	13	**David Evans**	7	69	10	22	69	32
40	179	22	**James Tate**	15	65	23	27	65	42
37	232	16	**Richard Hughes**	12	83	14	31	83	37
36	310	12	**Richard Fahey**	14	150	9	29	150	19
35	277	13	**David O'Meara**	14	90	16	28	90	31
33	240	14	**Stuart Williams**	12	67	18	23	67	34
33	303	11	**Marco Botti**	10	88	11	28	88	32
33	316	10	**Tony Carroll**	7	90	8	22	90	24
31	128	24	**Saeed bin Suroor**	18	75	24	28	75	37
29	203	14	**K R Burke**	11	84	13	21	84	25
28	112	25	**Sir Michael Stoute**	14	72	19	23	72	32
28	170	16	**James Fanshawe**	9	62	15	18	62	29
26	236	11	**Dean Ivory**	6	58	10	14	58	24
25	166	15	**Ed Walker**	9	65	14	20	65	31
25	235	11	**Antony Brittain**	3	28	11	14	28	50
24	194	12	**David Loughnane**	10	48	21	21	48	44
24	265	9	**John Butler**	4	57	7	19	57	33
23	141	16	**Charles Hills**	6	66	9	17	66	26
23	176	13	**Hugo Palmer**	12	83	14	17	83	20
23	213	11	**David Simcock**	7	85	8	18	85	21
23	222	10	**Jamie Osborne**	7	78	9	17	78	22
22	104	21	**Simon Crisford**	11	55	20	20	55	36
22	177	12	**Robert Cowell**	6	65	9	15	65	23
22	183	12	**Sir Mark Prescott Bt**	7	61	11	16	61	26
22	203	11	**Clive Cox**	11	94	12	17	94	18
21	134	16	**Roger Charlton**	11	71	15	16	71	23
21	159	13	**Keith Dalgleish**	7	64	11	13	64	20
20	67	30	**Charlie Appleby**	13	47	28	17	47	36
19	173	11	**Roger Fell**	4	52	8	17	52	33
19	205	9	**Charlie Wallis**	0	31	-	13	31	42
18	105	17	**Tom Dascombe**	10	49	20	15	49	31
18	112	16	**Ben Haslam**	4	36	11	12	36	33
18	121	15	**Tim Easterby**	8	77	10	13	77	17
17	81	21	**Michael Wigham**	3	19	16	7	19	37
17	166	10	**Shaun Keightley**	2	29	7	11	29	38
17	215	8	**Alexandra Dunn**	3	47	6	11	47	23
17	226	8	**Derek Shaw**	1	42	2	11	42	26
16	122	13	**Charlie Fellowes**	7	48	15	13	48	27
16	138	12	**Kevin Frost**	5	39	13	11	39	28

Top trainers by prize-money (AW)

Total prize-money	Trainer	Win prize-money	Wins	Class 1-3			Class 4-6		
				Won	Ran	%	Won	Ran	%
£979,492	**John Gosden**	£735,071	87	22	58	38	65	218	30
£873,978	**Mark Johnston**	£598,530	69	14	101	14	55	363	15
£701,780	**Richard Hannon**	£517,546	43	15	62	24	28	292	10
£656,592	**Michael Appleby**	£407,428	70	16	94	17	52	489	11
£539,522	**Archie Watson**	£373,568	66	9	59	15	57	315	18
£511,828	**William Haggas**	£317,967	42	11	56	20	31	129	24
£508,938	**Andrew Balding**	£373,917	44	7	54	13	37	212	17
£433,141	**Stuart Williams**	£237,773	33	11	81	14	21	156	13
£373,154	**Richard Fahey**	£208,477	36	7	47	15	29	263	11
£361,509	**Hugo Palmer**	£254,582	23	7	46	15	16	130	12
£360,245	**Roger Varian**	£211,719	43	4	40	10	39	153	25
£359,023	**David O'Meara**	£204,729	35	10	92	11	25	185	14
£329,136	**James Tate**	£247,735	40	7	39	18	33	140	24
£298,534	**Sir Michael Stoute**	£227,406	28	12	32	38	16	80	20
£295,379	**Saeed bin Suroor**	£220,199	31	10	43	23	21	85	25
£289,219	**Richard Hughes**	£166,084	37	3	32	9	34	200	17
£269,717	**Tom Dascombe**	£208,848	18	6	27	22	12	78	15
£266,747	**Clive Cox**	£175,084	22	6	31	19	16	172	9
£265,702	**Marco Botti**	£147,283	33	2	32	6	31	271	11
£263,066	**David Simcock**	£154,041	23	7	60	12	16	153	10
£258,418	**James Fanshawe**	£154,109	28	4	41	10	24	129	19
£255,532	**Robert Cowell**	£160,279	22	8	45	18	14	130	11
£251,539	**Tony Carroll**	£144,220	33	3	30	10	29	270	11
£239,765	**Ed Walker**	£166,091	25	6	20	30	19	146	13
£232,582	**David Evans**	£135,978	41	0	28	-	41	296	14
£220,277	**Roger Charlton**	£121,884	21	1	20	5	20	114	18
£219,111	**Alan King**	£155,351	14	3	30	10	11	92	12
£217,423	**Charles Hills**	£160,690	23	3	18	17	20	123	16
£201,345	**Dean Ivory**	£116,248	26	2	35	6	24	194	12
£194,509	**Charlie Fellowes**	£123,302	16	2	22	9	14	99	14
£190,535	**K R Burke**	£112,753	29	1	18	6	28	185	15
£177,355	**David Loughnane**	£108,198	24	1	14	7	23	180	13
£177,213	**Simon Crisford**	£123,662	22	4	21	19	18	83	22
£175,087	**Keith Dalgleish**	£104,590	21	5	40	13	16	119	13
£171,551	**Sir Mark Prescott Bt**	£99,288	22	1	7	14	21	176	12
£170,470	**Antony Brittain**	£90,792	25	0	2	-	25	230	11
£161,714	**Jamie Osborne**	£100,357	23	2	20	10	21	201	10
£148,942	**John Butler**	£86,671	24	0	1	-	24	256	9
£148,732	**Charlie Wallis**	£78,922	19	3	13	23	15	185	8
£145,565	**Charlie Appleby**	£88,582	20	1	12	8	19	55	35
£142,749	**Ralph Beckett**	£74,588	15	1	24	4	14	120	12
£138,589	**Roger Fell**	£78,256	19	0	14	-	19	159	12
£136,423	**Jane Chapple-Hyam**	£84,424	14	3	29	10	11	93	12
£136,095	**Kevin Frost**	£72,203	16	3	11	27	13	123	11
£134,441	**A P O'Brien**	£39,373	4	2	15	13	2	2	100
£133,677	**Richard Spencer**	£72,201	9	3	22	14	6	92	7
£132,083	**Eve Johnson Houghton**	£86,758	11	2	20	10	9	83	11

Top jockeys (Turf)

Won	Ran	%	Jockey	Best Trainer	Won	Ran
133	751	18	**Oisin Murphy**	Andrew Balding	24	142
129	647	20	**Daniel Tudhope**	David O'Meara	50	264
83	581	14	**Tom Marquand**	William Haggas	16	61
82	590	14	**Ben Curtis**	Roger Fell	21	148
80	496	16	**Silvestre De Sousa**	Andrew Balding	19	93
78	463	17	**Joe Fanning**	Mark Johnston	51	248
76	420	18	**James Doyle**	Charlie Appleby	21	89
73	562	13	**David Allan**	Tim Easterby	57	412
72	383	19	**Jim Crowley**	Charles Hills	12	39
69	483	14	**Jason Watson**	Roger Charlton	24	128
67	457	15	**Harry Bentley**	Ralph Beckett	35	216
67	484	14	**P J McDonald**	James Tate	14	49
66	490	13	**Paul Hanagan**	Richard Fahey	38	272
63	439	14	**Franny Norton**	Mark Johnston	44	262
60	369	16	**Ryan Moore**	Sir Michael Stoute	16	83
57	426	13	**Richard Kingscote**	Tom Dascombe	26	187
55	360	15	**Adam Kirby**	Clive Cox	26	153
55	462	12	**Graham Lee**	Bryan Smart	8	80
52	231	23	**Frankie Dettori**	John Gosden	37	138
52	362	14	**Andrea Atzeni**	Roger Varian	30	148
51	422	12	**Jason Hart**	John Quinn	20	154
51	523	10	**David Probert**	Andrew Balding	17	137
46	513	9	**Sean Davis**	Richard Fahey	25	261
45	351	13	**Hollie Doyle**	Archie Watson	20	117
44	329	13	**Rossa Ryan**	Richard Hannon	12	112
43	331	13	**Sean Levey**	Richard Hannon	29	210
43	473	9	**David Egan**	Roger Varian	14	118
42	292	14	**Cieren Fallon**	George Baker	7	20
41	236	17	**Dane O'Neill**	Simon Crisford	6	13
39	279	14	**Hector Crouch**	Clive Cox	12	95
38	247	15	**Jamie Spencer**	David Simcock	14	57
38	291	13	**Robert Havlin**	John Gosden	34	158
36	450	8	**Paul Mulrennan**	Michael Dods	12	128
35	232	15	**Jack Mitchell**	Roger Varian	11	55
35	344	10	**Kevin Stott**	Kevin Ryan	18	129
33	160	21	**William Buick**	Charlie Appleby	18	72
33	293	11	**Kieran O'Neill**	John Gosden	10	36
32	220	15	**Pat Cosgrave**	Saeed bin Suroor	7	30
32	299	11	**Tony Hamilton**	Richard Fahey	32	257
32	406	8	**Tom Eaves**	Kevin Ryan	15	123
31	245	13	**Pat Dobbs**	Richard Hannon	14	96
31	334	9	**Charles Bishop**	Eve Johnson Houghton	21	160
30	214	14	**Clifford Lee**	K R Burke	13	107
30	374	8	**James Sullivan**	Ruth Carr	10	167
29	278	10	**Liam Keniry**	Ed Walker	12	89
28	187	15	**Harrison Shaw**	Rebecca Menzies	6	10
28	325	9	**Rob Hornby**	Ralph Beckett	7	33
27	261	10	**Martin Dwyer**	Dean Ivory	6	18

Top jockeys (AW)

Won	Ran	%	Jockey	Best Trainer	Won	Ran
87	355	25	**Oisin Murphy**	Andrew Balding	12	43
82	906	9	**Luke Morris**	Sir Mark Prescott Bt	16	132
71	435	16	**Adam Kirby**	Clive Cox	13	83
71	468	15	**Hollie Doyle**	Archie Watson	26	120
65	417	16	**P J McDonald**	James Tate	18	68
61	686	9	**David Probert**	Ronald Harris	7	64
57	347	16	**Joe Fanning**	Mark Johnston	30	143
55	326	17	**Ben Curtis**	K R Burke	8	34
54	192	28	**Jim Crowley**	Owen Burrows	10	29
54	289	19	**Jack Mitchell**	Roger Varian	13	56
53	349	15	**Robert Havlin**	John Gosden	40	139
53	473	11	**Tom Marquand**	Richard Hannon	9	45
49	312	16	**Richard Kingscote**	Tom Dascombe	14	64
38	471	8	**Kieran O'Neill**	John Gosden	8	43
37	279	13	**Jason Hart**	John Quinn	7	60
35	411	9	**Shane Kelly**	Richard Hughes	22	127
34	215	16	**David Egan**	Roger Varian	7	30
31	252	12	**Alistair Rawlinson**	Michael Appleby	26	194
31	346	9	**Nicola Currie**	Jamie Osborne	16	124
30	145	21	**Daniel Tudhope**	William Haggas	6	12
29	141	21	**James Doyle**	Hugo Palmer	7	27
29	309	9	**Callum Shepherd**	Mick Channon	4	37
28	261	11	**Jason Watson**	Roger Charlton	10	76
28	261	11	**Franny Norton**	Michael Wigham	10	34
28	370	8	**Cam Hardie**	Antony Brittain	16	179
27	294	9	**Rob Hornby**	Jonathan Portman	5	54
26	168	15	**Barry McHugh**	Richard Fahey	9	37
26	283	9	**Andrew Mullen**	Ben Haslam	12	73
26	284	9	**Phil Dennis**	David C Griffiths	4	38
25	265	9	**Stevie Donohoe**	Charlie Fellowes	6	53
24	118	20	**Andrea Atzeni**	Roger Varian	12	55
24	230	10	**Hector Crouch**	Clive Cox	7	62
23	124	19	**Silvestre De Sousa**	Andrew Balding	6	21
23	154	15	**Sean Levey**	Richard Hannon	13	92
23	173	13	**Clifford Lee**	K R Burke	9	66
23	247	9	**Daniel Muscutt**	Marco Botti	6	35
22	108	20	**Nicky Mackay**	John Gosden	11	34
21	144	15	**Callum Rodriguez**	Keith Dalgleish	8	52
21	211	10	**George Wood**	James Fanshawe	12	64
21	218	10	**Paul Mulrennan**	Archie Watson	3	4
21	292	7	**Rossa Ryan**	Alexandra Dunn	5	62
20	187	11	**Cieren Fallon**	Charles Hills	4	10
20	278	7	**Josephine Gordon**	Shaun Keightley	9	69
19	323	6	**Liam Keniry**	Ed Walker	6	61
17	89	19	**Joshua Bryan**	Andrew Balding	7	26
17	126	13	**Robert Winston**	Dean Ivory	6	25
17	177	10	**Martin Dwyer**	Dean Ivory	4	30
17	252	7	**Joey Haynes**	Dean Ivory	4	37

Group 1 records

Year	Winner	Age (if all-aged race)	Trainer	Jockey	SP	draw/ran

2,000 Guineas (1m) Newmarket

Year	Winner	Age	Trainer	Jockey	SP	draw/ran
2010	**Makfi**		M Delzangles	C-P Lemaire	33-1	5/19
2011	**Frankel**		Sir H Cecil	T Queally	1-2f	1/13
2012	**Camelot**		A O'Brien	J O'Brien	15-8f	12/18
2013	**Dawn Approach**		J Bolger	K Manning	11-8f	6/13
2014	**Night Of Thunder**		R Hannon	K Fallon	40-1	3/14
2015	**Gleneagles**		A O'Brien	R Moore	4-1f	16/18
2016	**Galileo Gold**		H Palmer	F Dettori	14-1	1/13
2017	**Churchill**		A O'Brien	R Moore	6-4f	3/10
2018	**Saxon Warrior**		A O'Brien	D O'Brien	3-1	9/14
2019	**Magna Grecia**		A O'Brien	D O'Brien	11-2	17/19

THIS IS a specialist miler's race rather than a stepping stone to the Derby despite the relatively recent success of Camelot and Sea The Stars – prior to the latter's 2009 win there had been a 20-year wait for a horse to do the double. Most winners had proved themselves at two, with 19 of the last 28 having won a Group race including 14 at the highest level. Seven of those (Churchill, Dawn Approach, Frankel, Rock Of Gibraltar, Pennekamp, Zafonic and Rodrigo De Triano) had won the Dewhurst, while Magna Grecia, Saxon Warrior and Camelot have followed up victories in the Racing Post Trophy after a long blank since High Top in 1973. Favourites had a desperate record until five of the last nine winners hit back for punters. There have been just four British-trained winners in 15 years, with only Frankel and Haafhd following up victory in one of the domestic trials since Mystiko in 1991.

1,000 Guineas (1m) Newmarket

Year	Winner	Age	Trainer	Jockey	SP	draw/ran
2010	**Special Duty**		C Head-Maarek	S Pasquier	9-2f	18/17
2011	**Blue Bunting**		M Al Zarooni	F Dettori	16-1	16/18
2012	**Homecoming Queen**		A O'Brien	R Moore	25-1	16/17
2013	**Sky Lantern**		R Hannon Sr	R Hughes	9-1	7/15
2014	**Miss France**		A Fabre	M Guyon	7-1	4/17
2015	**Legatissimo**		D Wachman	R Moore	13-2	13/13
2016	**Minding**		A O'Brien	R Moore	11-10f	8/16
2017	**Winter**		A O'Brien	W Lordan	9-1	7/14
2018	**Billesdon Brook**		R Hannon	S Levey	66-1	8/15
2019	**Hermosa**		A O'Brien	W Lordan	14-1	4/15

COURSE FORM is the key factor in this race and is likely to become even more vital with the Fillies' Mile run at Newmarket for the first time in 2011. The 2016 winner Minding followed up victory in that race and Hermosa had been second in it, while five of the last 18 winners came via the Rockfel; four of the last 17 had been first or second in the Cheveley Park; 2006 winner Speciosa won the Nell Gwyn, in which Sky Lantern was second and Billesdon Brook fourth; Miss France landed the Oh So Sharp Stakes; and Blue Bunting won a Listed race over course and distance the previous October. Punters have hit back a little in recent years, but still 11 of the last 21 winners have been priced in double figures and Billesdon Brook was a real skinner in 2018 when the biggest-priced winner in the race's history. French fillies have a good record, with seven winners since 1993 and Miss France the only one of those not to have Group 1 form as a juvenile.

Lockinge Stakes (1m) Newbury

2010	**Paco Boy**	5	R Hannon Sr	R Hughes	8-11f	3/9
2011	**Canford Cliffs**	4	R Hannon Sr	R Hughes	4-5f	4/7
2012	**Frankel**	4	Sir H Cecil	T Queally	2-7f	6/6
2013	**Farhh**	5	S bin Suroor	S de Sousa	10-3	5/12
2014	**Olympic Glory**	4	R Hannon	F Dettori	11-8f	3/8
2015	**Night Of Thunder**	4	R Hannon	J Doyle	11-4jf	3/16
2016	**Belardo**	4	R Varian	A Atzeni	8-1	6/12
2017	**Ribchester**	4	R Fahey	W Buick	7-4f	5/8
2018	**Rhododendron**	4	A O'Brien	R Moore	10-3f	2/14
2019	**Mustashry**	6	Sir M Stoute	J Crowley	9-1	5/14

IT'S ESSENTIAL to look for horses who have already shown themselves to be Group 1 milers as 20 of the last 25 winners had won at the top level, all but one over the trip, and three of the exceptions had been second. Consequently it has been straightforward to identify the winner as 12 of the last 17 favourites have obliged and two of the exceptions were second in the market. Four-year-olds have by far the strongest record, accounting for 23 of the last 33 winners, and fillies can also do well with four winners in the last 14 years. The Sandown Mile is a popular prep race yet Belardo was only the second horse to do the double with 22 other Sandown winners failing.

Coronation Cup (1m4f) Epsom

2010	**Fame And Glory**	4	A O'Brien	J Murtagh	5-6f	8/9
2011	**St Nicholas Abbey**	4	A O'Brien	R Moore	Evsf	1/5
2012	**St Nicholas Abbey**	5	A O'Brien	J O'Brien	8-11f	4/6
2013	**St Nicholas Abbey**	6	A O'Brien	J O'Brien	3-10f	3/5
2014	**Cirrus Des Aigles**	8	C Barande Barbe	C Soumillon	10-11f	7/7
2015	**Pether's Moon**	5	R Hannon	P Dobbs	11-1	5/4
2016	**Postponed**	5	R Varian	A Atzeni	8-11f	3/8
2017	**Highland Reel**	5	A O'Brien	R Moore	9-4f	3/10
2018	**Cracksman**	4	J Gosden	F Dettori	2-7f	6/6
2019	**Defoe**	5	R Varian	A Atzeni	11-1	2/9

AIDAN O'BRIEN has trained eight of the last 15 winners, led by St Nicholas Abbey's hat-trick. That horse was favourite on every occasion, as were Cracksman, Highland Reel, Postponed, Cirrus Des Aigles and Fame And Glory in the last decade, although history shows that the traditionally small field can produce plenty of upsets, which was the case again in 2015 with the outsider of four in Pether's Moon. The key is to oppose four-year-

DEFOE (right): fourth winning five-year-old in the Coronation Cup in five years

olds as youngsters are often well fancied yet only 2-7 shot Cracksman has won since 2011, making it just five in 17 years overall. Four of the last five winners were aged five.

The Oaks (1m4f) Epsom

2010	**Snow Fairy**	E Dunlop	R Moore	9-1	15/15
2011	**Dancing Rain**	W Haggas	J Murtagh	20-1	7/13
2012	**Was**	A O'Brien	S Heffernan	20-1	10/12
2013	**Talent**	R Beckett	R Hughes	20-1	3/11
2014	**Taghrooda**	J Gosden	P Hanagan	5-1	9/17
2015	**Qualify**	A O'Brien	C O'Donoghue	50-1	2/11
2016	**Minding**	A O'Brien	R Moore	10-11f	4/9
2017	**Enable**	J Gosden	F Dettori	6-1	9/10
2018	**Forever Together**	A O'Brien	D O'Brien	7-1	3/9
2019	**Anapurna**	J Gosden	F Dettori	8-1	3/14

GUARANTEED STAMINA has been more important than proven top-class form in this race, which can make things tricky for punters with five of the last 12 winners priced at least 20-1. Two of Aidan O'Brien's seven winners came via the Guineas, but they are the only winners not to have been tried beyond a mile since Casual Look in 2003. It therefore follows that the 1,000 Guineas has become a weaker guide than was once the case, with Minding the only winner to follow up since Kazzia in 2002 and four failures in that time. Eleven of the last 13 winners had never been tried in a Group 1 and eight of them had triumphed over at least 1m2f, although none of the trials stands above any other and too much is often made of the Musidora winner, with three beaten favourites since 2008 and Sariska the only one to double up since Reams Of Verse in 1997.

The Derby (1m4f) Epsom

2010	**Workforce**	Sir M Stoute	R Moore	6-1	8/12
2011	**Pour Moi**	A Fabre	M Barzalona	4-1	7/13
2012	**Camelot**	A O'Brien	J O'Brien	8-13f	5/9
2013	**Ruler Of The World**	A O'Brien	R Moore	7-1	10/12
2014	**Australia**	A O'Brien	J O'Brien	11-8f	12/16

ANTHONY VAN DYCK (near): first Lingfield winner to add the Derby since 1998

2015	**Golden Horn**	J Gosden	F Dettori	13-8f	8/12
2016	**Harzand**	D Weld	P Smullen	13-2	9/16
2017	**Wings Of Eagles**	A O'Brien	P Beggy	40-1	14/18
2018	**Masar**	C Appleby	W Buick	16-1	10/12
2019	**Anthony Van Dyck**	A O'Brien	S Heffernan	13-2	7/13

JUST AS punters thought they had the Derby sussed, with 13 successive winners from the first three in the market including six favourites, along came the biggest-priced winner in more than 40 years in Wings Of Eagles in 2017 followed by a 16-1 surprise in Masar – and even last year's winner Anthony Van Dyck was only fourth choice in the market. Still, it's a decent outlook for punters overall and the resurgence of the 2,000 Guineas as a trial has played a big part in that, with Masar among five top-three finisher from Newmarket winning at Epsom in the last 12 years following Australia, Camelot, Sea The Stars and New Approach. Of the recognised trials, the Dante (five winners this century) and the Derrinstown (four) are better pointers than those at Chester and Lingfield, with Anthony Van Dyck the first winner to come via the latter race since High-Rise in 1998.

Queen Anne Stakes (1m) Royal Ascot

2010	**Goldikova**	5	F Head	O Peslier	11-8f	10/10
2011	**Canford Cliffs**	4	R Hannon Sr	R Hughes	11-8	6/7
2012	**Frankel**	4	Sir H Cecil	T Queally	1-10f	8/11
2013	**Declaration Of War**	4	A O'Brien	J O'Brien	15-2	6/13
2014	**Toronado**	4	R Hannon	R Hughes	4-5f	8/10
2015	**Solow**	5	F Head	M Guyon	11-8f	4/8
2016	**Tepin**	5	M Casse	J Leparoux	11-2	12/13
2017	**Ribchester**	4	R Fahey	W Buick	11-10f	1/16
2018	**Accidental Agent**	4	E Johnson Houghton	C Bishop	33-1	4/15
2019	**Lord Glitters**	6	D O'Meara	D Tudhope	14-1	1/16

LORD GLITTERS smashed one of the longest-running trends going last year when becoming the first horse older than five to win since 1976. The youngsters are still the way to go, though, with four-year-olds winning 23 of the last 31 runnings and several top-class horses aged six or older getting turned over, including Goldikova when defending her crown in 2011. Nine of the last 13 winners ran in the Lockinge at Newbury, which is obviously the key trial – Ribchester, Frankel and Canford Cliffs all did the double – and 13 of the last 16 winners had previously won a Group 1 at some stage. Toronado is the only horse to ever win the race first time out.

St James's Palace Stakes (1m) Royal Ascot

2010	**Canford Cliffs**	R Hannon Sr	R Hughes	11-4j	4/9
2011	**Frankel**	Sir H Cecil	T Queally	3-10f	5/9
2012	**Most Improved**	B Meehan	K Fallon	9-1	15/16
2013	**Dawn Approach**	J Bolger	K Manning	5-4f	5/9
2014	**Kingman**	J Gosden	J Doyle	8-11f	7/7
2015	**Gleneagles**	A O'Brien	R Moore	8-15f	5/5
2016	**Galileo Gold**	H Palmer	F Dettori	6-1	7/7
2017	**Barney Roy**	R Hannon	J Doyle	5-2	4/8
2018	**Without Parole**	J Gosden	F Dettori	9-4f	2/10
2019	**Circus Maximus**	A O'Brien	R Moore	10-1	1/11

GUINEAS FORM holds the key to this prize and ten of the last 15 winners had come out on top in one of the Classics. The Curragh is just about the best guide as six Irish 2,000 Guineas winners have followed up in that time compared to five from Newmarket and one from Longchamp. Gleneagles and Henrythenavigator had won at Newmarket and the Curragh and Frankel is the only Newmarket winner to follow up without a run in between since Bolkonski in 1975, although Barney Roy came straight from his Guineas second when winning last year. Without Parole was the first winner not to have run in a Group 1 at all since 1990, with Most Improved the only other winner to have skipped the Classics in 20 years. Circus Maximus and Dawn Approach were both dropping in trip after failing to stay in the Derby.

Prince of Wales's Stakes (1m2f) Royal Ascot

2010	**Byword**	4	A Fabre	M Guyon	5-2f	5/12
2011	**Rewilding**	4	M Al Zarooni	F Dettori	17-2	6/7
2012	**So You Think**	6	A O'Brien	J O'Brien	4-5f	7/11
2013	**Al Kazeem**	5	R Charlton	J Doyle	11-4	9/11
2014	**The Fugue**	5	J Gosden	W Buick	11-2	7/8
2015	**Free Eagle**	4	D Weld	P Smullen	5-2f	4/9
2016	**My Dream Boat**	4	C Cox	A Kirby	16-1	3/6
2017	**Highland Reel**	5	A O'Brien	R Moore	9-4	6/8
2018	**Poet's Word**	5	Sir M Stoute	J Doyle	11-2	1/7
2019	**Crystal Ocean**	5	Sir M Stoute	F Dettori	5-1	6/8

A RACE that has altered hugely since gaining Group 1 status in 2000 when Dubai Millennium provided one of the outstanding moments in Royal Ascot history. The race now attracts an international field and 12 of the last 20 winners had won a Group 1 outside Britain and Ireland. That also shows the quality required as three of the eight exceptions had won a Group 1 at home and Sir Michael Stoute's two recent winners, Crystal Ocean and Poet's Word, had both been second three times at the top level. The Tattersalls Gold Cup is the best pointer with four of the last eight horses to try it managing to complete the double and the last two both coming second.

Gold Cup (2m4f) Royal Ascot

2010	**Rite Of Passage**	6	D Weld	P Smullen	20-1	1/12
2011	**Fame And Glory**	5	A O'Brien	J Spencer	11-8f	3/15

2012	**Colour Vision**	4	S Bin Suroor	F Dettori	6-1	5/9
2013	**Estimate**	4	Sir M Stoute	R Moore	7-2f	5/14
2014	**Leading Light**	4	A O'Brien	J O'Brien	10-11f	14/13
2015	**Trip To Paris**	4	E Dunlop	G Lee	12-1	13/12
2016	**Order Of St George**	4	A O'Brien	R Moore	10-11f	10/17
2017	**Big Orange**	6	M Bell	J Doyle	5-1	7/14
2018	**Stradivarius**	4	J Gosden	F Dettori	7-4jf	6/9
2019	Stradivarius	5	J Gosden	F Dettori	Evsf	2/11

A HALF-MILE longer than any other British or Irish Group 1, this race understandably attracts plenty of real specialists, with Stradivarius, Royal Rebel, Kayf Tara, Drum Taps and Sadeem all dual winners since 1988 and Yeats becoming the first ever four-time winner in 2009. His trainer Aidan O'Brien has a stunning record as he has since won with Order Of St George, Leading Light and Fame And Glory, as well as finishing second with Order Of St George, Age Of Aquarius and Kingfisher, and five of his last six winners started their year in the Vintage Crop Stakes at Navan. The other strong trials are the Sagaro Stakes, which has come back into vogue with Estimate and Colour Vision winning both races to match Celeric, Double Trigger, Sadeem, Longboat and Gildoran since the mid-1980s, and the Henry II Stakes, the route taken by eight of the 13 winners prior to Yeats's reign plus Big Orange and Trip To Paris in the last five years. Wherever it's been, 16 of the last 19 winners had been successful over 2m. Four-year-olds have won six of the last eight renewals and any older horse has to have proved themselves at the top level already as nine of the last 12 older winners had previously landed a Group 1 (plus the 2017 winner Big Orange had won the last two runnings of the Goodwood Cup before it was upgraded to a Group 1).

Coronation Stakes (1m) Royal Ascot

2010	**Lillie Langtry**	A O'Brien	J Murtagh	7-2f	3/13
2011	**Immortal Verse**	R Collet	G Mosse	8-1	11/12
2012	**Fallen For You**	J Gosden	W Buick	12-1	11/10
2013	**Sky Lantern**	R Hannon Sr	R Hughes	9-2jf	16/17
2014	**Rizeena**	C Brittain	R Moore	11-2	7/12
2015	**Ervedya**	J-C Rouget	C Soumillon	3-1	7/9
2016	**Qemah**	J-C Rouget	G Benoist	6-1	11/13
2017	**Winter**	A O'Brien	R Moore	4-9f	7/7
2018	**Alpha Centauri**	J Harrington	C O'Donoghue	11-4f	9/12
2019	**Watch Me**	F-H Graffard	P-C Boudot	20-1	9/9

A CHAMPIONSHIP race for three-year-old fillies. French fillies have an outstanding recent record but the 1,000 Guineas at Newmarket is generally the best guide as ten of the last 18 winners had run on the Rowley Mile, with five doing the double (Winter, Sky Lantern, Ghanaati, Attraction and Russian Rhythm). It's generally best to have been off the track since then, though, as just three of the last 25 winners ran in the Newmarket Classic and the Irish 1,000 Guineas at the Curragh, which often counts against many in the field. Any horse who has been stepped up in trip can be opposed as Lush Lashes is the only winner in the last 25 years to have raced over further.

Diamond Jubilee Stakes (6f) Royal Ascot

2010	**Starspangledbanner**	4	A O'Brien	J Murtagh	13-2j	21/24
2011	**Society Rock**	4	J Fanshawe	P Cosgrave	25-1	3/16
2012	**Black Caviar**	5	P Moody	L Nolen	1-6f	15/14

2013	**Lethal Force**	4	C Cox	A Kirby	11-1	15/18
2014	**Slade Power**	5	E Lynam	W Lordan	7-2f	4/14
2015	**Undrafted**	5	W Ward	F Dettori	14-1	6/15
2016	**Twilight Son**	4	H Candy	R Moore	7-2	3/9
2017	**The Tin Man**	5	J Fanshawe	T Queally	9-2	3/19
2018	**Merchant Navy**	4	A O'Brien	R Moore	4-1	11/12
2019	**Blue Point**	5	C Appleby	J Doyle	6-4f	9/17

A RACE whose profile has risen steadily this century and which attracts the best sprinters from around the world, most notably the legendary Black Caviar in 2012. Yet despite Black Caviar and the American winner Undrafted in 2015, the percentage call is to side with domestic talent as they are the only winners trained outside Britain and Ireland since Cape Of Good Hope in 2005, during which time several fancied foreign raiders – Takeover Target (twice), J J The Jet Plane, Sacred Kingdom, Star Witness, Brazen Beau and Redkirk Warrior – have been beaten at 4-1 or shorter. In contrast, course form remains critical because, of the last 20 winners at Ascot, ten had already been successful at the course and the same number had managed a top-four finish at Royal Ascot. The race has thrown up more than its share of shocks, with four winners priced 20-1 or bigger in the last 12 years, but two of those were among a host of unfancied three-year-olds to run well and that age group is now barred from running because of the Commonwealth Cup.

Coral-Eclipse (1m2f) Sandown

2010	**Twice Over**	5	H Cecil	T Queally	13-8f	1/5
2011	**So You Think**	5	A O'Brien	S Heffernan	4-6f	3/5
2012	**Nathaniel**	4	J Gosden	W Buick	7-2	4/9
2013	**Al Kazeem**	5	R Charlton	J Doyle	15-8f	2/7
2014	**Mukhadram**	5	W Haggas	P Hanagan	14-1	10/9
2015	**Golden Horn**	3	J Gosden	F Dettori	4-9f	1/5
2016	**Hawkbill**	3	C Appleby	W Buick	6-1	3/7
2017	**Ulysses**	4	Sir M Stoute	J Crowley	8-1	6/9
2018	**Roaring Lion**	3	J Gosden	O Murphy	7-4f	7/7
2019	**Enable**	5	J Gosden	F Dettori	4-6f	8/8

TRADITIONALLY THE first clash of the generations. It has suffered a little in recent times from a lack of three-year-old representation, but the tide may be turning again, helped by Golden Horn and Sea The Stars following up Derby victories after the previous four to take their chance – Authorized, Motivator, Benny The Dip and Erhaab – were all beaten. Indeed, following Golden Horn's win, three-year-olds filled five of the six top-two positions from 2016 to 2018. For older horses, the Prince of Wales's Stakes is the key trial, although Al Kazeem is the only horse to do the double since Mtoto in 1987 with many horses beaten at Ascot – most recently Ulysses, Mukhadram, So You Think, Twice Over and David Junior – improving on that form.

July Cup (6f) Newmarket

2010	**Starspangledbanner**	4	A O'Brien	J Murtagh	2-1f	4/14
2011	**Dream Ahead**	3	D Simcock	H Turner	7-1	2/16
2012	**Mayson**	4	R Fahey	P Hanagan	20-1	11/12
2013	**Lethal Force**	4	C Cox	A Kirby	9-2	4/11
2014	**Slade Power**	5	E Lynam	W Lordan	7-4f	13/13
2015	**Muhaarar**	3	C Hills	P Hanagan	2-1jf	7/14

2016	**Limato**	4	H Candy	H Bentley	9-2f	16/18
2017	**Harry Angel**	3	C Cox	A Kirby	9-2	6/10
2018	**US Navy Flag**	3	A O'Brien	R Moore	8-1	12/13
2019	**Ten Sovereigns**	3	A O'Brien	R Moore	9-2	12/12

FIVE OF the last 14 winners were following up victories over the same trip at Royal Ascot – four in the Diamond Jubilee Stakes before Muhaarar from the inaugural Commonwealth Cup, in which subsequent winners Harry Angel and Ten Sovereigns had made the frame – but surprisingly it pays to ignore Group 1 form in other races as ten of the other 14 winners since 2001 were scoring for the first time at the top level. Indeed, this is a race in which stars are often born with 43 of the 52 winners being aged three or four. Often that's because horses are dropping into sprints having been tried over further as stamina is an important asset on this stiff uphill finish. Greats like Ajdal and Soviet Song are memorable for that many years ago and more recently the likes of US Navy Flag, Limato, Muhaarar and Dream Ahead had run over a mile earlier in the season.

King George VI and Queen Elizabeth Stakes (1m4f) Ascot

2010	**Harbinger**	4	Sir M Stoute	O Peslier	4-1	1/6
2011	**Nathaniel**	3	J Gosden	W Buick	11-2	3/5
2012	**Danedream**	4	P Schiergen	A Starke	9-1	4/10
2013	**Novellist**	4	A Wohler	J Murtagh	13-2	3/8
2014	**Taghrooda**	3	J Gosden	P Hanagan	7-2	7/8
2015	**Postponed**	4	L Cumani	A Atzeni	6-1	9/7
2016	**Highland Reel**	4	A O'Brien	R Moore	13-8f	3/7
2017	**Enable**	3	J Gosden	F Dettori	5-4f	7/10
2018	**Poet's Word**	5	Sir M Stoute	J Doyle	7-4	8/7
2019	**Enable**	5	J Gosden	F Dettori	8-15f	11/11

THIS RACE has suffered from a lack of three-year-old representation in recent years, with Enable, Taghrooda, Nathaniel, Alamshar and Galileo the only horses of that age to come out on top since Lammtarra in 1995. Taghrooda was an even bigger trends-buster as she became the first British-trained three-year-old filly to win any Group 1 over this trip against older males in the worldwide history of the sport – it therefore makes it all the more astonishing that Enable matched her just three years later and followed up in the Arc. Still, it generally pays to look for a four-year-old (the age of 11 of the last 16 winners, with Enable and Poet's Word the only older horses to score since 1999) and one proven at the top level and the trip because since Belmez in 1990 just four winners hadn't previously landed a Group 1 and just five hadn't been first or second in a Group 1 over 1m4f. The Coronation Cup is a poor guide, though, with only Opera House and Daylami doing the double in more than 40 years.

Sussex Stakes (1m) Goodwood

2010	**Canford Cliffs**	3	R Hannon Sr	R Hughes	4-6f	7/7
2011	**Frankel**	3	Sir H Cecil	T Queally	8-13f	3/4
2012	**Frankel**	4	Sir H Cecil	T Queally	1-20f	3/4
2013	**Toronado**	3	R Hannon Sr	R Hughes	11-4	7/7
2014	**Kingman**	3	J Gosden	J Doyle	2-5f	4/4
2015	**Solow**	5	F Head	M Guyon	2-5f	5/8
2016	**The Gurkha**	3	A O'Brien	R Moore	11-8f	1/10
2017	**Here Comes When**	7	A Balding	J Crowley	20-1	7/7

2018	**Lightning Spear**	7	D Simcock	O Murphy	9-1	4/8
2019	**Too Darn Hot**	3	J Gosden	F Dettori	Evsf	3/8

NOT MANY Group 1 races are won by seven-year-olds, let alone twice in a row, but that's what happened when Here Comes When and Lightning Spear won in 2017 and 2018. It was even more unlikely in the Sussex Stakes, which is generally a great race for glamorous three-year-olds as that age group has provided 30 of the 45 winners since it was opened to all ages in 1975. Ten of the last 13 triumphant three-year-olds were favourites and 12 of the last 14 had been at least placed in the St James's Palace Stakes, which is the key trial. Eight of the last 11 successful older horses had contested the Queen Anne Stakes, with Solow, Frankel and Ramonti doing the double since 2007. With Royal Ascot form holding up so well, it's perhaps little wonder that nine of the last 12 favourites have obliged, six of them at odds-on.

Nassau Stakes (1m1f192yds) Goodwood

2010	**Midday**	4	H Cecil	T Queally	15-8f	6/7
2011	**Midday**	5	Sir H Cecil	T Queally	6-4f	6/6
2012	**The Fugue**	3	J Gosden	R Hughes	11-4	7/8
2013	**Winsili**	3	J Gosden	W Buick	20-1	15/14
2014	**Sultanina**	4	J Gosden	W Buick	11-2	2/6
2015	**Legatissimo**	3	D Wachman	W Lordan	2-1f	8/9
2016	**Minding**	3	A O'Brien	R Moore	1-5f	1/5
2017	**Winter**	3	A O'Brien	R Moore	10-11f	6/6
2018	**Wild Illusion**	3	C Appleby	W Buick	4-1	6/6
2019	**Deirdre**	5	M Hashida	O Murphy	20-1	4/9

THIS IS another another fantastic race for punters as 23 of the last 26 winners emerged from the top three in the market including 14 favourites, although Deirdre was a real skinner when winning for Japan last year. The key is to side with a top-class three-year-old as the Classic generation have provided 34 of the 45 winners since the race was opened to older fillies in 1975, despite Midday's best efforts in racking up a hat-trick. Preferably they should be dropping down in trip rather than stepping up as Winter and Halfway To

TOO DARN HOT: a more typical Sussex Stakes winner than the two before him

JAPAN (left): just the eighth winning three-year-old in more than 35 years in the Juddmonte International – although four have come in the last six

Heaven are the only winners to have had their previous runs over a mile since 2004, during which time Minding has followed up victory in the Oaks while Wild Illusion, Legatissimo, The Fugue, Midday and Peeping Fawn all improved on placed efforts at Epsom.

Juddmonte International Stakes (1m2f85yds) York

2010	**Rip Van Winkle**	4	A O'Brien	J Murtagh	7-4f	7/9
2011	**Twice Over**	6	Sir H Cecil	I Mongan	11-2	4/5
2012	**Frankel**	4	Sir H Cecil	T Queally	1-10f	7/9
2013	**Declaration Of War**	4	A O'Brien	J O'Brien	7-1	2/6
2014	**Australia**	3	A O'Brien	J O'Brien	8-13f	6/6
2015	**Arabian Queen**	3	D Elsworth	S De Sousa	50-1	5/7
2016	**Postponed**	5	R Varian	A Atzeni	15-8f	6/12
2017	**Ulysses**	4	Sir M Stoute	J Crowley	4-1	3/7
2018	**Roaring Lion**	3	J Gosden	O Murphy	3-1	4/8
2019	**Japan**	3	A O'Brien	R Moore	5-1	7/9

FAMOUS FOR its many upsets since Brigadier Gerard suffered his only defeat to Roberto in 1972, this race rediscovered its teeth in 2015 when 50-1 shot Arabian Queen stunned the mighty Golden Horn. Otherwise, though, it has turned in punters' favour in recent times with no other winner returned bigger than 8-1 since Ezzoud in 1993 and seven of the last 13 favourites winning. Older horses have had the edge, with just eight younger horses triumphing since 1983, all of whom were recent Group 1 winners apart from Arabian Queen. The best trial is the Coral-Eclipse, which has provided ten of the last 25 winners, with 2018 winner Roaring Lion the eighth to complete the double in that time and the second in a row.

Yorkshire Oaks (1m3f195yds) York

2010	**Midday**	4	H Cecil	T Queally	11-4	6/8
2011	**Blue Bunting**	3	M Al Zarooni	F Dettori	11-4f	6/8
2012	**Shareta**	4	A de Royer-Dupre	C Lemaire	2-1	7/6
2013	**The Fugue**	4	J Gosden	W Buick	2-1f	6/7
2014	**Tapestry**	3	A O'Brien	R Moore	8-1	6/7
2015	**Pleascach**	3	J Bolger	K Manning	8-1	8/11
2016	**Seventh Heaven**	3	A O'Brien	C O'Donoghue	10-3	10/12
2017	**Enable**	3	J Gosden	F Dettori	1-4f	1/6
2018	**Sea Of Class**	3	W Haggas	J Doyle	7-4f	5/8
2019	**Enable**	5	J Gosden	F Dettori	1-4f	1/4

ALWAYS A top-class race, this has been won by the Classic generation 13 times in the last 20 years, including five in a row prior to Enable last year. However, with her first victory in 2017, Enable remains the only Oaks winner to follow up since Alexandrova in 2005, with four beaten in that time – Taghrooda, Was, Snow Fairy and Sariska – three of them when favourite. Significantly, Enable and Alexandrova had won the Irish Oaks in between because that has been a better guide – the last eight Curragh winners to take their chance have finished 11221211, while 2014 heroine Tapestry had finished second in Ireland.

Nunthorpe Stakes (5f) York

2010	**Sole Power**	3	E Lynam	W Lordan	100-1	11/12
2011	**Margot Did**	3	M Bell	H Turner	20-1	11/15
2012	**Ortensia**	7	P Messara	W Buick	7-2jf	8/19
2013	**Jwala**	4	R Cowell	S Drowne	40-1	8/17
2014	**Sole Power**	7	E Lynam	R Hughes	11-4f	10/13
2015	**Mecca's Angel**	4	M Dods	P Mulrennan	15-2	10/19
2016	**Mecca's Angel**	5	M Dods	P Mulrennan	9-2	7/19
2017	**Marsha**	4	Sir M Prescott	L Morris	8-1	8/11
2018	**Alpha Delphini**	7	B Smart	G Lee	40-1	7/15
2019	**Battaash**	5	C Hills	J Crowley	7-4	1/11

THIS HAS become a real race for upsets, none bigger than Sole Power at 100-1 in 2010, and there have been two 40-1 winners since then. This is because the race isn't often won by a proven top-level sprinter, with nine of the last 18 winners never having previously landed a Group race, let alone a Group 1, even though many had had long careers as six winners in this time were six or older. Furthermore, the King's Stand is less influential than many might think as only Sole Power has done the double since 2000.

Sprint Cup (6f) Haydock

2010	**Markab**	7	H Candy	P Cosgrave	12-1	14/13
2011	**Dream Ahead**	3	D Simcock	W Buick	4-1f	9/16
2012	**Society Rock**	5	J Fanshawe	K Fallon	10-1	3/13
2013	**Gordon Lord Byron**	5	T Hogan	J Murtagh	7-2	2/13
2014	**G Force**	3	D O'Meara	D Tudhope	11-1	10/17
2015	**Twilight Son**	3	H Candy	F Sweeney	10-1	5/15
2016	**Quiet Reflection**	3	K Burke	D Costello	7-2f	4/14
2017	**Harry Angel**	3	C Cox	A Kirby	2-1f	8/11

2018	**The Tin Man**	6	J Fanshawe	O Murphy	7-1	5/12
2019	**Hello Youmzain**	3	K Ryan	J Doyle	9-2cf	6/11

THREE-YEAR-OLDS have taken a firm grip on this race in recent times, winning five of the last six runnings and seven of the last 12 going back further from less than a third of the runners. That has turned the tide back in punters' favour – five of those winning three-year-olds were favourites – but the race is still known for plenty of upsets, with mid-summer form often misleading on much softer ground. Ten of the last 18 winners were returned in double figures, including 33-1 Red Clubs in 2007, and 11 were making their breakthrough at the highest level, with Harry Angel and Dream Ahead the only July Cup winners to follow up since Ajdal in 1987 and six others beaten in the meantime.

St Leger (1m6f132yds) Doncaster

2010	**Arctic Cosmos**	J Gosden	W Buick	12-1	8/10
2011	**Masked Marvel**	J Gosden	W Buick	15-2	3/9
2012	**Encke**	M Al Zarooni	M Barzalona	25-1	1/9
2013	**Leading Light**	A O'Brien	J O'Brien	7-2f	7/11
2014	**Kingston Hill**	R Varian	A Atzeni	9-4f	4/12
2015	**Simple Verse**	R Beckett	A Atzeni	8-1	1/7
2016	**Harbour Law**	L Mongan	G Baker	22-1	9/9
2017	**Capri**	A O'Brien	R Moore	3-1f	9/11
2018	**Kew Gardens**	A O'Brien	R Moore	3-1	8/12
2019	**Logician**	J Gosden	F Dettori	5-6f	4/8

TOP-CLASS horses tend to be kept to shorter trips these days and Capri was an unusual winner in 2017 given he already had an Irish Derby in the bag, making him the first Curragh winner to follow up since Nijinsky, while only one Derby winner has even tried since Reference Point in 1987, with Camelot beaten at 2-5 in 2012. Six of the nine winners to come via the Derby since 1997 finished outside the places at Epsom and even four of the ten to have warmed up in the Great Voltigeur in that time were beaten there, although 18 of the last 21 winners had won a Group race with the Gordon Stakes being the other key trial. Kingston Hill is the only winner in more than 25 years to have had his prep run over just 1m2f, though during that time only Leading Light warmed up beyond the Leger distance. Simple Verse is the only filly to prevail since User Friendly in 1992.

Prix de l'Arc de Triomphe (1m4f) Longchamp

2010	**Workforce**	3	Sir M Stoute	R Moore	6-1	8/19
2011	**Danedream**	3	P Schiergen	A Starke	20-1	2/16
2012	**Solemia**	4	C Laffon-Parias	O Peslier	33-1	6/18
2013	**Treve**	3	C Head-Maarek	T Jarnet	9-2	15/17
2014	**Treve**	4	C Head-Maarek	T Jarnet	11-1	3/20
2015	**Golden Horn**	3	J Gosden	F Dettori	9-2	14/17
2016	**Found**	4	A O'Brien	R Moore	6-1	12/16*
2017	**Enable**	3	J Gosden	F Dettori	10-11f	2/18*
2018	**Enable**	4	J Gosden	F Dettori	Evsf	6/19
2019	Waldgeist	5	A Fabre	P-C Boudot	131-10	3/12

**Run at Chantilly in 2016 and 2017*

THE PREMIER middle-distance championship of Europe is generally one for the French, with 18 of the last 30 winners trained at home, although the tide is turning as Waldgeist was the first French-trained colt to win since Rail Link in 2006 and eight of the 12 winners in between came from abroad. It follows that the big domestic trials have a poor record, with the Prix Niel, having thrown up ten winners in 13 years up to 2006, drawing a blank since then and Waldgeist the first winner to come via the Prix Foy since Subotica in 1992. Fillies are enjoying a remarkable period, with eight of the last 12 renewals going to the girls including brilliant dual winners Treve and Enable. Despite Waldgeist's win, it still makes sense to oppose anything older than four as only five such horses have won since the Second World War and the losers include three recent favourite in Enable, Treve and Orfevre.

Queen Elizabeth II Stakes (1m) Ascot

2010	**Poet's Voice**	3	S Bin Suroor	F Dettori	9-2	7/8
2011	**Frankel**	3	Sir H Cecil	T Queally	4-11f	2/8
2012	**Excelebration**	4	A O'Brien	J O'Brien	10-11f	6/8
2013	**Olympic Glory**	3	R Hannon Sr	R Hughes	11-2	7/12
2014	**Charm Spirit**	3	F Head	O Peslier	5-1	7/11
2015	**Solow**	5	F Head	M Guyon	11-10f	2/9
2016	**Minding**	3	A O'Brien	R Moore	7-4f	8/13
2017	**Persuasive**	4	J Gosden	F Dettori	8-1	6/15
2018	**Roaring Lion**	3	J Gosden	O Murphy	2-1f	15/13
2019	**King Of Change**	3	R Hannon	S Levey	12-1	12/16

THE MILE championship of Europe in which the Classic generation has held sway, with nine victories in the last 12 years extending a long period of superiority. That said, the time of year makes this a tough date for 2,000 Guineas winners, with Frankel and George Washington the only ones to do the double from ten to try in the last 17 years. Similarly, only Frankel and Bahri have followed up St James's Palace Stakes wins since 1995, but winners tend to be proven at the highest level, with 13 of the last 17 having already won a Group 1, and as a result King Of Change and Persuasive are the only ones not to come from the first three in the market since 2001. Fillies have won two of the last four runnings having previously drawn a blank since 1987.

Champion Stakes (1m2f) Ascot

2010	**Twice Over**	5	H Cecil	T Queally	7-2	4/10
2011	**Cirrus Des Aigles**	5	C Barande-Barbe	C Soumillon	12-1	1/12
2012	**Frankel**	4	Sir H Cecil	T Queally	2-11f	6/8
2013	**Farhh**	5	S Bin Suroor	S de Sousa	11-4	5/10
2014	**Noble Mission**	5	Lady Cecil	J Doyle	7-1	5/9
2015	**Fascinating Rock**	4	D Weld	P Smullen	10-1	7/13
2016	**Almanzor**	3	J-C Rouget	C Soumillon	11-8f	1/10
2017	**Cracksman**	3	J Gosden	F Dettori	13-8f	4/10
2018	**Cracksman**	4	J Gosden	F Dettori	5-6f	8/8
2019	**Magical**	4	A O'Brien	D O'Brien	Evsf	8/9

Run at Newmarket until 2011

THE SUBJECT of a big-money makeover when switched to Ascot in 2011. Older horses have increasingly come to the fore, accounting for nine of the last 11 winners including four five-year-olds. That's a trend likely to grow stronger because, among the 18 successful three-year-olds since 1980, mile form has proved a lot more influential than form over further – 12 of those 18 had won a Classic with New Approach the only one since Time Charter in 1982 to have done it over 1m4f – yet top milers now have the option of the QEII on the same day. This has been the best British Group 1 for French horses, with four winners in the last 14 years extending a long tradition of success.

Big handicap records

Lincoln (1m) Doncaster

Year	Winner	Age	Weight	Trainer	Jockey	SP	Draw/ran
2010	**Penitent**	4	9-2	W Haggas	J Murtagh	3-1f	1/21
2011	**Sweet Lightning**	6	9-4	M Dods	J Murtagh	16-1	16/21*
2012	**Brae Hill**	6	9-1	R Fahey	T Hamilton	25-1	12/22
2013	**Levitate**	5	8-7	J Quinn	D Egan (3)	20-1	3/22
2014	**Ocean Tempest**	5	9-3	J Ryan	A Kirby	20-1	3/17
2015	**Gabrial**	6	9-0	R Fahey	T Hamilton	12-1	15/22
2016	**Secret Brief**	4	9-4	C Appleby	W Buick	12-1	22/22
2017	**Bravery**	4	9-1	D O'Meara	D Tudhope	20-1	1/22
2018	**Addeybb**	4	9-2	W Haggas	J Doyle	5-1	10/20
2019	**Auxerre**	4	9-3	C Appleby	J Doyle	5-2f	17/19

Run at Newcastle in 2011

AS WITH all big handicaps, the rating required to get a run gets higher and higher, so long-standing trends about siding with a progressive horse on a low weight have been rendered obsolete. Even so, a big weight is still a huge disadvantage as the last winner to carry more than 9st 4lb was Babodana in 2004. It's common for runners to come via the all-weather or Dubai, but 14 of the last 18 winners were having their first run of the year and it's wise to side with trainers who have a proven track record of getting one ready as six of the last ten winning trainers – William Haggas (twice), Charlie Appleby, Richard Fahey, John Quinn and Mark Tompkins – had also won the race within the previous seven years. A high draw is a concern as 11 of the last 13 winners at Doncaster came from a stall no higher than 16.

Royal Hunt Cup (1m) Royal Ascot

Year	Winner	Age	Weight	Trainer	Jockey	SP	Draw/ran
2010	**Invisible Man**	4	8-9	S Bin Suroor	F Dettori	28-1	7/29
2011	**Julienas**	4	8-8	W Swinburn	E Ahern	12-1	24/28
2012	**Prince Of Johanne**	6	9-3	T Tate	J Fahy	16-1	33/30
2013	**Belgian Bill**	5	8-11	G Baker	J Doyle	33-1	6/28
2014	**Field Of Dream**	7	9-1	J Osborne	A Kirby	20-1	33/28
2015	**GM Hopkins**	4	9-3	J Gosden	R Moore	8-1	11/30
2016	**Portage**	4	9-5	M Halford	J Doyle	10-1	4/28
2017	**Zhui Feng**	4	9-0	A Perrett	M Dwyer	25-1	26/29
2018	**Settle For Bay**	4	9-1	D Marnane	W Lee	16-1	22/30
2019	**Afaak**	5	9-3	C Hills	J Crowley	20-1	21/28

A REAL puzzle for punters with Forgotten Voice in 2009 the only winning favourite in the last 22 years. A common mistake is to side with a lightly raced improver because

AUXERRE: another Lincoln won by a trainer with 'previous' in the race

experience is in fact a vital commodity – 20 of the last 22 winners had run at least eight times, which is more than many of the beaten favourites. The handicap tends to be condensed, especially after the demise of the Buckingham Palace Stakes, and few runners get in below the 9st barrier, so it's telling that only Portage (with just 9st 5lb) has carried more than 9st 3lb since 2008, making it just three in more than 30 years to have defied a greater burden. A high draw is generally essential, with only three of the last 17 winners at Ascot overcoming a single-figure berth.

Wokingham (6f) Royal Ascot

2010	**Laddies Poker Two**	5	8-11	J Noseda	J Murtagh	9-2f	26/27
2011	**Deacon Blues**	4	8-13	J Fanshawe	J Murtagh	15-2	11/25
2012	**Dandy Boy**	6	9-8	D Marnane	P Dobbs	33-1	15/28
2013	**York Glory**	5	9-2	K Ryan	J Spencer	14-1	22/26
2014	**Baccarat**	5	9-5	R Fahey	G Chaloner (3)	9-1	27/28
2015	**Interception**	5	9-3	D Lanigan	G Baker	10-1	21/25
2016	**Outback Traveller**	5	9-1	R Cowell	M Harley	10-1	28/28
2017	**Out Do**	8	8-13	D O'Meara	D Tudhope	25-1	1/27
2018	**Bacchus**	4	9-6	B Meehan	J Crowley	33-1	16/28
2019	**Cape Byron**	5	9-9	R Varian	A Atzeni	7-2f	10/26

THIS RACE is run at such a furious gallop that stamina comes to the fore and, while 14 of the last 16 winners had already triumphed over the big-race trip, both exceptions had done their winning over further and in all 11 of those 16 had a 7f victory to their name, with one of the exceptions, Interception, placed four times at 7f including in a Listed race. Therefore the Victoria Cup, run over 7f at the same track in May, is one of the key trials, along with the 6f handicaps at Newmarket's Guineas meeting and York's Dante meeting. Fresh horses are preferred, with 13 of the last 18 winners having run no more than twice that year, which is remarkable for a sprint handicap in June. There's nothing to fear about a big weight, but only two winners have been older than five since 1999.

Northumberland Plate (2m) Newcastle

2010	**Overturn**	6	8-7	D McCain	E Ahern	14-1	21/19
2011	**Tominator**	4	8-8	R Hollinshead	P Pickard (3)	25-1	14/19

2012	**Ile De Re**	6	9-3	D McCain	J Crowley	5-2f	9/16
2013	**Tominator**	6	9-10	J O'Neill	G Lee	8-1	4/18
2014	**Angel Gabrial**	5	9-1	R Fahey	G Chaloner (3)	4-1f	1/19
2015	**Quest For More**	5	9-4	R Charlton	G Baker	15-2	3/19
2016	**Antiquarium**	4	9-5	C Appleby	J McDonald	16-1	3/20
2017	**Higher Power**	5	9-9	J Fanshawe	T Queally	11-2	13/20
2018	**Withhold**	5	9-1	R Charlton	R Winston	5-1f	11/20
2019	**Who Dares Wins**	7	9-1	A King	T Marquand	12-1	7/19

WITH SO much of the season revolving around Royal Ascot and Newcastle's biggest day of the summer generally coming just a week later, this provides a good opportunity for horses laid out for the race rather than coming here as an afterthought. Just two of the last 17 winners had run at Royal Ascot despite several fancied runners in that time, including four beaten favourites, coming from the royal meeting. Furthermore, 12 of those 17 winners were opening their account for the season. The first bend comes shortly after the start so those drawn high can be disadvantaged, with 13 of the last 21 winners drawn seven or lower, and Overturn used controversial tactics to overcome that in 2010. The Chester Cup is traditionally a strong guide and that has been reinforced recently with Ile De Re doing the double before Tominator, Angel Gabrial and Who Dares Wins stepped up on placed efforts at Chester.

Bunbury Cup (7f) Newmarket

2010	**St Moritz**	4	9-1	M Johnston	F Dettori	4-1f	4/19
2011	**Brae Hill**	5	9-1	R Fahey	B McHugh	11-1	2/20
2012	**Bonnie Brae**	5	9-9	D Elsworth	R Moore	13-2	12/15
2013	**Field Of Dream**	6	9-7	J Osborne	A Kirby	14-1	20/19
2014	**Heaven's Guest**	4	9-3	R Fahey	T Hamilton	12-1	9/13
2015	**Rene Mathis**	5	9-1	R Fahey	P Hanagan	16-1	10/17
2016	**Golden Steps**	5	9-0	M Botti	F Dettori	7-1jf	14/16
2017	**Above The Rest**	6	9-1	D Barron	C Lee (5)	12-1	19/18
2018	**Burnt Sugar**	6	9-1	R Fell	P Hanagan	7-1	16/18
2019	**Vale Of Kent**	4	9-4	M Johnston	F Dettori	13-2	14/17

SEVEN FURLONGS tends to be a specialist trip and Golden Steps is the only winner since 2002 not to have already won a 7f handicap. Most major 7f handicaps over the season are run at Ascot, though, and not all horses act at the Berkshire track, so look for class horses who have struggled earlier in the campaign. The last ten winners hadn't won all year – just one of the last 26 had won more than once – and nine of them had been beaten at Ascot, most well down the field, but the last eight were still good enough to be rated at least 98, which tends to put them towards the top of the handicap given a mark of 91 got a run last year. Indeed, big weights shouldn't be feared at all given Mine, a three-time winner between 2002 and 2006, twice defied a burden of at least 9st 9lb and has been emulated by Bonnie Brae and Plum Pudding since then.

John Smith's Cup (1m2f85yds) York

2010	**Wigmore Hall**	3	8-5	M Bell	M Lane (3)	5-1	13/19
2011	**Green Destiny**	4	8-13	W Haggas	A Beschizza (3)	6-1	17-19
2012	**King's Warrior**	5	8-9	P Chapple-Hyam	R Havlin	33-1	19/18
2013	**Danchai**	4	8-11	W Haggas	A Atzeni	10-1	16/19
2014	**Farraaj**	5	9-11	R Varian	A Atzeni	6-1	22/16
2015	**Master Carpenter**	4	9-4	R Millman	P Makin	14-1	1/17

2016	**Educate**	7	9-8	I Mohammed	T Brown	18-1	14/19
2017	**Ballet Concerto**	4	9-3	Sir M Stoute	J Doyle	8-1	11/20
2018	**Euchen Glen**	5	9-3	J Goldie	A Rawlinson	20-1	3/19
2019	**Pivoine**	5	9-8	A Balding	R Hornby	14-1	6/21

LIKE THE Northumberland Plate, this is another handicap in which missing Royal Ascot helps, in keeping with 11 of the last 17 winners whereas 14 of the last 18 beaten favourites registered a top-four finish there. Combine that with a young improver and you might well be on to a winner, with Educate the only winner older than five – and just five of that age successful – since Vintage Premium in 2002 despite three-year-olds struggling desperately to get a run. Indeed, subsequent Grade 1 winner Wigmore Hall was the only three-year-old runner when successful in 2010 and just one has made the field since. This is run on one of the best Saturdays of the summer and, with many top jockeys engaged elsewhere, it provides an opportunity for some younger riders as six of the last 14 winners were partnered by an apprentice.

Stewards' Cup (6f) Goodwood

2010	**Evens And Odds**	6	9-1	D Nicholls	B Cray (5)	20-1	11/28
2011	**Hoof It**	4	10-0	M Easterby	K Fallon	13-2jf	18/27
2012	**Hawkeyethenoo**	6	9-9	J Goldie	G Lee	9-1	4/27
2013	**Rex Imperator**	4	9-4	W Haggas	N Callan	12-1	26/27
2014	**Intrinsic**	4	8-11	R Cowell	R Hughes	6-1	22/24
2015	**Magical Memory**	3	8-12	C Hills	F Dettori	6-1f	1/27
2016	**Dancing Star**	3	8-12	A Balding	D Probert	9-2f	4/27
2017	**Lancelot Du Lac**	7	9-5	D Ivory	F Dettori	25-1	15/26
2018	**Gifted Master**	5	9-11	H Palmer	J Watson (5)	20-1	25/26
2019	**Khaadem**	3	9-6	C Hills	J Crowley	4-1f	3/27

THIS IS a major betting heat with a strong ante-post market and the betting has become a good guide as eight of the last ten winners were 12-1 or shorter, with Khaadem getting favourite backers back on track last year after a bit of relief for bookmakers. This is a race for established sprint handicappers and, while there have been three three-year-old winners in the last five years, two of those had landed the big 6f handicap for that age group at Newmarket's July meeting. Fifteen of the last 21 older winners came via the

KHAADEM (left): the third winning favourite in five years in the Stewards' Cup

MUSTAJEER: campaigned in Group/Listed races all year until the Ebor

Wokingham, though none of them had won at Royal Ascot and all but two had another run in between. That run tends to have been a good one as ten of the last 17 winners finished first or second in their prep race, which is amazing given the competitiveness of sprint handicaps. Only two winners since 1984 carried more than 9st 7lb, with Jason Watson's 5lb claim taking Gifted Master below that threshold in 2018.

Ebor (1m6f) York

2010	**Dirar**	5	9-1	G Elliott	J Spencer	14-1	22/20
2011	**Moyenne Corniche**	6	8-13	B Ellison	D Swift (3)	25-1	10/20
2012	**Willing Foe**	5	9-2	S Bin Suroor	F Dettori	12-1	16/19
2013	**Tiger Cliff**	4	9-0	Lady Cecil	T Queally	5-1	18/14
2014	**Mutual Regard**	5	9-9	J Murtagh	L Steward (5)	20-1	16/19
2015	**Litigant**	7	9-1	J Tuite	O Murphy	33-1	6/19
2016	**Heartbreak City**	6	9-6	T Martin	A McNamara (5)	15-2	15/20
2017	**Nakeeta**	6	9-5	I Jardine	C Rodriguez (5)	12-1	18/19
2018	**Muntahaa**	5	9-9	J Gosden	J Crowley	11-1	21/20
2019	**Mustajeer**	6	9-5	G Lyons	C Keane	16-1	2/22

ONE OF the oldest and most famous handicaps, first run in 1847, this race received a massive cash injection in 2018, making it a £1 million race. The first two winners of the newly enriched Ebor, Muntahaa and Mustajeer, had been running in Group/Listed company all year and carried 9st 5lb or more, suggesting the new prize-money will change the strongest trend in the race because prior to that a light weight had been a big help - the pair are the only ones to defy such a burden (after taking into account claims) since Sea Pigeon in 1979 despite the handicap becoming more and more condensed. A shrewd trainer will use a claimer to bring the weight down, with five of the last 11 winners partnered by such a rider. Progressive horses have always been preferred as just six winners have been older than five since Sea Pigeon and ten of the last 16 had raced no more than nine times on the Flat in Britain or Ireland.

Ayr Gold Cup (6f) Ayr

2010	**Redford**	5	9-2	D Nicholls	F Dettori	14-1	17/26
2011	**Our Jonathan**	4	9-6	K Ryan	F Norton	11-1	12/26
2012	**Captain Ramius**	6	9-0	K Ryan	P Smullen	16-1	8/26
2013	**Highland Colori**	5	9-4	A Balding	O Murphy (5)	20-1	19/26
2014	**Louis The Pious**	6	9-4	D O'Meara	J Doyle	10-1	19/27
2015	**Don't Touch**	3	9-1	R Fahey	T Hamilton	6-1f	8/25
2016	**Brando**	4	9-10	K Ryan	T Eaves	11-1	8/23
2017	**Donjuan Triumphant**	4	9-10	A Balding	PJ McDonald	13-2	4/17*
2018	**Baron Bolt**	5	9-3	P Cole	C Noble (5)	28-1	21/25
2018	**Son Of Rest**	4	9-3	J Stack	C Hayes	5-1f	17/25
2019	**Angel Alexander**	3	8-13	T Dascombe	R Kingscote	28-1	24/24

**Run at Haydock as the 32Red Gold Cup in 2017*

A HISTORIC race first run in 1804, this produced a dead-heat in 2018 as Son Of Rest just about landed a massive gamble, continuing a fightback for punters after Don't Touch in 2015 had been the only other successful favourite in the last 20 years and Donjuan Triumphant in 2017 the only other winner priced in single figures in that time. While big weights have been defied more often in recent years, the percentage call is to avoid horses who have been hit by the handicapper for winning form – nine of the last 18 winners hadn't even won in any of their four most recent outings. Ten of the last 14 runnings have gone to major northern yards, with Kevin Ryan leading the way with four victories.

Cambridgeshire (1m1f) Newmarket

2010	**Credit Swap**	5	8-7	M Wigham	J Crowley	14-1	3/35
2011	**Prince Of Johanne**	5	8-12	T Tate	J Fahy (3)	40-1	31/32
2012	**Bronze Angel**	3	8-8	M Tregoning	W Buick	9-1	21/33
2013	**Educate**	4	9-9	I Mohammed	J Murtagh	8-1f	4/33
2014	**Bronze Angel**	5	8-13	M Tregoning	L Steward (5)	14-1	11/31
2015	**Third Time Lucky**	3	8-4	R Fahey	A Beschizza	14-1	7/34
2016	**Spark Plug**	5	9-4	B Meehan	J Fortune	12-1	28/31
2017	**Dolphin Vista**	4	8-10	M Meade	G Wood (3)	50-1	29/34
2018	**Wissahickon**	3	9-5	J Gosden	F Dettori	11-1	21/33
2019	**Lord North**	3	8-10	J Gosden	F Dettori	9-2f	29/30

THE FIRST leg of the Autumn Double. Because of its unusual distance and its straight course, this has thrown up a number of specialists down the years, with dual winner Bronze Angel being the most obvious recent example, so consider horses who have run well in the race before. Many of the runners are milers racing over an extra furlong, but stronger stayers often come to the fore and 12 of the last 18 winners had triumphed over 1m2f while Spark Plug had been second in a Listed race at the trip. Experience of a big field is vital and 14 of the last 16 winners had won a race of at least 12 runners, 11 of them in a handicap. Big weights spell trouble as Educate is the only horse to carry more than 9st 5lb to victory since Beauchamp Pilot in 2002.

Cesarewitch (2m2f) Newmarket

2010	**Aaim To Prosper**	7	8-2	B Meehan	L-P Beuzelin (3)	16-1	3/32
2011	**Never Can Tell**	4	8-11	J Osborne	F Dettori	25-1	36/33
2012	**Aaim To Prosper**	8	9-10	B Meehan	K Fallon	66-1	1/34
2013	**Scatter Dice**	4	8-8	M Johnston	S de Sousa	66-1	18/33
2014	**Big Easy**	7	8-7	P Hobbs	T Queally	10-1	2/33
2015	**Grumeti**	7	8-2	A King	A Beschizza	50-1	15/34
2016	**Sweet Selection**	4	8-8	H Morrison	S de Sousa	7-1	23/33
2017	**Withhold**	4	8-8	R Charlton	S de Sousa	5-1f	24/34
2018	**Low Sun**	5	9-2	W Mullins	S Heffernan	11-1	13/33
2019	**Stratum**	6	9-7	W Mullins	J Watson	25-1	20/30

THE SECOND leg of the Autumn Double. Generally punters are too swayed by a young improver as 2009 winner Darley Sun is one of only two successful three-year-olds in 25 years, with Southern France and St Michel the latest beaten favourites from the Classic generation in the last four years. Indeed, Darley Sun and Withhold in 2017 were rare winning favourites, with winners returned twice at 66-1 and twice at 50-1 since 2008. One of the big-priced winners, Aaim To Prosper, reinforced the significance of previous form in the race as he followed up his victory two years earlier. Scatter Dice is the only winner since 1995 not to have already been successful over at least 2m and the success of jumps yards reinforces the importance of proven stamina as just four of the last 24 runnings didn't have a recognised hurdler in the first two. The Northumberland Plate is the best trial having thrown up ten of the last 24 winners. Don't read too much into the draw as jockeys have increasingly worked out how to overcome a high berth, although seven of the last 12 winners were still drawn no higher than 18.

November Handicap (1m4f) Doncaster

2010	**Times Up**	4	8-13	J Dunlop	D O'Neill	14-1	9/22
2011	**Zuider Zee**	4	8-13	J Gosden	R Havlin	8-1	20/23
2012	**Art Scholar**	5	8-7	M Appleby	F Norton	20-1	9/23
2013	**Conduct**	6	9-2	W Haggas	S Sanders	8-1	21/23
2014	**Open Eagle**	5	8-12	D O'Meara	D Tudhope	15-2f	18/23
2015	**Litigant**	7	9-10	J Tuite	G Baker	10-1	12/22
2016	**Prize Money**	3	9-1	S bin Suroor	G Wood (5)	4-1	12/15
2017	**Saunter**	4	8-13	I Williams	J Crowley	6-1	14/23
2018	**Royal Line**	4	9-8	J Gosden	R Havlin	9-1	23/23
2019	*Abandoned*						

THE LAST big betting heat of the season and one that has changed in recent years due to the lack of three-year-olds able to get a run. When Malt Or Mash won in 2007 that age group had won 14 of the last 24 renewals and three-year-olds still have to be feared if getting in, as Prize Money proved in 2016 – bear in mind he had run just once as a two-year-old and four of the previous eight had been unraced, so all were therefore late developers. However, four of the last seven winners were at least five, a massive change given just five of the previous 32 had been older than four. A big weight remains a drawback as nine of the last 12 winners carried less than 9st once taking into account jockeys' claims. Favourites have a desperate record, with Open Eagle the only one to oblige since 1995.

Big-Race Dates, Fixtures and Track Facts

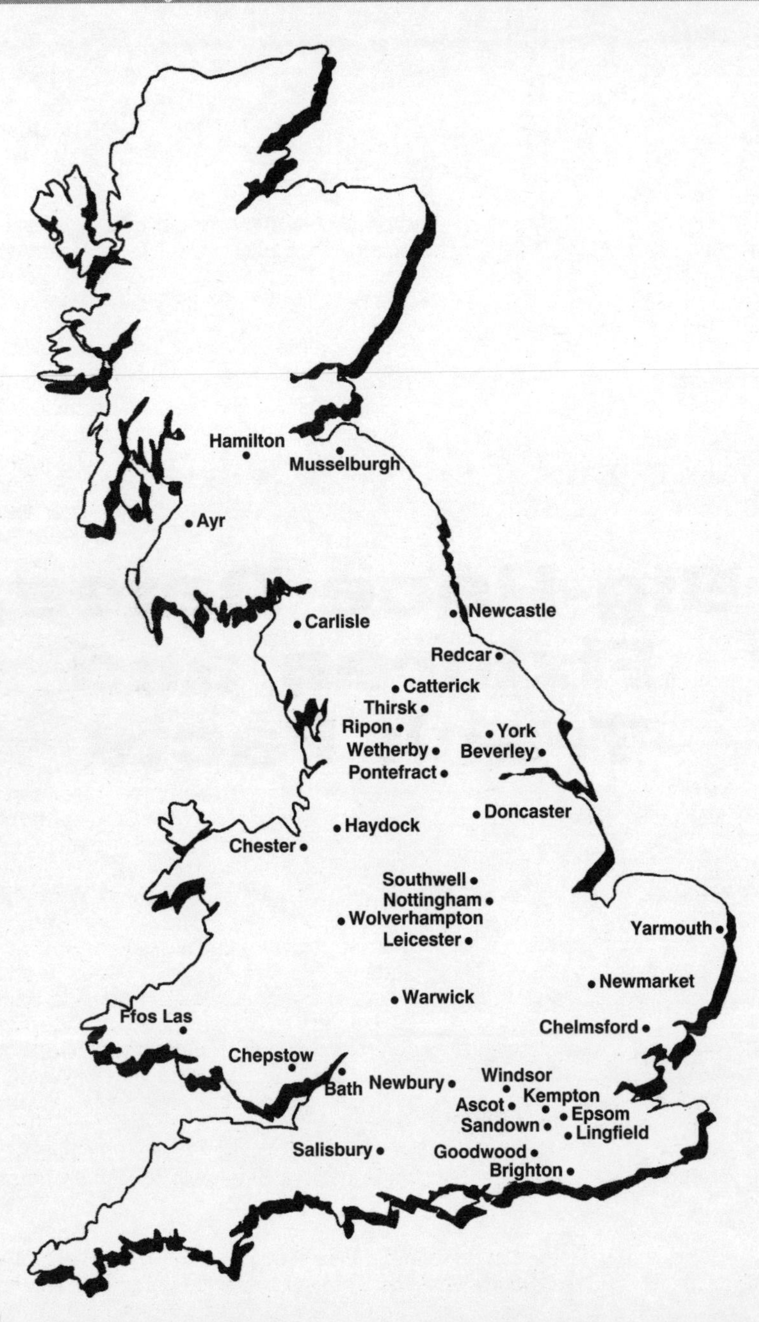
Hamilton
Musselburgh
Ayr
Carlisle
Newcastle
Redcar
Catterick
Thirsk
Ripon
York
Wetherby
Beverley
Pontefract
Doncaster
Haydock
Chester
Southwell
Nottingham
Wolverhampton
Leicester
Yarmouth
Newmarket
Warwick
Ffos Las
Chelmsford
Chepstow
Bath
Newbury
Windsor
Kempton
Ascot
Epsom
Sandown
Lingfield
Salisbury
Goodwood
Brighton

Fixtures

Key - Flat, **Jumps**

March

28 Sat..................Doncaster, Kempton, Wolverhampton, **Stratford**, **Uttoxeter**
29 Sun... Doncaster, **Ascot**
30 Mon...Bath, Newcastle, **Ludlow**
31 Tue ....Lingfield, Musselburgh, **Southwell**

April

1 Wed........................Lingfield, Wolverhampton, **Market Rasen**, **Wincanton**
2 Thu ....Southwell, Chelmsford, **Aintree**, **Taunton**
3 Fri ....Leicester, Kempton, **Aintree**, **Sedgefield**
4 Sat................. Lingfield, Wolverhampton, **Aintree**, **Chepstow**, **Newcastle**
5 Sun.. **Ffos Las**, **Plumpton**
6 Mon.. Redcar, Windsor, **Kelso**
7 Tue .... Pontefract, **Exeter**, **Southwell**
8 Wed...............................Catterick, Nottingham, Wolverhampton, Kempton
9 Thu..Bath, Chelmsford, **Wetherby**
10 Fri .... Chelmsford, Lingfield, Newcastle
11 Sat............. Kempton, Musselburgh, Wolverhampton, **Carlisle**, **Haydock**,
.... **Newton Abbot**
12 Sun................................ Southwell, **Ffos Las**, **Market Rasen**, **Plumpton**
13 Mon.......... Redcar, Wolverhampton, **Chepstow**, **Fakenham**, **Huntingdon**,
.... **Plumpton**
14 Tue ....Lingfield, Newmarket, **Warwick**
15 Wed.....................................Beverley, Newmarket, Kempton, **Cheltenham**
16 Thu.......................................Newmarket, Ripon, Newcastle, **Cheltenham**
17 Fri ....Newbury, Bath, **Ayr, Fontwell**, **Exeter**
18 Sat.......................... Newbury, Thirsk, Brighton, Nottingham, **Ayr, Bangor**
19 Sun.. **Stratford**, **Wincanton**
20 Mon....................Pontefract, Windsor, **Hexham**, **Newton Abbot**, **Kempton**
21 Tue .... Yarmouth, Wolverhampton, **Ludlow**, **Sedgefield**, **Southwell**
22 Wed...Catterick, Epsom, Lingfield, **Perth**, **Taunton**
23 Thu.................................... Beverley, Chelmsford, **Perth**, **Warwick**, **Exeter**
24 Fri .... Doncaster, Sandown, **Perth**, **Chepstow**
25 Sat.......Haydock, Leicester, Ripon, Doncaster, Wolverhampton, **Sandown**
26 Sun.. Salisbury, Wetherby
27 Mon... Ayr, Lingfield, Southwell, Thirsk, Windsor
28 Tue .... Brighton, Nottingham, Yarmouth, Ayr, Lingfield
29 Wed.................. Ascot, Pontefract, Wolverhampton, Brighton, Chelmsford
30 Thu........... Musselburgh, Redcar, Southwell, Chelmsford, Wolverhampton

May

1 Fri ....Chepstow, Lingfield, Musselburgh, Newcastle, **Cheltenham**
2 Sat...........Goodwood, Newmarket, Thirsk, Doncaster, **Uttoxeter**, **Hexham**

3 Sun.. Hamilton, Newmarket, Salisbury
4 Mon.................................Brighton, Nottingham, Windsor, **Kempton**
5 Tue ....Chester, Wolverhampton, **Ayr**, **Fakenham**, **Southwell**
6 Wed........................Chester, Kempton, **Kelso**, **Newton Abbot**, **Fontwell**
7 Thu..............Chester, Chelmsford, **Huntingdon**, **Worcester**, **Wincanton**
8 Fri.................. Ascot, Bath, Beverley, Wolverhampton, Ripon, **Warwick**,
....**Market Rasen**
9 Sat..................Ascot, Lingfield, Nottingham, Thirsk, **Hexham**, **Warwick**,
.... **Haydock (mixed)**
10 Sun.. **Ludlow**, **Plumpton**
11 Mon..........................Catterick, Musselburgh, Wolverhampton, Windsor
12 Tue ....Beverley, Chepstow, Ayr, Wetherby, **Sedgefield**
13 Wed................................York, Bath, **Newton Abbot**, **Worcester**, **Perth**
14 Thu................................ Salisbury, York, Newmarket, **Perth**, **Fontwell**
15 Fri ....Newbury, Newmarket, York, Hamilton, **Aintree**
16 Sat............. Newbury, Newmarket, Thirsk, Doncaster, **Bangor**, **Uttoxeter**
17 Sun..Ripon, **Stratford**
18 Mon... Carlisle, Redcar, Leicester, Windsor
19 Tue ....Lingfield, Nottingham, Wolverhampton, **Hexham**, **Huntingdon**
20 Wed..............................Ayr, Yarmouth, Kempton, **Warwick**, **Southwell**
21 Thu.......Lingfield, Wolverhampton, Chelmsford, Sandown, **Market Rasen**
22 Fri .... Bath, Brighton, Haydock, Pontefract, **Worcester**
23 Sat... Beverley, Catterick, Chester, Haydock, Salisbury, **Cartmel**, **Ffos Las**
24 Sun...**Fontwell**, **Kelso**, **Uttoxeter**
25 Mon.........Chelmsford, Leicester, Redcar, Windsor, **Cartmel**, **Huntingdon**
26 Tue ....Brighton, Leicester, Redcar, Lingfield, **Ludlow**
27 Wed......................Beverley, Hamilton, **Newton Abbot**, **Cartmel**, **Warwick**
28 Thu.............................Goodwood, Haydock, Ripon, Carlisle, Sandown
29 Fri ....Carlisle, Goodwood, Yarmouth, Catterick, Haydock, **Stratford**
30 Sat.............. Goodwood, Haydock, Newmarket, York, Lingfield, **Stratford**
31 Sun..Nottingham, **Fakenham**

June

1 Mon................................ Wolverhampton, Windsor, Yarmouth, **Southwell**
2 Tue .... Brighton, Lingfield, Newcastle, **Bangor**
3 Wed.................. Nottingham, Kempton, Ripon, **Fontwell**, **Newton Abbot**
4 Thu..............Hamilton, Chelmsford, Wolverhampton, **Ffos Las**, **Uttoxeter**
5 Fri ....Catterick, Epsom, Bath, Doncaster, Goodwood, **Market Rasen**
6 Sat......... Doncaster, Epsom, Musselburgh, Chepstow, Lingfield, **Hexham**,
.... **Worcester**
7 Sun... Goodwood, **Perth**
8 Mon... Ayr, Leicester, Pontefract, Windsor
9 Tue ....Lingfield, Salisbury, Chelmsford, Wetherby
10 Wed.........................Haydock, Yarmouth, Hamilton, Kempton, **Fontwell**
11 Thu..................... Newbury, Nottingham, Yarmouth, Haydock, **Uttoxeter**
12 Fri ....Chepstow, Sandown, York, Goodwood, **Aintree**, **Newton Abbot**
13 Sat............ Bath, Chester, Sandown, York, Leicester, **Hexham**, **Worcester**
14 Sun... Doncaster, Salisbury
15 Mon... Ayr, Thirsk, Nottingham, Windsor
16 Tue .... Royal Ascot, Thirsk, Beverley, Brighton, **Stratford**

17 Wed........................ Royal Ascot, Hamilton, Chelmsford, Ripon, **Uttoxeter**
18 Thu........................... Royal Ascot, Chelmsford, Ripon, Lingfield, **Ffos Las**
19 Fri......................... Royal Ascot, Redcar, Carlisle, Goodwood, Newmarket,
.... **Market Rasen**
20 Sat..........Royal Ascot, Ayr, Newmarket, Redcar, Haydock, Lingfield, **Perth**
21 Sun.. Pontefract, **Hexham**, **Worcester**
22 Mon............................... Chepstow, Windsor, Wolverhampton, **Southwell**
23 Tue .... Beverley, Brighton, Newbury, **Newton Abbot**
24 Wed.....................................Carlisle, Salisbury, Bath, Kempton, **Worcester**
25 Thu..................... Newcastle, Newmarket, Nottingham, Hamilton, Leicester
26 Fri........... Doncaster, Yarmouth, Chester, Newcastle, Newmarket, **Cartmel**
27 Sat... Chester, Newcastle, Newmarket, Windsor, York, Doncaster, Lingfield
28 Sun... Windsor, **Cartmel**, **Uttoxeter**
29 Mon.................................. Pontefract, Windsor, Wolverhampton, **Ffos Las**
30 Tue ....Brighton, Hamilton, Chepstow, **Stratford**

July

1 Wed.................................Musselburgh, Thirsk, Bath, Kempton, **Worcester**
2 Thu..Haydock, Yarmouth, Epsom, Newbury, **Perth**
3 Fri...........................Doncaster, Sandown, Beverley, Chelmsford, Haydock,
.... **Newton Abbot**
4 Sat.............Beverley, Chelmsford, Haydock, Leicester, Sandown, Carlisle,
.... Nottingham
5 Sun...Ayr, **Market Rasen**
6 Mon... Ayr, Ripon, Windsor, **Worcester**
7 Tue ....Pontefract, Wolverhampton, Brighton, **Uttoxeter**
8 Wed......................................Catterick, Lingfield, Yarmouth, Bath, Kempton
9 Thu..............................Carlisle, Doncaster, Newmarket, Epsom, Newbury
10 Fri......................... Ascot, Newmarket, York, Chepstow, Chester, **Ffos Las**
11 Sat..........................Ascot, Chester, Newmarket, York, Hamilton, Salisbury
12 Sun.. **Perth**, **Stratford**
13 Mon..Ayr, Brighton, Windsor, Wolverhampton
14 Tue .... Bath, Beverley, Chelmsford, **Southwell**
15 Wed................. Catterick, Lingfield, Wolverhampton, Yarmouth, **Uttoxeter**
16 Thu............................. Chepstow, Hamilton, Leicester, Epsom, **Worcester**
17 Fri....... Haydock, Newbury, Nottingham, Hamilton, Newmarket, Pontefract
18 Sat...............Newbury, Newmarket, Ripon, Doncaster, Haydock, **Cartmel**,
.... **Market Rasen**
19 Sun...Redcar, **Newton Abbot**, **Stratford**
20 Mon.. Ayr, Beverley, Windsor, **Cartmel**
21 Tue .... Musselburgh, Chelmsford, Nottingham, **Southwell**
22 Wed.. Bath, Catterick, Lingfield, Leicester, Sandown
23 Thu........................ Sandown, Yarmouth, Doncaster, Newbury, **Worcester**
24 Fri...........................Ascot, Thirsk, Chepstow, Newmarket, York, **Uttoxeter**
25 Sat.........Ascot, Chester, Newcastle, Newmarket, York, Lingfield, Salisbury
26 Sun... Pontefract, **Uttoxeter**
27 Mon................................. Ayr, Windsor, Wolverhampton, **Newton Abbot**
28 Tue .... Beverley, Goodwood, Yarmouth, **Perth**, **Worcester**
29 Wed.................................Goodwood, Redcar, Leicester, Sandown, **Perth**
30 Thu..........................Goodwood, Nottingham, Epsom, Ffos Las, **Stratford**

31 Fri .... Goodwood, Wolverhampton, Bath, Musselburgh, Newmarket, ... **Bangor**

August

1 Sat...... Chelmsford, Doncaster, Goodwood, Newmarket, Thirsk, Hamilton, ... Lingfield
2 Sun.. Chester, **Market Rasen**
3 Mon..Kempton, Ripon, Carlisle, Windsor
4 Tue .... Catterick, Ffos Las, Nottingham
5 Wed.................................. Bath, Brighton, Pontefract, Kempton, Yarmouth
6 Thu........................... Brighton, Haydock, Yarmouth, Newcastle, Sandown
7 Fri ....Brighton, Musselburgh, Thirsk, Chelmsford, Haydock, Newmarket
8 Sat.......... Ascot, Chelmsford, Haydock, Newmarket, Redcar, Ayr, Lingfield
9 Sun..Leicester, Windsor
10 Mon.. Ayr, Ripon, Windsor, Wolverhampton
11 Tue ....Chepstow, Nottingham, Lingfield
12 Wed.. Beverley, Salisbury, Kempton, Newcastle
13 Thu................................Beverley, Lingfield, Salisbury, Ffos Las, Yarmouth
14 Fri .... Newbury, Nottingham, Wolverhampton, Chelmsford, Newmarket, ... Thirsk
15 Sat........................... Doncaster, Newbury, Newmarket, Ripon, Bath, **Perth**, ...**Market Rasen**
16 Sun..Pontefract, **Southwell**
17 Mon..Catterick, Lingfield, Windsor, **Bangor**
18 Tue .... Hamilton, Kempton, Carlisle
19 Wed..Bath, Carlisle, York, Kempton, **Worcester**
20 Thu.................................. Chepstow, York, Leicester, **Stratford**, **Fontwell**
21 Fri ... Musselburgh, Sandown, York, Newcastle, Salisbury, Wolverhampton
22 Sat......... Chester, Sandown, Wolverhampton, York, Chelmsford, Lingfield, ... **Newton Abbot**
23 Sun..Brighton, **Worcester**
24 Mon..Brighton, Chepstow, Ripon
25 Tue ....Yarmouth, Salisbury, **Bangor**
26 Wed......................... Catterick, Lingfield, Musselburgh, Kempton, **Stratford**
27 Thu............................. Carlisle, Ffos Las, Newbury, **Fontwell**, **Sedgefield**
28 Fri ....Ffos Las, Newmarket, Thirsk, Chelmsford, Goodwood, Hamilton
29 Sat.........Beverley, Chelmsford, Goodwood, Newmarket, Redcar, Windsor, ...**Cartmel**
30 Sun.. Beverley, Goodwood, Yarmouth
31 Mon..................................Chepstow, Epsom, Ripon, Southwell, **Cartmel**

September

1 Tue ....Epsom, Ripon, **Newton Abbot**
2 Wed......................................Bath, Lingfield, Hamilton, **Uttoxeter**, **Hexham**
3 Thu.................... Haydock, Salisbury, Chelmsford, **Sedgefield**, **Worcester**
4 Fri ....Ascot, Haydock, Newcastle, Kempton, Musselburgh
5 Sat............. Ascot, Haydock, Kempton, Thirsk, Wolverhampton, **Stratford**
6 Sun.. York, **Fontwell**
7 Mon..Brighton, Windsor, **Newton Abbot**, **Perth**
8 Tue ....Catterick, Goodwood, Leicester, Newcastle

9 Wed.......Carlisle, Doncaster, Wolverhampton, **Uttoxeter**
10 Thu.......Chepstow, Doncaster, Epsom, Chelmsford
11 Fri.......Chester, Doncaster, Sandown, Salisbury
12 Sat.......Bath, Chelmsford, Chester, Doncaster, Lingfield, Musselburgh
13 Sun.......Bath, Ffos Las
14 Mon.......Brighton, Thirsk, Wolverhampton, **Worcester**
15 Tue.......Redcar, Yarmouth, Kempton, **Southwell**
16 Wed.......Beverley, Sandown, Yarmouth, **Kelso**
17 Thu.......Ayr, Pontefract, Yarmouth, Chelmsford
18 Fri.......Ayr, Newbury, Kempton, **Newton Abbot**
19 Sat.......Ayr, Catterick, Chelmsford, Newbury, Newmarket, Wolverhampton
20 Sun.......Hamilton, **Plumpton**
21 Mon.......Hamilton, Leicester, Wolverhampton, **Warwick**
22 Tue.......Beverley, Lingfield, Newcastle, **Warwick**
23 Wed.......Goodwood, Redcar, Kempton, **Perth**
24 Thu.......Newmarket, Pontefract, Kempton, **Perth**
25 Fri.......Haydock, Newmarket, Newcastle, **Worcester**
26 Sat.......Chester, Haydock, Newmarket, Ripon, Chelmsford, **Market Rasen**
27 Sun.......Epsom, Musselburgh
28 Mon.......Bath, Hamilton, Newcastle, **Newton Abbot**
29 Tue.......Ayr, Wolverhampton, **Sedgefield**, **Worcester**
30 Wed.......Nottingham, Kempton, **Bangor**, **Huntingdon**

October

1 Thu.......Salisbury, Chelmsford, **Southwell**, **Warwick**
2 Fri.......Ascot, Newcastle, **Fontwell**, **Hexham**
3 Sat.......Ascot, Newmarket, Redcar, Wolverhampton, **Fontwell**
4 Sun.......**Kelso**, **Uttoxeter**
5 Mon.......Pontefract, Windsor, Wolverhampton, **Stratford**
6 Tue.......Brighton, Catterick, Leicester, Southwell
7 Wed.......Nottingham, Kempton, **Ludlow**
8 Thu.......Ayr, Chelmsford, Southwell, **Exeter**, **Worcester**
9 Fri.......Newmarket, York, Kempton, **Chepstow**
10 Sat.......Newmarket, York, Chelmsford, **Chepstow**, **Hexham**
11 Sun.......Goodwood, **Newton Abbot**
12 Mon.......Musselburgh, Windsor, Yarmouth, Wolverhampton
13 Tue.......Leicester, Newcastle, **Hereford**, **Huntingdon**
14 Wed.......Bath, Nottingham, Kempton, **Wetherby**
15 Thu.......Brighton, Chelmsford, Southwell, **Carlisle**, **Wincanton**
16 Fri.......Haydock, Redcar, Newcastle, **Fakenham**, **Uttoxeter**
17 Sat.......Ascot, Catterick, Wolverhampton, **Ffos Las**, **Market Rasen**,
.......**Stratford**
18 Sun.......**Kempton**, **Sedgefield**
19 Mon.......Pontefract, Windsor, Wolverhampton, **Plumpton**
20 Tue.......Newcastle, Yarmouth, Kempton, **Exeter**
21 Wed.......Newmarket, Kempton, **Fontwell**, **Worcester**
22 Thu.......Chelmsford, Wolverhampton, **Carlisle**, **Ludlow**, **Southwell**
23 Fri.......Doncaster, Newbury, Newcastle, **Cheltenham**
24 Sat.......Doncaster, Newbury, Chelmsford, **Cheltenham**, **Kelso**
25 Sun.......**Aintree**, **Wincanton**

26 Mon .... Leicester, Redcar, Newcastle, **Ayr**
27 Tue .... Catterick, Southwell, **Bangor**, **Chepstow**
28 Wed .... Nottingham, Kempton, **Fakenham**, **Taunton**
29 Thu .... Lingfield, Chelmsford, Southwell, **Newton Abbot**, **Stratford**
30 Fri .... Newmarket, Newcastle, **Uttoxeter**, **Wetherby**
31 Sat .... Newmarket, Wolverhampton, **Ascot**, **Ayr**, **Wetherby**

November

1 Sun .... **Carlisle**, **Huntingdon**
2 Mon .... Kempton, Wolverhampton, **Hereford**, **Plumpton**
3 Tue .... Redcar, Southwell, Newcastle, **Exeter**
4 Wed .... Lingfield, Nottingham, Kempton, **Musselburgh**
5 Thu .... Chelmsford, Kempton, **Market Rasen**, **Newbury**, **Sedgefield**
6 Fri .... Newcastle, **Fontwell**, **Hexham**, **Warwick**
7 Sat .... Doncaster, Chelmsford, **Aintree**, **Kelso**, **Wincanton**
8 Sun .... **Ffos Las**, **Sandown**
9 Mon .... **Carlisle**, **Chepstow**, **Kempton**
10 Tue .... **Hereford**, **Huntingdon**, **Lingfield**
11 Wed .... **Ayr**, **Bangor**, **Exeter**
12 Thu .... **Ludlow**, **Sedgefield**, **Taunton**
13 Fri .... **Cheltenham**, **Newcastle**, **Southwell**
14 Sat .... Lingfield, Wolverhampton, **Cheltenham**, **Uttoxeter**, **Wetherby**
15 Sun .... **Cheltenham**, **Fontwell**
16 Mon .... Wolverhampton, Kempton, **Leicester**, **Plumpton**
17 Tue .... Southwell, Newcastle, **Fakenham**, **Lingfield**
18 Wed .... Kempton, **Ffos Las**, **Hexham**, **Warwick**
19 Thu .... Newcastle, Chelmsford, **Market Rasen**, **Wincanton**
20 Fri .... Newcastle, **Ascot**, **Catterick**, **Chepstow**
21 Sat .... Lingfield, Wolverhampton, **Ascot**, **Haydock**, **Huntingdon**
22 Sun .... **Exeter**, **Uttoxeter**
23 Mon .... **Kempton**, **Ludlow**, **Musselburgh**
24 Tue .... Wolverhampton, **Sedgefield**, **Southwell**
25 Wed .... Lingfield, Kempton, **Hereford**, **Wetherby**
26 Thu .... Southwell, Chelmsford, **Taunton**
27 Fri .... Southwell, Chelmsford, **Doncaster**, **Newbury**
28 Sat .... Wolverhampton, **Bangor**, **Doncaster**, **Newbury**, **Newcastle**
29 Sun .... **Carlisle**, **Leicester**
30 Mon .... Wolverhampton, **Ayr**, **Fakenham**

December

1 Tue .... Wolverhampton, **Lingfield**, **Southwell**
2 Wed .... Lingfield, Kempton, **Haydock**, **Ludlow**
3 Thu .... Chelmsford, **Leicester**, **Market Rasen**, **Wincanton**
4 Fri .... Newcastle, **Exeter**, **Sandown**, **Sedgefield**
5 Sat .... Wolverhampton, **Aintree**, **Chepstow**, **Sandown**, **Wetherby**
6 Sun .... **Huntingdon**, **Kelso**
7 Mon .... Wolverhampton, **Musselburgh**, **Plumpton**
8 Tue .... Southwell, **Fontwell**, **Uttoxeter**
9 Wed .... Lingfield, Kempton, **Hexham**, **Leicester**
10 Thu .... Chelmsford, **Newcastle**, **Taunton**, **Warwick**

ROYAL LINE: won the last November Handicap to be run in 2018 – let's hope the race can go ahead this year on November 7 after last year's abandonment

11 Fri.. Southwell, **Bangor**, **Cheltenham**, **Doncaster**
12 Sat......... Newcastle, Wolverhampton, **Cheltenham**, **Doncaster**, **Hereford**
13 Sun.. **Carlisle**, **Southwell**
14 Mon.. **Ayr**, **Ffos Las**, **Plumpton**
15 Tue .... Wolverhampton, **Catterick**, **Wincanton**
16 Wed.. Lingfield, Kempton, **Ludlow**, **Newbury**
17 Thu ....Southwell, Chelmsford, **Exeter**
18 Fri.. Southwell, Wolverhampton, **Ascot**, **Uttoxeter**
19 Sat...................... Lingfield, Wolverhampton, **Ascot**, **Haydock**, **Newcastle**
20 Sun...Southwell, **Fakenham**
21 Mon.. **Lingfield**, **Musselburgh**
26 Sat.....Wolverhampton, **Fontwell**, **Huntingdon**, **Kempton**, **Market Rasen**,
.... **Sedgefield**, **Wetherby**, **Wincanton**
27 Sun..............................Wolverhampton, **Chepstow**, **Kempton**, **Wetherby**
28 Mon... Lingfield, **Catterick**, **Leicester**
29 Tue ....Southwell, **Doncaster**, **Kelso**, **Newbury**
30 Wed.. Lingfield, **Haydock**, **Taunton**
31 Thu ....Lingfield, **Uttoxeter**, **Warwick**

Big-race dates

March

28 Mar Doncaster........ Lincoln (Heritage Handicap)

April

10 Apr Lingfield........ All-Weather Championship Finals
14 Apr Newmarket........ Nell Gwyn Stakes (Group 3)
15 Apr Newmarket........ Earl of Sefton Stakes (Group 3)
16 Apr Newmarket........ Craven Stakes (Group 3)
18 Apr Newbury........ Fred Darling Stakes (Group 3)
18 Apr Newbury........ Greenham Stakes (Group 3)
18 Apr Newbury........ John Porter Stakes (Group 3)
24 Apr Sandown........ Gordon Richards Stakes (Group 3)
24 Apr Sandown........ bet365 Mile (Group 2)
29 Apr Ascot........ Sagaro Stakes (Group 3)

May

2 May Newmarket........ 2,000 Guineas (Group 1)
2 May Newmarket........ Dahlia Stakes (Group 3)
3 May Newmarket........ 1,000 Guineas (Group 1)
3 May Newmarket........ Jockey Club Stakes (Group 2)
6 May Chester........ Chester Vase (Group 3)
7 May Chester........ Ormonde Stakes (Group 3)
8 May Chester........ Chester Cup (Heritage Handicap)
8 May Chester........ Huxley Stakes (Group 3)
9 May Ascot........ Victoria Cup (Heritage Handicap)
9 May Lingfield........ Derby Trial (Group 3)
13 May York........ Duke of York Stakes (Group 2)
13 May York........ Musidora Stakes (Group 3)
14 May York........ Dante Stakes (Group 2)
14 May York........ Middleton Stakes (Group 3)
15 May York........ Yorkshire Cup (Group 2)
16 May Newbury........ Lockinge Stakes (Group 1)
23 May Haydock........ Temple Stakes (Group 2)
28 May Sandown........ Henry II Stakes (Group 2)
28 May Sandown........ Brigadier Gerard Stakes (Group 3)
30 May Haydock........ Sandy Lane Stakes (Group 2)
30 May Haydock........ John of Gaunt Stakes (Group 3)
30 May Haydock........ Pinnacle Stakes (Group 3)

June

5 Jun Epsom........ The Oaks (Group 1)
5 Jun Epsom........ Coronation Cup (Group 1)
6 Jun Epsom........ The Derby (Group 1)
6 Jun Epsom........ Princess Elizabeth Stakes (Group 3)
16 Jun Royal Ascot........ King's Stand Stakes (Group 1)
16 Jun Royal Ascot........ Queen Anne Stakes (Group 1)
16 Jun Royal Ascot........ St James's Palace Stakes (Group 1)
16 Jun Royal Ascot........ Coventry Stakes (Group 2)
17 Jun Royal Ascot........ Prince of Wales's Stakes (Group 1)
17 Jun Royal Ascot........ Queen Mary Stakes (Group 2)
17 Jun Royal Ascot........ Duke of Cambridge Stakes (Group 2)
17 Jun Royal Ascot........ Jersey Stakes (Group 3)

17 Jun Royal Ascot .... Royal Hunt Cup (Heritage Handicap)
18 Jun Royal Ascot .... Gold Cup (Group 1)
18 Jun Royal Ascot .... Ribblesdale Stakes (Group 2)
18 Jun Royal Ascot .... Norfolk Stakes (Group 2)
19 Jun Royal Ascot .... Coronation Stakes (Group 1)
19 Jun Royal Ascot .... Commonwealth Cup (Group 1)
19 Jun Royal Ascot .... King Edward VII Stakes (Group 2)
19 Jun Royal Ascot .... Albany Stakes (Group 3)
20 Jun Royal Ascot .... Diamond Jubilee Stakes (Group 1)
20 Jun Royal Ascot .... Hardwicke Stakes (Group 2)
20 Jun Royal Ascot .... Wokingham (Heritage Handicap)
27 Jun Newcastle .... Northumberland Plate (Heritage Handicap)
27 Jun Newcastle .... Chipchase Stakes (Group 3)
27 Jun Newmarket .... Criterion Stakes (Group 3)

July

4 Jul Sandown .... Coral-Eclipse Stakes (Group 1)
4 Jul Haydock .... Lancashire Oaks (Group 2)
9 Jul Newmarket .... Princess of Wales's Stakes (Group 2)
9 Jul Newmarket .... July Stakes (Group 2)
10 Jul Newmarket .... Falmouth Stakes (Group 1)
10 Jul Newmarket .... Duchess of Cambridge Stakes (Group 2)
10 Jul York .... Summer Stakes (Group 3)
11 Jul Newmarket .... July Cup (Group 1)
11 Jul Newmarket .... Superlative Stakes (Group 2)
11 Jul Newmarket .... Bunbury Cup (Heritage Handicap)
11 Jul York .... John Smith's Cup (Heritage Handicap)
18 Jul Newbury .... Hackwood Stakes (Group 3)
25 Jul Ascot .... King George VI and Queen Elizabeth Stakes (Group 1)
25 Jul Ascot .... Summer Mile (Group 2)
25 Jul York .... York Stakes (Group 2)
28 Jul Goodwood .... Goodwood Cup (Group 2)
28 Jul Goodwood .... Lennox Stakes (Group 2)
28 Jul Goodwood .... Vintage Stakes (Group 2)
29 Jul Goodwood .... Sussex Stakes (Group 1)
29 Jul Goodwood .... Molecomb Stakes (Group 3)
30 Jul Goodwood .... Nassau Stakes (Group 1)
30 Jul Goodwood .... Richmond Stakes (Group 2)
31 Jul Goodwood .... Betfred Mile (Heritage Handicap)
31 Jul Goodwood .... King George Stakes (Group 2)
31 Jul Goodwood .... Oak Tree Stakes (Group 3)

August

1 Aug Goodwood .... Stewards' Cup (Heritage Handicap)
1 Aug Goodwood .... Gordon Stakes (Group 3)
8 Aug Ascot .... Shergar Cup Day
8 Aug Haydock .... Rose of Lancaster Stakes (Group 3)
8 Aug Newmarket .... Sweet Solera Stakes (Group 3)
13 Aug Salisbury .... Sovereign Stakes (Group 3)
15 Aug Newbury .... Hungerford Stakes (Group 2)
15 Aug Newbury .... Geoffrey Freer Stakes (Group 3)
19 Aug York .... Juddmonte International (Group 1)
19 Aug York .... Great Voltigeur Stakes (Group 2)
19 Aug York .... Acomb Stakes (Group 3)
20 Aug York .... Yorkshire Oaks (Group 1)
20 Aug York .... Lowther Stakes (Group 2)
21 Aug York .... Nunthorpe Stakes (Group 1)

21 Aug York .... Lonsdale Cup (Group 2)
21 Aug York .... Gimcrack Stakes (Group 2)
22 Aug York .... Ebor (Heritage Handicap)
22 Aug York .... City of York Stakes (Group 2)
22 Aug Goodwood .... Celebration Mile (Group 2)
22 Aug Goodwood .... Prestige Stakes (Group 3)
22 Aug Windsor .... Winter Hill Stakes (Group 3)
29 Aug Sandown .... Solario Stakes (Group 3)

September

5 Sep Haydock .... Sprint Cup (Group 1)
5 Sep Kempton .... Sirenia Stakes (Group 3)
5 Sep Kempton .... September Stakes (Group 3)
10 Sep Doncaster .... May Hill Stakes (Group 2)
10 Sep Doncaster .... Park Hill Stakes (Group 2)
11 Sep Doncaster .... Doncaster Cup (Group 2)
11 Sep Doncaster .... Flying Childers Stakes (Group 2)
12 Sep Doncaster .... St Leger (Group 1)
12 Sep Doncaster .... Park Stakes (Group 2)
12 Sep Doncaster .... Champagne Stakes (Group 2)
12 Sep Doncaster .... Portland (Heritage Handicap)
19 Sep Ayr .... Ayr Gold Cup (Heritage Handicap)
19 Sep Ayr .... Firth Of Clyde Stakes (Group 3)
19 Sep Newbury .... Mill Reef Stakes (Group 2)
19 Sep Newbury .... World Trophy (Group 3)
19 Sep Newbury .... Arc Trial (Group 3)
24 Sep Newmarket .... Tattersalls Stakes (Group 3)
25 Sep Newmarket .... Rockfel Stakes (Group 2)
25 Sep Newmarket .... Joel Stakes (Group 2)
26 Sep Newmarket .... Cambridgeshire (Heritage Handicap)
26 Sep Newmarket .... Middle Park Stakes (Group 1)
26 Sep Newmarket .... Cheveley Park Stakes (Group 1)
26 Sep Newmarket .... Royal Lodge Stakes (Group 2)

October

3 Oct Newmarket .... Sun Chariot Stakes (Group 1)
3 Oct Ascot .... Cumberland Lodge Stakes (Group 3)
3 Oct Ascot .... Bengough Stakes (Group 3)
9 Oct Newmarket .... Fillies' Mile (Group 1)
9 Oct Newmarket .... Challenge Stakes (Group 2)
9 Oct Newmarket .... Cornwallis Stakes (Group 3)
9 Oct Newmarket .... Oh So Sharp Stakes (Group 3)
10 Oct Newmarket .... Cesarewitch (Heritage Handicap)
10 Oct Newmarket .... Dewhurst Stakes (Group 1)
10 Oct Newmarket .... Autumn Stakes (Group 3)
10 Oct Newmarket .... Darley Stakes (Group 3)
17 Oct Ascot .... Queen Elizabeth II Stakes (Group 1)
17 Oct Ascot .... Champion Stakes (Group 1)
17 Oct Ascot .... Champions Sprint (Group 1)
17 Oct Ascot .... Champions Filly & Mare Stakes (Group 1)
17 Oct Ascot .... Champions Long Distance Cup (Group 2)
24 Oct Doncaster .... Vertem Futurity Trophy (Group 1)
24 Oct Newbury .... Horris Hill Stakes (Group 3)
24 Oct Newbury .... St Simon Stakes (Group 3)

November

7 Nov Doncaster .... November (Heritage Handicap)

Track Facts

WANT TO size up the layout and undulations of the course where your fancy's about to line up? Over the next 30-odd pages, we bring you three-dimensional maps of all Britain's Flat tracks, allowing you to see at a glance the task facing your selection. The maps come to you courtesy of the Racing Post's website (www.racingpost.com).

We've listed the top dozen trainers and jockeys at each course, ranked by strike-rate, with a breakdown of their relevant statistics over the last five years. We've also included addresses, phone numbers, directions and fixture lists for each track, together with Racing Post standard times for all you clock-watchers.

ASCOT

Ascot, Berkshire SL5 7JX
Tel 0870 7227 227

How to get there Road: M4 junction 6 or M3 junction 3 on to A332. Rail: Frequent service from Reading or Waterloo

Features RH, stiff climb for final mile on round course

Winning Post
Startpoint
Highest Point
Lowest Point
Open ditch
Water jump
Fence

2m 5 1/2f
1m (Royal Hunt Cup)
6 1/2f 6f
7f 2m 4f 5 1/2f
5f
2m
1m 4f
1m
1m 2f

2020 Fixtures April 29, May 8-9, June 16-20, July 10-11, 24-25, August 8, September 4-5, October 2-3, 16

Racing Post standard times

5f	59.5	1m2f	2min5
6f	1min12.4	1m4f	2min28.9
7f	1min25.6	2m	3min22
1m (str)	1min38.8	2m4f	4min20
1m (rnd)	1min39.8	2m5f159yds	4min45

Trainers	*Wins-Runs*	*%*	*2yo*	*3yo+*	*£1 level stks*
John Gosden	47-277	17	9-29	38-248	-22.43
A P O'Brien	34-244	14	9-47	25-197	-19.71
Charlie Appleby	26-167	16	11-38	15-129	-18.60
Richard Hannon	26-331	8	14-117	12-214	-124.75
Mark Johnston	25-253	10	12-68	13-185	-99.00
William Haggas	24-188	13	3-25	21-163	-45.31
Sir Michael Stoute	23-166	14	2-10	21-156	+6.32
Roger Varian	19-139	14	3-24	16-115	-48.39
Andrew Balding	19-204	9	0-20	19-184	-77.00
Clive Cox	14-130	11	4-32	10-98	-18.25
Jamie Osborne	12-64	19	0-16	12-48	+41.25
Saeed bin Suroor	12-103	12	3-16	9-87	-34.20
Roger Charlton	10-69	14	3-8	7-61	-25.25

Jockeys	*Wins-Rides*	*%*	*£1 level stks*	*Best Trainer*	*W-R*
Ryan Moore	49-268	18	-48.11	A P O´Brien	28-123
William Buick	39-226	17	-13.35	Charlie Appleby	15-91
Frankie Dettori	38-185	21	+19.74	John Gosden	22-86
James Doyle	29-207	14	-36.22	Charlie Appleby	5-39
Jamie Spencer	24-217	11	-12.68	David Simcock	4-26
Andrea Atzeni	22-188	12	-51.22	Roger Varian	10-72
Adam Kirby	21-196	11	-18.80	Clive Cox	12-77
Silvestre De Sousa	18-218	8	-71.30	Andrew Balding	4-24
Oisin Murphy	14-182	8	-64.13	Andrew Balding	3-25
Jim Crowley	14-215	7	-79.25	Owen Burrows	3-16
Martin Harley	12-109	11	+22.00	William Haggas	3-4
Daniel Tudhope	10-72	14	+43.00	William Haggas	4-10
Robert Havlin	10-79	13	-7.75	John Gosden	10-63

Favourites

2yo 32.4 -13.11 3yo 32 -13.25 Total 32.7 +8.91

Whitletts Road Ayr KA8 0JE.
Tel 01292 264 179

AYR

How to get there
Road: south from Glasgow on A77 or A75, A70, A76.
Rail: Ayr, bus service from station on big race days

Features LH

2020 Fixtures
April 27-28, May 12, 20, June 8, 15, 20, July 5-6, 13, 20, 27, August 8, 10, September 17-19, 29, October 8

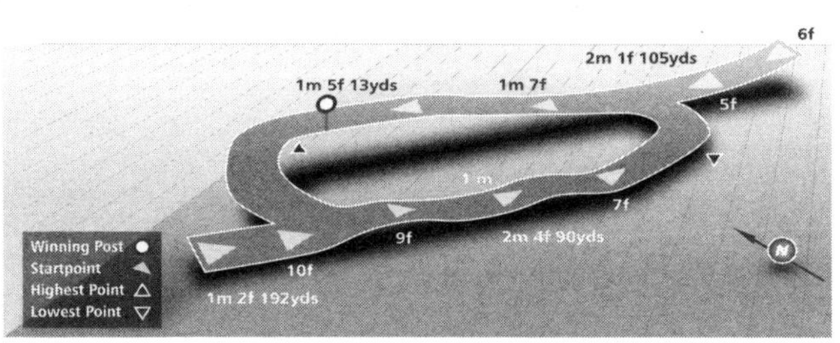

Racing Post standard times

5f	57.7	1m2f192yds	2min17.5
6f	1min10	1m5f13yds	2min47
7f50yds	1min28	1m7f	3min15
1m	1min38	2m1f105yds	3min49
1m1f20yds	1min51	2m4f90yds	4min31
1m2f	2min6		

Trainers	*Wins-Runs*	*%*	*2yo*	*3yo+*	*£1 level stks*
Keith Dalgleish	60-506	12	15-92	45-414	-8.93
Jim Goldie	51-577	9	0-8	51-569	-122.17
David O'Meara	34-207	16	1-17	33-190	-12.25
Richard Fahey	34-366	9	9-90	25-276	-138.12
Michael Dods	30-285	11	7-54	23-231	-37.13
K R Burke	25-133	19	10-42	15-91	-0.27
Ruth Carr	22-182	12	0-0	22-182	-17.05
R Mike Smith	21-189	11	0-7	21-182	+47.50
Iain Jardine	21-211	10	1-23	20-188	-63.75
Linda Perratt	17-316	5	0-12	17-304	-161.50
Mark Johnston	16-140	11	10-58	6-82	-79.92
Adrian Paul Keatley	14-72	19	0-3	14-69	+9.88
Tim Easterby	14-152	9	0-14	14-138	-19.09

Jockeys	*Wins-Rides*	*%*	*£1 level stks*	*Best Trainer*	*W-R*
Daniel Tudhope	40-218	18	+45.35	David O´Meara	18-94
Paul Mulrennan	33-241	14	-23.96	Michael Dods	12-106
Phillip Makin	31-168	18	+46.35	Keith Dalgleish	19-94
Joe Fanning	27-225	12	-87.19	Mark Johnston	9-69
James Sullivan	27-245	11	-7.97	Ruth Carr	18-120
P J McDonald	26-219	12	-29.35	R Mike Smith	8-40
Graham Lee	26-223	12	+11.45	Keith Dalgleish	6-35
Ben Curtis	21-129	16	-12.31	K R Burke	8-25
Jamie Gormley	16-119	13	+16.50	Iain Jardine	8-59
Jason Hart	16-134	12	+25.75	John Quinn	5-49
Paul Hanagan	16-149	11	-56.12	Richard Fahey	10-88
Connor Beasley	16-173	9	-92.19	Keith Dalgleish	6-47
Callum Rodriguez	14-105	13	+22.58	Michael Dods	7-49

Favourites

2yo	31.4	-20.19	3yo	26.5	-44.63	Total	29.3	-108.1

BATH

Lansdown, Bath, Glos BA1 9BU
Tel 01291 622 260

How to get there Road: M4, Jctn 18, then A46 south. Rail: Bath Spa, special bus service to course on race days

Features LH uphill 4f straight

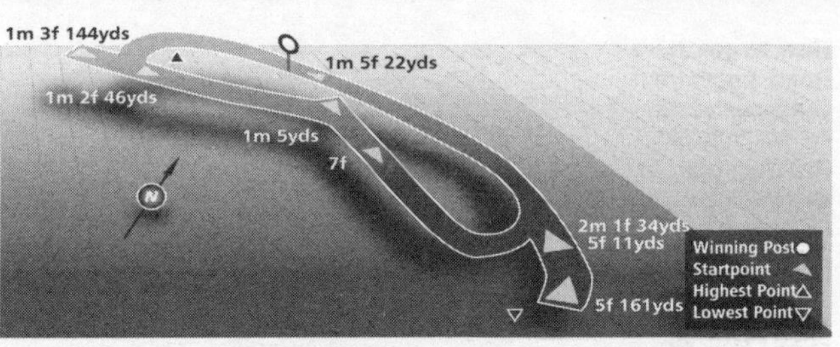

2020 Fixtures March 30, April 9, 17, May 8, 13, 22, June 5, 13, 24, July 1, 8, 14, 22, 31, August 5, 15, 19, September 2, 12-13, 28, October 14

Racing Post standard times

5f11yds	1min0.8	1m3f144yds	2min28
5f161yds	1min9.6	1m5f22yds	2min48.5
1m5yds	1min39	2m1f34yds	3min40
1m2f46yds	2min8		

Trainers	*Wins-Runs*	*%*	*2yo*	*3yo+*	*£1 level stks*
Malcolm Saunders	29-158	18	0-4	29-154	-2.34
Richard Hannon	27-179	15	12-79	15-100	-55.08
Mick Channon	25-135	19	8-37	17-98	-3.00
Clive Cox	24-122	20	9-26	15-96	-19.00
Tony Carroll	23-166	14	0-8	23-158	-15.36
Mark Johnston	21-89	24	6-27	15-62	-20.34
Ronald Harris	21-171	12	2-21	19-150	-6.92
Charles Hills	20-89	22	5-24	15-65	+1.22
Roger Charlton	17-49	35	3-7	14-42	+24.83
Rod Millman	17-123	14	1-18	16-105	+34.63
Sir Mark Prescott Bt	15-42	36	0-4	15-38	-6.51
Brian Meehan	15-58	26	5-24	10-34	+26.10
Marcus Tregoning	13-42	31	1-4	12-38	+9.24

Jockeys	*Wins-Rides*	*%*	*£1 level stks*	*Best Trainer*	*W-R*
Silvestre De Sousa	29-135	21	-25.34	Mark Johnston	6-14
Tom Marquand	26-130	20	+81.34	Tony Carroll	7-19
Luke Morris	26-189	14	-75.59	Sir Mark Prescott Bt	13-33
Franny Norton	24-114	21	-22.25	Mark Johnston	8-35
Adam Kirby	21-78	27	+23.02	Clive Cox	11-36
Steve Drowne	19-108	18	+57.88	George Baker	5-19
David Probert	17-161	11	-60.03	Ronald Harris	4-29
Josephine Gordon	16-98	16	+40.17	Malcolm Saunders	3-12
Oisin Murphy	15-114	13	-5.07	Rod Millman	3-9
Martin Dwyer	15-145	10	-51.33	William Muir	3-39
George Baker	13-37	35	+8.58	Roger Charlton	3-7
Dane O'Neill	13-78	17	-0.20	Richard Hannon	2-3
Charles Bishop	13-96	14	-2.25	Mick Channon	7-24

Favourites

2yo	43.6	+3.08	3yo	38.3	-38.95	Total	35.5	-78.61

York Road, Beverley, E Yorkshire
HU17 8QZ. Tel 01482 867 488

BEVERLEY

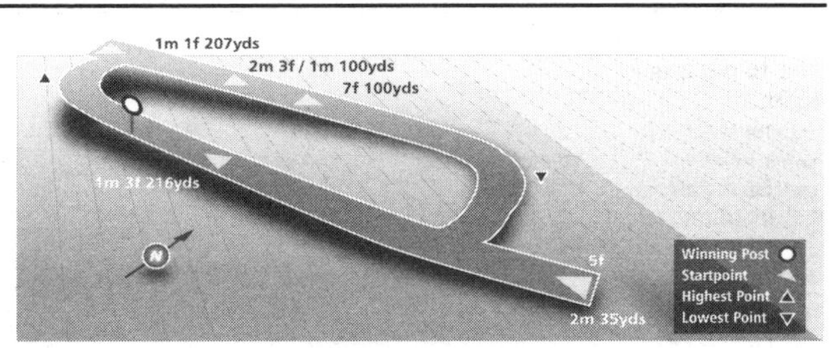

How to get there Road: Course is signposted from the M62. Rail: Beverley, bus service to course on race days

Features RH, uphill finish

2020 Fixtures
April 15, 23, May 8, 12, 23, 27, June 16, 23, July 3-4, 14, 20, 28, August 12-13, 29-30, September 16, 22

Racing Post standard times

5f	1min1	1m4f16yds	2min34.2
7f100yds	1min30	2m35yds	3min30
1m100yds	1min43	2m3f100yds	4min17
1m1f207yds	2min1.3		

Trainers	*Wins-Runs*	*%*	*2yo*	*3yo+*	*£1 level stks*
Mark Johnston	52-262	20	27-90	25-172	-54.80
Richard Fahey	52-380	14	22-139	30-241	-122.06
Tim Easterby	46-401	11	6-108	40-293	-151.11
David O'Meara	44-261	17	4-53	40-208	-1.21
Kevin Ryan	22-174	13	10-64	12-110	+4.33
Nigel Tinkler	20-170	12	5-65	15-105	-56.17
Karen Tutty	14-85	16	0-1	14-84	+32.75
Richard Guest	13-62	21	2-4	11-58	+45.75
Les Eyre	13-109	12	1-11	12-98	-14.20
Michael Bell	12-43	28	2-9	10-34	+0.41
David Loughnane	12-56	21	0-8	12-48	+70.25
Michael Dods	12-87	14	6-31	6-56	-21.75
Ollie Pears	12-152	8	2-35	10-117	-32.75

Jockeys	*Wins-Rides*	*%*	*£1 level stks*	*Best Trainer*	*W-R*
Joe Fanning	48-266	18	-56.57	Mark Johnston	35-165
Daniel Tudhope	45-184	24	+50.39	David O´Meara	22-98
David Allan	40-311	13	-119.98	Tim Easterby	26-191
Paul Hanagan	28-157	18	-29.92	Richard Fahey	20-103
Ben Curtis	28-164	17	-7.06	Brian Ellison	5-23
Tony Hamilton	24-173	14	-34.73	Richard Fahey	16-113
Graham Lee	24-220	11	-93.64	Bryan Smart	7-46
Paul Mulrennan	23-178	13	-59.19	Michael Dods	9-48
P J McDonald	19-191	10	-90.13	Ann Duffield	7-50
Tom Eaves	16-225	7	-78.59	Kevin Ryan	7-50
Andrew Mullen	13-178	7	-58.65	Mark Walford	3-7
Kevin Stott	12-86	14	-14.30	Kevin Ryan	6-38
Jason Hart	11-100	11	-32.53	John Quinn	6-39

Favourites

2yo	37.7	-25.43	3yo	41.3	+14.12	Total	36.5	-26.2

BRIGHTON

Freshfield Road, Brighton, E Sussex
BN2 2XZ. Tel 01273 603 580

How to get there Road: Signposted from A23 London Road and A27. Rail: Brighton, bus to course on race days

Features LH, undulating, sharp

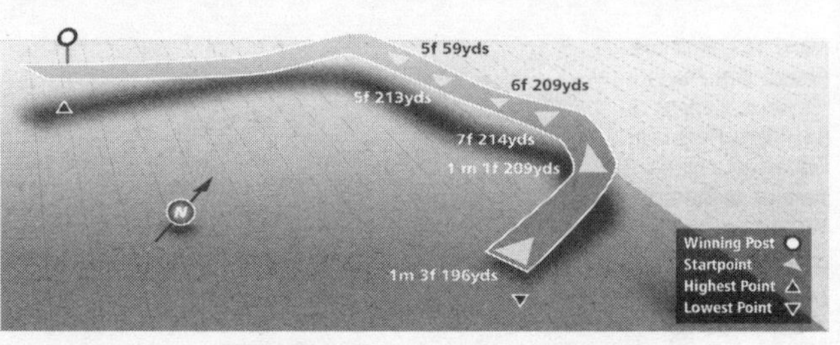

2020 Fixtures April 18, 28-29, May 4, 22, 26, June 2, 16, 23, 30, July 7, 13, August 5-7, 23-24, September 7, 14, October 6, 15

Racing Post standard times

5f59yds	1min0.4	7f214yds	1min33
5f213yds	1min8.4	1m1f209yds	1min59.4
6f209yds	1min20.5	1m3f196yds	2min28.8

Trainers	*Wins-Runs*	*%*	*2yo*	*3yo+*	*£1 level stks*
Tony Carroll	46-274	17	0-7	46-267	+5.16
Richard Hannon	36-153	24	16-67	20-86	+50.82
Gary Moore	33-227	15	4-25	29-202	+3.10
Eve Johnson Houghton	24-107	22	3-23	21-84	+21.04
Richard Hughes	20-92	22	4-21	16-71	-3.44
John Gallagher	19-115	17	1-8	18-107	+18.63
Mark Johnston	18-108	17	9-42	9-66	-46.15
Mick Channon	16-145	11	4-42	12-103	-35.92
Paul Cole	14-45	31	4-9	10-36	+27.50
Philip Hide	14-74	19	1-4	13-70	-10.81
Andrew Balding	13-66	20	3-15	10-51	-22.12
John Bridger	13-120	11	0-6	13-114	-25.67
Stuart Williams	12-66	18	2-6	10-60	-21.31

Jockeys	*Wins-Rides*	*%*	*£1 level stks*	*Best Trainer*	*W-R*
Jim Crowley	35-141	25	-0.67	Paul Cole	3-4
Tom Marquand	35-189	19	+143.25	Richard Hannon	12-47
Silvestre De Sousa	29-137	21	-18.39	Mark Johnston	3-17
Adam Kirby	26-86	30	+34.89	Clive Cox	8-17
Hector Crouch	26-195	13	+3.38	Gary Moore	16-117
Jason Watson	25-110	23	-2.09	Amanda Perrett	3-11
David Probert	25-132	19	+12.61	Andrew Balding	5-21
Shane Kelly	24-142	17	-31.94	Richard Hughes	16-58
Luke Morris	24-165	15	-29.26	Sir Mark Prescott Bt	7-21
Pat Cosgrave	22-116	19	+15.72	George Baker	4-29
J F Egan	16-107	15	-30.05	John Berry	6-19
William Carson	16-142	11	-39.48	John Bridger	8-52
Charles Bishop	15-105	14	+2.25	Eve Johnson Houghton	7-42

Favourites

2yo	41.7	-18.82	3yo	31.8	-57.07	Total	33.2	-126.54

Durdar Road, Carlisle, Cumbria, CA2 4TS. Tel 01228 554 700

CARLISLE

How to get there Road: M6 Jctn 42, follow signs on Dalston Road. Rail: Carlisle, 66 bus to course on race days

Features RH, undulating, uphill finish

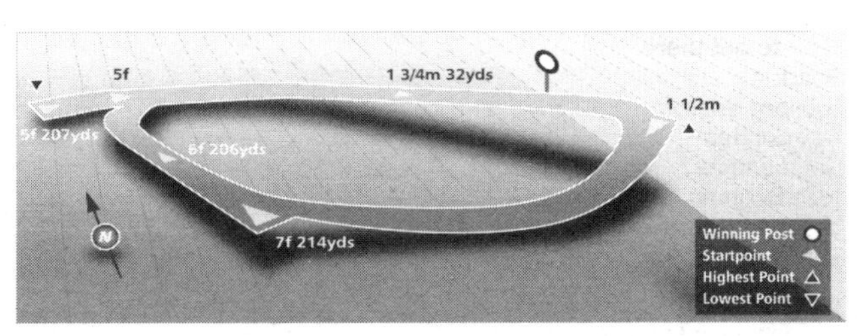

2020 Fixtures May 18, 28-29, June 19, 24, July 4, 9, August 3, 18-19, 27, September 9

Racing Post standard times

5f	1min	1m1f61yds	1min55.2
5f193yds	1min12.2	1m3f107yds	2min23.5
6f192yds	1min25.7	1m6f32yds	3min2.5
7f200yds	1min38.5	2m1f52yds	3min46

Trainers	Wins-Runs	%	2yo	3yo+	£1 level stks
Keith Dalgleish	35-263	13	4-50	31-213	-34.38
Richard Fahey	34-261	13	14-102	20-159	-77.60
Tim Easterby	32-293	11	3-76	29-217	-91.82
K R Burke	25-122	20	17-60	8-62	+35.47
Mark Johnston	24-123	20	8-45	16-78	-19.36
Michael Dods	19-157	12	9-49	10-108	-59.63
Kevin Ryan	14-103	14	5-36	9-67	-27.95
Brian Ellison	11-76	14	1-17	10-59	-15.82
Nigel Tinkler	10-38	26	2-11	8-27	+51.00
Roger Fell	10-63	16	0-3	10-60	+3.00
Ann Duffield	10-67	15	6-30	4-37	+3.98
Dianne Sayer	10-75	13	0-1	10-74	+32.13
Iain Jardine	9-88	10	0-16	9-72	-22.17

Jockeys	Wins-Rides	%	£1 level stks	Best Trainer	W-R
Ben Curtis	39-154	25	+132.36	K R Burke	9-35
Paul Mulrennan	31-183	17	-12.68	Michael Dods	13-63
Tony Hamilton	20-129	16	-7.51	Richard Fahey	13-85
Joe Fanning	19-127	15	-21.78	Mark Johnston	12-55
Graham Lee	19-151	13	-39.00	Keith Dalgleish	2-13
P J McDonald	14-97	14	-25.52	Ann Duffield	4-29
Phillip Makin	12-93	13	-13.18	Keith Dalgleish	9-61
David Allan	12-101	12	-40.90	Tim Easterby	10-77
Kevin Stott	11-67	16	+4.10	Kevin Ryan	6-34
Shane Gray	11-79	14	-0.67	Keith Dalgleish	8-32
Rachel Richardson	11-104	11	-20.00	Tim Easterby	7-74
Daniel Tudhope	10-74	14	-25.58	Archie Watson	2-5
Franny Norton	10-75	13	-41.38	Mark Johnston	7-44

Favourites

2yo 44.6 +7.45 3yo 39.5 +18.79 Total 34.8 -13.49

CATTERICK

Catterick Bridge, Richmond, N Yorks DL10 7PE. Tel 01748 811 478

How to get there Road: A1, exit 5m south of Scotch Corner. Rail: Darlington or Northallerton and bus

Features LH, undulating, tight

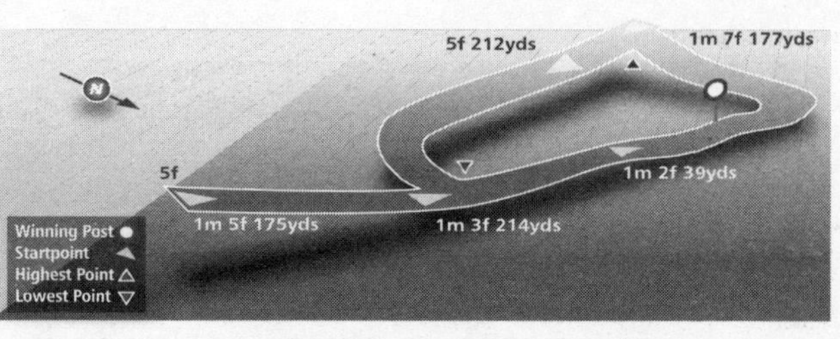

2020 Fixtures
April 8, 22, May 11, 23, 29, June 5, July 8, 15, 22, August 4, 17, 26, September 8, 19, October 6, 17, 27

Racing Post standard times

5f	58.3	1m3f214yds	2min33
5f212yds	1min11.3	1m5f175yds	2min57
7f	1min23.3	1m7f177yds	3min23

Trainers	*Wins-Runs*	*%*	*2yo*	*3yo+*	*£1 level stks*
Richard Fahey	41-222	18	16-89	25-133	+2.32
Tim Easterby	32-267	12	4-59	28-208	-47.40
John Quinn	29-177	16	9-53	20-124	-0.95
David O'Meara	28-200	14	8-48	20-152	-72.63
Mark Johnston	23-146	16	15-71	8-75	-68.89
Keith Dalgleish	22-118	19	6-38	16-80	+42.17
Ruth Carr	21-157	13	1-4	20-153	-30.50
Brian Ellison	15-97	15	3-15	12-82	-7.69
Kevin Ryan	13-92	14	4-23	9-69	-18.87
Michael Easterby	13-139	9	1-22	12-117	+19.13
Michael Bell	12-37	32	1-8	11-29	+12.64
Michael Appleby	11-107	10	1-9	10-98	-38.29
K R Burke	10-57	18	4-25	6-32	+16.38

Jockeys	*Wins-Rides*	*%*	*£1 level stks*	*Best Trainer*	*W-R*
P J McDonald	29-167	17	+16.87	Mark Johnston	5-20
Jason Hart	29-175	17	+17.78	John Quinn	16-91
Daniel Tudhope	28-134	21	-32.24	David O´Meara	17-80
James Sullivan	27-214	13	-10.22	Ruth Carr	16-112
David Allan	22-201	11	-22.71	Tim Easterby	11-102
Paul Mulrennan	21-124	17	-26.08	Paul Midgley	3-9
Ben Curtis	21-153	14	-25.91	Brian Ellison	5-25
Joe Fanning	16-140	11	-54.68	Mark Johnston	7-60
Graham Lee	16-182	9	-95.40	Rebecca Menzies	2-5
Connor Beasley	13-74	18	+96.75	Keith Dalgleish	6-16
Jack Garritty	12-80	15	-0.75	Richard Fahey	2-11
Tom Eaves	12-123	10	-11.51	Michael Dods	2-4
Phillip Makin	11-82	13	-34.46	Keith Dalgleish	5-26

Favourites

2yo	43.9	-3.04	3yo	33.7	-28.06	Total	34.7	-40.57

CHELMSFORD

Great Leighs, CM3 1QP.
Tel 01245 362 412

How to get there Road: M11 Jctn 8, A120 towards Chelmsford, signposted from A131. Rail: Chelmsford, bus to course on racedays

Features LH, Polytrack, 1m circuit with wide sweeping bends

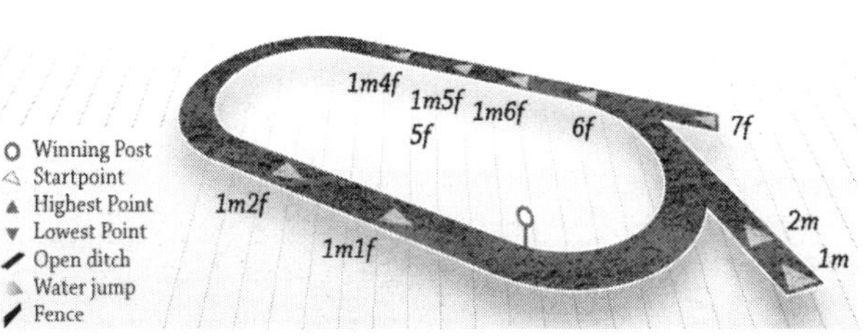

2020 Fixtures April 2, 9, 10, 23, 29-30, May 7, 21, 25, June 4, 9, 17-18, July 3-4, 14, 21, August 1, 7-8, 14, 22, 28-29, September 3, 10, 12, 17, 19, 26, October 1, 8, 10, 15, 22, 24, 29, November 5, 7, 19, 26-27, December 3, 10, 17

Racing Post standard times

5f	59.6
6f	1min12.3
1m	1min39
1m2f	2min6.5
1m6f	3min0.6
2m	3min28

Trainers	*Wins-Runs*	*%*	*2yo*	*3yo+*	*£1 level stks*
Mark Johnston	73-474	15	31-163	42-311	-141.34
John Gosden	64-255	25	15-89	49-166	-53.71
Michael Appleby	57-544	10	0-31	57-513	-200.24
Saeed bin Suroor	56-184	30	12-44	44-140	-4.10
David Simcock	55-301	18	6-36	49-265	+6.38
Stuart Williams	55-356	15	6-31	49-325	-9.90
William Haggas	48-213	23	13-59	35-154	-39.90
Marco Botti	45-350	13	16-99	29-251	-54.44
Derek Shaw	43-345	12	1-32	42-313	-25.83
Sir Michael Stoute	41-173	24	8-43	33-130	-11.59
Richard Hannon	40-341	12	19-150	21-191	-104.74
Dean Ivory	39-285	14	0-27	39-258	-23.83
Jamie Osborne	38-305	12	9-99	29-206	-43.98

Jockeys	*Wins-Rides*	*%*	*£1 level stks*	*Best Trainer*	*W-R*
Luke Morris	92-881	10	-387.89	Sir Mark Prescott Bt	24-132
Adam Kirby	76-431	18	-92.27	Clive Cox	6-17
Oisin Murphy	75-366	20	-21.74	Andrew Balding	13-52
Jim Crowley	74-317	23	+32.88	Sir Michael Stoute	9-16
Silvestre De Sousa	68-340	20	-13.89	Chris Dwyer	15-66
Martin Harley	48-324	15	-35.98	David Simcock	8-21
Ryan Moore	45-125	36	+23.78	Sir Michael Stoute	16-40
Robert Havlin	44-288	15	-82.01	John Gosden	28-106
James Doyle	41-176	23	-52.68	William Haggas	9-27
P J McDonald	35-169	21	+71.91	Mark Johnston	11-47
Franny Norton	34-279	12	-79.39	Mark Johnston	16-120
Josephine Gordon	34-384	9	-120.22	Phil McEntee	9-85
Shane Kelly	33-292	11	-78.16	Richard Hughes	17-82

Favourites

2yo 44 +18.63 3yo 36.4 -118.78 Total 36.7 -168.29

CHEPSTOW

Chepstow, Monmouthshire, NP16 6BE. Tel 01291 622 260

How to get there Road: M4 Jct 22 on west side of Severn Bridge, A48 north, A446. Rail: Chepstow, bus to course on race days

Features LH, undulating

2020 Fixtures May 1, 12, June 6, 12, 22, 30, July 10, 16, 24, August 11, 20, 24, 31, September 10

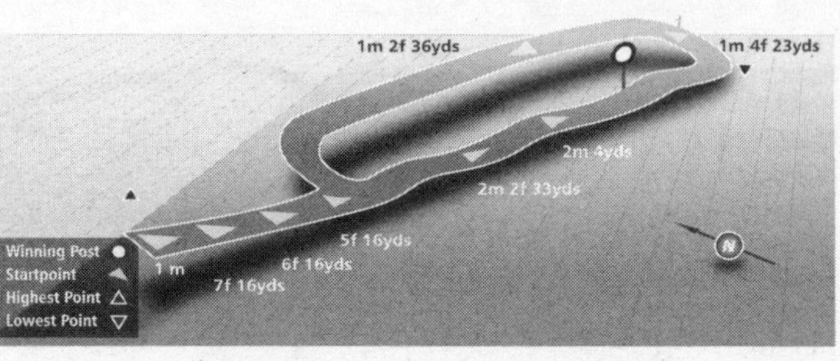

Racing Post standard times

5f16yds	58.3	1m2f36yds	2min6.5
6f16yds	1min9.8	1m4f23yds	2min34
7f16yds	1min21.5	2m49yds	3min28
1m14yds	1min33.5	2m2f	3min52

Trainers	*Wins-Runs*	*%*	*2yo*	*3yo+*	*£1 level stks*
David Evans	25-219	11	6-66	19-153	-44.45
Richard Hannon	24-150	16	15-62	9-88	-24.44
John O'Shea	21-148	14	0-0	21-148	+17.08
Andrew Balding	19-108	18	2-17	17-91	-17.87
Eve Johnson Houghton	18-77	23	5-25	13-52	+2.59
Ralph Beckett	17-64	27	2-17	15-47	+1.68
Mick Channon	16-105	15	3-31	13-74	+12.35
Ronald Harris	16-148	11	1-30	15-118	+19.60
Ed de Giles	15-69	22	0-4	15-65	+42.25
Clive Cox	14-61	23	4-15	10-46	-3.29
Bernard Llewellyn	13-110	12	0-0	13-110	-5.08
Richard Price	11-84	13	0-2	11-82	-36.18
Grace Harris	11-93	12	0-3	11-90	+63.50

Jockeys	*Wins-Rides*	*%*	*£1 level stks*	*Best Trainer*	*W-R*
David Probert	25-184	14	-22.58	Andrew Balding	5-38
Rossa Ryan	23-100	23	+57.90	David Evans	6-11
Tom Marquand	22-140	16	-9.37	Richard Price	7-22
Luke Morris	20-170	12	-45.76	John O´Shea	4-17
Oisin Murphy	19-89	21	+2.51	Rod Millman	4-8
Franny Norton	19-94	20	+24.22	Mark Johnston	5-31
Callum Shepherd	16-79	20	+42.50	Ed de Giles	8-26
Richard Kingscote	15-60	25	+11.04	K R Burke	2-3
Dane O'Neill	14-72	19	-7.06	Richard Hannon	2-4
Pat Dobbs	11-63	17	-14.20	Richard Hannon	4-26
John Fahy	11-64	17	+38.38	Eve Johnson Houghton	5-13
Liam Keniry	11-104	11	-34.90	Neil Mulholland	2-3
Charles Bishop	10-87	11	-21.25	Eve Johnson Houghton	7-26

Favourites

2yo 40 -9.52 3yo 34.6 -39.45 Total 34.7 -59.39

Steam Mill Street, Chester, CH1 2LY
Tel 01244 304 600

CHESTER

How to get there Road: Inner Ring Road and A458 Queensferry Road.
Rail: Chester General, bus to city centre

Features LH, flat, very sharp

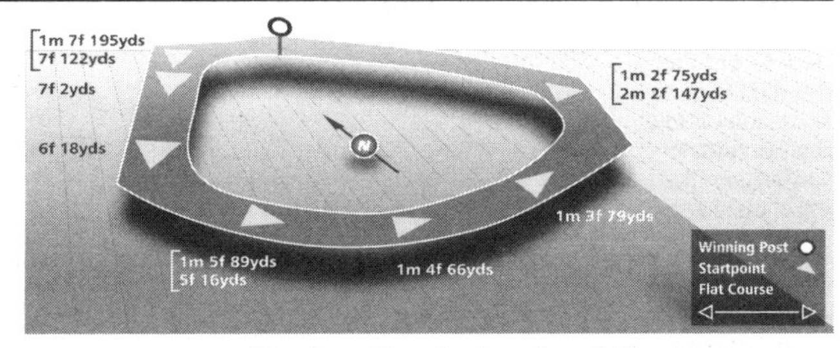

2020 Fixtures May 5-7, 23, June 13, 26-27, July 10-11, 25, August 2, 22, September 11-12, 26

Racing Post standard times

5f16yds	59.6	1m3f79yds	2min22.7
5f110yds	1min5.6	1m4f66yds	2min34.6
6f18yds	1min13.1	1m5f89yds	2min48
7f2yds	1min24.3	1m7f195yds	3min24
7f122yds	1min31.4	2m2f147yds	4min1
1m2f75yds	2min7.9		

Trainers	*Wins-Runs*	*%*	*2yo*	*3yo+*	*£1 level stks*
Richard Fahey	67-537	12	12-98	55-439	-34.55
Andrew Balding	42-203	21	8-28	34-175	+32.10
Mark Johnston	40-246	16	15-77	25-169	-35.40
Tom Dascombe	39-331	12	20-120	19-211	-140.09
Tim Easterby	19-141	13	1-21	18-120	-9.00
Richard Hannon	15-86	17	10-39	5-47	-11.84
Sir Michael Stoute	13-44	30	1-3	12-41	-2.04
Ian Williams	13-117	11	1-4	12-113	-40.25
A P O'Brien	12-36	33	0-0	12-36	-1.33
Ralph Beckett	12-63	19	1-5	11-58	-17.93
Kevin Ryan	11-70	16	4-11	7-59	-13.84
William Haggas	9-36	25	3-6	6-30	-8.18
John Gosden	8-33	24	0-1	8-32	-5.25

Jockeys	*Wins-Rides*	*%*	*£1 level stks*	*Best Trainer*	*W-R*
Franny Norton	43-287	15	-81.15	Mark Johnston	25-152
Richard Kingscote	40-225	18	-17.96	Tom Dascombe	25-151
David Probert	19-124	15	-35.78	Andrew Balding	15-82
Ryan Moore	14-47	30	-10.58	A P O´Brien	11-22
Paul Hanagan	14-108	13	-26.40	Richard Fahey	9-82
Paddy Mathers	11-89	12	-20.50	Richard Fahey	11-68
Silvestre De Sousa	10-53	19	+6.19	Richard Hannon	2-2
Shane Gray	10-72	14	+0.75	Kevin Ryan	6-26
J F Egan	10-108	9	-38.00	Saeed bin Suroor	2-5
Harry Bentley	9-32	28	+25.75	Ralph Beckett	4-12
Rob Hornby	9-44	20	+21.75	Andrew Balding	7-24
Adam McNamara	8-37	22	+6.17	Richard Fahey	8-31
Graham Lee	8-52	15	+9.85	Ed Dunlop	1-1

Favourites

2yo	36.2	-17.78	3yo	33.8	-13.82	Total	31.5	-64.9

DONCASTER

Leger Way, Doncaster
DN2 6BB. Tel 01302 320066/7

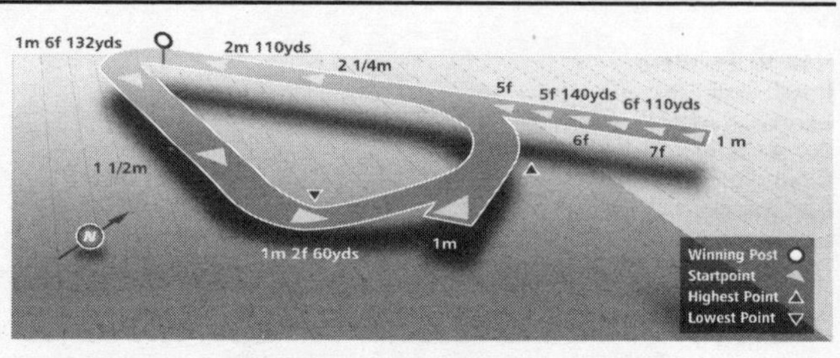

How to get there
Road: M18 Jct 3, A638, A18 to Hull.
Rail: Doncaster Central

Features LH, flat

2020 Fixtures
March 28-29, April 24-25, May 2, 16, June 5-6, 14, 26-27, July 3, 9, 18, 23, August 1, 15, September 9-12, October 23-24, November 7

Racing Post standard times

5f	57.9	1m (Rnd)	1min36.2
5f140yds	1min6.2	1m2f60yds	2m6
6f	1min10.5	1m4f	2min29
6f110yds	1min17	1m6f132yds	3min3
7f	1min23.3	2m110yds	3min33
1m (Str)	1min36	2m2f	3min52

Trainers	*Wins-Runs*	*%*	*2yo*	*3yo+*	*£1 level stks*
Richard Fahey	41-433	9	13-112	28-321	-121.17
Roger Varian	40-156	26	5-37	35-119	+30.30
Richard Hannon	35-299	12	15-134	20-165	-60.03
John Gosden	29-136	21	9-43	20-93	-35.94
Sir Michael Stoute	27-75	36	4-15	23-60	+52.75
Mark Johnston	27-182	15	13-81	14-101	-40.25
Charlie Appleby	25-102	25	11-44	14-58	-2.73
David O'Meara	24-252	10	4-14	20-238	-78.34
Saeed bin Suroor	23-68	34	5-17	18-51	+15.45
William Haggas	23-112	21	11-36	12-76	-13.44
David Simcock	20-88	23	2-13	18-75	+12.70
Ralph Beckett	19-105	18	7-33	12-72	+4.39
Ian Williams	17-89	19	0-3	17-86	+37.53

Jockeys	*Wins-Rides*	*%*	*£1 level stks*	*Best Trainer*	*W-R*
Andrea Atzeni	45-194	23	+40.77	Roger Varian	20-71
Jamie Spencer	32-158	20	+41.52	David Simcock	11-33
Ryan Moore	27-124	22	-16.28	Sir Michael Stoute	8-20
Daniel Tudhope	27-164	16	+14.88	David O´Meara	9-75
P J McDonald	26-192	14	+42.38	Mark Johnston	6-29
William Buick	24-122	20	+2.58	Charlie Appleby	10-51
James Doyle	22-138	16	-60.56	Charlie Appleby	5-18
Silvestre De Sousa	21-137	15	-28.28	Mark Johnston	3-16
Paul Hanagan	20-170	12	-48.48	Richard Fahey	8-81
Jim Crowley	19-114	17	-29.21	Ian Williams	3-4
Oisin Murphy	18-131	14	-39.10	Ralph Beckett	5-13
Frankie Dettori	17-77	22	-15.30	John Gosden	10-37
Graham Lee	16-169	9	-52.38	Jedd O´Keeffe	2-19

Favourites
2yo 46.6 +24.53 3yo 40.1 +14.5 Total 36.6 -5.26

EPSOM

Epsom Downs, Surrey, KT18 5LQ
Tel 01372 726 311

How to get there Road: M25 Jct 8 (A217) or 9 (A24), 2m south of Epsom on B290. Rail: Epsom and bus, Epsom Downs or Tattenham Corner

Features LH, undulating

2020 Fixtures April 22, June 5-6, July 2, 9, 16, 30, August 31, September 1, 10, 27

Racing Post standard times

5f	54.9	1m114yds	1min41.8
6f	1min7	1m2f18yds	2min5.3
7f	1min20	1m4f10yds	2min33.6

Trainers	*Wins-Runs*	*%*	*2yo*	*3yo+*	*£1 level stks*
Mark Johnston	21-128	16	13-31	8-97	-38.08
Andrew Balding	15-100	15	2-12	13-88	+13.29
Mick Channon	14-64	22	3-20	11-44	+16.07
John Gosden	12-51	24	0-7	12-44	-5.96
Jim Boyle	12-79	15	0-13	12-66	-3.75
Roger Varian	11-34	32	0-3	11-31	+18.63
Ralph Beckett	10-55	18	3-8	7-47	-6.13
Richard Fahey	10-105	10	1-16	9-89	-26.13
Eve Johnson Houghton	9-48	19	0-7	9-41	+1.48
Richard Hannon	9-86	10	6-34	3-52	-37.00
Gary Moore	8-79	10	0-9	8-70	+12.10
Charlie Appleby	7-31	23	3-7	4-24	-1.41
John Quinn	7-31	23	0-3	7-28	+21.50

Jockeys	*Wins-Rides*	*%*	*£1 level stks*	*Best Trainer*	*W-R*
Silvestre De Sousa	35-136	26	+40.62	Mark Johnston	6-32
Charles Bishop	14-36	39	+37.64	Eve Johnson Houghton	5-14
Franny Norton	13-58	22	+11.43	Mark Johnston	10-36
Andrea Atzeni	12-71	17	-9.87	Roger Varian	8-22
Jim Crowley	12-73	16	-12.10	Owen Burrows	2-3
Frankie Dettori	10-39	26	-0.51	John Gosden	9-21
Oisin Murphy	10-97	10	-38.29	Andrew Balding	4-27
James Doyle	9-50	18	-18.05	Charlie Appleby	3-9
Harry Bentley	9-59	15	-18.08	David O´Meara	3-9
David Probert	9-66	14	-16.25	Andrew Balding	3-26
Jason Watson	8-36	22	+2.79	Hughie Morrison	2-3
Pat Dobbs	7-34	21	+19.28	Richard Hannon	3-13
Edward Greatrex	6-31	19	+28.46	Andrew Balding	4-9

Favourites

2yo	38.9	-8.83	3yo	32.6	-17.53	Total 32.2	-48.84

FFOS LAS

Trimsaran, Carmarthenshire, SA17 4DE
Tel: 01554 811092

How to get there
Road: M4 Jctn 48 and follow the A4138 to Llanelli.
Rail: Llanelli, Kidwelly or Carmarthen

Features LH, flat, galloping

2020 Fixtures
July 30, August 4, 13, 27-28, September 13

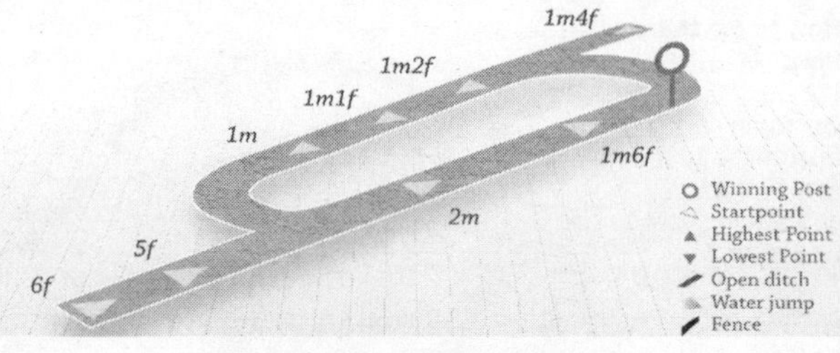

Racing Post standard times

5f	57	1m4f	2min34
6f	1min8.5	1m6f	3min
1m	1min38	2m	3min28.5
1m2f	2min6		

Trainers	*Wins-Runs*	*%*	*2yo*	*3yo+*	*£1 level stks*
Andrew Balding	16-61	26	4-16	12-45	+24.52
David Evans	16-152	11	7-60	9-92	-13.75
Rod Millman	11-60	18	1-22	10-38	-11.25
Roger Charlton	9-28	32	4-9	5-19	+36.82
Archie Watson	8-24	33	3-11	5-13	+5.40
Richard Hughes	6-37	16	2-16	4-21	+6.18
Ralph Beckett	6-38	16	2-16	4-22	-5.84
William Muir	6-43	14	4-15	2-28	-9.25
Stuart Kittow	5-24	21	0-1	5-23	-0.10
Hughie Morrison	5-26	19	0-5	5-21	-1.00
Richard Hannon	5-53	9	4-40	1-13	-35.00
Sir Mark Prescott Bt	4-10	40	2-5	2-5	+1.48
Hugo Palmer	4-14	29	0-2	4-12	-5.67

Jockeys	*Wins-Rides*	*%*	*£1 level stks*	*Best Trainer*	*W-R*
Oisin Murphy	12-45	27	+3.63	Archie Watson	3-5
Liam Keniry	11-72	15	+20.50	Andrew Balding	3-13
David Probert	10-44	23	-0.28	Andrew Balding	7-19
Luke Morris	9-35	26	+8.25	Sir Mark Prescott Bt	3-7
Kieran Shoemark	9-45	20	+13.13	David Evans	2-7
Tom Marquand	8-47	17	+1.35	Ali Stronge	2-3
Shane Kelly	8-49	16	-20.08	Richard Hughes	4-24
Martin Dwyer	8-52	15	-6.92	William Muir	3-16
Rossa Ryan	7-33	21	+27.88	David Flood	1-1
Fran Berry	7-40	18	-7.09	David Evans	3-6
Jim Crowley	6-24	25	-10.13	David Evans	2-3
Finley Marsh	6-38	16	-6.50	Rod Millman	3-6
Edward Greatrex	5-26	19	+4.45	Ed Dunlop	1-1

Favourites

2yo	32.2	-15.96	3yo	32.5	-27.83	Total	34.6	-36.71

Chichester, W Sussex,
PO18 0PS. Tel 01243 755 022

GOODWOOD

How to get there
Road: signposted from A27 south and A285 north. Rail: Chichester, bus to course on race days

Features RH, undulating

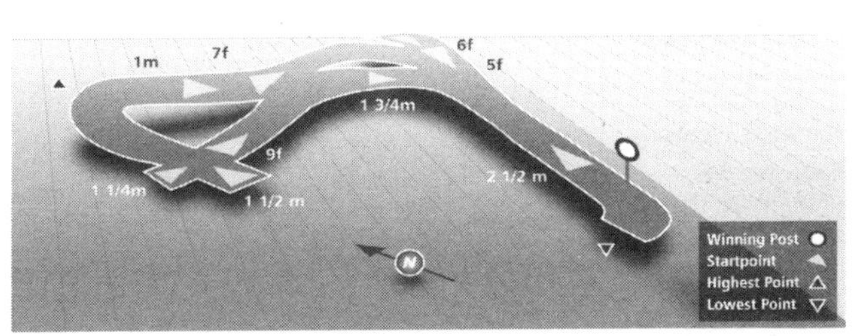

2020 Fixtures
May 2, 28-30, June 5, 7, 12, 19, July 28-31, August 1, 28-30, September 8, 23, October 11

Racing Post standard times

5f	57	1m3f	2min21
6f	1min9.7	1m4f	2min34
7f	1min24	1m6f	2min58.5
1m	1min36.7	2m	3min21
1m1f	1min51.4	2m4f	4min14
1m1f192yds	2min4		

Trainers	*Wins-Runs*	*%*	*2yo*	*3yo+*	*£1 level stks*
Mark Johnston	51-321	16	17-99	34-222	+30.49
Richard Hannon	38-353	11	19-157	19-196	-101.97
John Gosden	25-121	21	4-18	21-103	-32.99
William Haggas	25-126	20	3-19	22-107	-13.43
Mick Channon	25-203	12	14-68	11-135	-16.92
Sir Michael Stoute	22-113	19	1-5	21-108	-35.13
Charlie Appleby	21-99	21	13-33	8-66	-24.48
Andrew Balding	21-189	11	2-44	19-145	-79.14
David Simcock	17-118	14	1-7	16-111	+17.91
Ralph Beckett	16-100	16	3-20	13-80	+7.38
Charles Hills	15-138	11	5-51	10-87	-49.30
Roger Varian	13-97	13	3-17	10-80	-38.25
Henry Candy	11-57	19	0-9	11-48	-2.33

Jockeys	*Wins-Rides*	*%*	*£1 level stks*	*Best Trainer*	*W-R*
Jim Crowley	37-242	15	-69.65	Charles Hills	8-24
Oisin Murphy	25-198	13	-52.09	Andrew Balding	6-48
Ryan Moore	23-137	17	-51.46	Sir Michael Stoute	7-31
Harry Bentley	23-158	15	+27.03	Ralph Beckett	10-47
James Doyle	23-160	14	-9.40	Mark Johnston	5-18
William Buick	22-99	22	+30.16	Charlie Appleby	14-44
Andrea Atzeni	22-165	13	+18.76	Roger Varian	7-53
Silvestre De Sousa	22-168	13	-31.77	Mick Channon	8-33
Frankie Dettori	21-118	18	+5.48	John Gosden	8-38
Joe Fanning	21-132	16	-5.94	Mark Johnston	17-95
Jamie Spencer	16-101	16	+4.38	David Simcock	5-27
Adam Kirby	15-102	15	-6.50	Clive Cox	5-33
Pat Cosgrave	13-85	15	+118.50	William Haggas	6-20

Favourites

2yo	41.3	+2.87	3yo	38.2	+24.98	Total	38.5	+60.57

HAMILTON

Bothwell Road, Hamilton, Lanarkshire
ML3 0DW. Tel 01698 283 806

How to get there Road: M74 Jct 5, off the A74. Rail: Hamilton West

Features RH, undulating, dip can become testing in wet weather

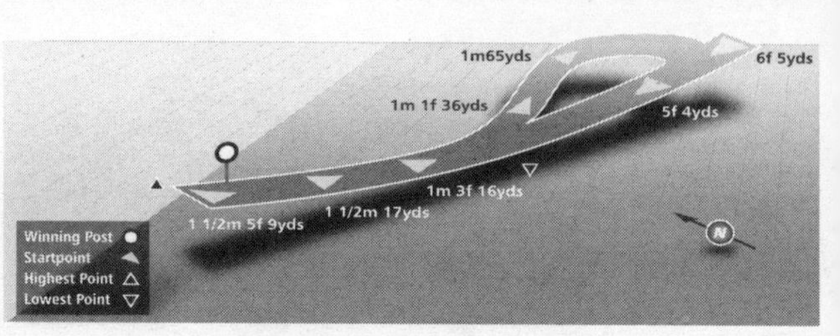

2020 Fixtures
May 3, 15, 27, June 4, 10, 17, 25, 30, July 11, 16-17, August 1, 18, 28, September 2, 20-21, 28

Racing Post standard times

5f4yds	58.2	1m3f16yds	2min20
6f5yds	1min10	1m4f17yds	2min33.7
1m65yds	1min45	1m5f9yds	2min47.5
1m1f36yds	1min55.5		

Trainers	*Wins-Runs*	*%*	*2yo*	*3yo+*	*£1 level stks*
Keith Dalgleish	60-486	12	12-92	48-394	-95.82
Mark Johnston	38-200	19	17-71	21-129	-39.47
Richard Fahey	38-293	13	11-95	27-198	-95.88
Kevin Ryan	34-140	24	12-37	22-103	+30.64
David O'Meara	28-143	20	1-17	27-126	-23.15
Tim Easterby	24-121	20	3-11	21-110	+12.65
Iain Jardine	20-180	11	3-19	17-161	+15.30
John Patrick Shanahan	19-96	20	0-3	19-93	+4.14
Jim Goldie	17-179	9	0-3	17-176	-53.00
Michael Dods	14-77	18	3-13	11-64	-9.09
Jedd O'Keeffe	11-42	26	1-7	10-35	+8.47
Rebecca Bastiman	11-88	13	0-0	11-88	+15.38
Paul Midgley	10-78	13	0-2	10-76	+4.25

Jockeys	*Wins-Rides*	*%*	*£1 level stks*	*Best Trainer*	*W-R*
Joe Fanning	44-270	16	-44.78	Mark Johnston	25-133
Daniel Tudhope	27-135	20	+5.25	David O´Meara	11-52
Graham Lee	25-174	14	-56.52	Keith Dalgleish	4-32
P J McDonald	24-140	17	-20.30	Mark Johnston	8-17
Connor Beasley	23-162	14	+3.50	Keith Dalgleish	11-53
James Sullivan	20-184	11	+11.00	Ruth Carr	5-67
Paul Mulrennan	19-150	13	-43.73	Michael Dods	5-23
Rowan Scott	19-158	12	-27.58	Keith Dalgleish	7-57
Jamie Gormley	17-116	15	-18.21	Iain Jardine	6-61
Shane Gray	17-125	14	-8.47	Kevin Ryan	8-25
Tom Eaves	17-191	9	-81.80	Kevin Ryan	5-32
David Allan	16-77	21	-14.77	Tim Easterby	14-40
Tony Hamilton	16-110	15	-22.58	Richard Fahey	10-65

Favourites

2yo	41.3	-9.42	3yo	40.7	-7.21	Total	33.1	-91.27

HAYDOCK

Newton-Le-Willows, Merseyside
WA12 0HQ. Tel 01942 725 963

How to get there
Road: M6 Jct 23, A49 to Wigan.
Rail: Wigan & 320 bus or Newton-le-Willows

Features LH, flat, easy turns, suits the galloping type

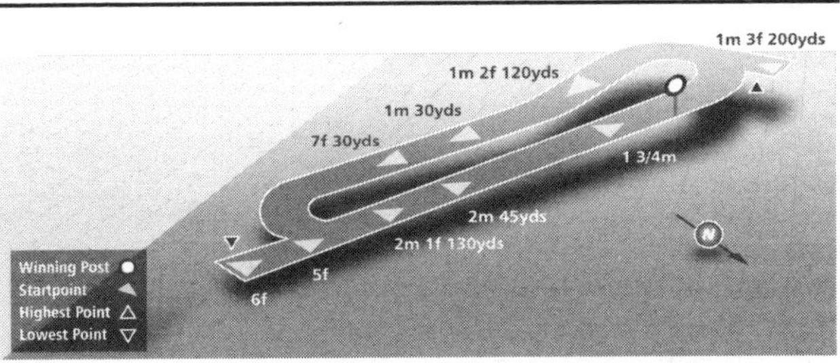

2020 Fixtures
April 25, May 9, 22-23, 28-30, June 10-11, 20, July 2-4, 17-18, August 6-8, September 3-5, 25-26, October 16

Racing Post standard times

5f	58.5	1m2f95yds	2min9
5f (Inner)	58	1m3f200yds	2min26.5
6f	1min11	1m6f	2min54
6f (Inner)	1min10.3	2m45yds	3min24
7f	1min26	2m1f130yds	3min51
1m	1min38		

Trainers	*Wins-Runs*	*%*	*2yo*	*3yo+*	*£1 level stks*
Tom Dascombe	68-384	18	22-132	46-252	+197.72
Mark Johnston	43-242	18	17-81	26-161	-12.09
William Haggas	38-142	27	4-28	34-114	-10.58
Richard Fahey	31-355	9	12-97	19-258	-150.89
John Gosden	26-101	26	10-33	16-68	+9.53
David O'Meara	25-221	11	0-5	25-216	-7.53
Richard Hannon	24-208	12	9-87	15-121	-53.44
K R Burke	23-203	11	6-65	17-138	-34.79
Tim Easterby	23-236	10	3-49	20-187	-35.40
Kevin Ryan	20-162	12	7-57	13-105	-23.75
Hugo Palmer	18-63	29	7-15	11-48	+77.20
Charles Hills	15-84	18	3-21	12-63	+9.77
Andrew Balding	15-103	15	4-9	11-94	-25.35

Jockeys	*Wins-Rides*	*%*	*£1 level stks*	*Best Trainer*	*W-R*
Richard Kingscote	74-393	19	+40.15	Tom Dascombe	53-269
Franny Norton	29-168	17	-4.00	Mark Johnston	22-96
Daniel Tudhope	29-187	16	-16.72	David O´Meara	14-88
Paul Hanagan	21-180	12	-77.78	Richard Fahey	9-67
Jim Crowley	19-87	22	+3.14	Charles Hills	4-10
Pat Cosgrave	17-57	30	+28.99	William Haggas	10-26
William Buick	16-76	21	-13.26	Charlie Appleby	7-32
Ben Curtis	16-151	11	-18.38	K R Burke	5-33
Graham Lee	16-159	10	-68.46	Kevin Ryan	3-12
Frankie Dettori	15-45	33	+0.56	John Gosden	7-19
James Doyle	15-71	21	-22.42	Hugo Palmer	5-5
Adam Kirby	14-84	17	+1.37	Clive Cox	9-18
Oisin Murphy	14-105	13	-27.25	Andrew Balding	8-33

Favourites

2yo	39.5	-15.27	3yo	34.6	-42.97	Total	34	-88.43

KEMPTON

Staines Rd East, Sunbury-On-Thames
TW16 5AQ. Tel 01932 782 292

How to get there
Road: M3 Jct 1, A308 to Kingston-on-Thames. Rail: Kempton Park from Waterloo

Features RH, Polytrack, sharp

2020 Fixtures
March 28, April 3, 8, 11, 15, May 6, 20, June 3, 10, 24, July 1, 8, August 3, 5, 12, 18-19, 26, September 4-5, 15, 18, 23-24, 30, October 7, 9, 14, 20-21, 28, November 2, 4-5, 16, 18, 25, December 2, 9, 16

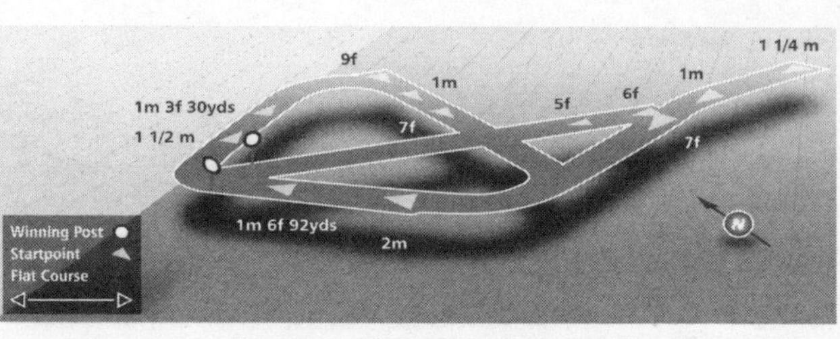

Racing Post standard times

5f	58.8	1m2f	2min4
6f	1min10.6	1m3f	2min17
7f	1min23.7	1m4f	2min30
1m	1min36.6	2m	3min22.5

Trainers	*Wins-Runs*	*%*	*2yo*	*3yo+*	*£1 level stks*
John Gosden	80-306	26	30-153	50-153	+28.16
Richard Hannon	73-637	11	33-298	40-339	-166.02
Roger Varian	53-245	22	19-97	34-148	-9.64
James Fanshawe	49-308	16	6-44	43-264	-88.94
Charlie Appleby	46-139	33	28-84	18-55	-24.06
Andrew Balding	42-341	12	10-74	32-267	-56.67
Roger Charlton	41-239	17	12-92	29-147	-20.17
Ralph Beckett	40-283	14	17-122	23-161	-25.88
Archie Watson	38-172	22	14-73	24-99	-1.46
Clive Cox	37-300	12	9-84	28-216	-26.48
Saeed bin Suroor	36-161	22	13-62	23-99	-51.28
Hugo Palmer	36-214	17	16-93	20-121	-6.54
Mark Johnston	35-283	12	18-114	17-169	-103.47

Jockeys	*Wins-Rides*	*%*	*£1 level stks*	*Best Trainer*	*W-R*
Oisin Murphy	96-603	16	-81.98	Andrew Balding	15-93
Jim Crowley	89-548	16	-117.40	Amanda Perrett	9-45
Adam Kirby	89-658	14	-189.38	Clive Cox	20-133
Luke Morris	84-945	9	-276.40	Sir Mark Prescott Bt	17-120
James Doyle	67-265	25	+22.62	Hugo Palmer	12-44
Robert Havlin	59-424	14	-106.39	John Gosden	37-150
Tom Marquand	56-597	9	-95.05	Richard Hannon	11-136
David Probert	49-557	9	-119.50	Andrew Balding	9-97
Liam Keniry	48-622	8	-160.91	Ed Walker	10-87
Andrea Atzeni	47-213	22	+17.47	Roger Varian	19-78
Martin Harley	42-281	15	+22.94	James Tate	6-23
George Baker	41-262	16	-65.13	Gary Moore	7-37
William Buick	39-141	28	-31.47	Charlie Appleby	26-69

Favourites

2yo	39.8	-39.33	3yo	35.8	-72.62	Total	35.1	-138.17

London Road, Oadby, Leicester, LE2 4QH. Tel 0116 271 6515

LEICESTER

How to get there Road: M1 Jct 21, A6, 2m south of city. Rail: Leicester, bus

Features RH, straight mile is downhill for first 4f, then uphill to finish

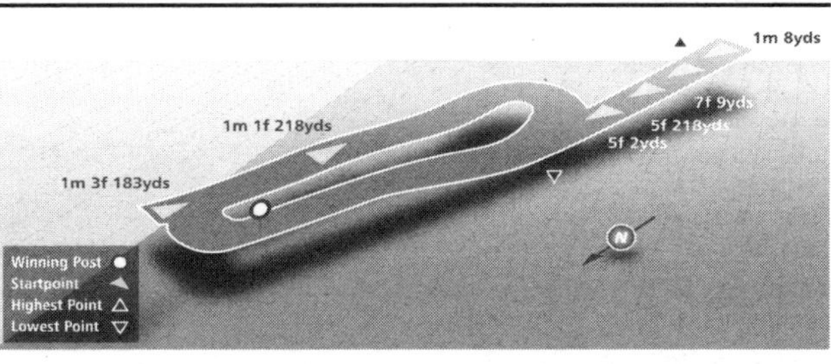

2020 Fixtures April 3, 25, May 18, 25-26, June 8, 13, 25, July 4, 16, 22, 29, August 9, 20, September 8, 21, October 6, 13

Racing Post standard times

5f2yds	59	1m60yds	1min42.5
5f218yds	1min10.5	1m1f218yds	2min4.5
7f9yds	1min23	1m3f183yds	2min29.3
1m8yds	1min41		

Trainers	*Wins-Runs*	*%*	*2yo*	*3yo+*	*£1 level stks*
Richard Fahey	35-171	20	13-64	22-107	+42.05
Mark Johnston	29-138	21	10-57	19-81	-12.36
Richard Hannon	29-204	14	17-99	12-105	-47.85
Sir Michael Stoute	17-76	22	3-29	14-47	-11.57
Mick Channon	17-93	18	8-39	9-54	+20.43
Saeed bin Suroor	15-51	29	5-16	10-35	+0.79
Charles Hills	15-84	18	4-36	11-48	+3.63
Michael Bell	13-67	19	4-25	9-42	+13.07
Roger Varian	13-77	17	2-22	11-55	-32.58
David Evans	13-119	11	5-44	8-75	-38.09
Ralph Beckett	11-63	17	5-20	6-43	-14.39
Clive Cox	11-103	11	3-35	8-68	-33.02
David O'Meara	10-81	12	0-8	10-73	-36.00

Jockeys	*Wins-Rides*	*%*	*£1 level stks*	*Best Trainer*	*W-R*
Silvestre De Sousa	33-144	23	+27.99	Mark Johnston	9-28
Jim Crowley	25-127	20	+19.49	Charles Hills	7-15
Paul Hanagan	19-89	21	+19.93	Richard Fahey	9-34
Andrea Atzeni	17-95	18	-32.54	Roger Varian	9-41
Adam Kirby	15-124	12	-34.11	Clive Cox	7-51
James Doyle	14-63	22	+3.93	Saeed bin Suroor	4-10
Fran Berry	13-70	19	+14.75	David Evans	3-10
Jamie Spencer	13-75	17	-20.01	Luca Cumani	4-8
Ryan Moore	13-77	17	-38.29	Sir Michael Stoute	5-27
Sean Levey	12-54	22	+17.13	Richard Hannon	8-38
Oisin Murphy	12-103	12	-53.87	Martyn Meade	2-2
William Buick	11-54	20	-17.03	Charlie Appleby	5-22
P J McDonald	11-62	18	-16.63	Mark Johnston	8-22

Favourites

2yo	33.8	-35.16	3yo	36.1	-12.5	Total	33.4	-74.82

LINGFIELD Turf

Racecourse Road, Lingfield
RH7 6PQ. Tel 01342 834 800

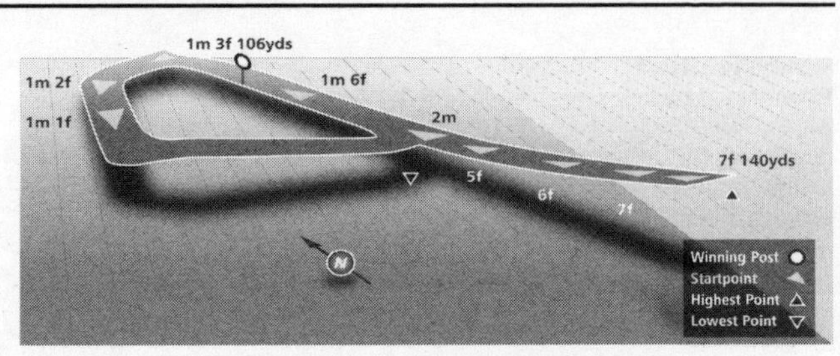

How to get there Road: M25 Jctn 6, south on A22, then B2029. Rail: Lingfield from London Bridge or Victoria

Features LH, undulating

2020 Fixtures
May 1, 9, 21, 26, 30, June 6, 9, 20, 27, July 8, 15, 22, 25, August 1, 8, 13, 26, September 2, 12

Racing Post standard times

5f	56.9	1m2f	2min6.7
6f	1min9.4	1m3f106yds	2min27
7f	1min21	1m6f	3min
7f140yds	1min28	2m	3min27.5
1m1f	1min53		

Trainers	*Wins-Runs*	*%*	*2yo*	*3yo+*	*£1 level stks*
William Haggas	26-62	42	11-19	15-43	+38.36
Richard Hannon	25-155	16	8-60	17-95	-31.84
John Bridger	16-134	12	3-25	13-109	+67.13
Jim Boyle	15-71	21	2-11	13-60	+51.50
Gary Moore	13-111	12	1-9	12-102	-28.75
Mick Channon	13-113	12	6-38	7-75	-52.04
Roger Varian	12-44	27	2-10	10-34	-4.34
Andrew Balding	12-59	20	1-7	11-52	-7.36
David Evans	12-82	15	7-37	5-45	+2.28
Charles Hills	11-52	21	4-15	7-37	-25.39
John Best	10-58	17	1-15	9-43	+0.48
Richard Hughes	10-60	17	3-18	7-42	-16.85
Sylvester Kirk	9-46	20	1-11	8-35	-4.27

Jockeys	*Wins-Rides*	*%*	*£1 level stks*	*Best Trainer*	*W-R*
Silvestre De Sousa	29-114	25	-30.54	Ed Dunlop	3-5
Oisin Murphy	27-130	21	-32.49	Archie Watson	5-15
Pat Cosgrave	24-98	24	-0.36	William Haggas	10-20
Jim Crowley	23-81	28	+3.02	Charles Hills	3-8
Harry Bentley	15-68	22	+6.92	Ed Vaughan	5-12
Tom Marquand	14-96	15	-22.06	Richard Hannon	6-32
Hector Crouch	14-97	14	+18.48	Gary Moore	6-46
Adam Kirby	13-57	23	+0.31	David Evans	2-4
David Probert	13-99	13	+22.13	Andrew Balding	3-15
Luke Morris	13-101	13	-57.35	Sir Mark Prescott Bt	6-16
James Doyle	11-42	26	-11.68	William Haggas	3-8
Hollie Doyle	11-73	15	-1.02	Richard Hannon	4-15
Martin Dwyer	11-82	13	-36.64	Sylvester Kirk	2-2

Favourites

2yo	47	-0.4	3yo	33.5	-55.88	Total	37.3	-65.93

LINGFIELD AW

Features LH, Polytrack, tight

2020 Fixtures
March 31, April 1, 4, 10, 14, 22, 27-28, May 19, June 2, 18, August 11, 17, 22, September 22, October 29, November 4, 14, 21, 25, December 2, 9, 16, 19, 28, 30-31

Racing Post standard times

5f	57.5	1m2f	2min1.8
6f	1min9.6	1m4f	2min28
7f	1min22.2	1m5f	2min40.5
1m	1min35.3	2m	3min16

Trainers	*Wins-Runs*	*%*	*2yo*	*3yo+*	*£1 level stks*
Richard Hannon	68-396	17	21-115	47-281	+26.34
Mark Johnston	62-317	20	10-54	52-263	-7.27
John Gosden	55-223	25	11-55	44-168	-26.38
Charlie Appleby	45-141	32	3-25	42-116	+5.78
Archie Watson	42-204	21	12-40	30-164	-7.70
David Evans	39-291	13	6-36	33-255	-58.01
William Haggas	37-142	26	13-41	24-101	+4.69
Simon Dow	36-258	14	5-25	31-233	+30.65
Andrew Balding	35-248	14	2-20	33-228	-86.37
Gary Moore	34-298	11	0-20	34-278	-87.55
Ralph Beckett	31-158	20	6-29	25-129	-35.50
Stuart Williams	29-193	15	2-11	27-182	+25.03
Jamie Osborne	29-250	12	3-47	26-203	-53.36

Jockeys	*Wins-Rides*	*%*	*£1 level stks*	*Best Trainer*	*W-R*
Adam Kirby	125-679	18	-146.19	Charlie Appleby	16-36
Luke Morris	114-919	12	-243.09	Sir Mark Prescott Bt	22-114
Jim Crowley	70-333	21	-7.66	Amanda Perrett	10-28
Oisin Murphy	65-355	18	-5.62	Andrew Balding	12-61
George Baker	58-304	19	-12.53	Gary Moore	9-52
Joe Fanning	57-270	21	+43.72	Mark Johnston	35-137
Tom Marquand	57-386	15	+32.29	Richard Hannon	16-77
Robert Havlin	46-361	13	-106.26	John Gosden	30-104
Shane Kelly	43-443	10	-183.73	Richard Hughes	18-129
James Doyle	41-140	29	-8.16	Saeed bin Suroor	8-15
Richard Kingscote	40-235	17	-34.67	Tom Dascombe	14-60
David Probert	39-403	10	-163.27	Andrew Balding	10-71
Martin Harley	38-270	14	-43.39	Tom Dascombe	4-5

Favourites

2yo 35.7 -32.34 3yo 38 -89.9 Total 36.4 -177.41

MUSSELBURGH

Linkfield Road EH21 7RG
Tel 0131 665 2859

How to get there Road: M8 Jct 2, A8 east, follow Ring Road, A1 east. Rail: Musselburgh from Edinburgh Waverley

Features RH, flat, tight

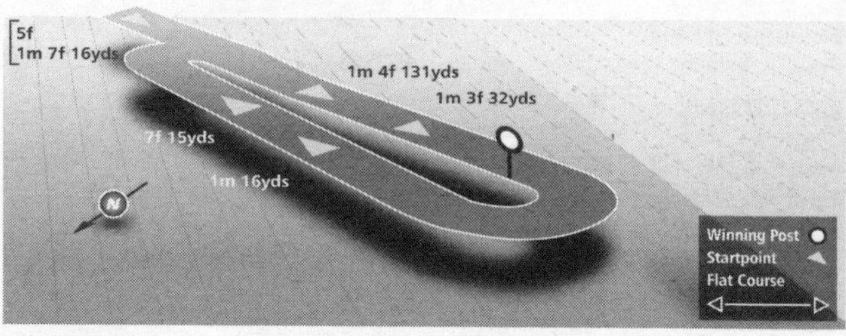

2020 Fixtures March 31, April 11, 30, May 1, 11, June 6, July 1, 21, 31, August 7, 21, 26, September 4, 12, 27, October 12

Racing Post standard times

5f	58	1m3f32yds	2min22
7f30yds	1min26.8	1m4f100yds	2min40
1m	1min38.8	1m6f	1min59.2
1m1f	1min51.1	2m	3min25

Trainers	*Wins-Runs*	*%*	*2yo*	*3yo+*	*£1 level stks*
Keith Dalgleish	60-473	13	14-91	46-382	-123.49
Mark Johnston	46-227	20	16-78	30-149	-22.86
Richard Fahey	46-253	18	12-63	34-190	+20.53
Iain Jardine	23-210	11	3-22	20-188	-80.30
Kevin Ryan	21-104	20	6-25	15-79	+15.13
Tim Easterby	21-193	11	4-29	17-164	-58.80
Jim Goldie	19-301	6	0-11	19-290	-127.88
Rebecca Bastiman	17-128	13	0-2	17-126	-18.75
David O'Meara	16-141	11	5-34	11-107	-52.85
Linda Perratt	13-206	6	1-11	12-195	-41.50
Bryan Smart	12-76	16	3-23	9-53	+17.70
John Quinn	12-79	15	3-23	9-56	-10.22
Paul Midgley	12-105	11	1-10	11-95	+0.91

Jockeys	*Wins-Rides*	*%*	*£1 level stks*	*Best Trainer*	*W-R*
Joe Fanning	63-331	19	-58.27	Mark Johnston	36-144
Paul Mulrennan	29-199	15	-46.57	Alistair Whillans	4-13
Daniel Tudhope	26-102	25	+34.89	David O´Meara	8-45
David Allan	23-144	16	+1.88	Tim Easterby	10-78
Connor Beasley	22-151	15	+25.79	Keith Dalgleish	7-49
Phillip Makin	21-129	16	+5.59	Keith Dalgleish	12-63
Jason Hart	20-146	14	-14.25	John Quinn	7-38
Ben Curtis	18-98	18	+10.71	William Haggas	3-5
Graham Lee	18-159	11	-49.68	Bryan Smart	5-21
P J McDonald	17-150	11	-44.37	Linda Perratt	3-22
James Sullivan	17-153	11	+6.50	Ruth Carr	7-63
Paul Hanagan	16-91	18	+1.18	Richard Fahey	13-61
Andrew Mullen	13-121	11	-33.43	Michael Appleby	5-15

Favourites

2yo 37.9% -8.84 | 3yo 35.1% -8.14 | Total 33% -44.62

Newbury, Berkshire, RG14 7NZ
Tel: 01635 400 15 or 01635 550 354

NEWBURY

How to get there
Road: M4 Jct 13 and A34 south.
Rail: Newbury Racecourse

Features LH, wide, flat

2020 Fixtures
April 17-18, May 15-16, June 11, 23, July 2, 9, 17-18, 23, August 14-15, 27, September 18-19, October 23-24

Racing Post standard times

5f34yds	59.6	1m1f	1min50
6f8yds	1min10.5	1m2f6yds	2min3
7f	1min22.8	1m3f5yds	2min17
7f64yds	1min28	1m4f4yds	2min30.3
1m	1min35.8	1m5f61yds	2min47.5
1m7yds	1min36.5	2m	3min23.5

Trainers	*Wins-Runs*	*%*	*2yo*	*3yo+*	*£1 level stks*
Richard Hannon	57-506	11	32-280	25-226	-59.41
John Gosden	43-192	22	18-63	25-129	+0.84
William Haggas	39-174	22	13-76	26-98	+7.25
Andrew Balding	23-202	11	5-65	18-137	-17.43
Roger Charlton	21-125	17	7-44	14-81	+23.24
Sir Michael Stoute	19-117	16	5-26	14-91	-33.07
Charles Hills	18-188	10	10-80	8-108	-25.63
Ralph Beckett	16-137	12	6-53	10-84	-29.63
Brian Meehan	16-179	9	8-97	8-82	+8.75
Charlie Appleby	15-58	26	4-20	11-38	-0.43
Roger Varian	15-118	13	5-39	10-79	-38.25
Mark Johnston	14-97	14	7-39	7-58	-16.65
Eve Johnson Houghton	14-121	12	3-45	11-76	+22.88

Jockeys	*Wins-Rides*	*%*	*£1 level stks*	*Best Trainer*	*W-R*
James Doyle	38-206	18	-18.82	William Haggas	9-36
Frankie Dettori	35-137	26	+24.44	John Gosden	19-67
Jim Crowley	34-252	13	+9.34	William Haggas	5-19
Ryan Moore	30-178	17	-53.82	Sir Michael Stoute	11-54
Silvestre De Sousa	24-157	15	+18.87	Mick Channon	4-20
Oisin Murphy	22-236	9	-96.23	John Gosden	3-6
William Buick	21-93	23	+32.74	Charlie Appleby	9-21
Jason Watson	17-90	19	+39.13	Roger Charlton	9-32
Paul Hanagan	15-78	19	+13.50	William Haggas	3-8
Jamie Spencer	15-115	13	-14.38	Luca Cumani	4-14
Pat Dobbs	15-160	9	-7.25	Richard Hannon	8-82
David Probert	14-148	9	-5.33	Andrew Balding	12-65
Andrea Atzeni	14-161	9	-24.50	Roger Varian	7-54

Favourites

2yo 32.7% -35.92 3yo 28.9% -43.28 Total 28.9% -123.76

NEWCASTLE

High Gosforth Park NE3 5HP
Tel: 0191 236 2020 or 236 5508

How to get there Road: Signposted from A1. Rail: Newcastle Central, metro to Regent Centre or Four Lane End and bus

Features LH, Tapeta, easy bends with uphill straight

2020 Fixtures March 30, April 10, 16, May 1, June 2, 25-27, July 25, August 6, 12, 21, September 4, 8, 22, 25, 28, October 2, 13, 16, 20, 26, 30, November 3, 6, 17, 19-20, December 4, 12

Racing Post standard times

5f	58	1m4f98yds	2min36.5
6f	1min10.2	2m56yds	3min27
7f	1min24		
1m	1min36.5		
1m2f	2min6		

Trainers	*Wins-Runs*	*%*	*2yo*	*3yo+*	*£1 level stks*
Richard Fahey	63-514	12	17-163	46-351	-27.63
John Gosden	42-110	38	19-42	23-68	+8.93
Jim Goldie	42-377	11	1-4	41-373	-6.21
Mark Johnston	34-330	10	13-141	21-189	-95.42
William Haggas	31-86	36	9-27	22-59	+13.41
Ben Haslam	29-206	14	4-51	25-155	+75.58
Michael Easterby	28-224	13	5-33	23-191	+53.58
Roger Varian	27-120	23	6-41	21-79	-32.51
Kevin Ryan	26-221	12	5-50	21-171	-32.94
K R Burke	26-235	11	12-86	14-149	+45.69
David O'Meara	26-314	8	3-46	23-268	-97.65
James Bethell	25-154	16	2-26	23-128	+32.33
Brian Ellison	25-302	8	1-39	24-263	-47.34

Jockeys	*Wins-Rides*	*%*	*£1 level stks*	*Best Trainer*	*W-R*
Ben Curtis	61-385	16	+23.14	K R Burke	11-40
P J McDonald	59-509	12	-89.74	James Bethell	10-51
Joe Fanning	54-387	14	-54.28	Mark Johnston	14-120
Luke Morris	43-357	12	-113.41	Sir Mark Prescott Bt	17-79
Andrew Mullen	43-464	9	-49.83	Ben Haslam	14-74
Daniel Tudhope	42-260	16	-77.44	Jim Goldie	7-18
Callum Rodriguez	39-215	18	+80.31	Michael Dods	12-50
Kevin Stott	31-191	16	-9.08	Kevin Ryan	11-69
Josephine Gordon	29-167	17	-22.44	Hugo Palmer	10-39
Paul Mulrennan	29-398	7	-175.45	Michael Dods	7-76
Paul Hanagan	28-241	12	-86.30	Richard Fahey	14-109
Graham Lee	28-452	6	-235.69	Bryan Smart	7-65
Tony Hamilton	26-288	9	-69.88	Richard Fahey	17-166

Favourites

2yo 39.7% -21.02 3yo 39.3% -8.14 Total 35.1% -96.35

Westfield House, The Links,
Newmarket, Suffolk. CB8 0TG

NEWMARKET

Rowley Mile

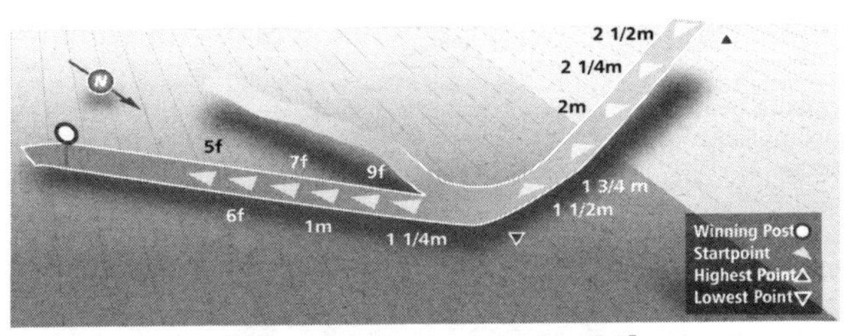

How to get there Road: from south M11 Jct 9, then A11, otherwise A14 and A11. Rail: Newmarket

Features RH, wide, galloping, uphill finish

2020 Fixtures April 14-16, May 2-3, 14-16, 30, September 19, 24-26, October 3, 9-10, 21, 30-31

Racing Post standard times

5f	57.5	1m2f	2min0.5
6f	1min10.1	1m4f	2min28
7f	1min22.5	1m6f	2min53.5
1m	1min35.1	2m	3min19
1m1f	1min47.8	2m2f	3min45

Trainers	Wins-Runs	%	2yo	3yo+	£1 level stks
John Gosden	62-328	19	24-118	38-210	-6.42
Charlie Appleby	54-200	27	19-81	35-119	+28.06
A P O'Brien	34-175	19	20-102	14-73	+22.42
Roger Varian	31-215	14	10-67	21-148	-26.66
Mark Johnston	31-264	12	15-107	16-157	-19.75
Richard Hannon	31-367	8	9-167	22-200	-58.38
Saeed bin Suroor	24-140	17	9-46	15-94	-0.88
Ralph Beckett	21-130	16	11-46	10-84	+30.41
William Haggas	21-195	11	7-82	14-113	-41.76
Sir Michael Stoute	19-158	12	1-43	18-115	-50.88
Andrew Balding	15-167	9	2-53	13-114	-46.53
Mick Channon	12-114	11	1-51	11-63	-27.38
Charles Hills	12-161	7	2-56	10-105	-89.93

Jockeys	Wins-Rides	%	£1 level stks	Best Trainer	W-R
William Buick	64-286	22	+53.49	Charlie Appleby	41-137
Ryan Moore	52-319	16	-94.06	A P O´Brien	22-93
Frankie Dettori	46-239	19	+28.46	John Gosden	35-129
James Doyle	29-249	12	-112.28	Saeed bin Suroor	9-40
Jim Crowley	28-229	12	-80.88	Sir Michael Stoute	3-9
Oisin Murphy	25-208	12	-45.28	Saeed bin Suroor	9-19
Silvestre De Sousa	25-211	12	-48.83	Mark Johnston	5-27
Andrea Atzeni	24-231	10	-72.59	Roger Varian	13-92
Harry Bentley	20-136	15	-16.09	Ralph Beckett	12-43
Pat Cosgrave	16-111	14	-24.67	William Haggas	6-39
Richard Kingscote	14-89	16	+46.38	Tom Dascombe	5-33
Joe Fanning	13-122	11	+34.00	Mark Johnston	8-88
Adam Kirby	13-151	9	+1.10	Charlie Appleby	4-13

Favourites

2yo 35.6% -25.50 3yo 33.9% -5.76 Total 33.8% -35.75

NEWMARKET

Westfield House, The Links, Newmarket, Suffolk. CB8 0TG

July Course

How to get there See previous page

Features RH, wide, galloping, uphill finish

2020 Fixtures June 19-20, 25-27, July 9-11, 17-18, 24-25, 31, August 1, 7-8, 14-15, 28-29

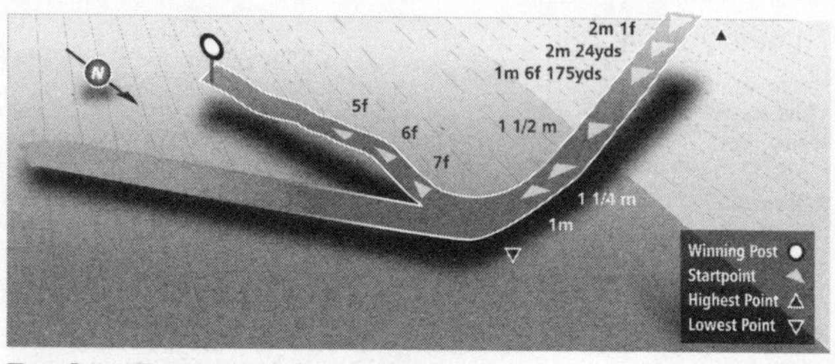

Racing Post standard times

5f	57.2	1m110yds	1min43	1m6f175yds	3min3
6f	1min10.1	1m2f	2min1.5	2m24yds	3min20
7f	1min23	1m4f	2min26.5		
1m	1min36	1m5f	2min40		

Trainers	*Wins-Runs*	*%*	*2yo*	*3yo+*	*£1 level stks*
Richard Hannon	50-371	13	25-189	25-182	-63.53
Mark Johnston	49-225	22	16-72	33-153	+33.89
Charlie Appleby	48-196	24	31-110	17-86	-14.41
John Gosden	40-217	18	13-85	27-132	-52.11
William Haggas	22-148	15	3-36	19-112	-50.94
Saeed bin Suroor	21-94	22	5-27	16-67	+2.25
Charles Hills	17-139	12	6-45	11-94	-32.38
Richard Fahey	17-143	12	5-36	12-107	+2.75
Sir Michael Stoute	16-120	13	5-41	11-79	-57.83
Ralph Beckett	15-90	17	5-34	10-56	-14.18
Andrew Balding	15-108	14	3-26	12-82	-4.71
Hugo Palmer	14-111	13	6-44	8-67	-26.95
Roger Varian	14-122	11	1-28	13-94	-47.84

Jockeys	*Wins-Rides*	*%*	*£1 level stks*	*Best Trainer*	*W-R*
James Doyle	58-254	23	+5.11	Charlie Appleby	16-48
William Buick	30-159	19	-47.36	Charlie Appleby	15-74
Harry Bentley	30-170	18	-3.52	Ralph Beckett	5-28
Ryan Moore	28-153	18	-24.88	A P O'Brien	8-28
Dane O'Neill	26-149	17	+4.50	Charles Hills	5-17
Jim Crowley	22-118	19	-15.27	Mark Johnston	4-12
Andrea Atzeni	22-148	15	-27.65	Roger Varian	7-40
Silvestre De Sousa	22-165	13	-44.31	Mark Johnston	4-16
Frankie Dettori	21-132	16	-32.78	John Gosden	8-47
Oisin Murphy	20-121	17	+1.14	Andrew Balding	5-14
Robert Havlin	18-88	20	-11.26	John Gosden	17-50
Adam Kirby	18-146	12	-63.99	Charlie Appleby	4-11
Sean Levey	15-133	11	-48.54	Richard Hannon	12-91

Favourites

2yo 44.9% +10.13   3yo 32.9% -43.09   Total 37% -8.27

COMMUNIQUE: winning last year's Princess of Wales's Stakes for Mark Johnston, whose horses go phenomenally well on Newmarket's July Course

NOTTINGHAM

Colwick Park, Nottingham, NG2 4BE. Tel 0115 958 0620

How to get there Road: M1 Jct 25, A52 east to B686, signs for Trent Bridge, then Colwick Park. Rail: Nottingham

Features LH, flat, easy turns

2020 Fixtures April 8, 18, 28, May 4, 9, 19, 31, June 3, 11, 15, 25, July 4, 17, 21, 30, August 4, 11, 14, September 30, October 7, 14, 28, November 4

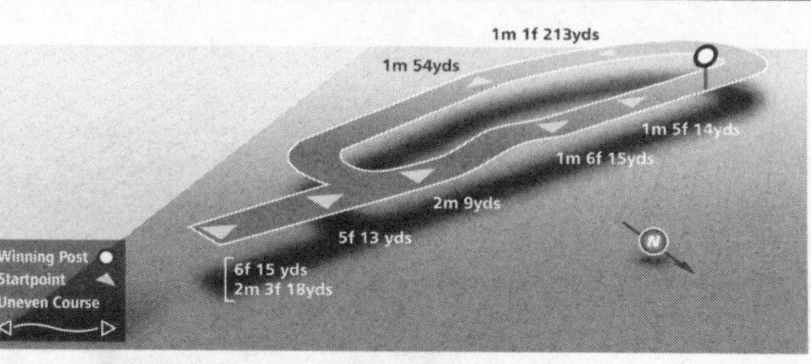

Racing Post standard times

5f13yds	58.4	1m2f50yds (Inner)	2min8.6
5f13yds (Inner)	59.8	1m6f15yds	2min57
6f15yds	1min12.2	2m9yds	3min24
1m75yds	1min42	2m9yds (Inner)	3min32
1m75yds (Inner)	1min43.5	2m2f18yds	3min55
1m2f50yds	2min6		

Trainers	*Wins-Runs*	*%*	*2yo*	*3yo+*	*£1 level stks*
Richard Fahey	38-232	16	13-82	25-150	+31.01
Michael Appleby	37-264	14	2-26	35-238	-9.55
Richard Hannon	27-178	15	11-83	16-95	-32.24
Roger Varian	21-115	18	5-39	16-76	-16.55
John Gosden	21-122	17	10-51	11-71	-11.15
Sir Michael Stoute	20-88	23	2-16	18-72	+21.01
Mick Channon	20-131	15	9-48	11-83	+52.76
Mark Johnston	18-149	12	12-75	6-74	-71.68
William Haggas	17-81	21	5-30	12-51	-18.43
Saeed bin Suroor	16-35	46	9-15	7-20	+24.41
Ian Williams	16-74	22	0-4	16-70	+6.29
K R Burke	16-109	15	8-33	8-76	-3.51
Hughie Morrison	13-70	19	0-15	13-55	+24.50

Jockeys	*Wins-Rides*	*%*	*£1 level stks*	*Best Trainer*	*W-R*
Jim Crowley	35-101	35	+82.62	Ian Williams	5-7
Silvestre De Sousa	32-194	16	-38.63	Mick Channon	5-19
Paul Hanagan	26-132	20	+3.37	Richard Fahey	12-53
Oisin Murphy	23-121	19	+38.17	Hughie Morrison	4-9
Andrea Atzeni	22-98	22	+8.06	Roger Varian	12-46
Sean Levey	19-76	25	+39.57	Richard Hannon	16-56
James Doyle	17-59	29	+1.19	John Gosden	3-8
Andrew Mullen	17-127	13	+26.57	Michael Appleby	10-62
Franny Norton	17-130	13	+3.32	Mark Johnston	9-58
Adam Kirby	14-93	15	-31.50	Clive Cox	7-33
Ben Curtis	14-95	15	+8.74	K R Burke	6-16
Graham Lee	14-106	13	-23.38	Jennie Candlish	2-2
Luke Morris	14-151	9	-27.79	Scott Dixon	2-3

Favourites

2yo 37.6% -18.25 3yo 36.6% +1.21 Total 35.1% -23.92

33 Ropergate, Pontefract,
WF8 1LE. Tel 01977 703 224

PONTEFRACT

How to get there Road: M62 Jct 32, then A539. Rail: Pontefract Monkhill or Pontefract Baghill from Leeds

Features LH, undulating, sharp home turn, last half-mile all uphill

2020 Fixtures April 7, 20, 29, May 22, June 8, 21, 29, July 7, 17, 26, August 5, 16, September 17, 24, October 5, 19

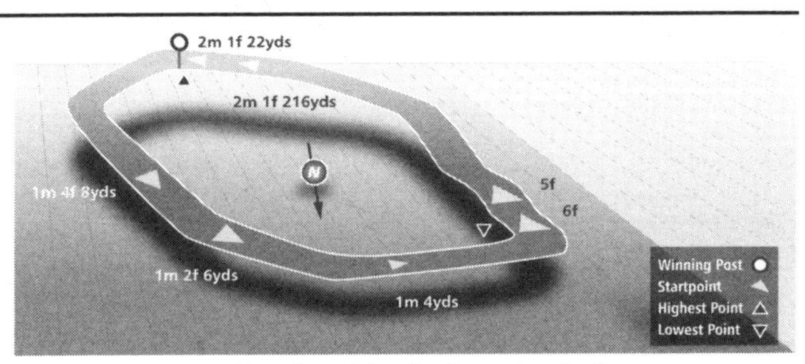

Racing Post standard times

5f	1min1.8	1m4f8yds	2min35.5
6f	1min14.6	2m1f22yds	3min41
1m4yds	1min42.6	2m1f216yds	3min51
1m2f6yds	2min9.4	2m5f122yds	4min41

Trainers	*Wins-Runs*	*%*	*2yo*	*3yo+*	*£1 level stks*
Richard Fahey	51-331	15	22-105	29-226	-5.93
Mark Johnston	39-199	20	15-64	24-135	-49.54
Tim Easterby	28-228	12	2-48	26-180	-27.92
David O'Meara	20-174	11	0-20	20-154	-53.75
Kevin Ryan	18-123	15	5-29	13-94	-10.97
Mick Channon	17-70	24	7-23	10-47	+48.50
Sir Michael Stoute	15-54	28	1-6	14-48	-7.41
Richard Whitaker	14-69	20	2-6	12-63	+22.58
Micky Hammond	14-161	9	1-11	13-150	-56.25
Michael Easterby	13-100	13	0-11	13-89	+0.08
Paul Midgley	13-122	11	0-7	13-115	-31.25
Ralph Beckett	12-26	46	6-11	6-15	+11.96
Les Eyre	11-76	14	0-7	11-69	-10.00

Jockeys	*Wins-Rides*	*%*	*£1 level stks*	*Best Trainer*	*W-R*
Silvestre De Sousa	33-136	24	-8.44	Mark Johnston	10-33
Daniel Tudhope	31-177	18	-31.20	David O´Meara	13-89
Graham Lee	27-239	11	-31.75	Mick Channon	5-17
Franny Norton	24-121	20	-16.31	Mark Johnston	16-71
David Allan	24-151	16	+43.25	Tim Easterby	19-108
Ben Curtis	21-120	18	+19.92	Roger Fell	5-15
Paul Hanagan	21-130	16	+37.05	Richard Fahey	14-89
Tony Hamilton	20-146	14	-38.89	Richard Fahey	20-99
P J McDonald	18-153	12	-37.32	Mark Johnston	4-22
Joe Fanning	16-94	17	+32.53	Mark Johnston	5-35
Paul Mulrennan	14-151	9	-47.33	Michael Dods	7-55
Richard Kingscote	13-73	18	-10.41	Tom Dascombe	4-39
Graham Gibbons	11-72	15	-17.55	Michael Easterby	3-12

Favourites

2yo 43% +0.54 3yo 34.8% -30.91 Total 34.4% -51.68

REDCAR

Redcar, Teesside,
TS10 2BY. Tel 01642 484 068

How to get there
Road: A1, A168, A19, then A174.
Rail: Redcar Central from Darlington

Features LH, flat, galloping

2020 Fixtures
April 6, 13, 30, May 18, 25-26, June 19-20, July 19, 29, August 8, 29, September 15, 23, October 3, 16, 26, November 3

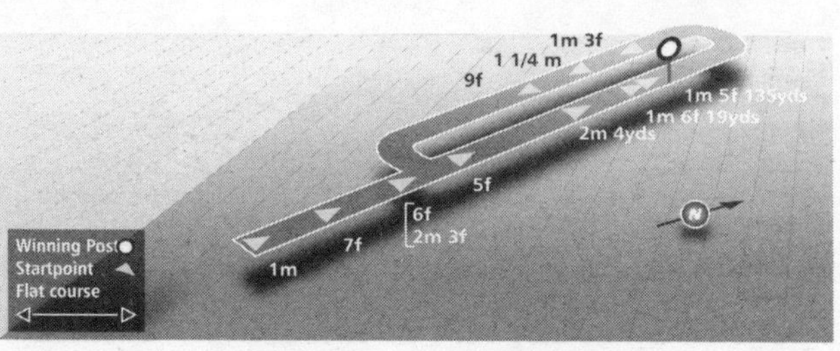

Racing Post standard times

5f	57	1m3f	2min16
6f	1min9.5	1m5f135yds	2min51
7f	1min22	1m6f19yds	2min57.5
1m	1min35	2m4yds	3min22
1m1f	1min48	2m3f	4min8
1m2f	2min3		

Trainers	*Wins-Runs*	*%*	*2yo*	*3yo+*	*£1 level stks*
Richard Fahey	48-333	14	20-142	28-191	-43.23
David O'Meara	38-257	15	7-44	31-213	-26.54
Tim Easterby	35-434	8	3-118	32-316	-137.26
Michael Dods	24-223	11	8-73	16-150	-12.34
Mark Johnston	22-132	17	7-50	15-82	-18.82
Kevin Ryan	22-159	14	8-62	14-97	-53.65
William Haggas	17-39	44	6-18	11-21	+5.92
David Barron	17-117	15	4-24	13-93	+17.45
Keith Dalgleish	13-95	14	6-40	7-55	+15.75
Michael Easterby	13-135	10	1-33	12-102	-47.13
Ruth Carr	12-167	7	0-2	12-165	-78.75
Archie Watson	11-35	31	5-16	6-19	+0.45
Declan Carroll	11-84	13	4-18	7-66	+16.25

Jockeys	*Wins-Rides*	*%*	*£1 level stks*	*Best Trainer*	*W-R*
Daniel Tudhope	34-157	22	+37.40	David O´Meara	16-88
David Allan	33-277	12	-63.34	Tim Easterby	18-162
Graham Lee	24-239	10	-75.44	Keith Dalgleish	3-10
Jason Hart	23-161	14	-11.14	John Quinn	6-43
Paul Mulrennan	22-219	10	-106.25	Michael Dods	10-68
Kevin Stott	20-121	17	-4.63	Kevin Ryan	12-44
Paul Hanagan	20-129	16	-35.83	Richard Fahey	8-63
Tony Hamilton	20-150	13	-43.24	Richard Fahey	18-86
Joe Fanning	19-112	17	+6.03	Mark Johnston	9-47
Ben Curtis	19-160	12	-67.07	William Haggas	3-4
Andrew Mullen	19-204	9	+7.63	Michael Dods	5-30
Phillip Makin	15-114	13	-33.89	David O´Meara	4-18
P J McDonald	15-173	9	-66.38	Ann Duffield	3-32

Favourites
2yo 38.1% -6.63 3yo 38.2% +5.86 Total 35.5% -1.70

RIPON

77 North Street, Ripon, N Yorkshire
HG4 1DS. Tel 01765 602 156 or 01765 603 696

How to get there Road: A1, then B6265. Rail: Harrogate, bus to Ripon centre, 1m walk

Features RH, sharp

2020 Fixtures April 16, 25, May 8, 17, 28, June 3, 17-18, July 6, 18, August 3, 10, 15, 24, 31, September 1, 26

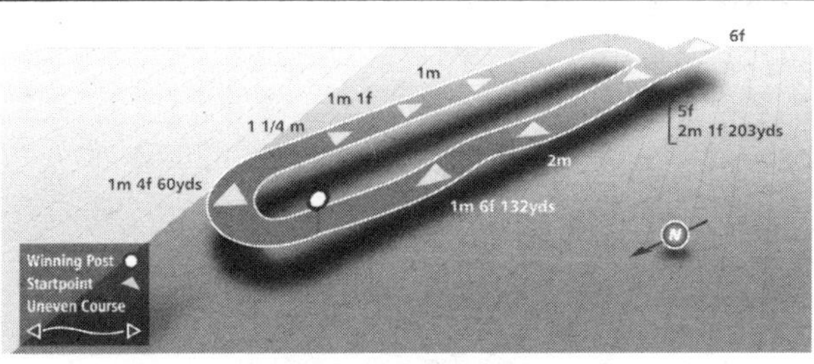

Racing Post standard times

5f	58	1m2f	2min4.5
6f	1min10.3	1m4f10yds	2min33.4
1m	1min38.1	2m	3min26.5
1m1f	1min52	2m1f203yds	3min53
1m1f170yds	2min1.3		

Trainers	*Wins-Runs*	*%*	*2yo*	*3yo+*	*£1 level stks*
Tim Easterby	52-459	11	11-110	41-349	-57.67
Richard Fahey	47-344	14	16-110	31-234	-83.89
David O'Meara	45-297	15	8-38	37-259	+29.58
Mark Johnston	37-217	17	16-60	21-157	+1.88
William Haggas	20-48	42	3-10	17-38	+5.26
Ruth Carr	16-124	13	0-2	16-122	+67.50
Keith Dalgleish	12-92	13	0-29	12-63	-28.30
Roger Varian	11-43	26	1-6	10-37	-11.96
Nigel Tinkler	11-87	13	2-29	9-58	-10.17
James Tate	10-21	48	3-7	7-14	+3.06
Kevin Ryan	10-118	8	1-26	9-92	-33.25
Saeed bin Suroor	9-29	31	3-5	6-24	+6.67
Jedd O'Keeffe	9-50	18	2-16	7-34	-5.18

Jockeys	*Wins-Rides*	*%*	*£1 level stks*	*Best Trainer*	*W-R*
Daniel Tudhope	41-175	23	+8.73	David O´Meara	18-110
David Allan	37-249	15	-44.19	Tim Easterby	29-209
Silvestre De Sousa	32-84	38	+34.84	Mark Johnston	6-16
Paul Mulrennan	24-137	18	-5.72	Michael Dods	4-31
Tony Hamilton	23-149	15	-9.58	Richard Fahey	18-100
Franny Norton	20-109	18	+20.72	Mark Johnston	14-69
P J McDonald	19-159	12	-39.17	Ann Duffield	4-32
Graham Lee	16-123	13	-25.96	Jedd O´Keeffe	3-8
Paul Hanagan	15-115	13	-41.77	Richard Fahey	11-76
Jason Hart	14-101	14	+2.42	John Quinn	6-37
Joe Fanning	13-95	14	-48.58	Mark Johnston	7-56
Kevin Stott	11-57	19	+38.25	Kevin Ryan	4-29
David Nolan	11-80	14	-7.96	David O´Meara	6-43

Favourites

2yo 42.3% -2.38 3yo 39.4% -1.34 Total 37.1% -8.50

SALISBURY

Netherhampton, Salisbury, Wilts
SP2 8PN. Tel 01722 326 461

How to get there Road: 2m west of Salisbury on A3094. Rail: Salisbury, bus

Features RH, uphill finish

2020 Fixtures April 26, May 3, 14, 23, June 9, 14, 24, July 11, 25, August 12-13, 21, 25, September 3, 11, October 1

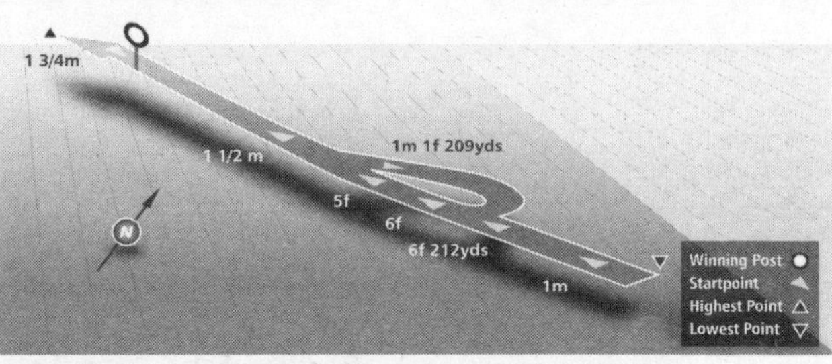

Racing Post standard times

5f	59.8	1m1f198yds	2min5.8
6f	1min12.3	1m4f	2min33
6f212yds	1min26.5	1m6f21yds	3min
1m	1min39.5		

Trainers	*Wins-Runs*	%	*2yo*	*3yo+*	*£1 level stks*
Richard Hannon	48-387	12	28-194	20-193	-93.24
Andrew Balding	30-191	16	11-60	19-131	-39.29
Clive Cox	22-121	18	10-44	12-77	-13.98
Ralph Beckett	20-145	14	6-51	14-94	-25.96
John Gosden	15-53	28	2-9	13-44	+32.69
Henry Candy	15-94	16	2-25	13-69	-13.74
Mick Channon	15-150	10	5-61	10-89	-38.40
Rod Millman	15-162	9	6-55	9-107	-65.47
William Haggas	14-49	29	3-19	11-30	-5.66
Roger Varian	13-74	18	4-21	9-53	-2.28
Roger Charlton	12-70	17	2-24	10-46	-27.63
Sir Michael Stoute	12-74	16	2-17	10-57	-8.19
Charles Hills	12-85	14	0-29	12-56	-13.40

Jockeys	*Wins-Rides*	%	*£1 level stks*	*Best Trainer*	*W-R*
Oisin Murphy	29-159	18	+30.13	Andrew Balding	8-44
Tom Marquand	22-170	13	-9.22	Richard Hannon	11-72
David Probert	21-137	15	+5.35	Andrew Balding	11-68
Jim Crowley	20-155	13	-42.72	Charles Hills	3-16
Pat Dobbs	18-156	12	-77.08	Richard Hannon	10-61
Andrea Atzeni	16-60	27	+16.62	Roger Varian	5-19
Silvestre De Sousa	14-76	18	-18.01	Mark Johnston	3-7
Robert Havlin	13-57	23	+27.44	John Gosden	11-32
Ryan Moore	13-59	22	-23.51	Sir Michael Stoute	4-18
Charles Bishop	13-113	12	-39.62	Eve Johnson Houghton	5-38
Sean Levey	13-115	11	-42.70	Richard Hannon	12-98
Harry Bentley	11-89	12	-35.71	Ralph Beckett	4-35
James Doyle	10-34	29	+14.33	William Haggas	3-7

Favourites

2yo 34% -32.29 3yo 33.3% -40.78 Total 34% -69.65

SANDOWN

Esher, Surrey, KT10 9AJ.
Tel 01372 463 072 or 01372 464 348

How to get there Road: M25 Jct 10 then A3. Rail: Esher from Waterloo

Features RH, last 7f uphill

2020 Fixtures April 24, May 21, 28, June 12-13, July 3-4, 22-23, 29, August 6, 21-22, September 11, 16

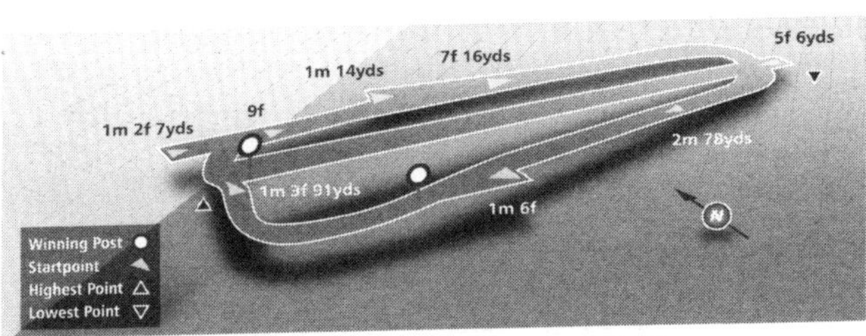

Racing Post standard times

5f6yds	59.8	1m2f7yds	2min5.8
7f16yds	1min27	1m3f91yds	2min23
1m14yds	1min39.9	1m6f	2min58.3
1m1f	1min52.9	2m78yds	3min34

Trainers	Wins-Runs	%	2yo	3yo+	£1 level stks
John Gosden	37-149	25	11-42	26-107	-14.05
Richard Hannon	35-273	13	15-106	20-167	-33.52
Sir Michael Stoute	28-124	23	1-21	27-103	-2.12
Andrew Balding	21-172	12	5-41	16-131	-2.49
Roger Varian	18-83	22	1-15	17-68	-18.13
Clive Cox	18-116	16	5-26	13-90	+1.11
William Haggas	17-77	22	6-19	11-58	-9.99
Mark Johnston	17-125	14	9-41	8-84	-56.87
Roger Charlton	14-67	21	1-12	13-55	+2.39
Charlie Appleby	12-76	16	7-32	5-44	-17.57
Henry Candy	10-66	15	2-11	8-55	+8.79
Ralph Beckett	10-87	11	1-21	9-66	-24.64
William Muir	8-41	20	0-3	8-38	+21.75

Jockeys	Wins-Rides	%	£1 level stks	Best Trainer	W-R
Ryan Moore	38-177	21	-4.39	Sir Michael Stoute	18-60
Silvestre De Sousa	32-119	27	+29.77	Mark Johnston	8-29
Oisin Murphy	29-211	14	-39.88	Andrew Balding	4-50
Frankie Dettori	27-103	26	-4.22	John Gosden	15-53
Jim Crowley	26-197	13	-22.13	Richard Hannon	3-11
James Doyle	25-153	16	-51.96	William Haggas	4-15
Andrea Atzeni	22-136	16	-55.95	Roger Varian	8-40
William Buick	18-119	15	-31.32	Charlie Appleby	8-43
Adam Kirby	16-136	12	-55.67	Clive Cox	10-51
Fran Berry	11-73	15	+14.08	David Menuisier	3-7
Charles Bishop	11-80	14	+17.25	Eve Johnson Houghton	6-39
George Baker	10-38	26	+1.16	Roger Charlton	3-4
Jason Watson	10-56	18	+37.20	Roger Charlton	3-10

Favourites

2yo 41.8% -2.34 3yo 41.4% +31.35 Total 41.6% +55.41

SOUTHWELL

Rolleston, Newark, Notts
NG25 0TS. Tel 01636 814 481

How to get there Road: A1 to Newark, then A617 or M1 to Nottingham, then A612. Rail: Rolleston

Features LH, Fibresand, sharp

Please note there are no turf fixtures scheduled this year. Stats relate to all-weather only.

2020 Fixtures April 2, 12, 27, 30, August 31, October 6, 8, 15, 27, 29, November 3, 17, 26-27, December 8, 11, 17-18, 20, 29

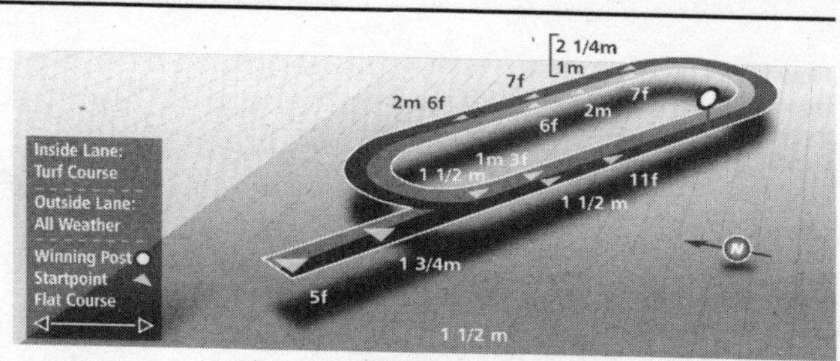

Racing Post standard times

5f	58	1m4f	2min35
6f	1min14	1m5f	2min50.5
7f	1min27	1m6f	3min2
1m	1min39.8	2m	3min34
1m3f	2min22.3	2m2f	4min4

Trainers	*Wins-Runs*	*%*	*2yo*	*3yo+*	*£1 level stks*
Michael Appleby	107-767	14	5-49	102-718	-229.33
Scott Dixon	51-620	8	3-45	48-575	-65.98
K R Burke	35-184	19	5-32	30-152	+136.11
Richard Fahey	34-200	17	6-44	28-156	-11.04
David Evans	34-227	15	3-27	31-200	+26.04
Declan Carroll	27-141	19	0-4	27-137	+27.20
Derek Shaw	27-233	12	1-5	26-228	+73.58
David Barron	25-118	21	3-8	22-110	+3.23
Andrew Balding	21-103	20	0-7	21-96	-24.01
Mark Johnston	19-114	17	5-29	14-85	-14.61
Conor Dore	19-133	14	0-1	19-132	+3.63
Roger Fell	17-109	16	1-6	16-103	+64.13
Tony Carroll	17-112	15	0-0	17-112	+123.23

Jockeys	*Wins-Rides*	*%*	*£1 level stks*	*Best Trainer*	*W-R*
Luke Morris	59-498	12	-179.17	Michael Appleby	12-99
Ben Curtis	47-289	16	+38.16	K R Burke	8-27
Andrew Mullen	45-418	11	-169.04	Michael Appleby	18-168
Alistair Rawlinson	39-253	15	-31.03	Michael Appleby	33-202
Kieran O'Neill	33-317	10	+59.33	Scott Dixon	23-203
Joe Fanning	26-218	12	-75.78	Mark Johnston	7-45
Paul Mulrennan	25-189	13	+16.09	Conor Dore	7-34
P J McDonald	23-187	12	-63.93	Philip Kirby	3-6
J F Egan	22-118	19	+4.88	David Evans	8-41
Barry McHugh	22-144	15	+7.07	James Given	5-12
Tony Hamilton	22-188	12	+5.25	Derek Shaw	8-47
Tom Eaves	22-267	8	-40.33	James Given	4-37
Silvestre De Sousa	19-92	21	+4.85	Chris Dwyer	5-17

Favourites

2yo 35.2% -13.82 3yo 36.1% -43.95 Total 33.2% -156.83

THIRSK

Station Road, Thirsk, N Yorkshire, YO7 1QL. Tel 01845 522 276

How to get there Road: A61 from A1 in the west or A19 in the east. Rail: Thirsk, 10min walk

Features LH, sharp, tight turns

2020 Fixtures April 18, 27, May 2, 9, 16, June 15-16, July 1, 24, August 1, 7, 14, 28, September 5, 14

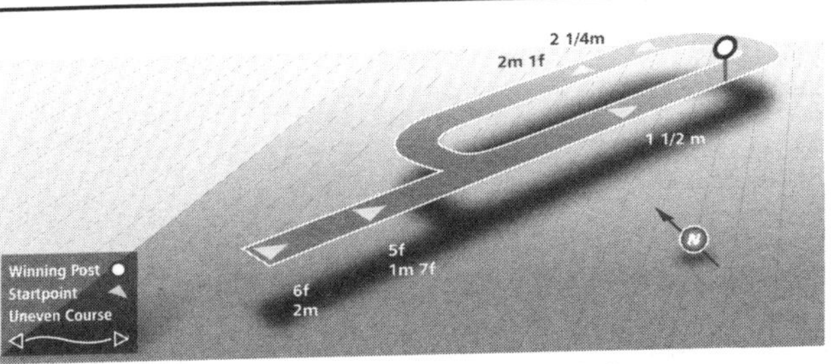

Racing Post standard times

5f	58	1m	1min36.5
6f	1min10.6	1m4f	2min32
7f	1min24	2m	3min23

Trainers	Wins-Runs	%	2yo	3yo+	£1 level stks
Richard Fahey	53-318	17	21-118	32-200	+26.28
David O'Meara	33-263	13	4-41	29-222	-33.67
Tim Easterby	33-417	8	5-113	28-304	-69.28
Kevin Ryan	27-211	13	8-56	19-155	-5.21
Michael Dods	26-257	10	7-67	19-190	-50.78
Paul Midgley	18-110	16	0-8	18-102	+29.25
William Haggas	13-45	29	4-14	9-31	-14.80
Brian Ellison	13-100	13	1-19	12-81	+1.60
John Quinn	13-118	11	4-37	9-81	-10.47
Keith Dalgleish	12-67	18	3-21	9-46	+37.96
Ruth Carr	12-208	6	0-3	12-205	-76.14
Michael Appleby	11-71	15	1-5	10-66	+101.25
Michael Easterby	11-143	8	0-29	11-114	-59.00

Jockeys	Wins-Rides	%	£1 level stks	Best Trainer	W-R
Daniel Tudhope	35-181	19	-3.75	David O´Meara	20-103
David Allan	31-250	12	+7.25	Tim Easterby	17-167
Paul Mulrennan	29-232	13	-25.88	Michael Dods	12-97
Paul Hanagan	21-131	16	+14.26	Richard Fahey	15-74
Graham Lee	20-224	9	-81.18	Bryan Smart	4-29
Ben Curtis	18-170	11	-38.58	Brian Ellison	4-24
Kevin Stott	17-107	16	+1.48	Kevin Ryan	9-41
Tom Eaves	17-197	9	+25.57	Kevin Ryan	4-49
P J McDonald	17-211	8	-72.68	Ann Duffield	4-22
Joe Fanning	16-78	21	-2.38	Mark Johnston	5-22
Tony Hamilton	16-172	9	-64.33	Richard Fahey	13-94
Phillip Makin	14-97	14	-16.13	John Davies	3-14
Jason Hart	13-155	8	-36.44	John Quinn	6-59

Favourites

2yo 40.8% +1.66 3yo 38% -10.28 Total 36.4% +22.08

WETHERBY

York Road, Wetherby, West Yorks
L22 5EJ. Tel: 01937 582 035

How to get there Road: A1, A58 from Leeds, B1224 from York. Rail: Leeds, Harrogate, York.

Features LH, 1m4f circuit

2020 Fixtures April 26, May 12, June 9

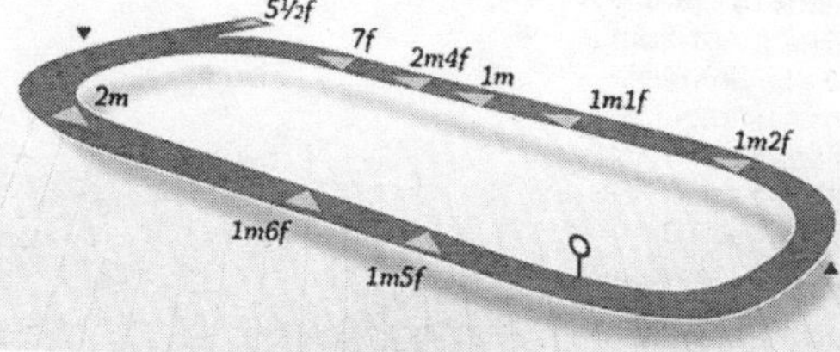

Racing Post standard times

5f110yds	1min4.8	1m2f	2min4.5
7f	1min25.2	1m6f	2min56
1m	1min38.3		

Trainers	Wins-Runs	%	2yo	3yo+	£1 level stks
Richard Fahey	8-38	21	2-11	6-27	+23.75
David O'Meara	6-36	17	0-3	6-33	+39.11
John Gosden	5-10	50	0-0	5-10	+5.79
Tim Easterby	5-49	10	0-5	5-44	-5.20
Declan Carroll	4-17	24	0-0	4-17	+18.00
Roger Fell	4-20	20	0-1	4-19	+4.00
Kevin Ryan	4-21	19	1-3	3-18	+30.50
David Brown	3-4	75	0-1	3-3	+36.00
David Loughnane	3-8	38	0-0	3-8	+41.50
William Haggas	3-11	27	0-0	3-11	+1.17
Jedd O'Keeffe	3-12	25	0-0	3-12	+6.00
Mark Johnston	3-21	14	1-6	2-15	+4.10
Ruth Carr	3-25	12	0-0	3-25	-6.00

Jockeys	Wins-Rides	%	£1 level stks	Best Trainer	W-R
Daniel Tudhope	7-24	29	+57.61	David O´Meara	4-14
P J McDonald	7-49	14	+30.50	David Loughnane	2-3
Ben Curtis	6-39	15	-5.50	Roger Fell	1-1
Tony Hamilton	6-43	14	-4.50	Roger Fell	2-13
Paul Hanagan	5-29	17	+1.67	Richard Fahey	3-11
Tom Eaves	5-33	15	+42.50	Kevin Ryan	3-7
James Sullivan	5-36	14	+13.00	Ruth Carr	3-19
Paul Mulrennan	5-36	14	-4.90	John Mackie	1-1
Jack Garritty	4-22	18	+6.00	Jedd O´Keeffe	3-9
Cam Hardie	4-24	17	+6.38	David Brown	1-1
Phillip Makin	4-25	16	+3.00	David O´Meara	2-4
David Allan	4-33	12	-6.45	Alan Swinbank	1-1
Joe Fanning	4-34	12	+19.00	Mark Johnston	2-11

Favourites

2yo 45.5% +2.73 3yo 30.2% -15.86 Total 28.7% -25.02

WINDSOR

Maidenhead Road, Windsor, Berks
SL4 5JJ. Tel 01753 498 400

How to get there Road: M4 Jctn 6, A355, A308. Rail: Paddington to Windsor Central/ Waterloo to Windsor Riverside

Features Figure of eight, flat, long straight

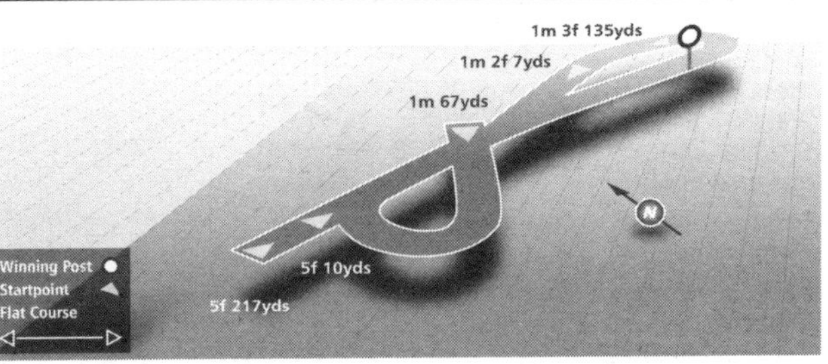

2020 Fixtures April 6, 20, 27, May 4, 11, 18, 25, June 1, 8, 15, 22, 27-29, July 6, 13, 20, 27, August 3, 9-10, 17, 29, September 7, October 5, 12, 19

Racing Post standard times

5f10yds	59.2	1m2f7yds	2min5
6f	1min10.5	1m3f135yds	2min25
1m67yds	1min41.1		

Trainers	*Wins-Runs*	*%*	*2yo*	*3yo+*	*£1 level stks*
Richard Hannon	61-380	16	32-165	29-215	-61.26
Clive Cox	42-211	20	13-44	29-167	-0.76
Roger Varian	24-86	28	1-9	23-77	-9.75
Ed Walker	24-116	21	4-29	20-87	-15.65
David Evans	22-245	9	11-96	11-149	-101.99
William Haggas	21-81	26	5-28	16-53	-22.46
Ralph Beckett	20-125	16	5-30	15-95	-40.91
Charles Hills	20-139	14	5-49	15-90	-4.65
Andrew Balding	20-161	12	6-30	14-131	-67.19
Saeed bin Suroor	19-55	35	4-12	15-43	+4.64
John Gosden	19-76	25	4-11	15-65	-23.22
Henry Candy	18-105	17	2-18	16-87	-16.63
Mark Johnston	17-73	23	10-27	7-46	-5.40

Jockeys	*Wins-Rides*	*%*	*£1 level stks*	*Best Trainer*	*W-R*
Adam Kirby	56-290	19	-21.07	Clive Cox	30-113
Oisin Murphy	51-298	17	-69.19	Andrew Balding	7-51
James Doyle	40-157	25	-26.92	Saeed bin Suroor	7-15
Tom Marquand	32-275	12	-86.94	Richard Hannon	13-104
Jamie Spencer	29-166	17	-1.91	Ed Walker	6-12
Silvestre De Sousa	26-117	22	+9.70	Mick Channon	5-15
Sean Levey	24-150	16	+13.47	Richard Hannon	18-106
David Probert	23-231	10	-33.36	Andrew Balding	9-65
Andrea Atzeni	22-105	21	-18.88	Roger Varian	10-39
Harry Bentley	22-133	17	-20.63	Henry Candy	4-9
Jim Crowley	21-127	17	-27.41	Ralph Beckett	4-4
Pat Dobbs	21-131	16	-25.20	Ralph Beckett	4-19
George Baker	20-102	20	-16.21	Ed Walker	4-10

Favourites

2yo 47.3% +9.47 3yo 39% -7.28 Total 38.5% -9.60

WOLVES

Dunstall Park, Gorsebrook Road, Wolverhampton, West Midlands. WV6 0PE. Tel 08702 202 442

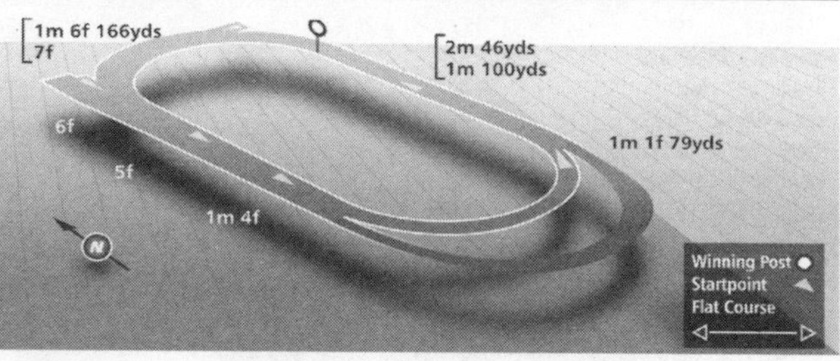

How to get there Road: A449, close to M6, M42 and M54. Rail: Wolverhampton

Features LH, sharp, relaid with Tapeta in 2014

2020 Fixtures March 28, April 1, 4, 8, 11, 13, 21, 25, 29-30, May 5, 8, 11, 19, 21, June 1, 4, 22, 29, July 7, 13, 15, 27, 31, August 10, 14, 21-22, September 5, 9, 14, 19, 21, 29, October 3, 5, 12, 17, 19, 22, 31, November 2, 14, 16, 21, 24, 28, 30, December 1, 5, 7, 12, 15, 18-19, 26-27

Racing Post standard times

5f20yds	1min0.5	1m1f103yds	1min57.3
5f216yds	1min13.2	1m4f50yds	2min35.3
7f32yds	1min27	1m5f194yds	2min58.5
1m141yds	1min46.7	2m119yds	3min36

Trainers	*Wins-Runs*	*%*	*2yo*	*3yo+*	*£1 level stks*
David Evans	85-697	12	12-140	73-557	-114.72
Richard Fahey	68-562	12	13-167	55-395	-116.81
Michael Appleby	64-622	10	2-20	62-602	-160.87
Mark Johnston	63-468	13	18-151	45-317	-141.62
Tom Dascombe	62-410	15	14-122	48-288	+57.12
Mark Loughnane	58-659	9	1-56	57-603	-168.64
John Gosden	54-180	30	20-74	34-106	-19.12
Marco Botti	51-342	15	14-93	37-249	+39.10
David O'Meara	51-451	11	5-63	46-388	-114.81
Tony Carroll	50-495	10	1-25	49-470	-126.42
William Haggas	46-143	32	16-55	30-88	-3.15
Charlie Appleby	46-144	32	12-49	34-95	-24.93
Jamie Osborne	44-360	12	12-95	32-265	-158.38

Jockeys	*Wins-Rides*	*%*	*£1 level stks*	*Best Trainer*	*W-R*
Luke Morris	157-1276	12	-324.20	Sir Mark Prescott Bt	28-149
Adam Kirby	126-600	21	-32.42	Jamie Osborne	10-32
Richard Kingscote	91-566	16	-104.07	Tom Dascombe	42-239
Joe Fanning	76-565	13	-128.71	Mark Johnston	27-186
Oisin Murphy	71-347	20	-37.94	Andrew Balding	9-34
Stevie Donohoe	58-468	12	+15.47	Ian Williams	14-92
Martin Harley	56-342	16	-11.22	Marco Botti	6-15
David Probert	56-503	11	-36.52	Ronald Harris	10-81
Silvestre De Sousa	52-248	21	-28.29	Chris Dwyer	7-22
Jack Mitchell	49-248	20	+22.85	Roger Varian	19-78
P J McDonald	49-411	12	-91.50	Mark Johnston	7-54
Robert Havlin	47-239	20	-34.28	John Gosden	25-87
Shane Kelly	47-488	10	-190.16	Richard Hughes	19-124

Favourites

2yo 41.2% -4.69 3yo 37% -113.86 Total 35.5% -211.05

YARMOUTH

North Denes, Great Yarmouth, Norfolk NR30 4AU. Tel 01493 842 527

How to get there Road: A47 to end, A1064. Rail: Great Yarmouth, bus

Features LH, flat

2020 Fixtures April 21, 28, May 20, 29, June 1, 10-11, 26, July 2, 8, 15, 23, 28, August 5-6, 13, 25, 30, September 15-17, October 12, 20

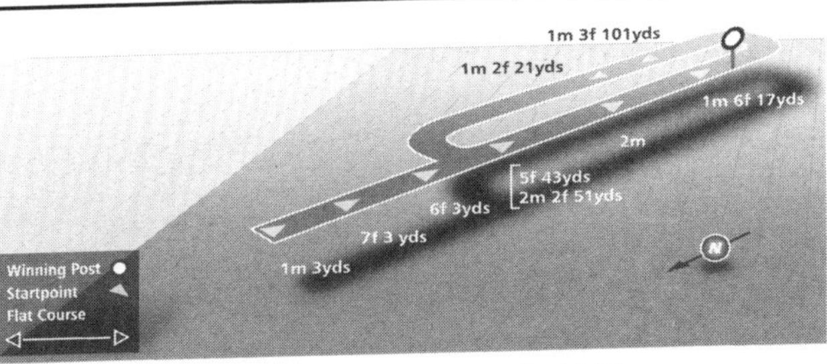

Racing Post standard times

5f43yds	1min0.5	1m2f21yds	2min5
6f3yds	1min11	1m3f101yds	2min23.5
7f3yds	1min23.6	1m6f17yds	2min59
1m3yds	1min36.5	2m	3min24.5
1m1f	1min50	2m2f51yds	3min56

Trainers	*Wins-Runs*	*%*	*2yo*	*3yo+*	*£1 level stks*
William Haggas	31-132	23	12-59	19-73	-16.63
John Gosden	30-81	37	12-44	18-37	+32.13
David Simcock	29-123	24	6-28	23-95	+28.13
Roger Varian	23-102	23	8-41	15-61	-14.72
Michael Bell	19-100	19	8-44	11-56	+9.23
Stuart Williams	19-122	16	0-14	19-108	-28.50
Mark Johnston	18-79	23	8-27	10-52	+45.40
Chris Wall	16-89	18	1-15	15-74	-21.32
Chris Dwyer	16-92	17	2-14	14-78	+40.63
Sir Michael Stoute	12-64	19	5-30	7-34	-28.33
Philip McBride	11-53	21	2-13	9-40	+47.63
Hugo Palmer	11-61	18	4-26	7-35	+2.19
James Tate	11-61	18	5-20	6-41	-8.38

Jockeys	*Wins-Rides*	*%*	*£1 level stks*	*Best Trainer*	*W-R*
Jamie Spencer	48-197	24	+62.84	David Simcock	18-49
Silvestre De Sousa	46-200	23	+16.02	Chris Dwyer	7-40
Andrea Atzeni	27-107	25	-6.06	Roger Varian	13-46
Ryan Moore	23-76	30	-13.69	Sir Michael Stoute	6-24
James Doyle	20-82	24	-0.09	Charlie Appleby	5-13
Pat Cosgrave	19-113	17	+35.57	William Haggas	6-28
Jim Crowley	17-83	20	-15.78	Owen Burrows	4-9
Luke Morris	17-159	11	-70.20	Sir Mark Prescott Bt	4-30
Frankie Dettori	16-37	43	+19.27	John Gosden	9-18
Jack Mitchell	15-104	14	-8.92	Olly Williams	2-5
Robert Havlin	14-74	19	-8.76	John Gosden	12-29
David Egan	13-106	12	-28.27	John Butler	2-5
Stevie Donohoe	13-108	12	-16.00	Charlie Fellowes	7-30

Favourites

2yo 46% +4.63 | 3yo 40.8% +18.00 | Total 39.1% -6.99

YORK

Knavesmire Road, York, YO23 1EX
Tel 01904 620 911

How to get there Road: Course is south of city. From north, A1, A59 to York, northern bypass from A19 to A64. Otherwise, A64. Rail: York, bus

Features LH, flat

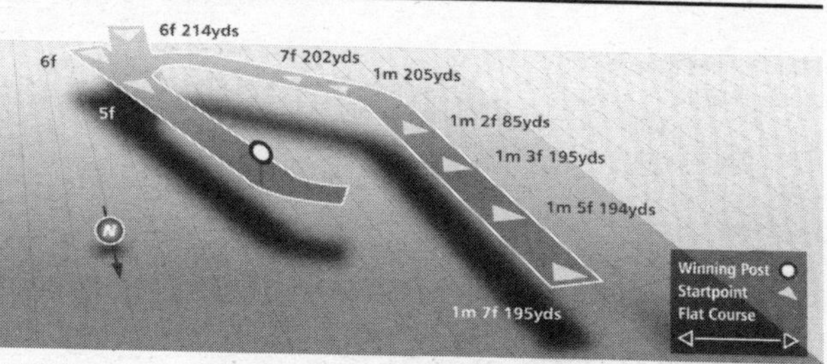

2020 Fixtures May 13-15, 30, June 12-13, 27, July 10-11, 24-25, August 19-22, September 6, October 9-10

Racing Post standard times

5f	57.5	1m208yds	1min49
5f89yds	1min2.7	1m2f88yds	2min7
6f	1min10	1m4f	2min28.1
7f	1min22.3	1m6f	2min57
1m	1min37	2m88yds	3min29

Trainers	*Wins-Runs*	*%*	*2yo*	*3yo+*	*£1 level stks*
Richard Fahey	42-644	7	17-206	25-438	-244.38
William Haggas	35-188	19	12-50	23-138	-27.11
John Gosden	30-103	29	1-6	29-97	+12.39
Tim Easterby	30-385	8	5-68	25-317	-33.50
Mark Johnston	28-279	10	13-108	15-171	-25.74
David O'Meara	28-419	7	0-39	28-380	-137.25
Kevin Ryan	23-288	8	14-103	9-185	-125.88
Michael Dods	20-122	16	1-15	19-107	+21.29
Sir Michael Stoute	17-99	17	1-2	16-97	-8.79
Charlie Appleby	15-71	21	6-14	9-57	-0.70
Ralph Beckett	13-82	16	4-15	9-67	+24.08
Andrew Balding	13-118	11	1-22	12-96	+22.20
Richard Hannon	13-146	9	10-75	3-71	-43.60

Jockeys	*Wins-Rides*	*%*	*£1 level stks*	*Best Trainer*	*W-R*
Frankie Dettori	29-120	24	+2.96	John Gosden	19-52
James Doyle	27-147	18	+17.10	Saeed bin Suroor	5-17
Daniel Tudhope	26-264	10	-67.96	David O´Meara	12-156
Paul Hanagan	21-243	9	-70.75	Richard Fahey	12-152
P J McDonald	19-163	12	+53.85	Mark Johnston	6-39
Andrea Atzeni	16-145	11	-41.00	Roger Varian	8-48
David Allan	16-207	8	-48.50	Tim Easterby	12-163
Oisin Murphy	15-94	16	+30.18	Andrew Balding	4-19
Jim Crowley	15-114	13	+36.50	Sir Michael Stoute	3-14
William Buick	14-104	13	-10.58	Charlie Appleby	8-35
Phillip Makin	14-127	11	+12.13	David O´Meara	5-39
Jamie Spencer	14-148	9	-73.28	Kevin Ryan	4-35
James Sullivan	12-113	11	+20.83	Tom Tate	3-21

Favourites

2yo 32.9% -11.62 3yo 35.7% +23.04 Total 30.8% -3.09

BLUE POINT: the subsequent multiple Group 1 winner took the 2016 Gimcrack – among nearly half of Charlie Appleby's juvenile runners at the track to win

Win - free form!

THIS YEAR'S QUIZ could hardly be more simple, and the prize should prove invaluable to our lucky winner. We're offering a free subscription to The Flat Form Book, the BHA's official form book – every week from May to November, you could be getting the previous week's results in full, together with notebook comments highlighting future winners, adjusted Official Ratings and Racing Post Ratings. The winner will also get a copy of last year's complete form book.

All you have to do is this: identify the three horses pictured on the following pages. And here's a clue – they were newly crowned British champion jockey Oisin Murphy's only three Group 1 winners in Britain during 2019. If you think you know the answer, write their names in the box below in the order in which they appear.

Send your answers along with your details on the entry form below, to:

2020 Flat Guide Competition, Racing & Football Outlook, Floor 7, Vivo Building, South Bank Central, 30 Stamford Street, London, SE1 9LS.

Entries must reach us no later than first post on May 7. The winner's name and the right answers will be printed in the RFO's May 12 edition.

Six runners-up will each receive a copy of last year's form book.

Name..

Address..

....

Town..

Postcode..

In the event of more than one correct entry, the winner will be drawn at random from the correct entries. The Editor's decision is final and no correspondence will be entered into.

QATAR

BETTING CHART

ON	ODDS	AGAINST
50	Evens	50
52.4	11-10	47.6
54.5	6-5	45.5
55.6	5-4	44.4
58	11-8	42
60	6-4	40
62	13-8	38
63.6	7-4	36.4
65.3	15-8	34.7
66.7	2-1	33.3
68	85-40	32
69.2	9-4	30.8
71.4	5-2	28.6
73.4	11-4	26.6
75	3-1	25
76.9	100-30	23.1
77.8	7-2	22.2
80	4-1	20
82	9-2	18
83.3	5-1	16.7
84.6	11-2	15.4
85.7	6-1	14.3
86.7	13-2	13.3
87.5	7-1	12.5
88.2	15-2	11.8
89	8-1	11
89.35	100-12	10.65
89.4	17-2	10.6
90	9-1	10
91	10-1	9
91.8	11-1	8.2
92.6	12-1	7.4
93.5	14-1	6.5
94.4	16-1	5.6
94.7	18-1	5.3
95.2	20-1	4.8
95.7	22-1	4.3
96.2	25-1	3.8
97.2	33-1	2.8
97.6	40-1	2.4
98.1	50-1	1.9
98.5	66-1	1.3
99.0	100-1	.0.99

The table above (often known as the 'Field Money Table') shows both bookmakers' margins and how much a backer needs to invest to win £100. To calculate a bookmaker's margin, simply add up the percentages of all the odds on offer. The sum by which the total exceeds 100% gives the 'over-round' on the book. To determine what stake is required to win £100 (includes returned stake) at a particular price, just look at the relevant row, either odds-against or odds-on.

RULE 4 DEDUCTIONS

When a horse is withdrawn before coming under starter's orders, but after a market has been formed, bookmakers are entitled to make the following deductions from win and place returns (excluding stakes) in accordance with Tattersalls' Rule 4(c).

	Odds of withdrawn horse	*Deduction from winnings*
(1)	3-10 or shorter	75p in the £
(2)	2-5 to 1-3	70p in the £
(3)	8-15 to 4-9	65p in the £
(4)	8-13 to 4-7	60p in the £
(5)	4-5 to 4-6	55p in the £
(6)	20-21 to 5-6	50p in the £
(7)	Evens to 6-5	45p in the £
(8)	5-4 to 6-4	40p in the £
(9)	13-8 to 7-4	35p in the £
(10)	15-8 to 9-4	30p in the £
(11)	5-2 to 3-1	25p in the £
(12)	100-30 to 4-1	20p in the £
(13)	9-2 to 11-2	15p in the £
(14)	6-1 to 9-1	10p in the £
(15)	10-1 to 14-1	5p in the £
(16)	longer than 14-1	no deductions

(17) .... When more than one horse is withdrawn without coming under starter's orders, total deductions shall not exceed 75p in the £.

**Starting-price bets are affected only when there was insufficient time to form a new market.*

Feedback!

If you have any comments or criticism about this book, or suggestions for future editions, please tell us.

Write Nick Watts/Dylan Hill
2020 Flat Guide
Racing & Football Outlook
Floor 7, Vivo Building, South Bank Central
30 Stamford Street
London SE1 9LS

email rfo@rfoutlook.co.uk

Horse index

All horses discussed, with page numbers, except for references in the Group 1 and two-year-old form sections (pages 80-111), which have their own indexes